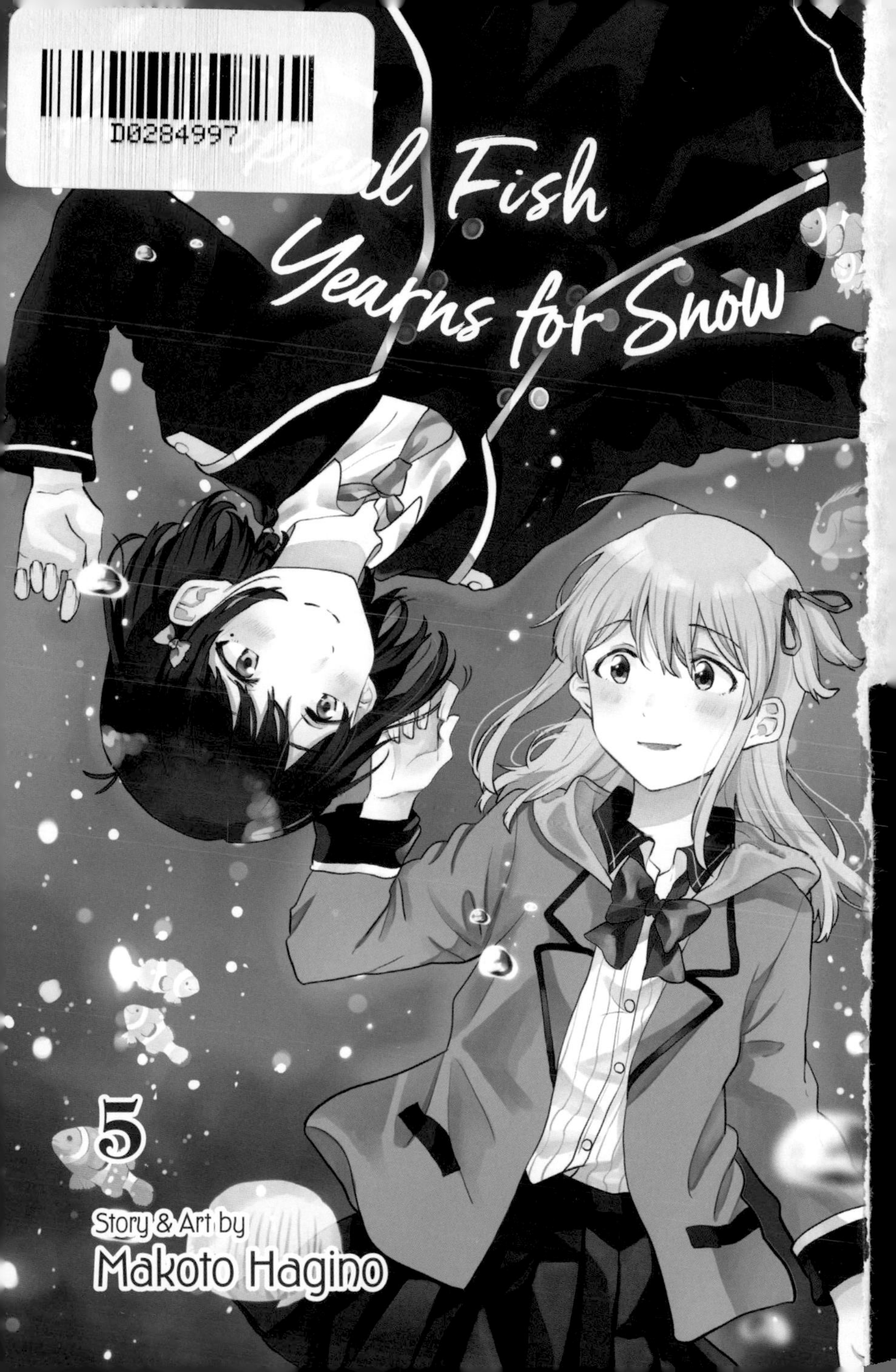
al Fish
Yearns for Snow
5
Story & Art by
Makoto Hagino

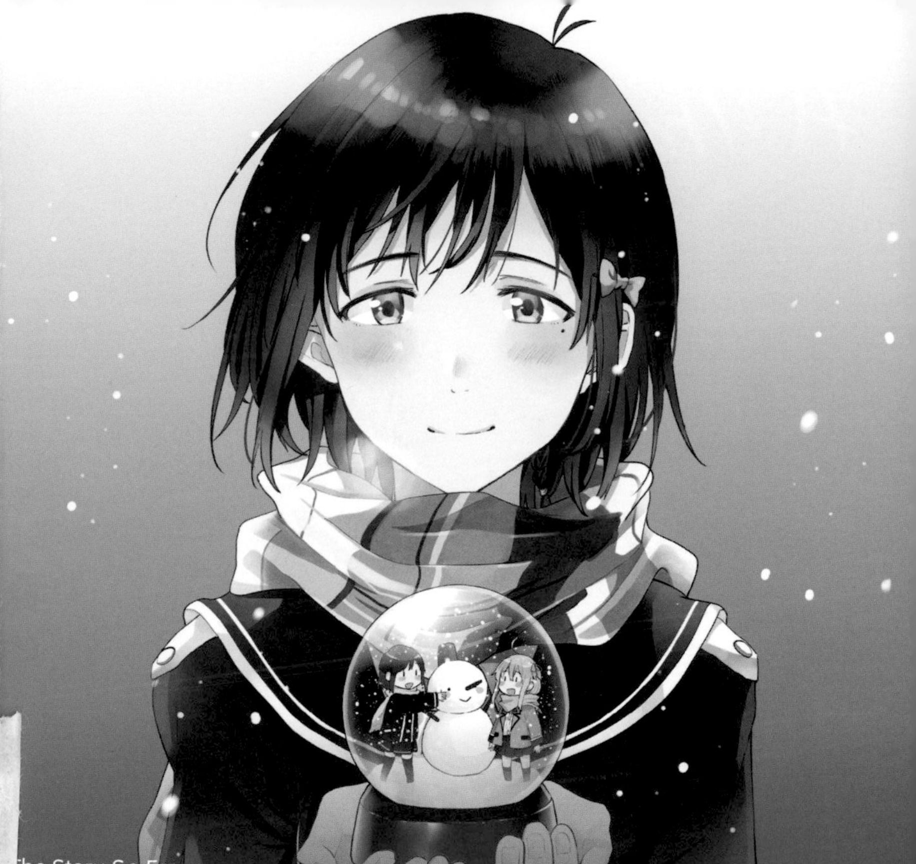

The Story So Far

Konatsu transfers to Nanahama High School from the city and meets Koyuki, the only member of the Aquarium Club. The two girls naturally take a liking to each other because they're both lonely, so Konatsu nds up joining the club. At the aquarium's winter open house, Koyuki jumps for joy when the shark uccessfully swims through a hoop, but then she runs away in embarrassment at having so openly splayed her emotions. Konatsu finds Koyuki and tells her that she accepts her just the way she is.

haracters

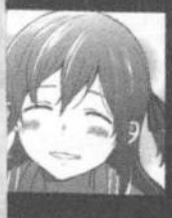

Konatsu Amano

A first-year transfer student. She has trouble adapting her new surroundings until she ecides to join her new friend Koyuki the Aquarium Club.

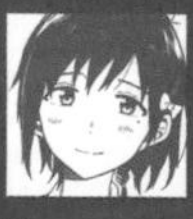

Koyuki Honami

Head of the Aquarium Club. Everyone puts her on a pedestal, and she tries to satisfy their expectations even though she finds them suffocating and feels lonely.

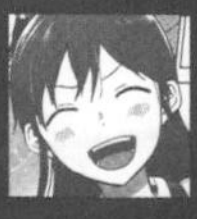

Kaede Hirose

Konatsu's classmate. Due to her perky personality, she has many friends and doesn't hesitate to extend a hearty welcome to Konatsu.

A Tropical Fish Yearns for Snow

Tank 17: Koyuki Honami Isn't Cold.....5

Tank 18: Koyuki Honami Isn't Bored.....39

Tank 19: Koyuki Honami Doesn't Move Forward.....75

Tank 20: Kaede Hirose Doesn't Notice.....119

Afterword.....161

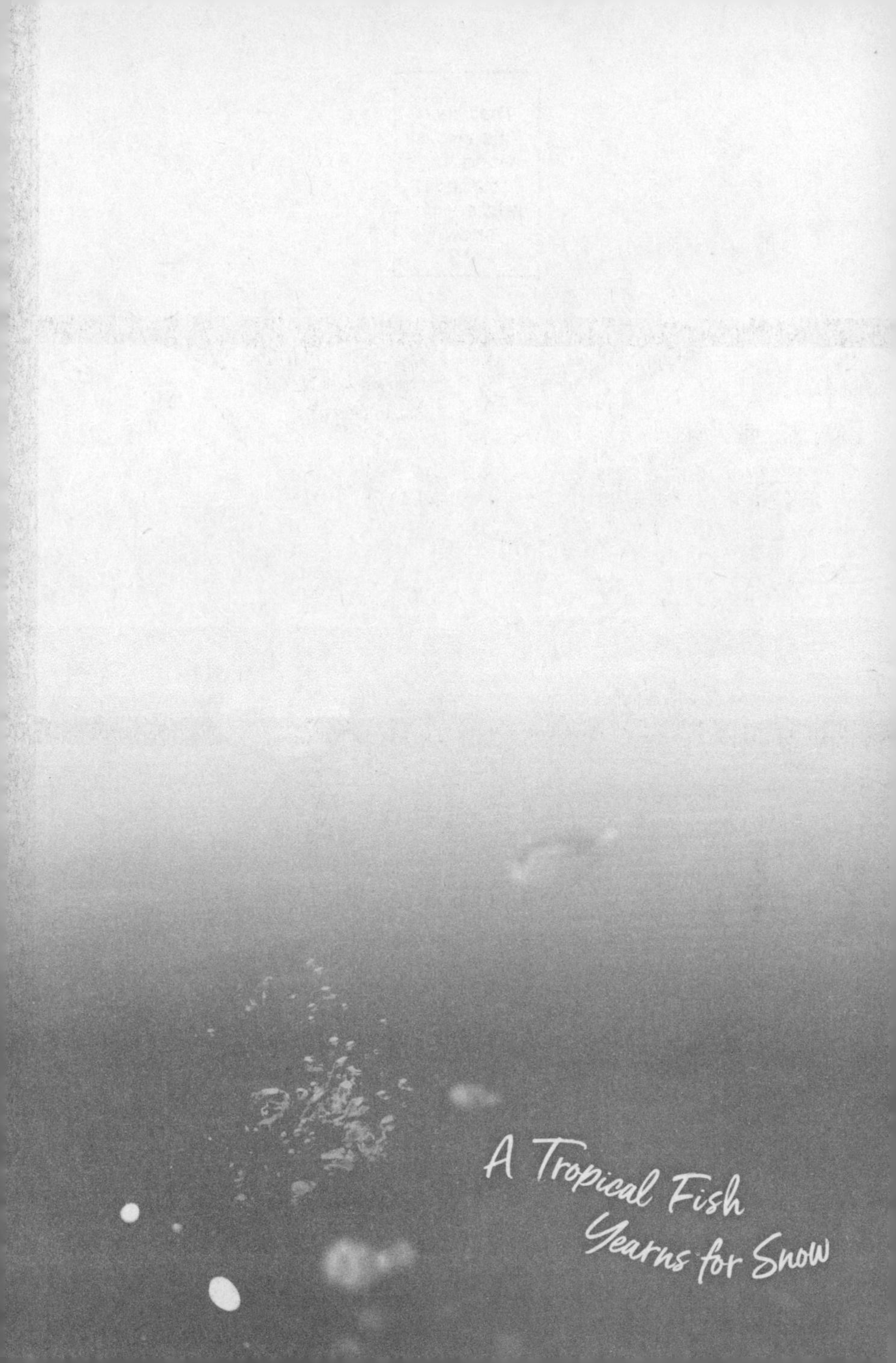
A Tropical Fish
Yearns for Snow

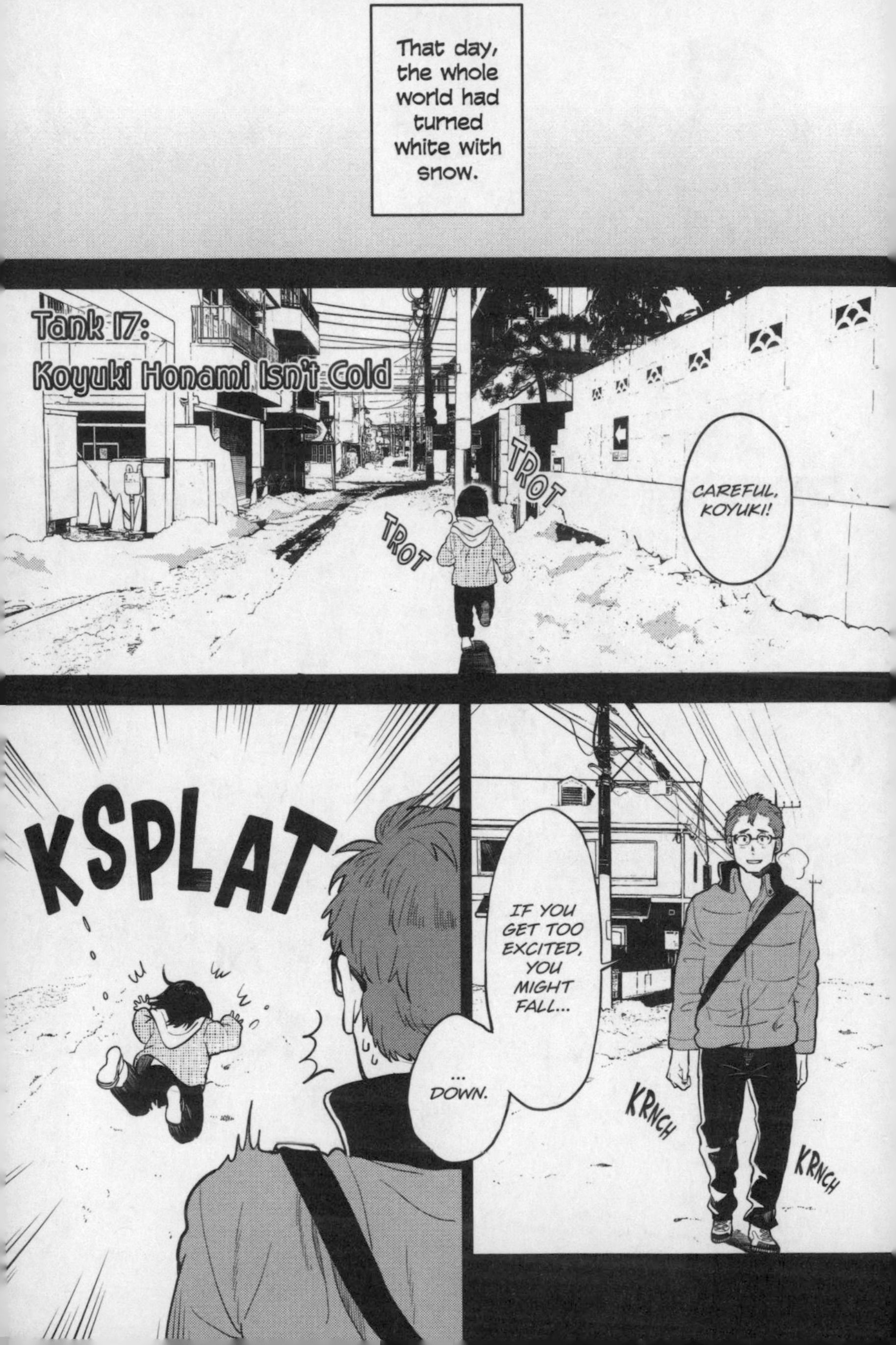
That day, the whole world had turned white with snow.
Tank 17: Koyuki Honami Isn't Cold
CAREFUL, KOYUKI!
TROT
TROT
IF YOU GET TOO EXCITED, YOU MIGHT FALL...
KRNCH
KRNCH
... DOWN.
KSPLAT

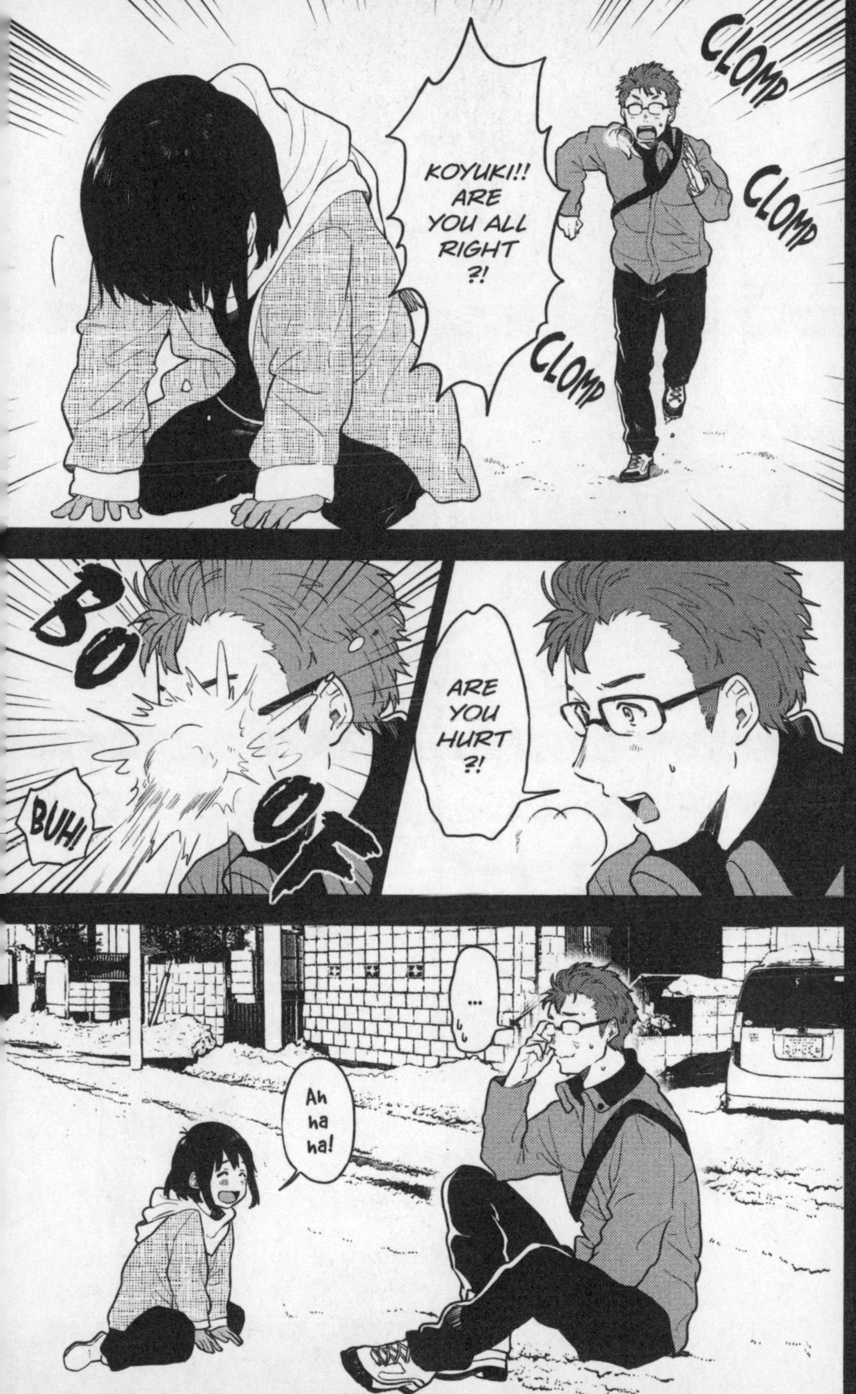
CLOMP
CLOMP
CLOMP
KOYUKI!! ARE YOU ALL RIGHT ?!
ARE YOU HURT ?!
BOO
BUH!
...
Ah ha ha!

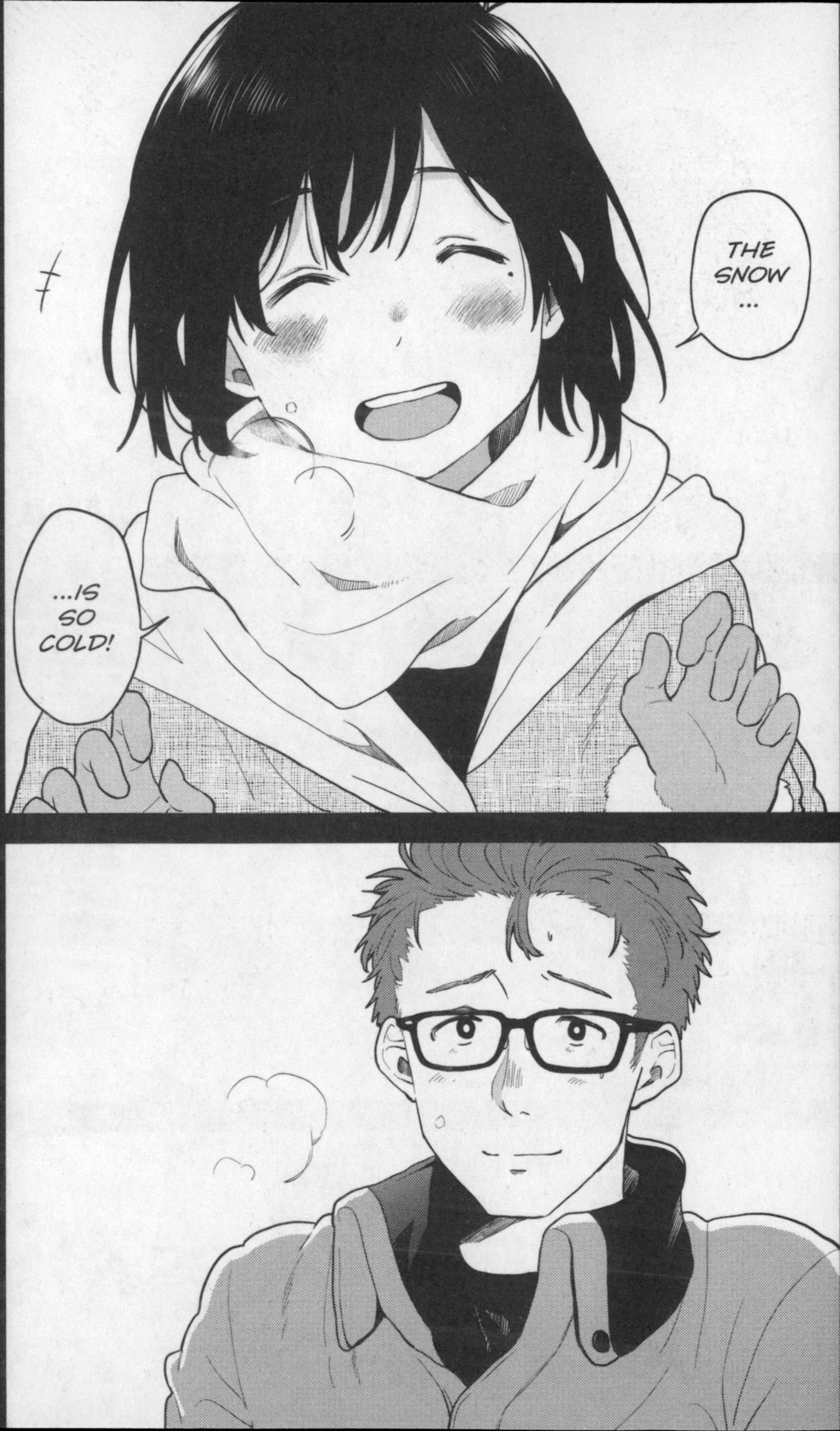
THE SNOW ...
...IS SO COLD!

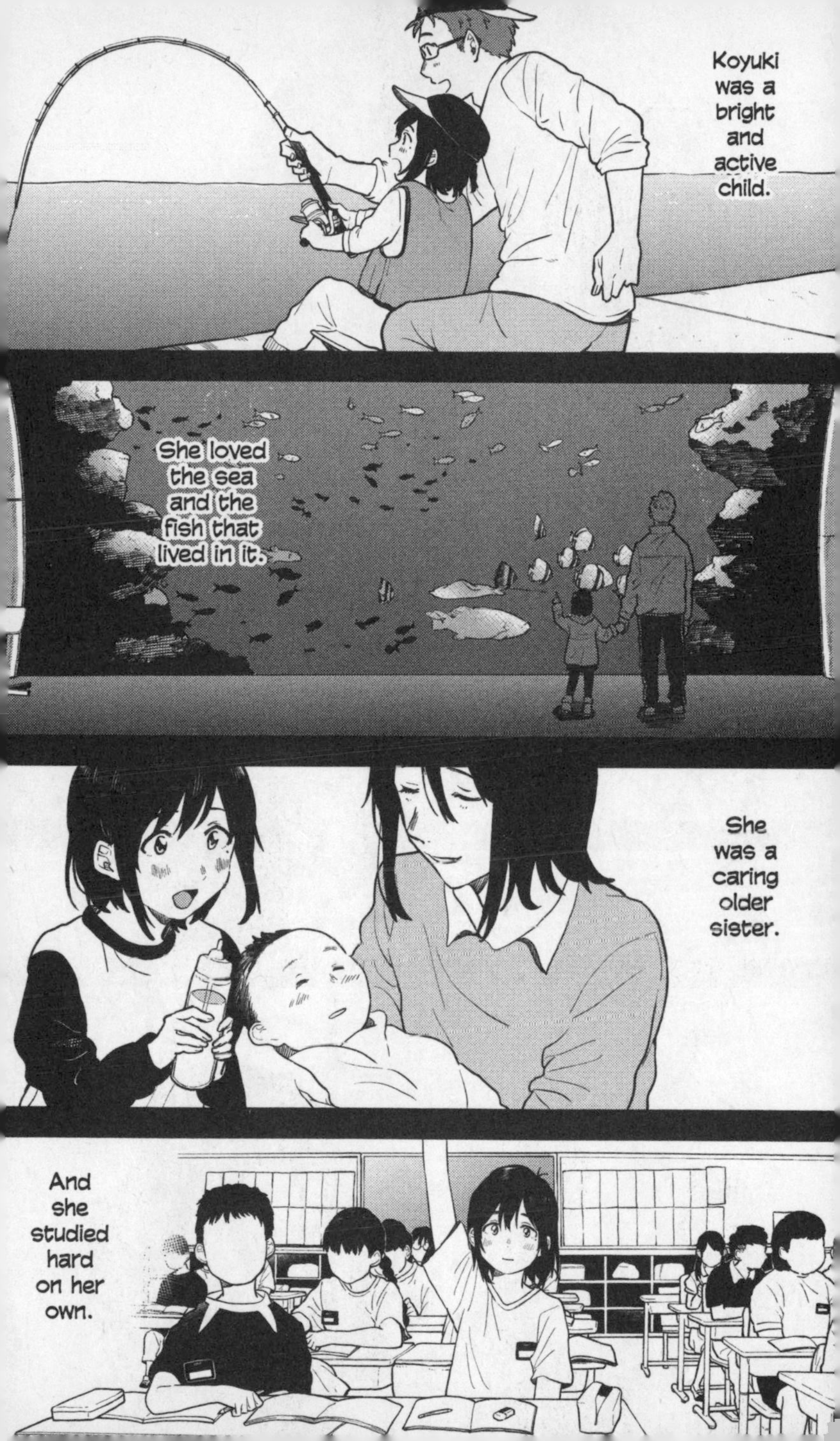
Koyuki was a bright and active child.
She loved the sea and the fish that lived in it.
She was a caring older sister.
And she studied hard on her own.

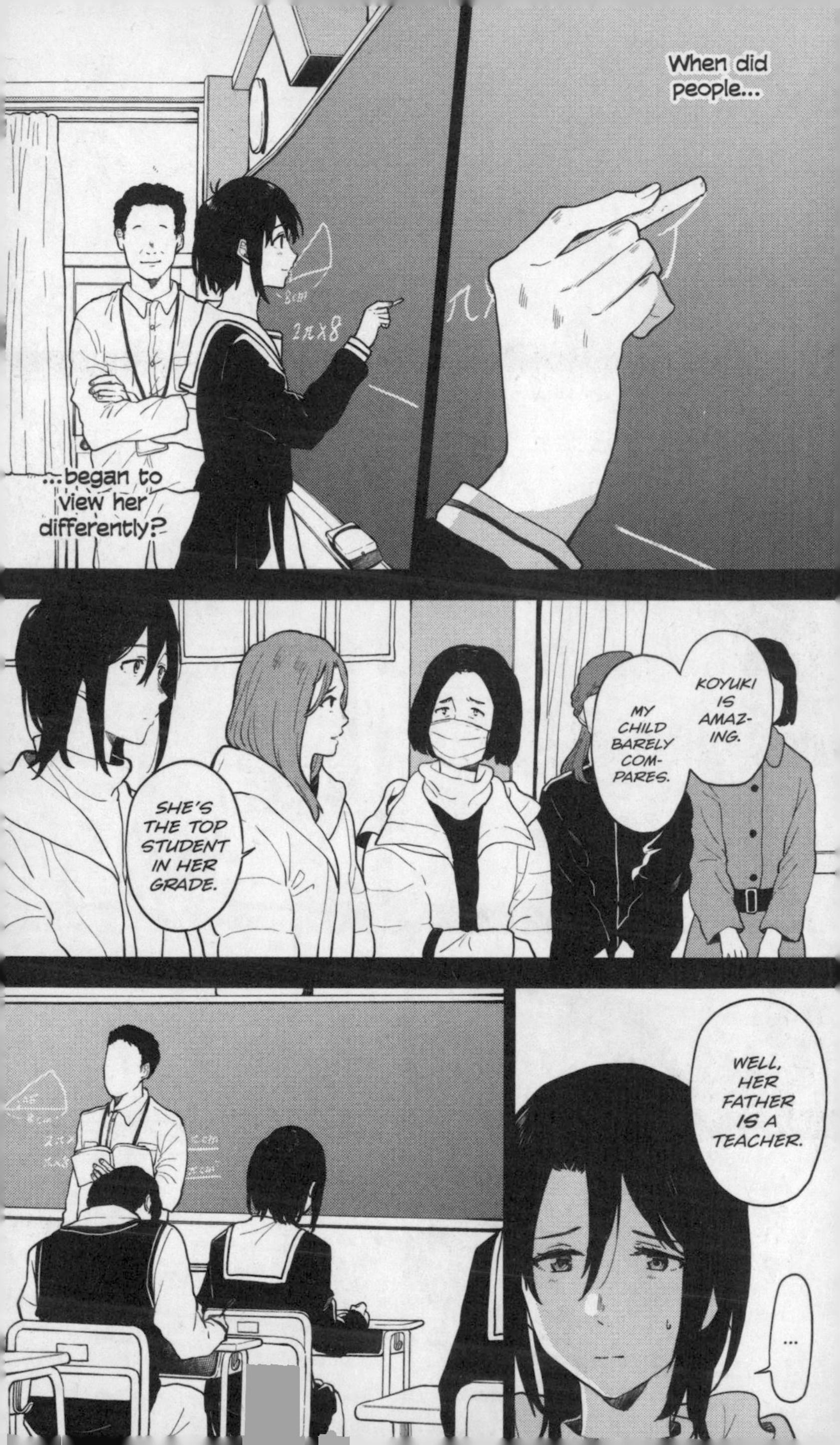
When did people...
...began to view her differently?
KOYUKI IS AMAZING.
MY CHILD BARELY COMPARES.
SHE'S THE TOP STUDENT IN HER GRADE.
WELL, HER FATHER IS A TEACHER.
...

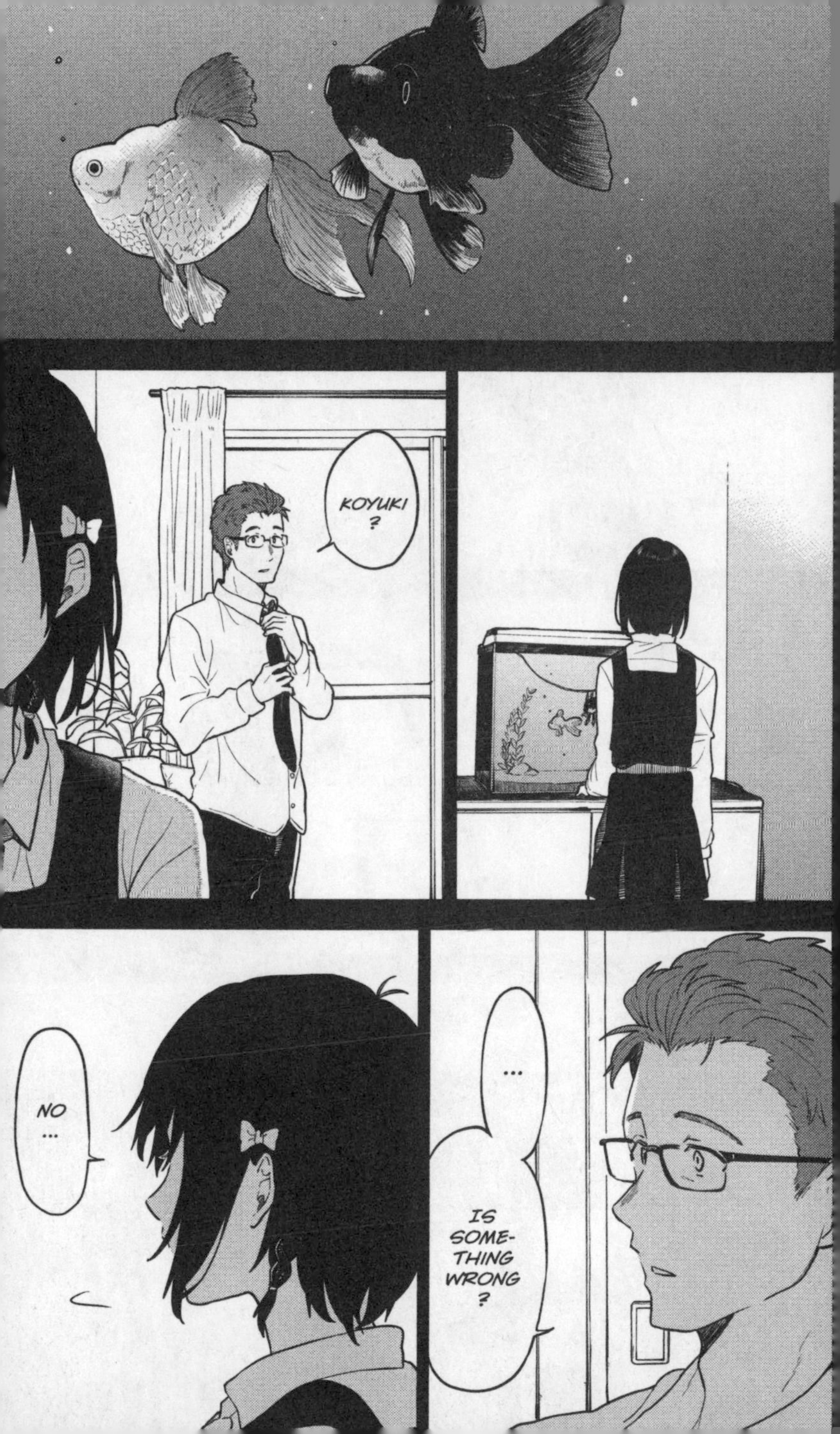
KOYUKI?
...
IS SOME-THING WRONG?
NO ...

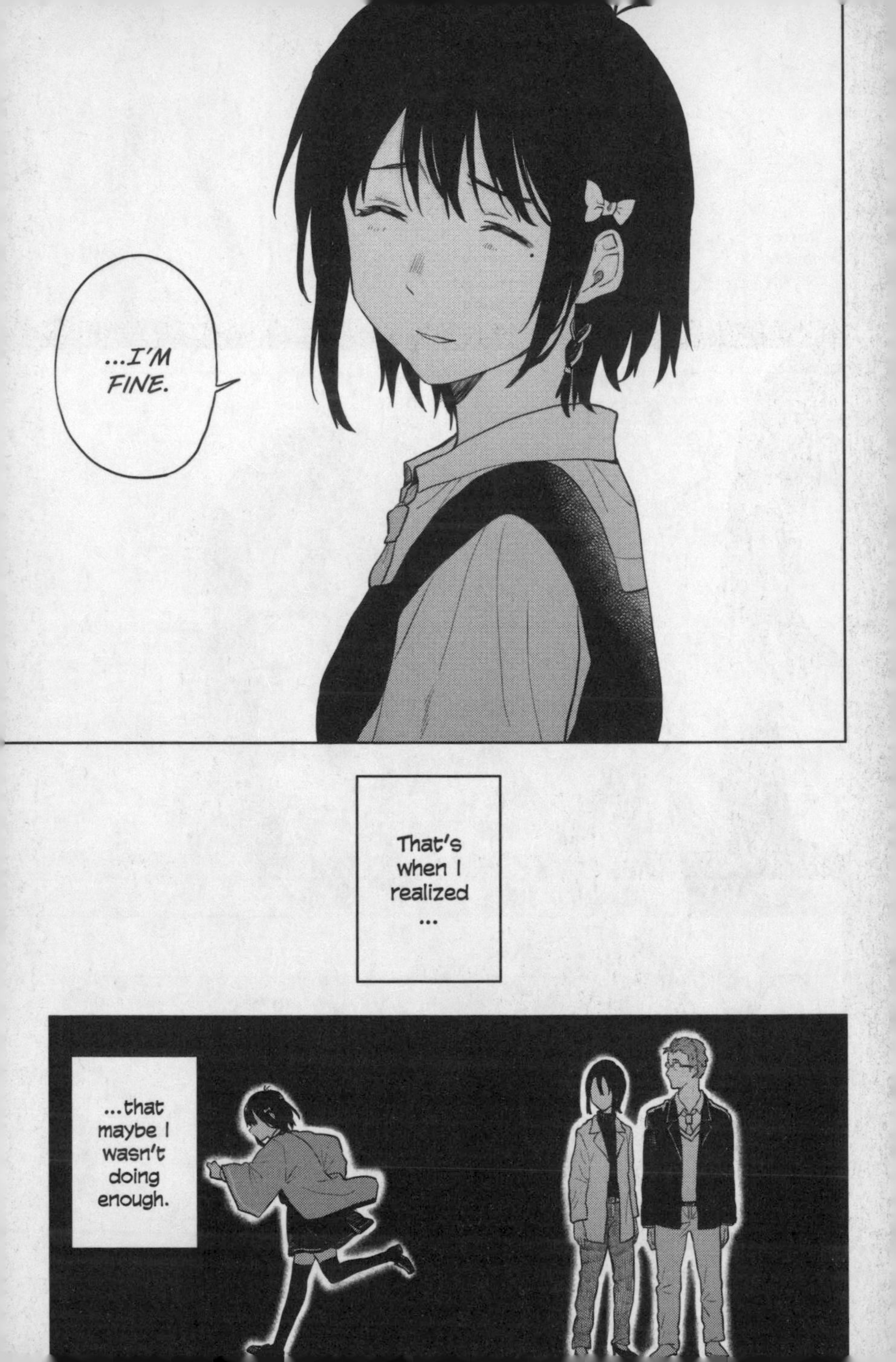
...I'M FINE.
That's when I realized ...
...that maybe I wasn't doing enough.

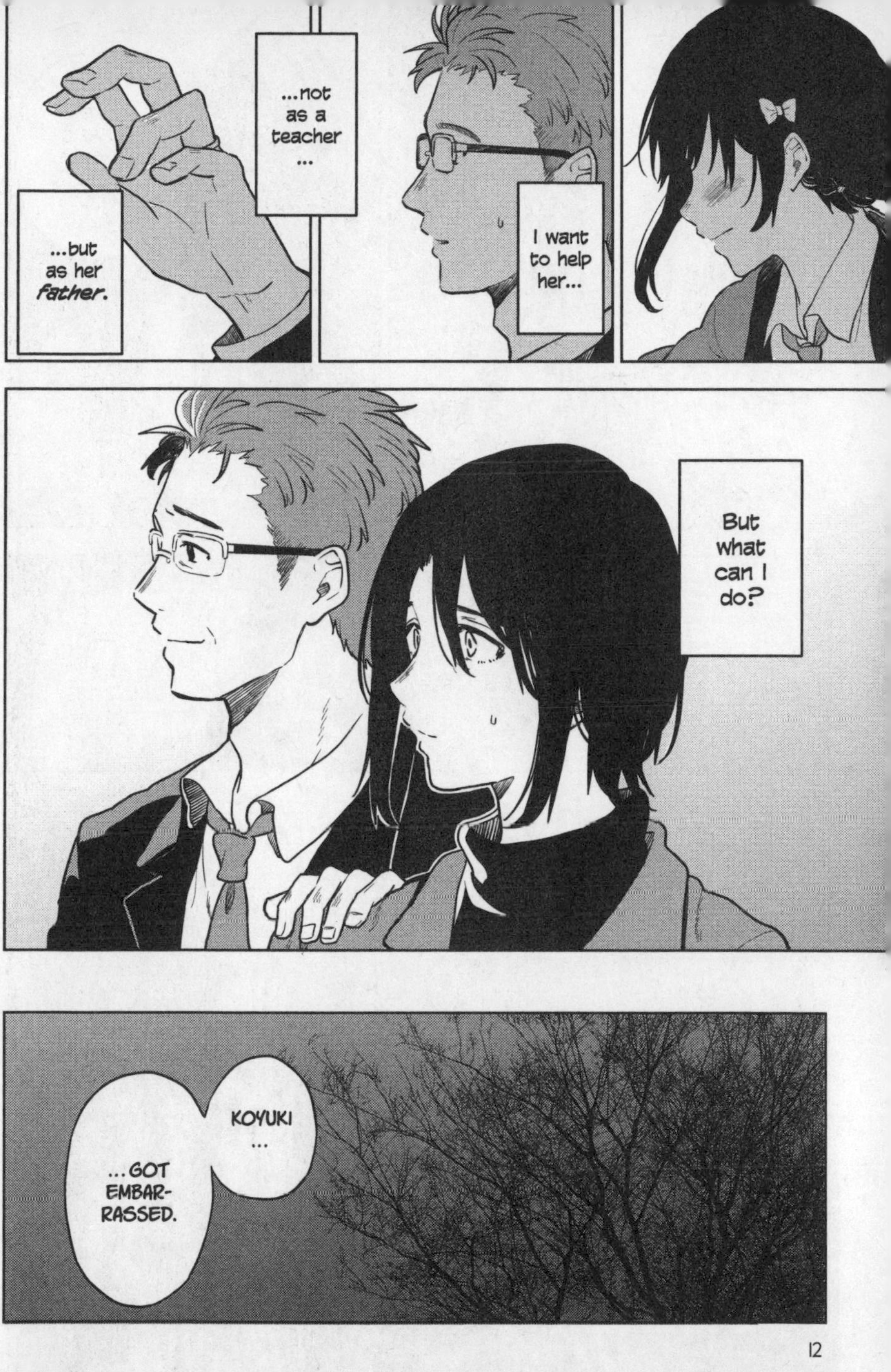
I want to help her...
...not as a teacher ...
...but as her *father*.
But what can I do?
KOYUKI ...
...GOT EMBARRASSED.

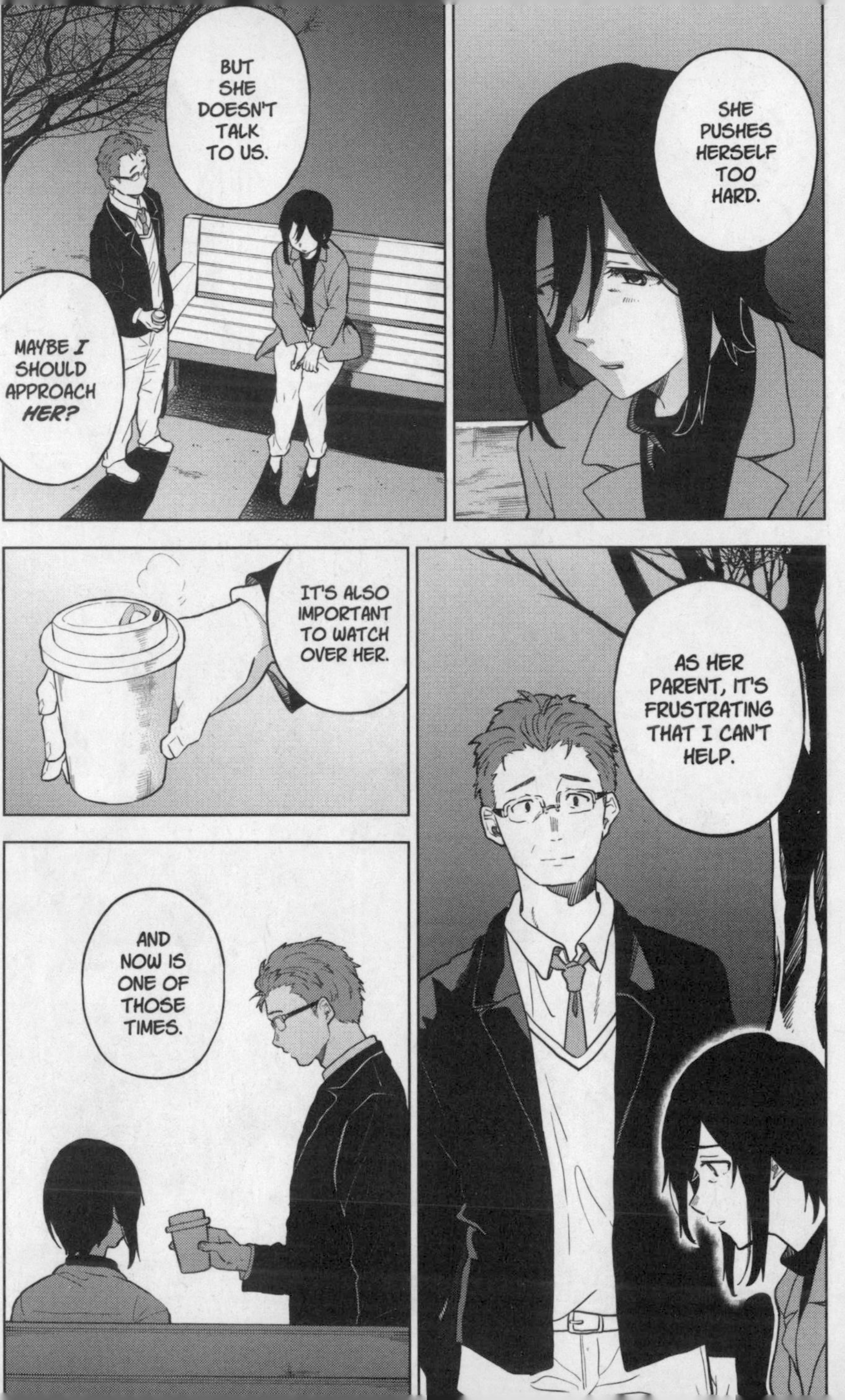
SHE PUSHES HERSELF TOO HARD.
BUT SHE DOESN'T TALK TO US.
MAYBE I SHOULD APPROACH HER?
AS HER PARENT, IT'S FRUSTRATING THAT I CAN'T HELP.
IT'S ALSO IMPORTANT TO WATCH OVER HER.
AND NOW IS ONE OF THOSE TIMES.

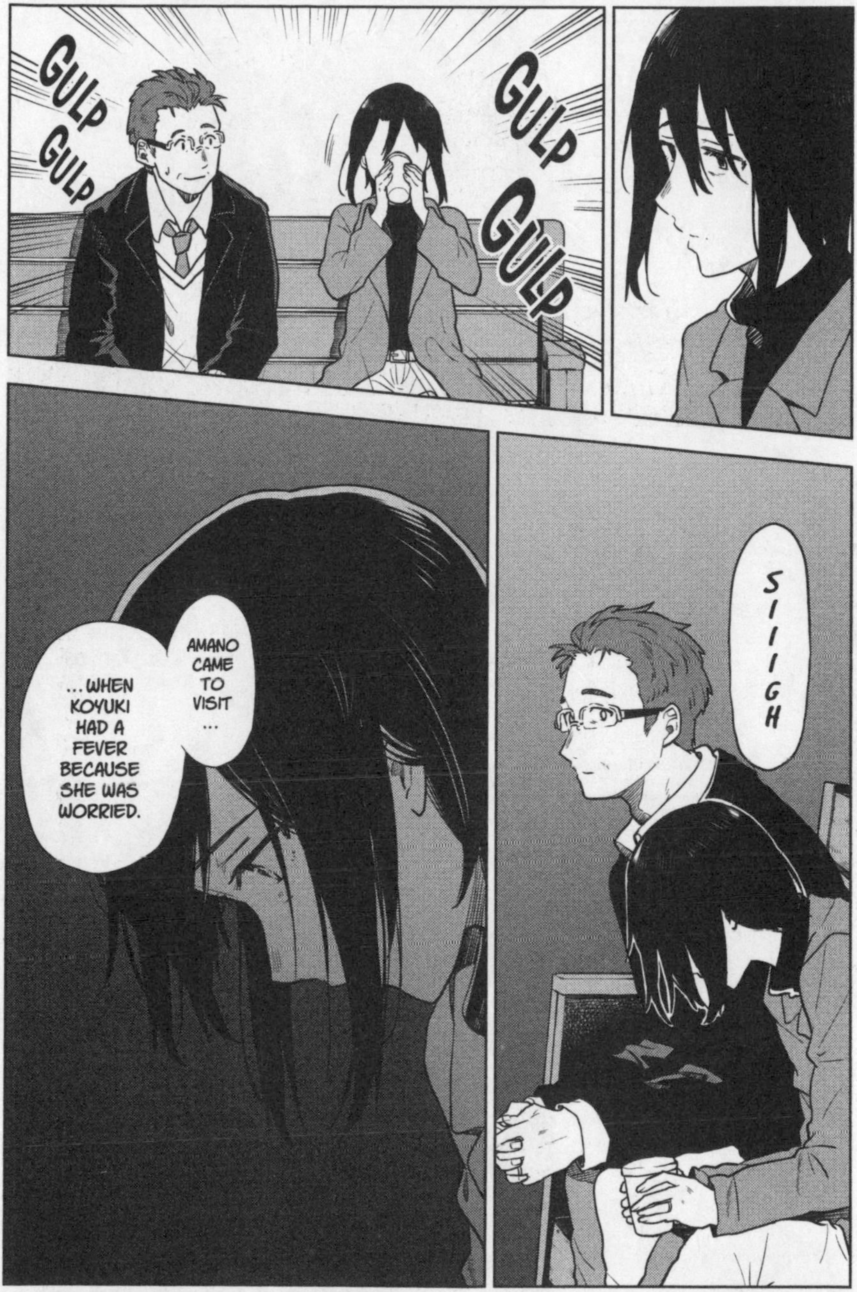
GULP GULP
GULP GULP
SIIIGH
AMANO CAME TO VISIT ...
...WHEN KOYUKI HAD A FEVER BECAUSE SHE WAS WORRIED.

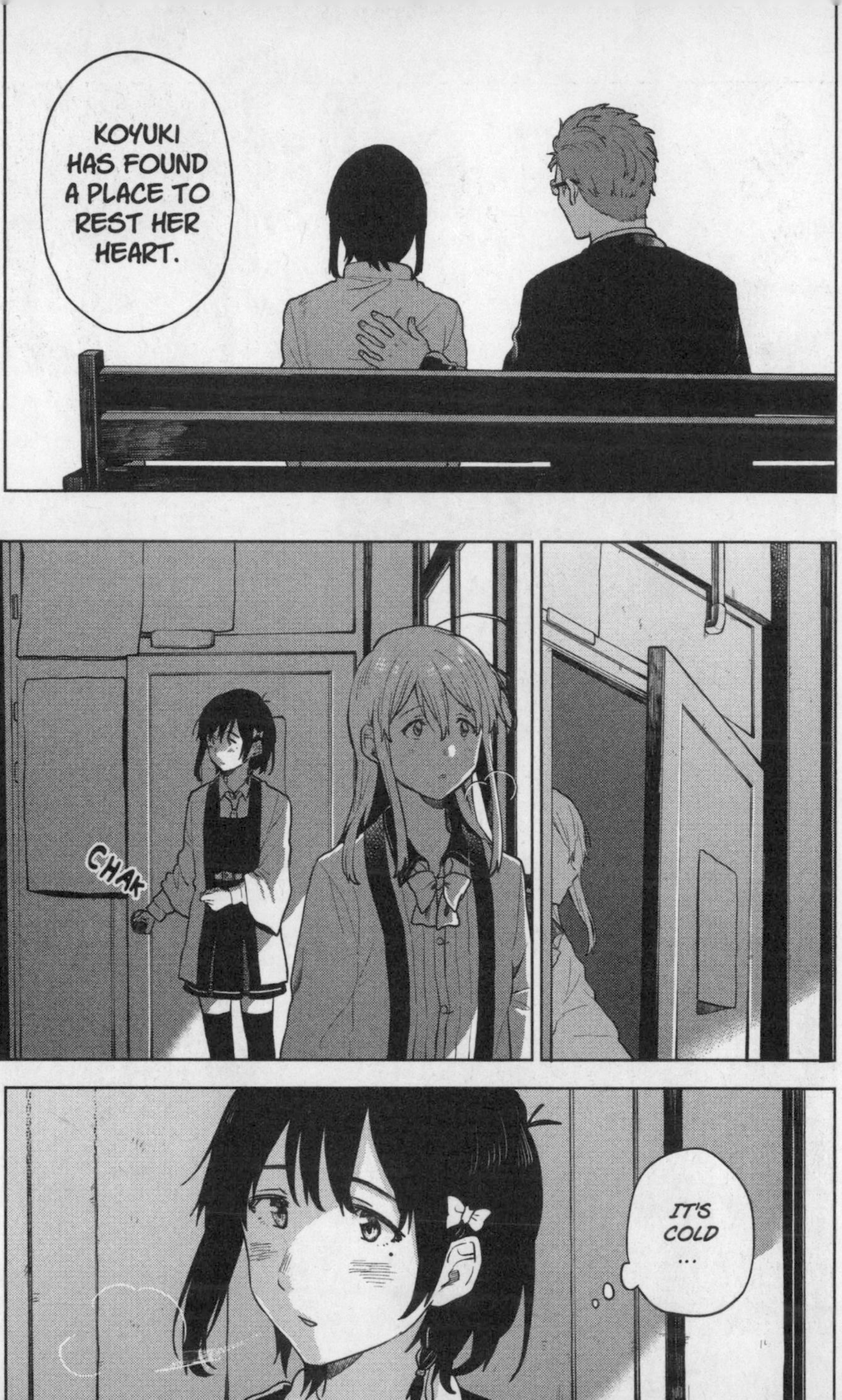
KOYUKI HAS FOUND A PLACE TO REST HER HEART.
CHAK
IT'S COLD ...

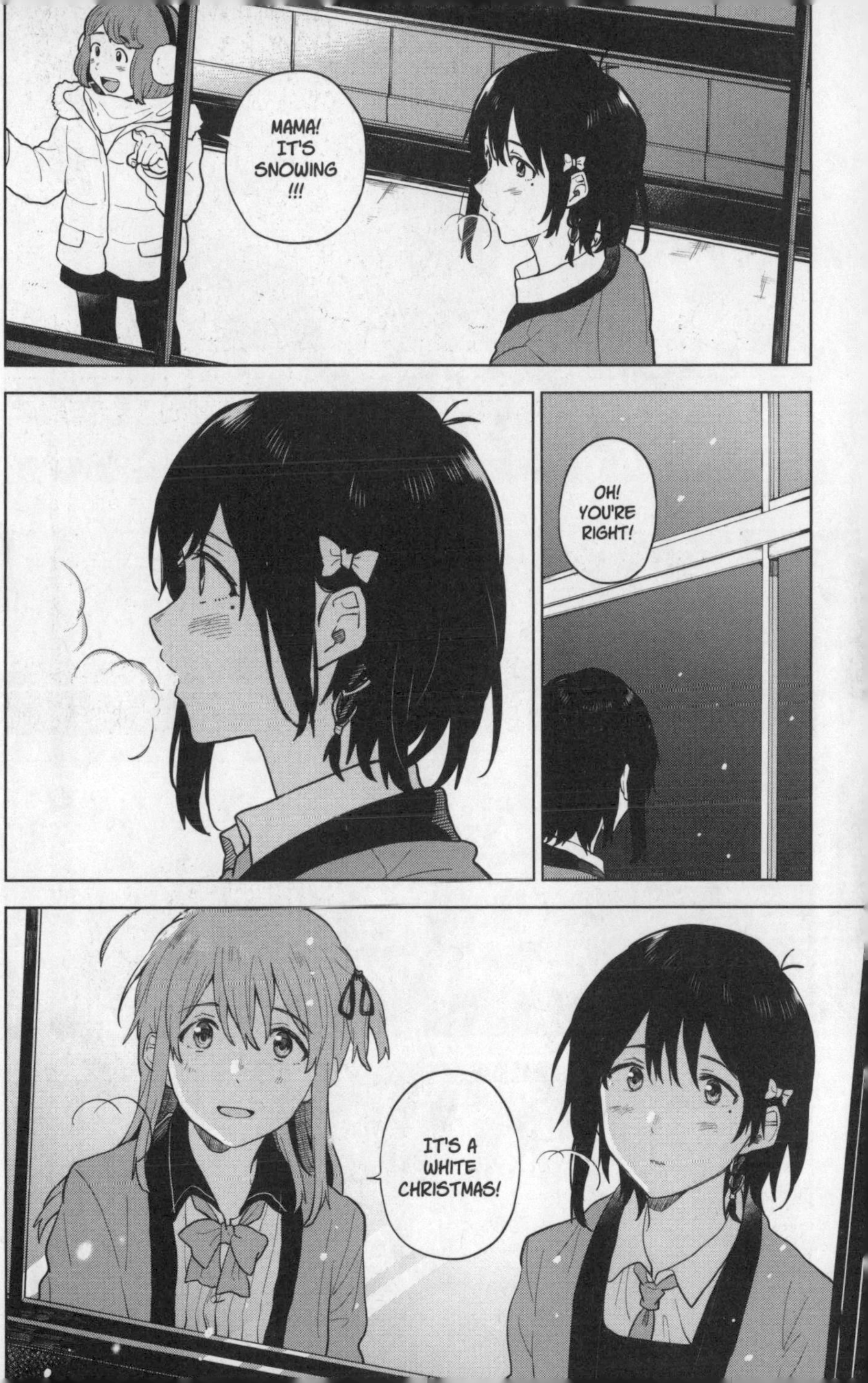
MAMA! IT'S SNOWING !!!
OH! YOU'RE RIGHT!
IT'S A WHITE CHRISTMAS!

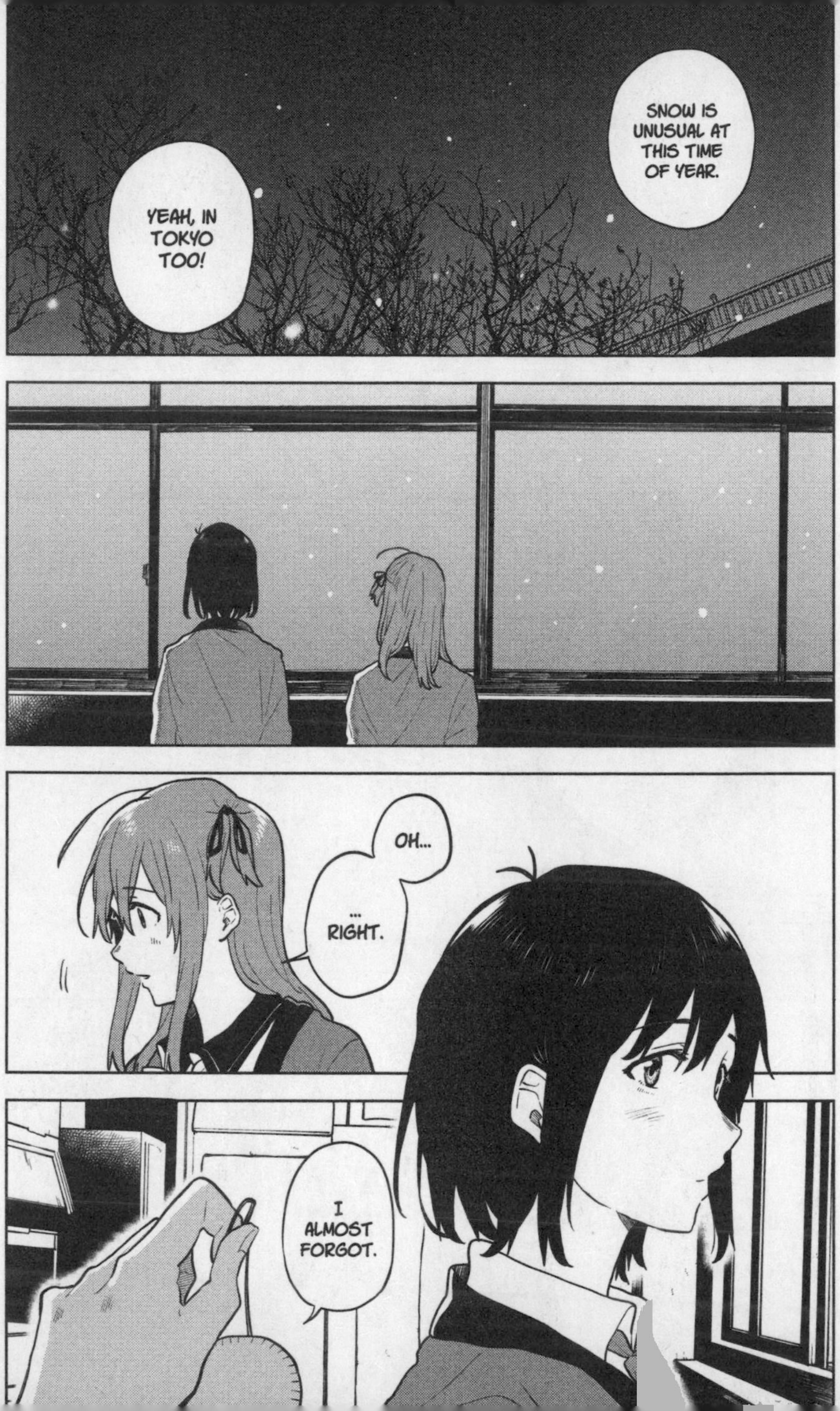
SNOW IS UNUSUAL AT THIS TIME OF YEAR.
YEAH, IN TOKYO TOO!
OH...
... RIGHT.
I ALMOST FORGOT.

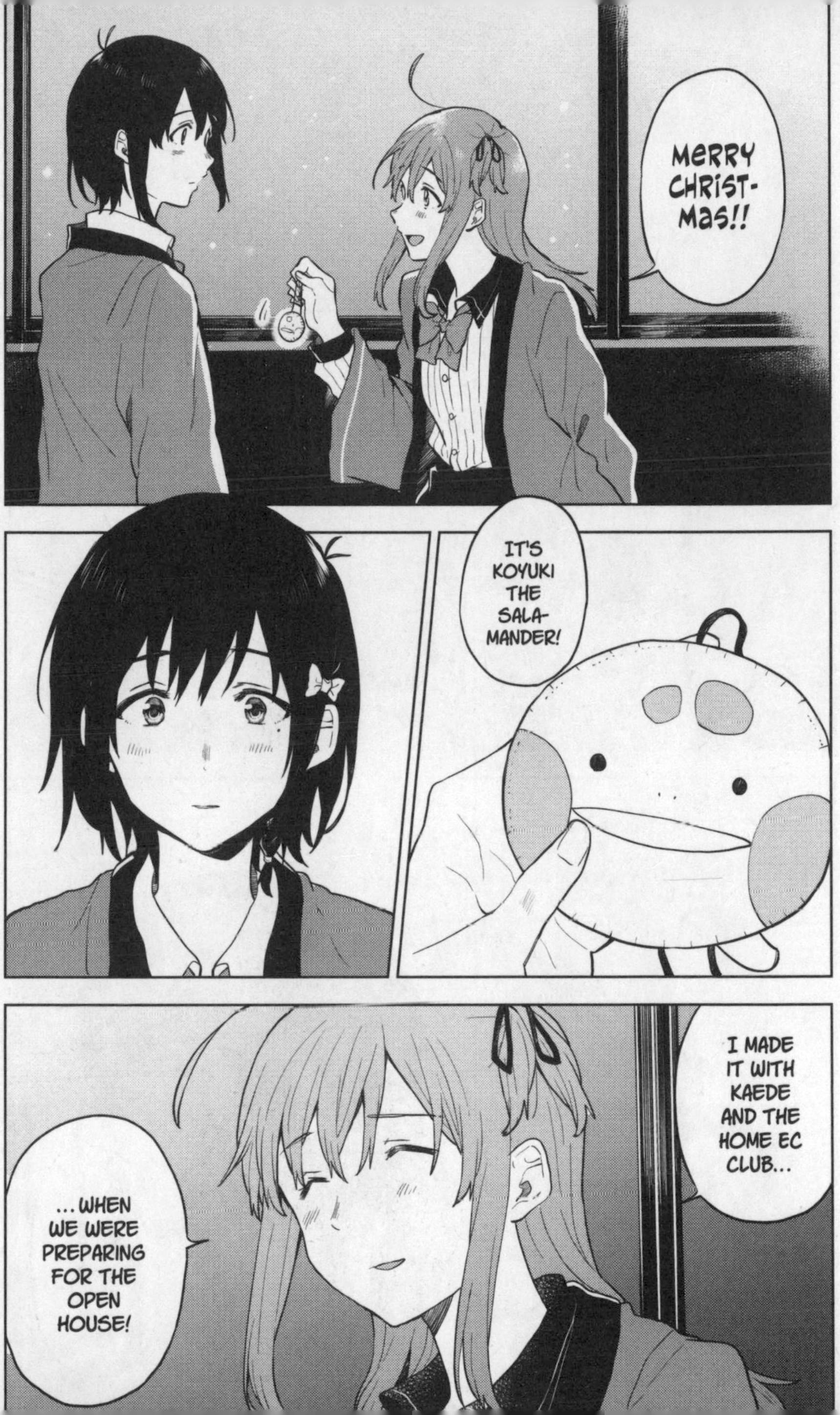
MERRY CHRIST-MAS!!
IT'S KOYUKI THE SALA-MANDER!
I MADE IT WITH KAEDE AND THE HOME EC CLUB...
...WHEN WE WERE PREPARING FOR THE OPEN HOUSE!

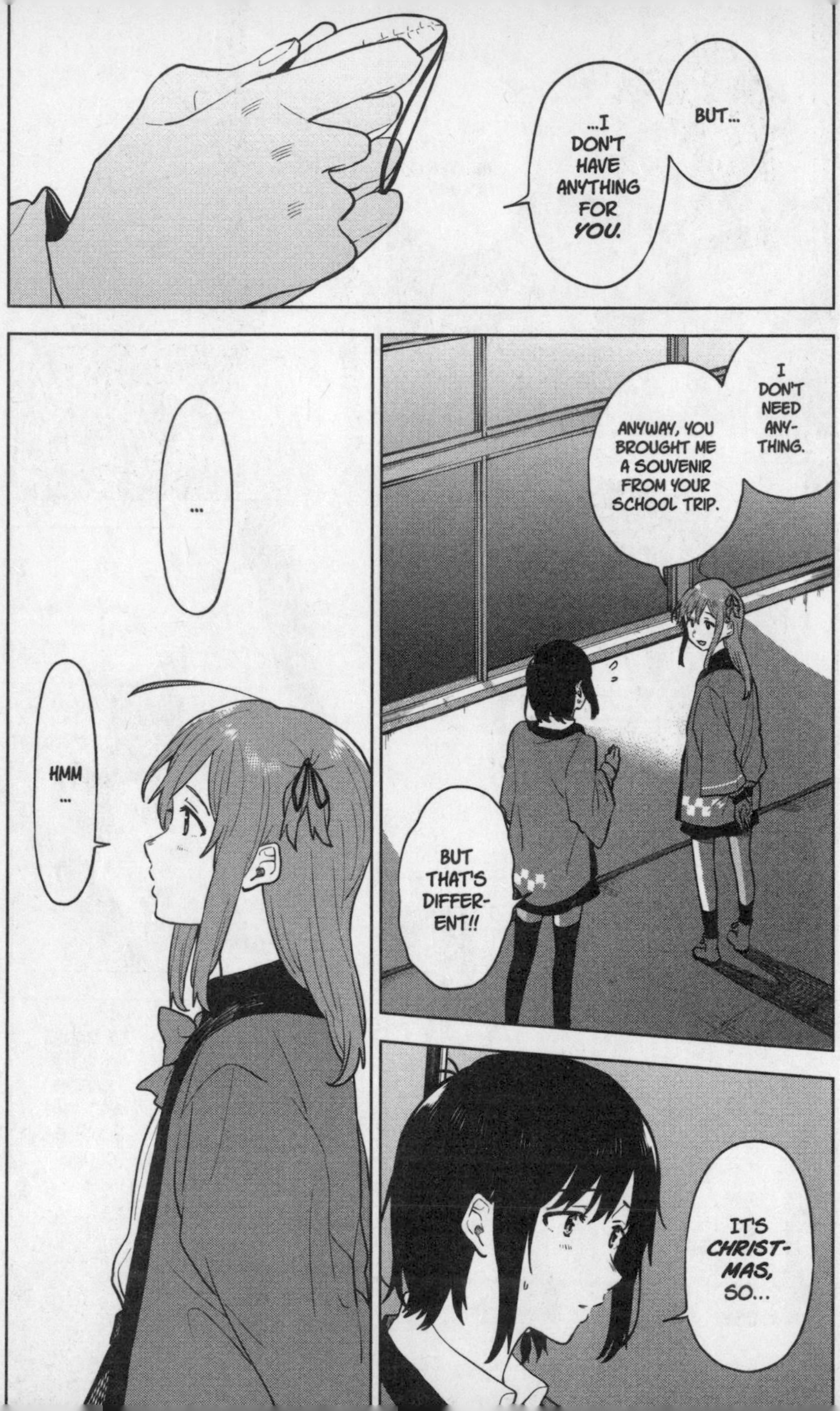
BUT...
...I DON'T HAVE ANYTHING FOR YOU.
I DON'T NEED ANY-THING.
ANYWAY, YOU BROUGHT ME A SOUVENIR FROM YOUR SCHOOL TRIP.
BUT THAT'S DIFFER-ENT!!
IT'S CHRIST-MAS, SO...
...
HMM...

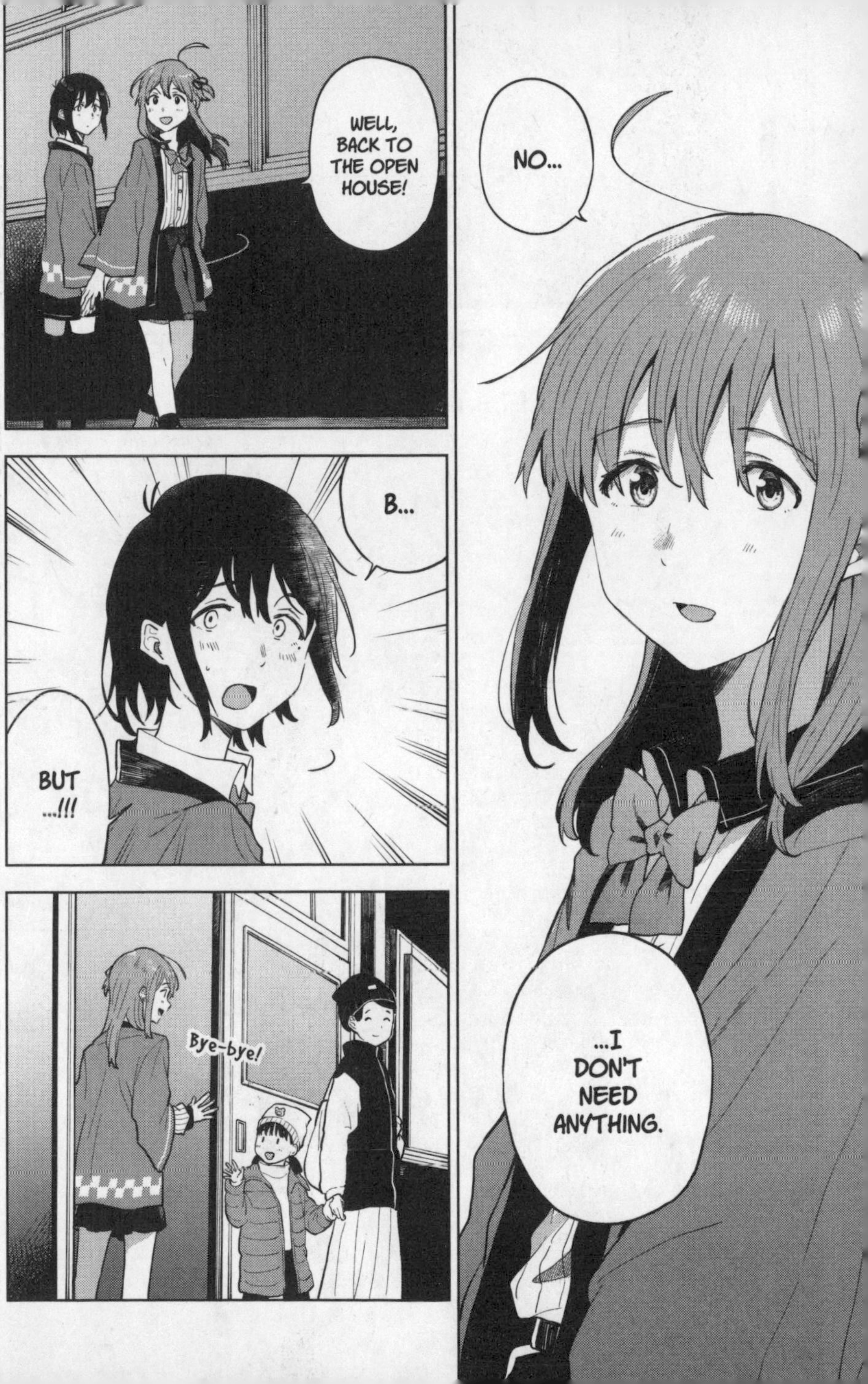
NO...
...I DON'T NEED ANYTHING.
WELL, BACK TO THE OPEN HOUSE!
B...
BUT ...!!!
Bye-bye!

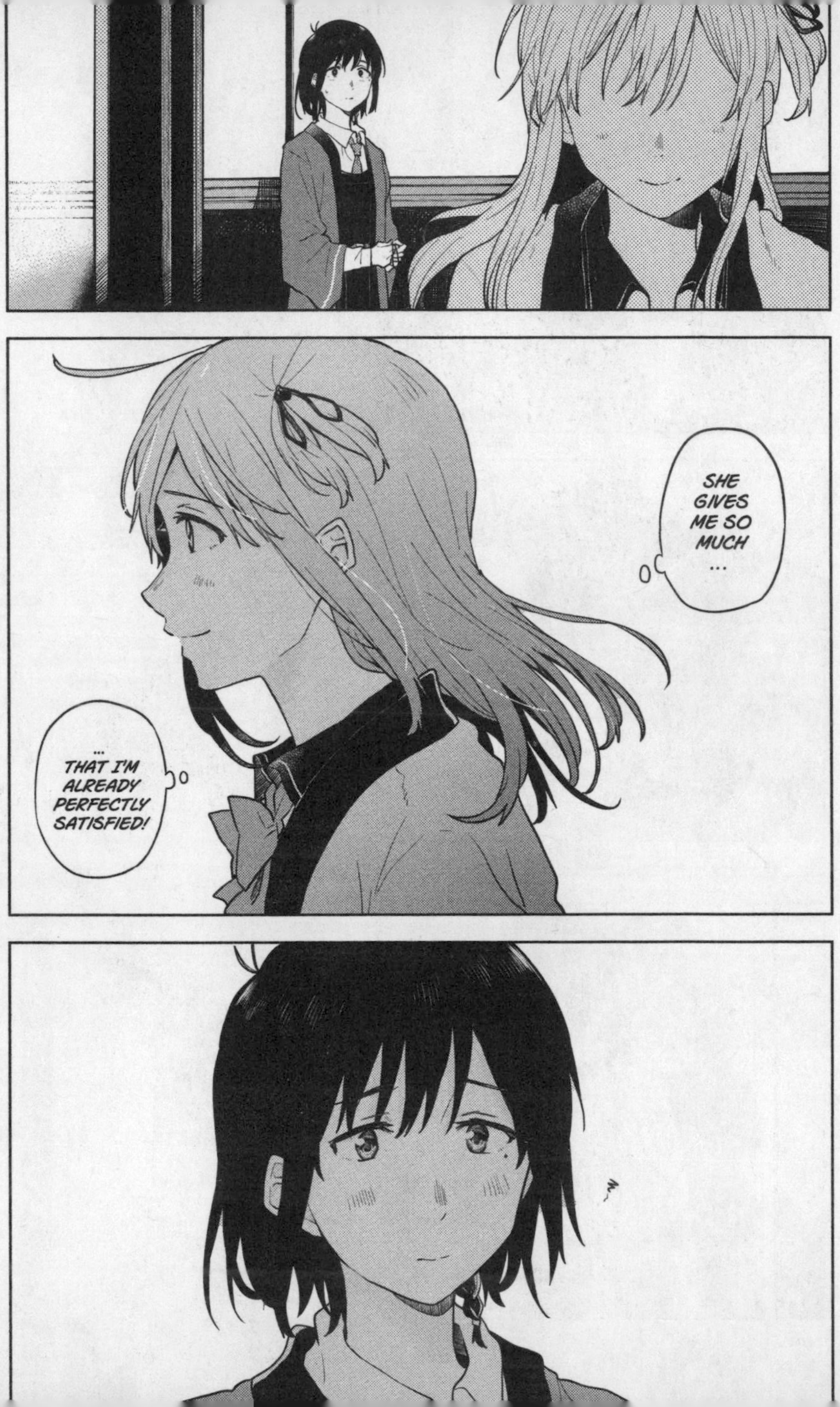
SHE GIVES ME SO MUCH ...
... THAT I'M ALREADY PERFECTLY SATISFIED!

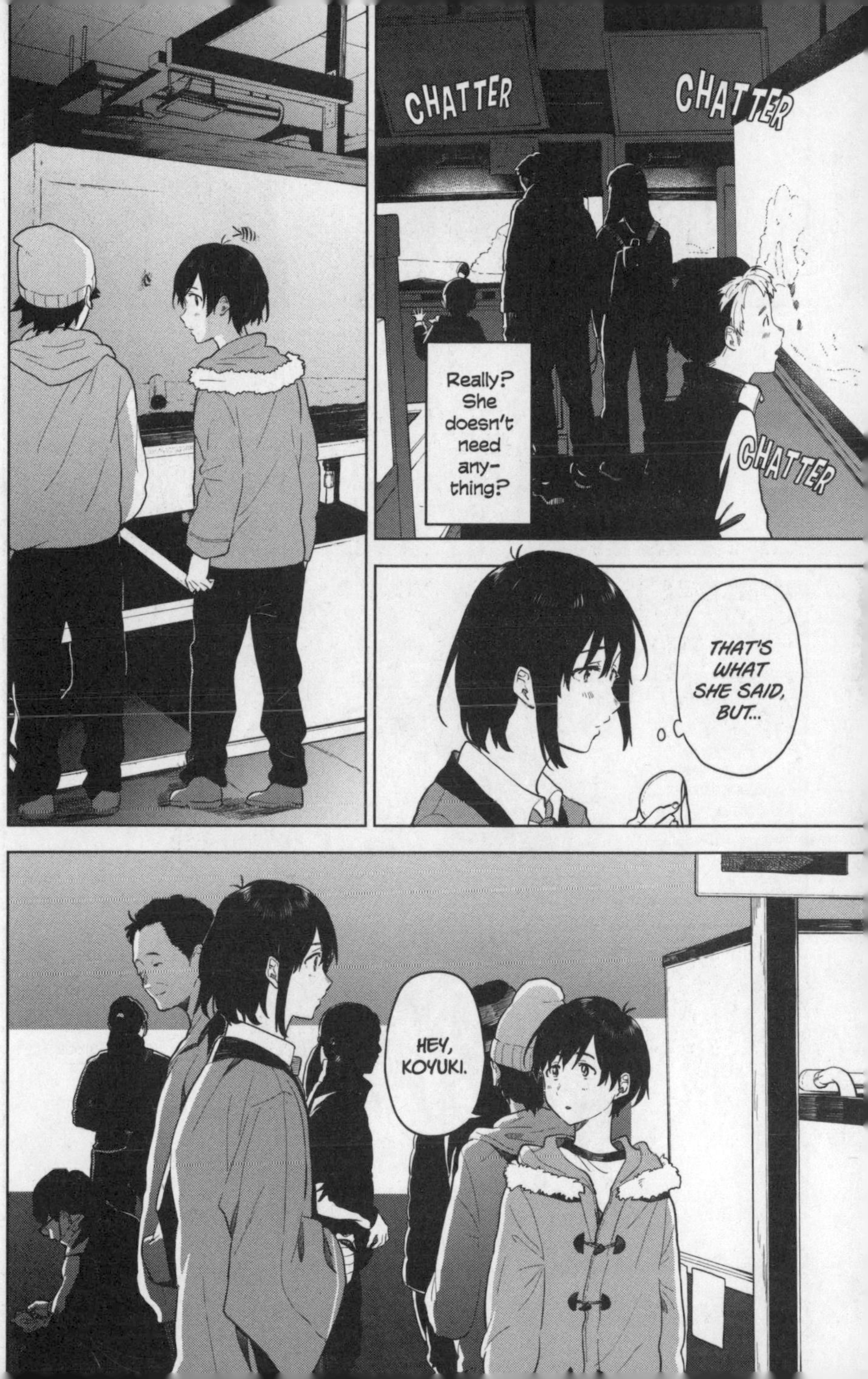
CHATTER
CHATTER
Really? She doesn't need any-thing?
CHATTER
THAT'S WHAT SHE SAID, BUT...
HEY, KOYUKI.

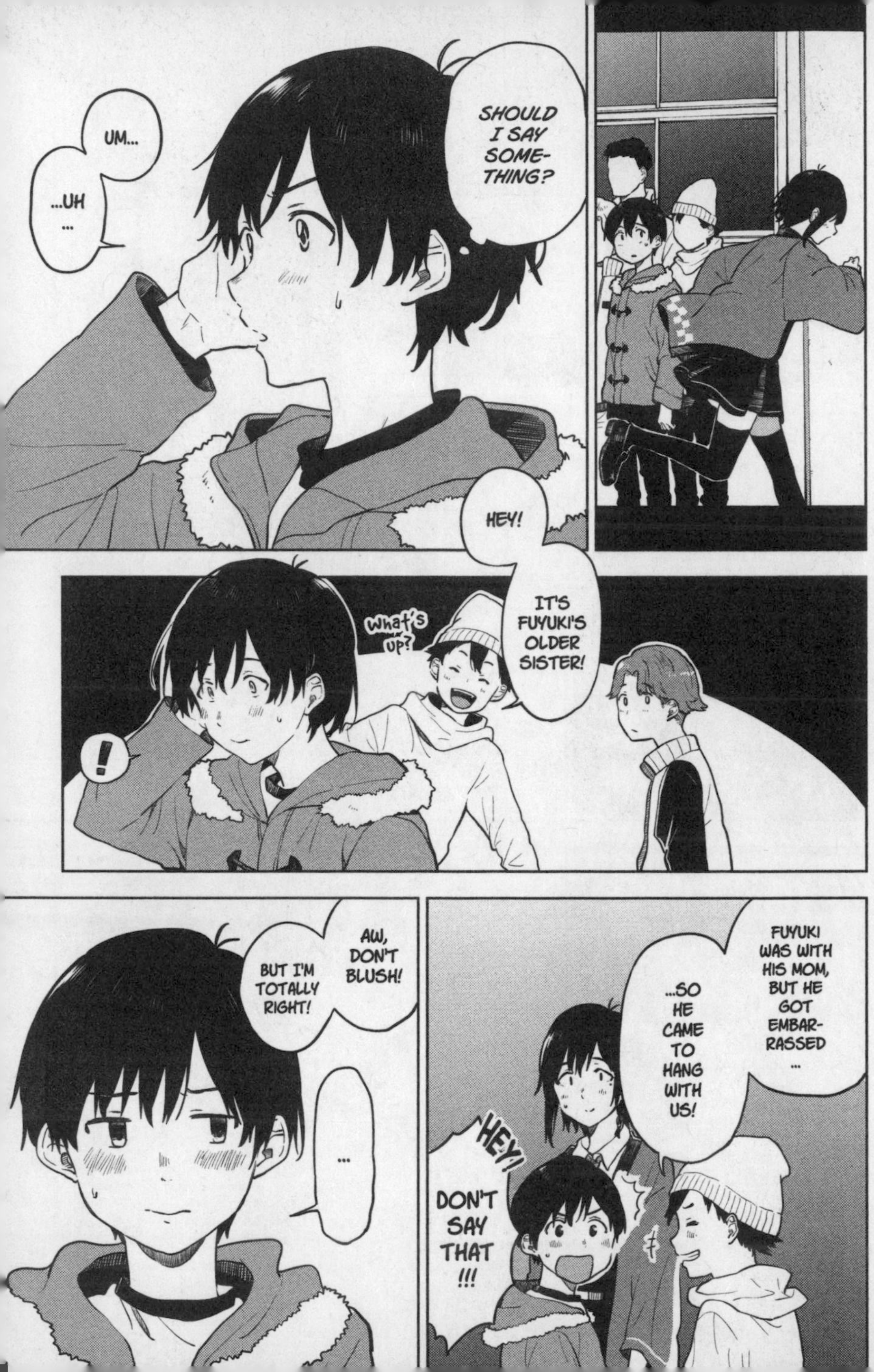
SHOULD I SAY SOME-THING?
UM...
...UH ...
HEY!
IT'S FUYUKI'S OLDER SISTER!
What's up?
!
FUYUKI WAS WITH HIS MOM, BUT HE GOT EMBAR-RASSED ...
...SO HE CAME TO HANG WITH US!
HEY!
DON'T SAY THAT !!!
AW, DON'T BLUSH!
BUT I'M TOTALLY RIGHT!
...

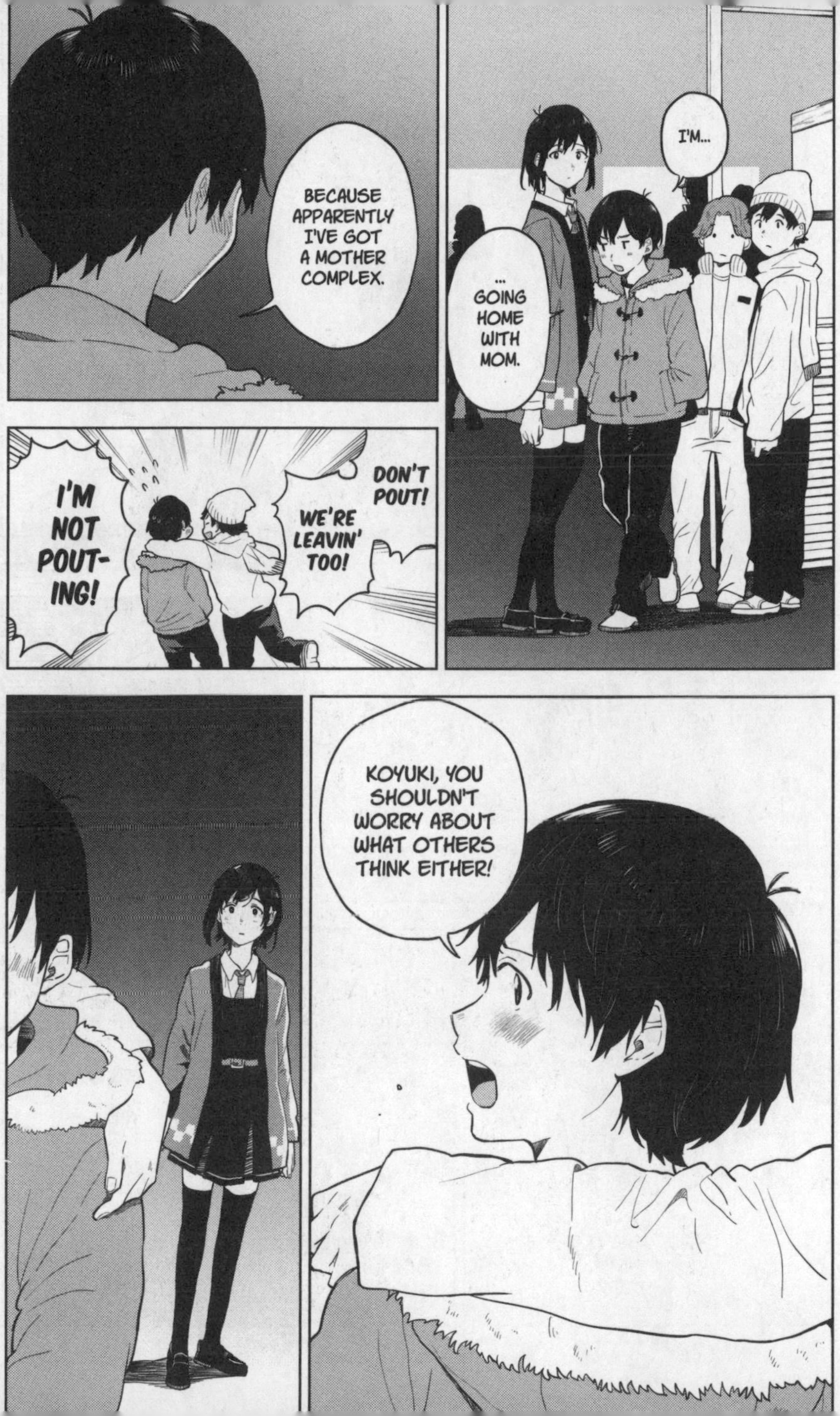
I'M...
...GOING HOME WITH MOM.
BECAUSE APPARENTLY I'VE GOT A MOTHER COMPLEX.
DON'T POUT!
WE'RE LEAVIN' TOO!
I'M NOT POUT-ING!
KOYUKI, YOU SHOULDN'T WORRY ABOUT WHAT OTHERS THINK EITHER!

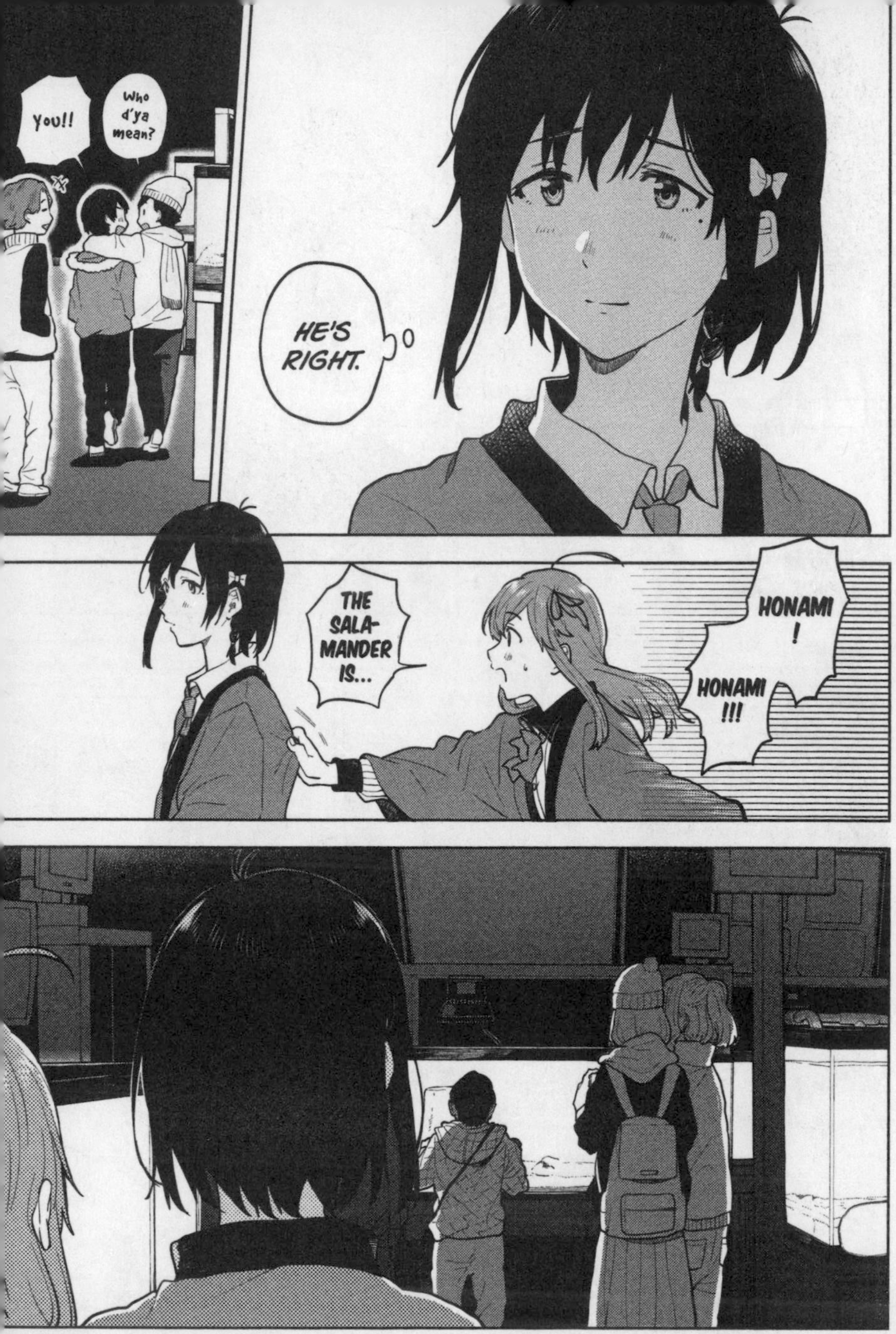
HE'S RIGHT.
Who d'ya mean?
You!!
HONAMI!
HONAMI!!!
THE SALAMANDER IS...

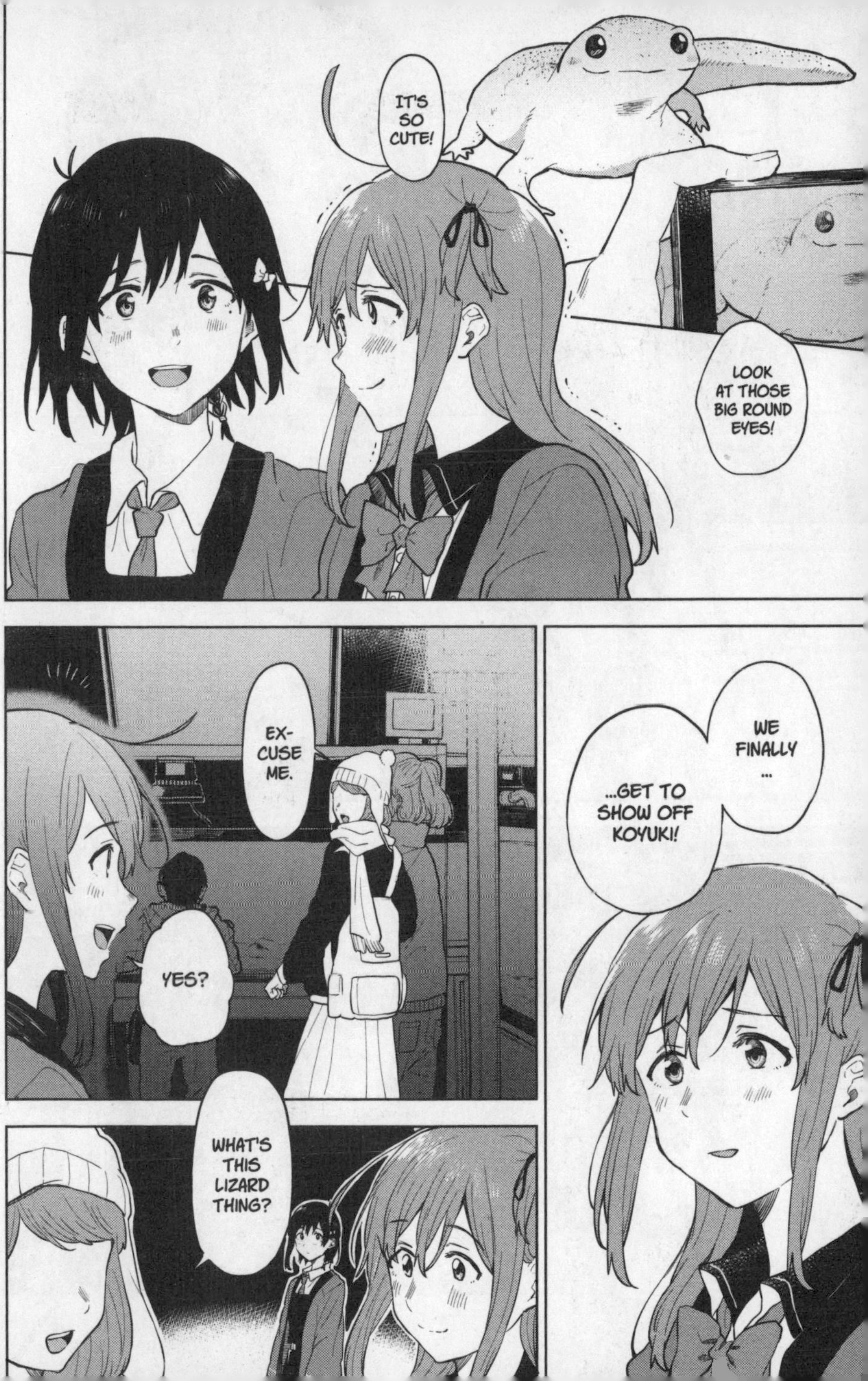
IT'S SO CUTE!
LOOK AT THOSE BIG ROUND EYES!
WE FINALLY ...
...GET TO SHOW OFF KOYUKI!
EX-CUSE ME.
YES?
WHAT'S THIS LIZARD THING?

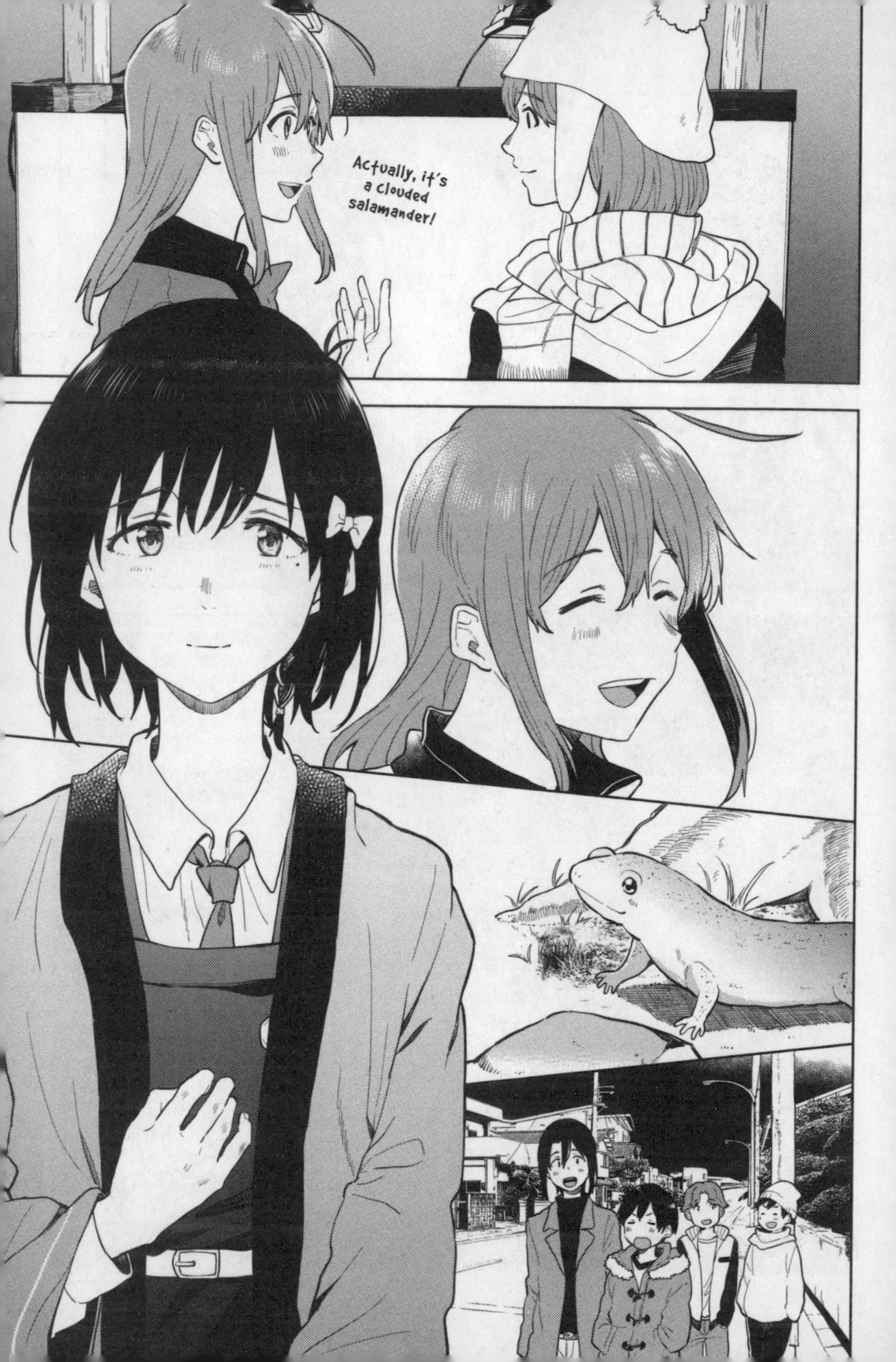
Actually, it's a clouded salamander!

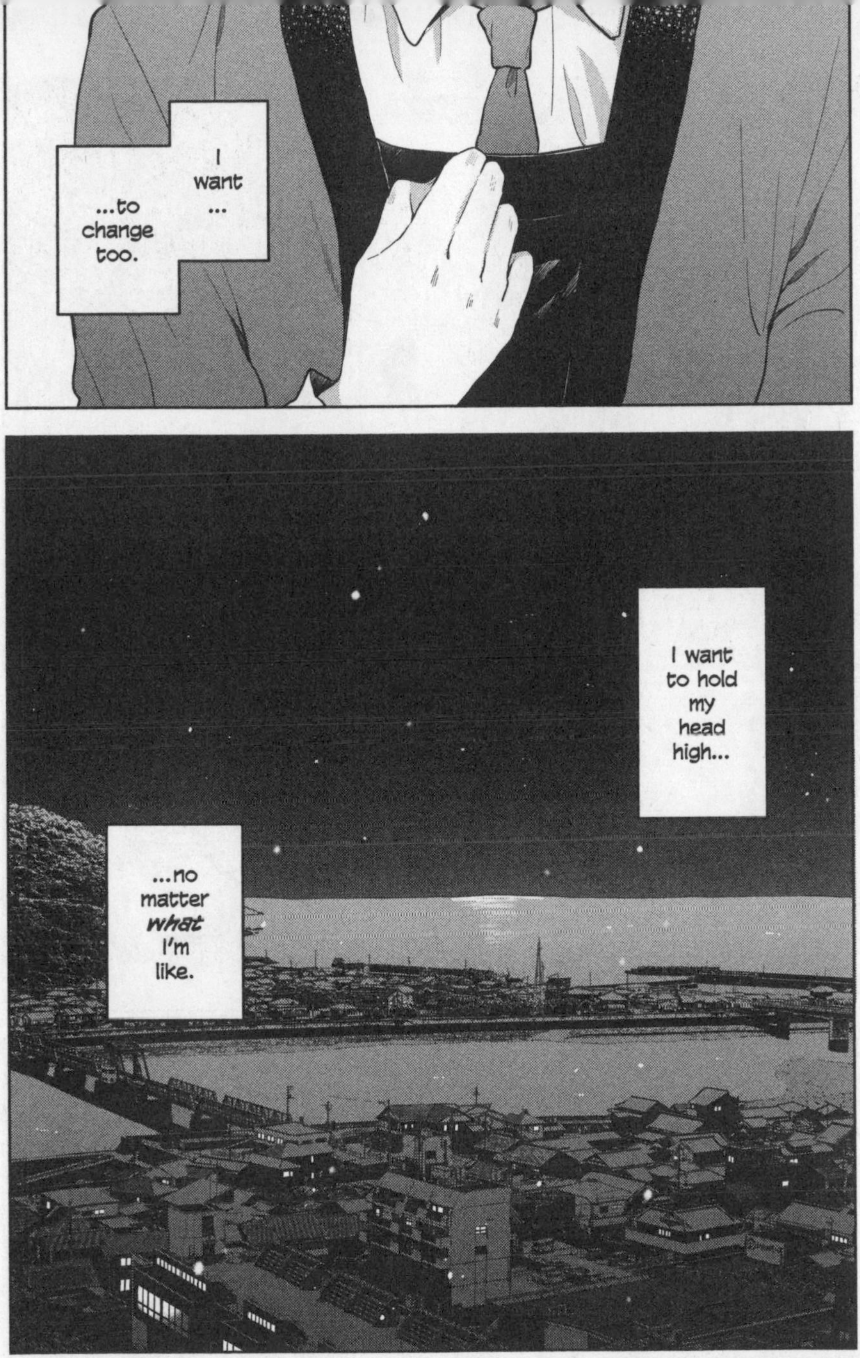
I want ...
...to change too.
I want to hold my head high...
...no matter *what* I'm like.

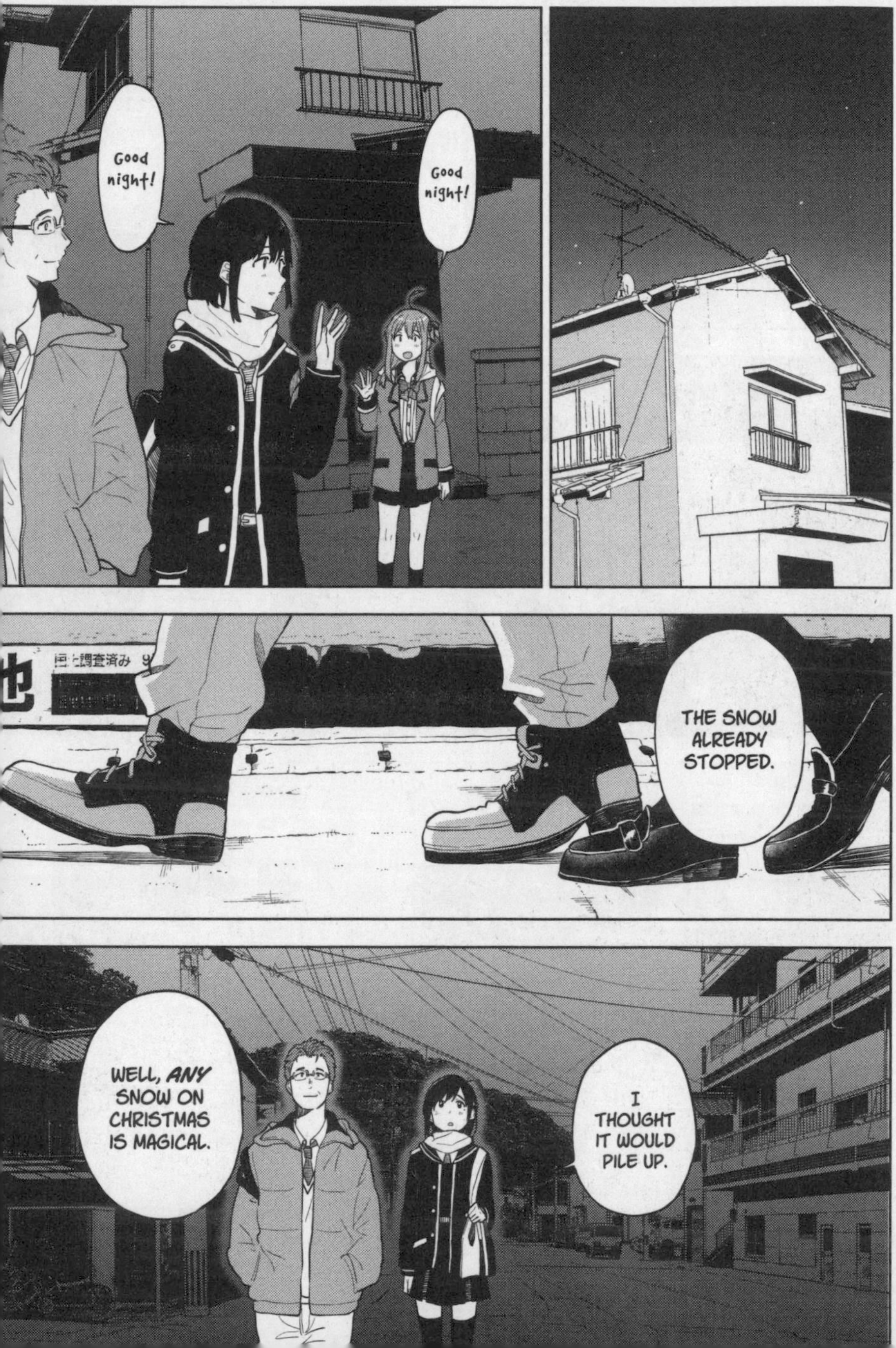
Good night!
Good night!
THE SNOW ALREADY STOPPED.
I THOUGHT IT WOULD PILE UP.
WELL, *ANY* SNOW ON CHRISTMAS IS MAGICAL.

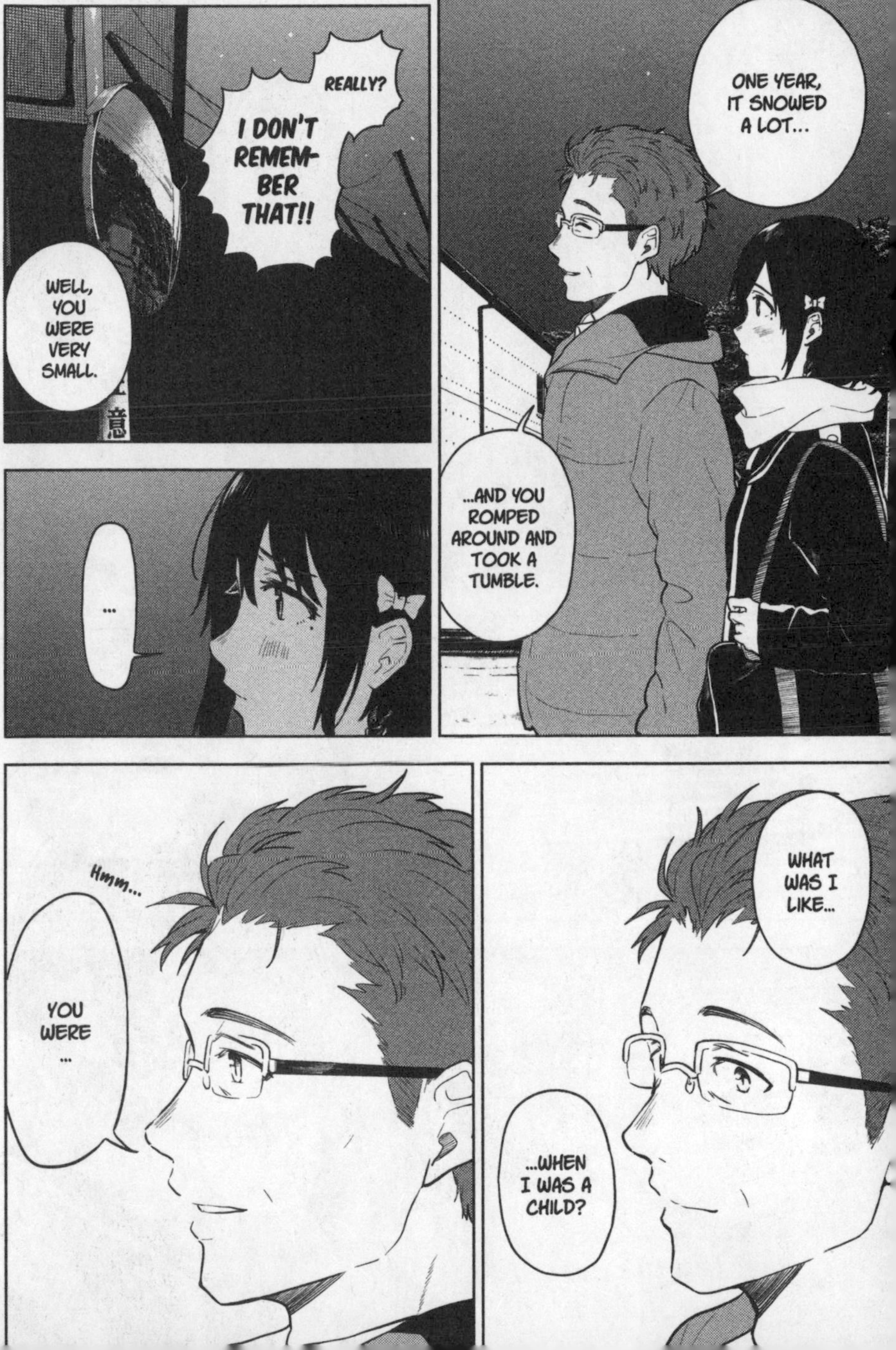
ONE YEAR, IT SNOWED A LOT...
...AND YOU ROMPED AROUND AND TOOK A TUMBLE.
REALLY?
I DON'T REMEMBER THAT!!
WELL, YOU WERE VERY SMALL.
...
WHAT WAS I LIKE...
...WHEN I WAS A CHILD?
Hmm...
YOU WERE ...

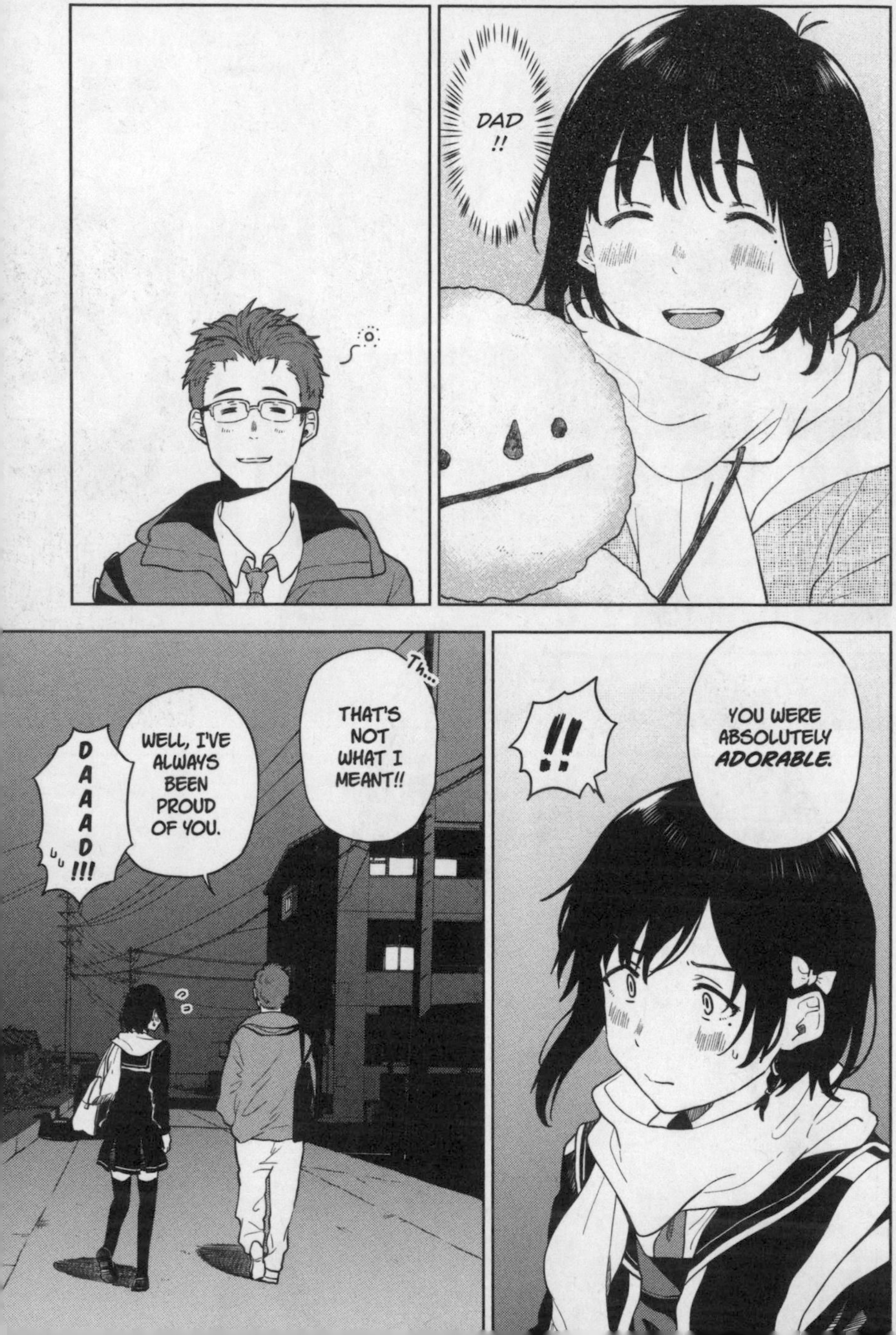
DAD !!
YOU WERE ABSOLUTELY ADORABLE.
!!
Th...
THAT'S NOT WHAT I MEANT!!
WELL, I'VE ALWAYS BEEN PROUD OF YOU.
DAAAAD!!!

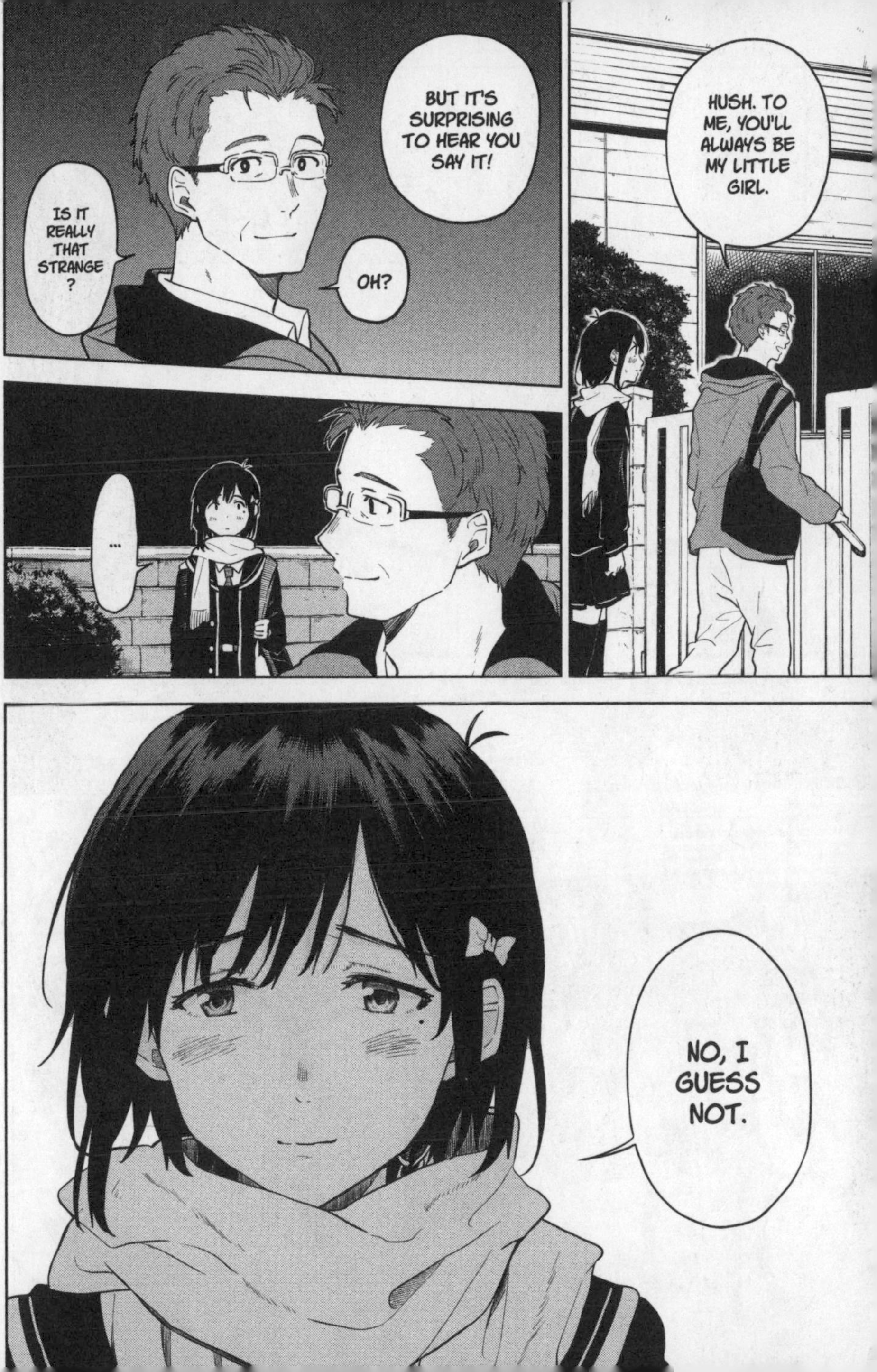
HUSH. TO ME, YOU'LL ALWAYS BE MY LITTLE GIRL.
BUT IT'S SURPRISING TO HEAR YOU SAY IT!
IS IT REALLY THAT STRANGE?
OH?
...
NO, I GUESS NOT.

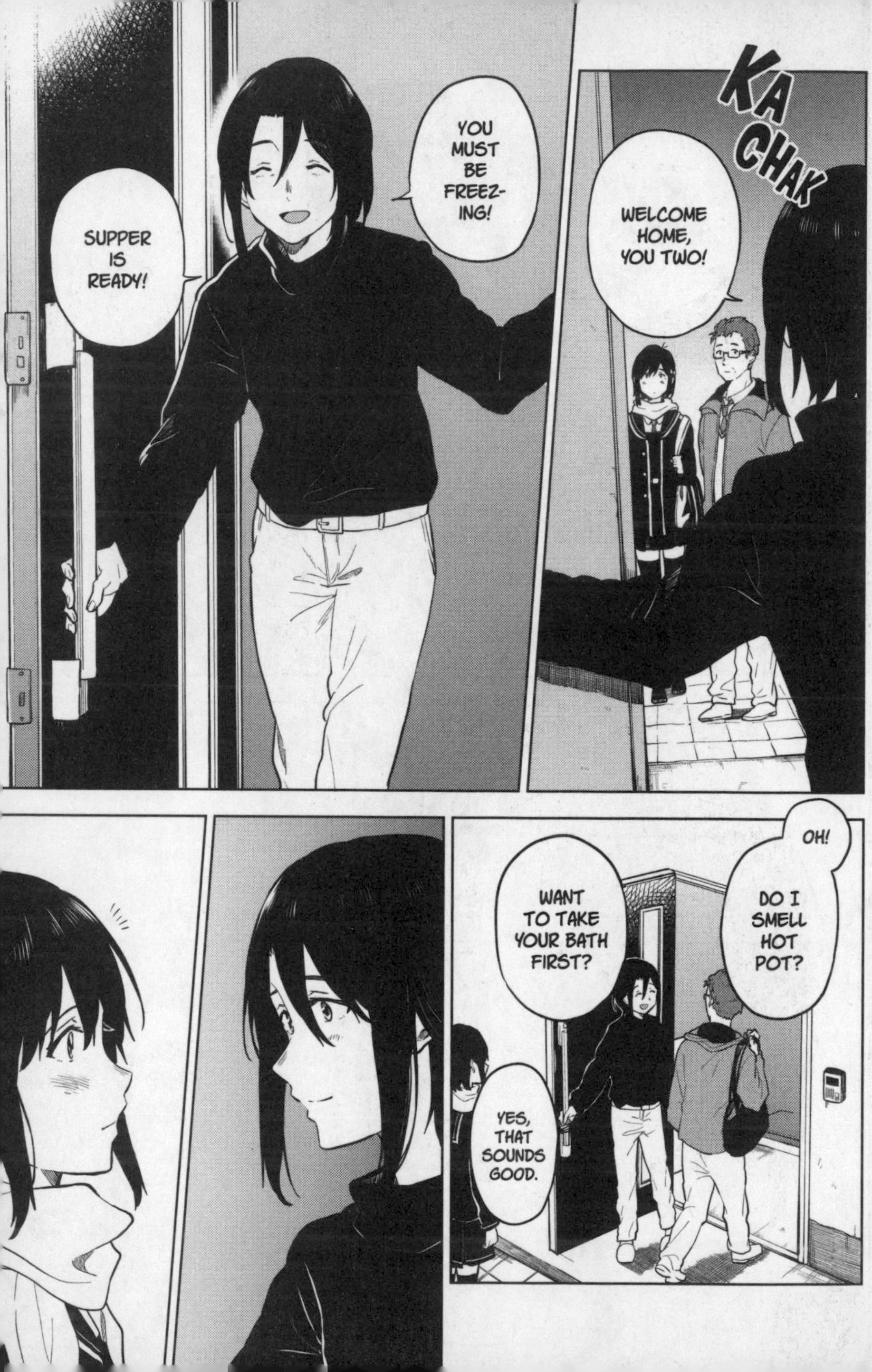
KA CHAK
WELCOME HOME, YOU TWO!
YOU MUST BE FREEZ-ING!
SUPPER IS READY!
OH!
DO I SMELL HOT POT?
WANT TO TAKE YOUR BATH FIRST?
YES, THAT SOUNDS GOOD.

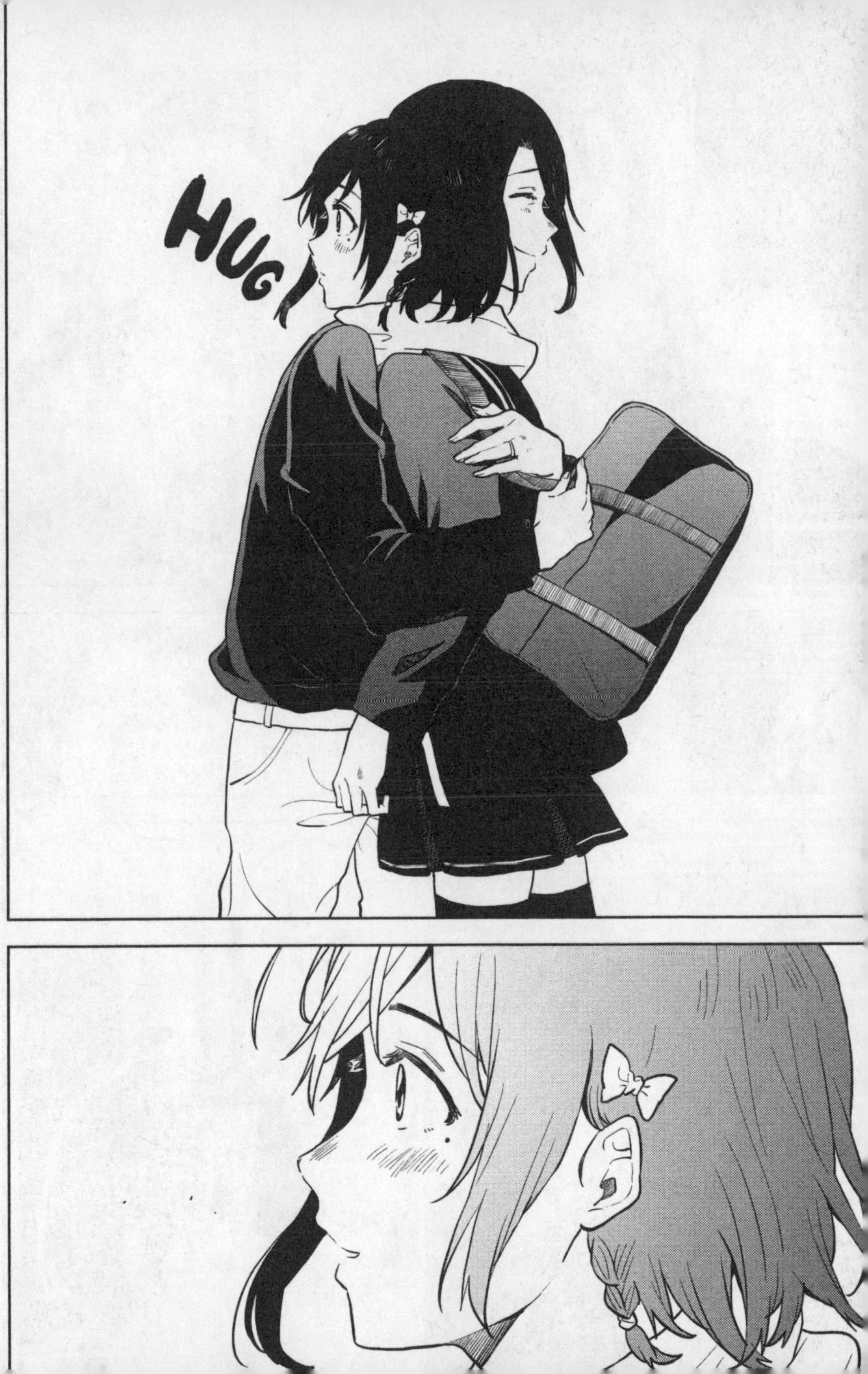
HUG

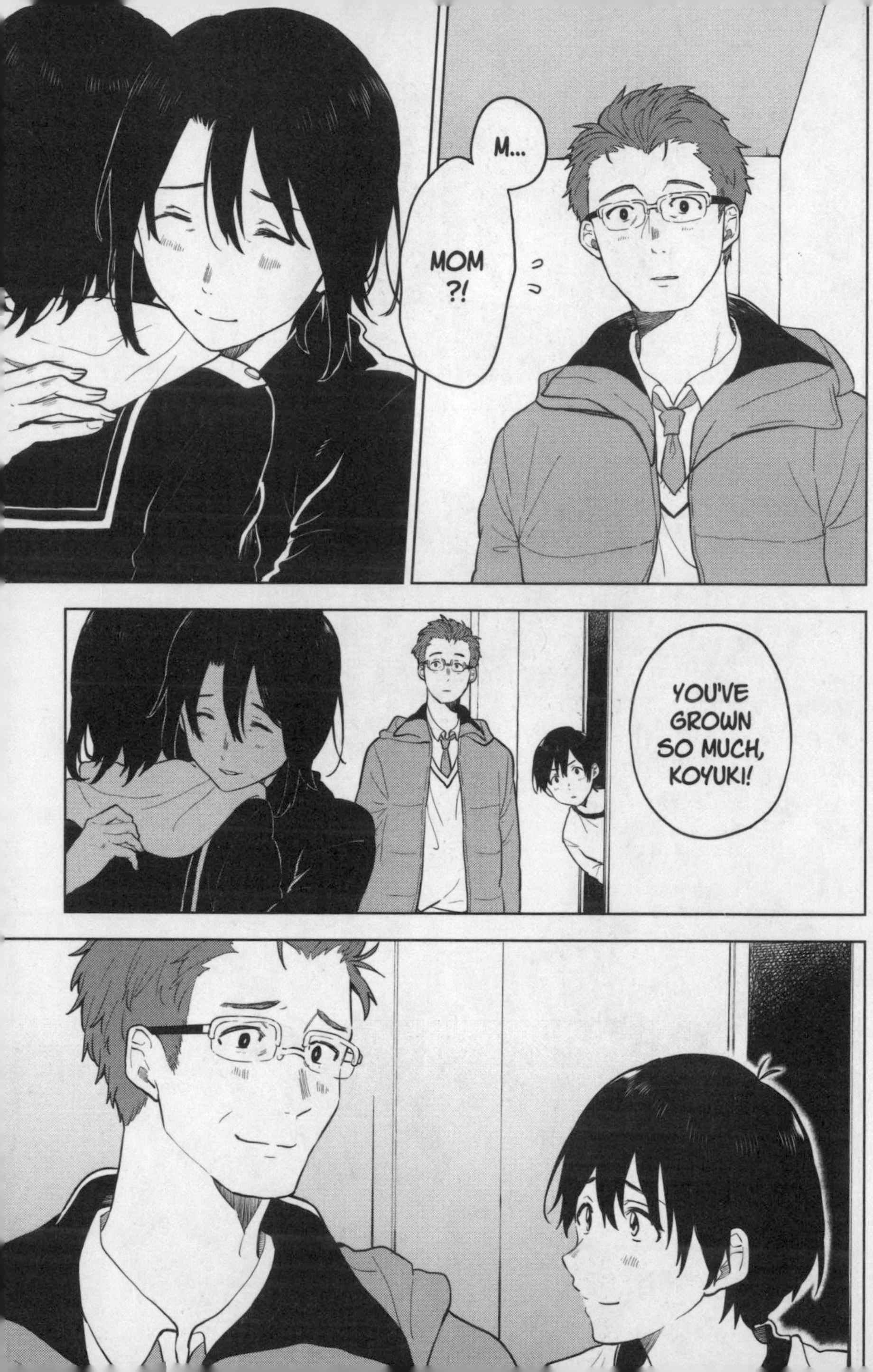
M...
MOM ?!
YOU'VE GROWN SO MUCH, KOYUKI!

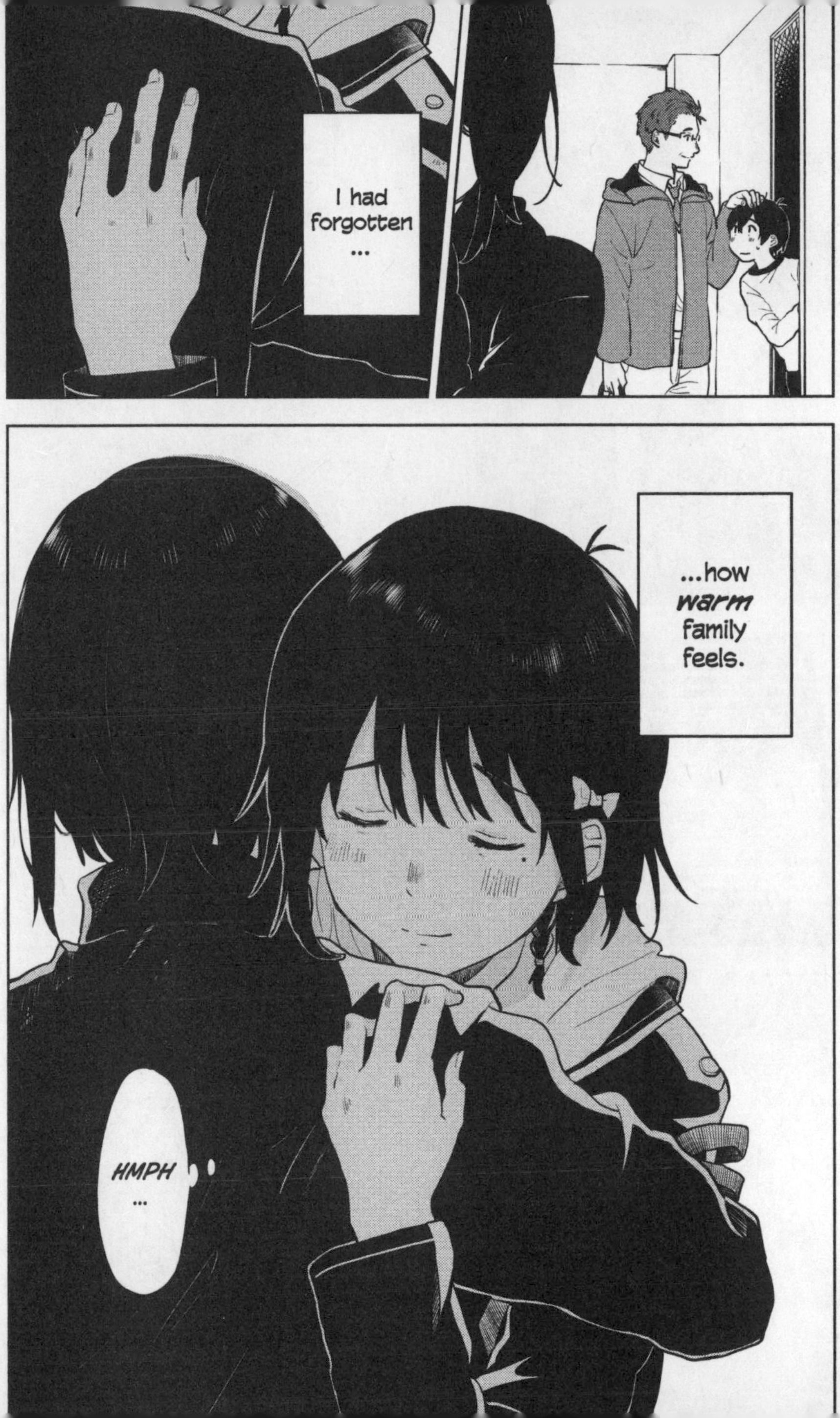
I had forgotten ...
...how *warm* family feels.
HMPH ...

A Tropical Fish
Yearns for Snow

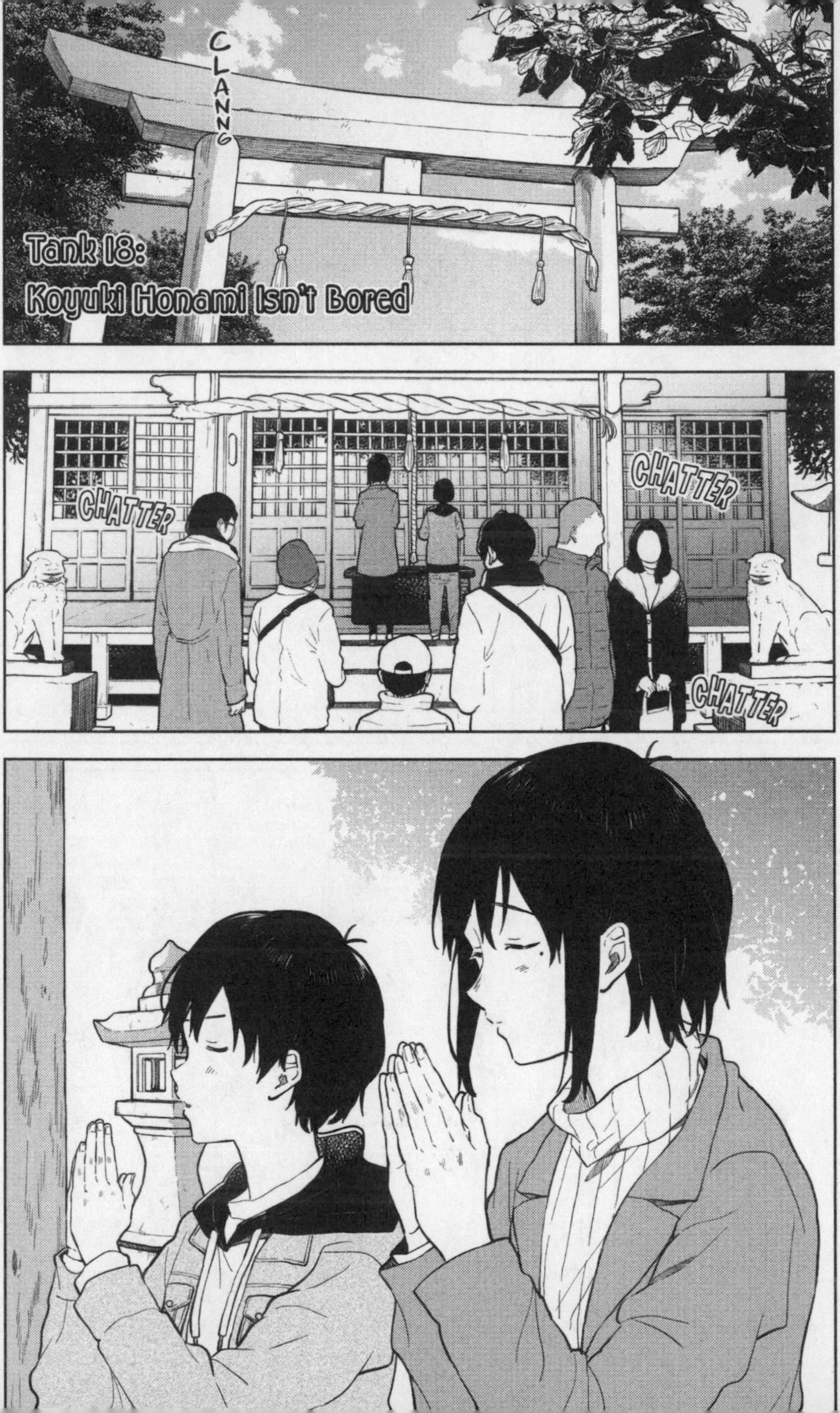
CLANNG
Tank 18:
Koyuki Honami Isn't Bored
CHATTER
CHATTER
CHATTER

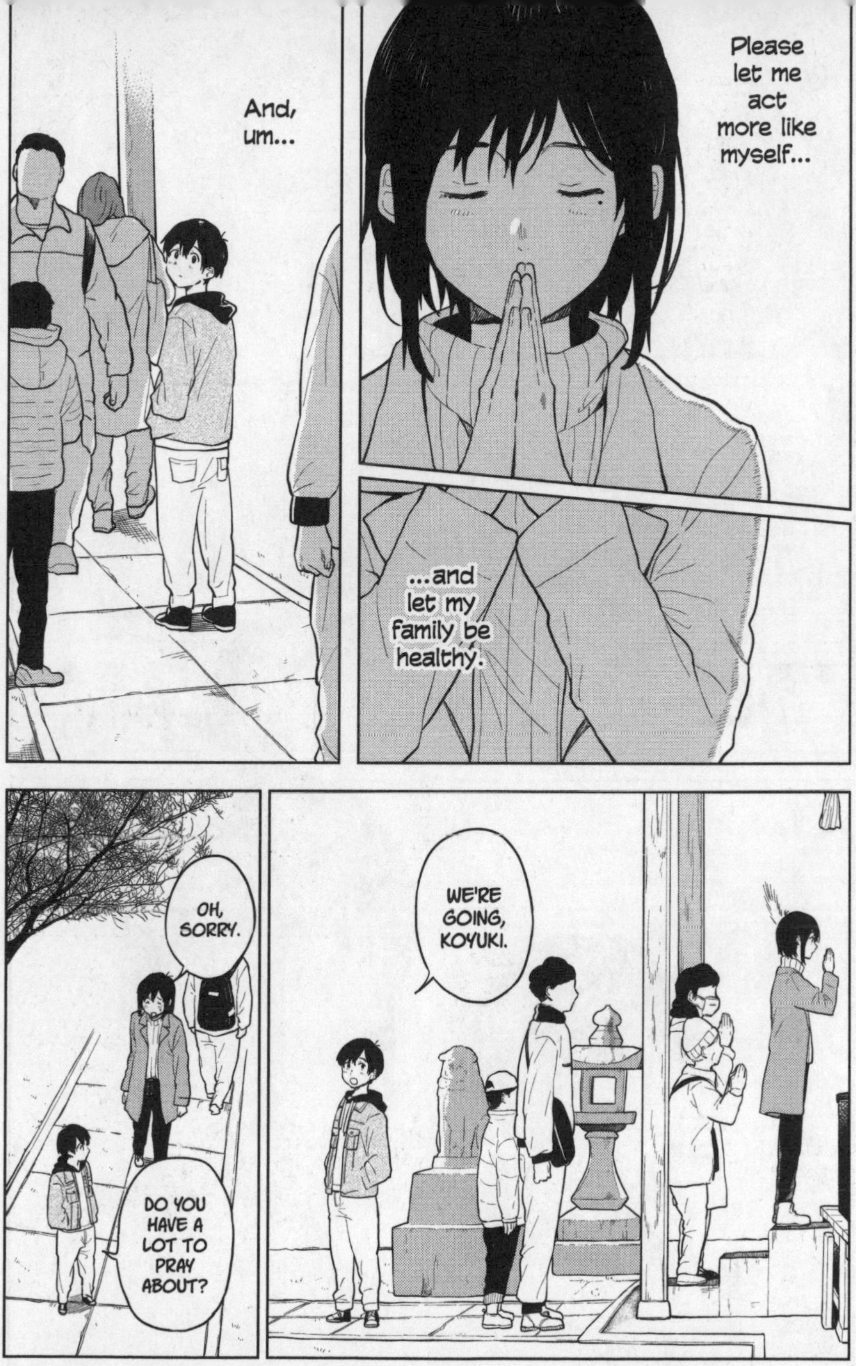
Please let me act more like myself...
...and let my family be healthy.
And, um...
WE'RE GOING, KOYUKI.
OH, SORRY.
DO YOU HAVE A LOT TO PRAY ABOUT?

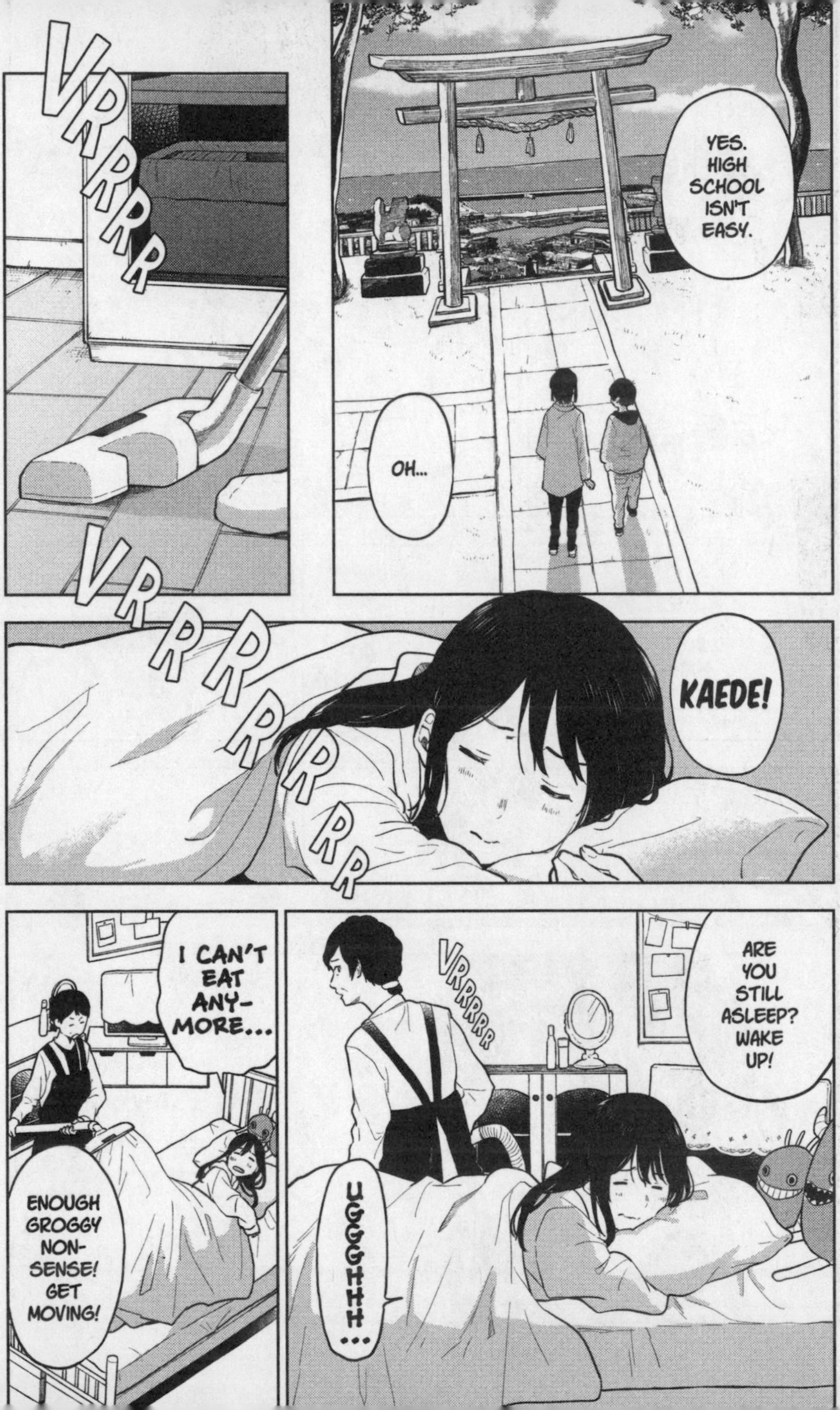
YES. HIGH SCHOOL ISN'T EASY.
OH...
VRRRRR
VRRRRRRRRR
KAEDE!
ARE YOU STILL ASLEEP? WAKE UP!
VRRRRR
UGGGHHH...
I CAN'T EAT ANY-MORE...
ENOUGH GROGGY NON-SENSE! GET MOVING!

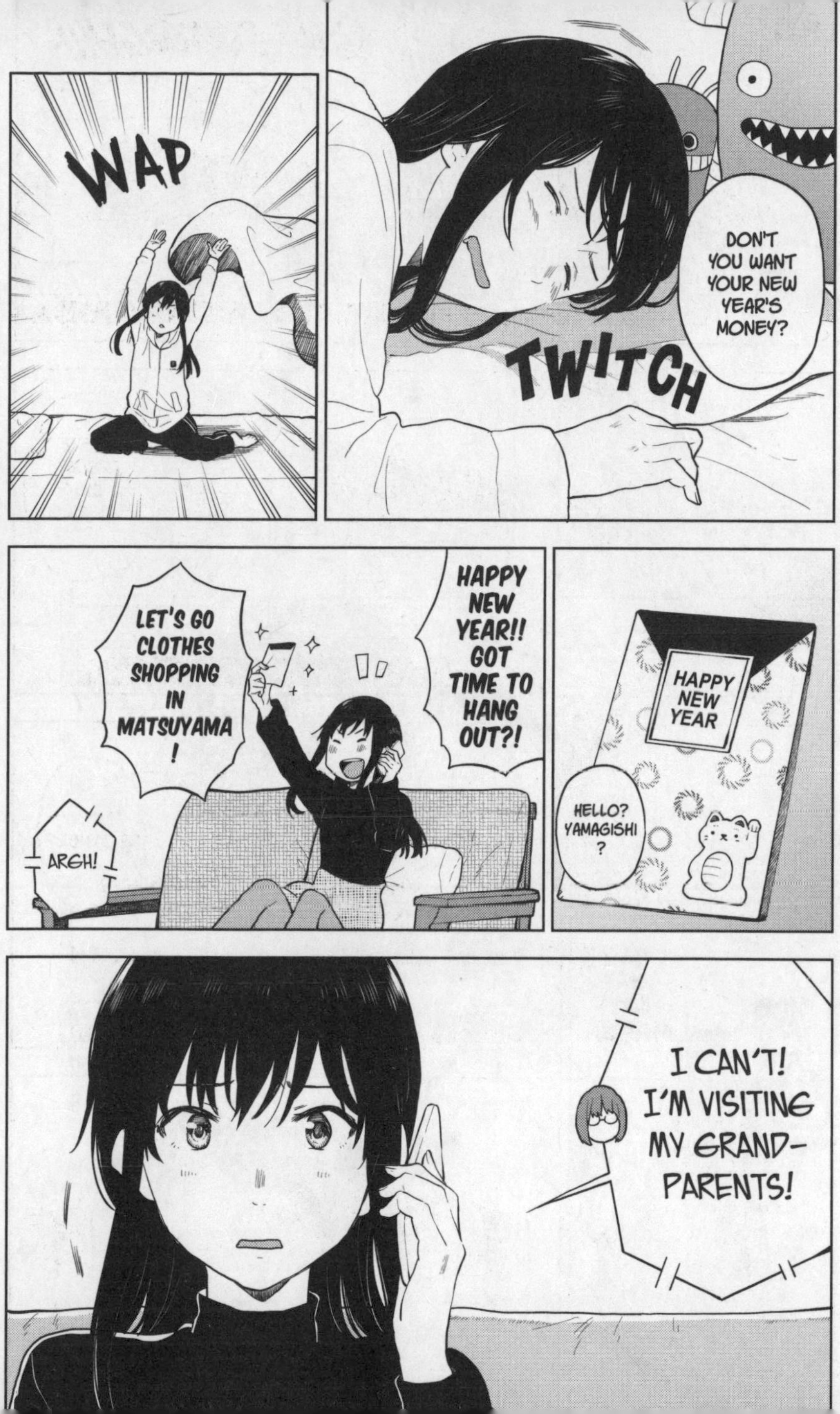
DON'T YOU WANT YOUR NEW YEAR'S MONEY?
TWITCH
WAP
HAPPY NEW YEAR
HELLO? YAMAGISHI?
HAPPY NEW YEAR!! GOT TIME TO HANG OUT?!
LET'S GO CLOTHES SHOPPING IN MATSUYAMA!
ARGH!
I CAN'T! I'M VISITING MY GRAND-PARENTS!

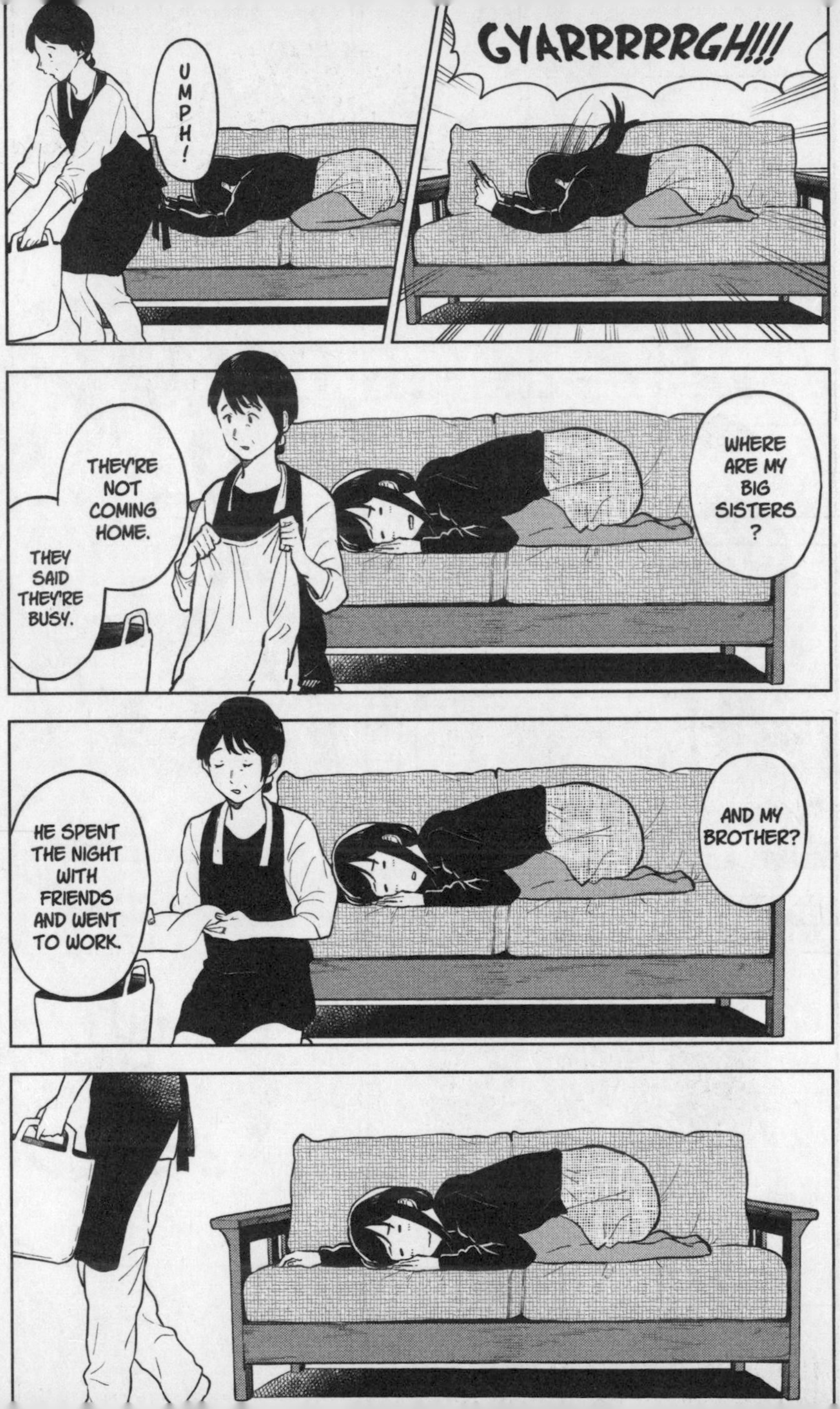
GYARRRRRGH!!!
UMPH!
WHERE ARE MY BIG SISTERS?
THEY'RE NOT COMING HOME.
THEY SAID THEY'RE BUSY.
AND MY BROTHER?
HE SPENT THE NIGHT WITH FRIENDS AND WENT TO WORK.

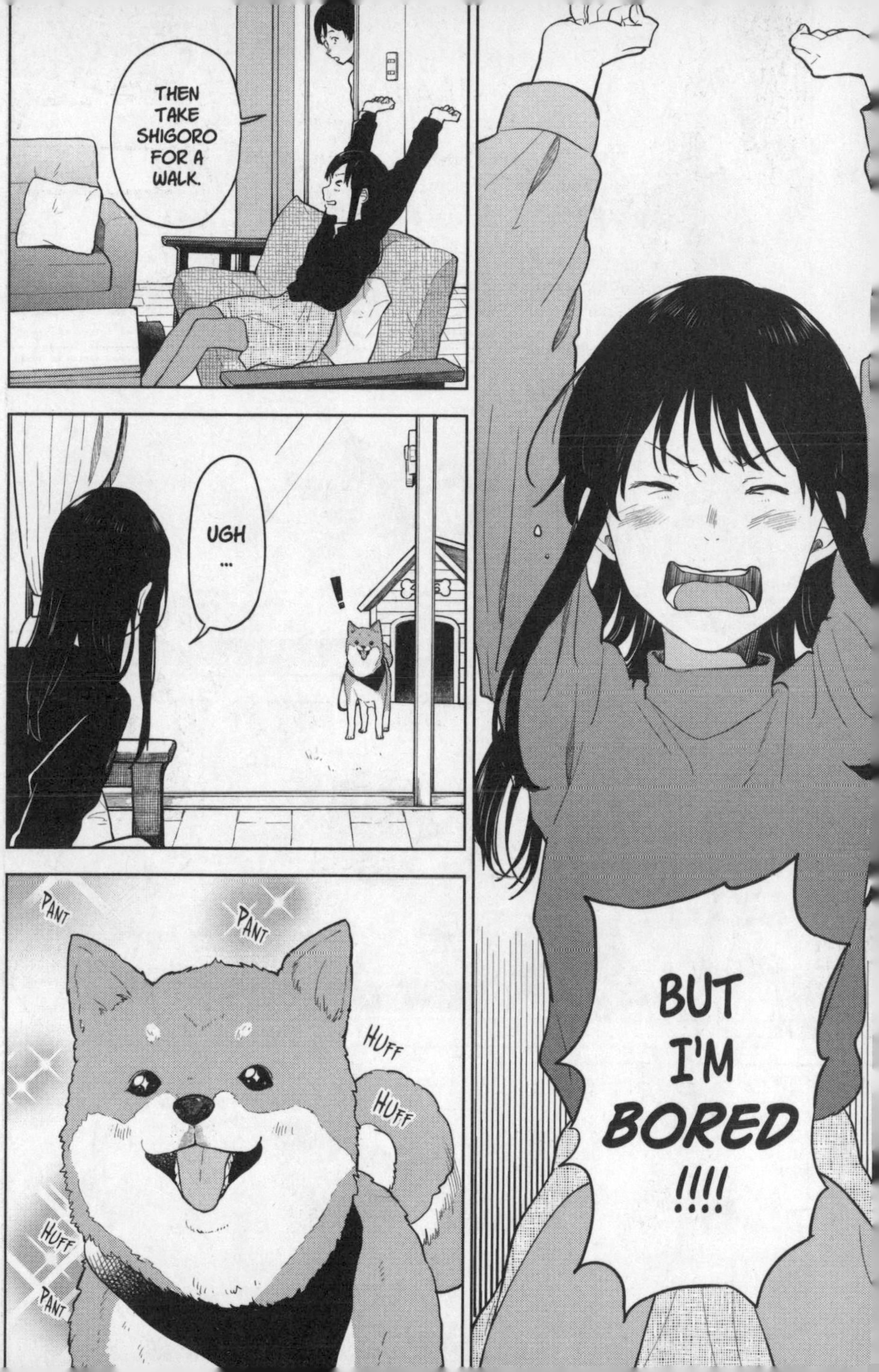
BUT I'M BORED !!!!
THEN TAKE SHIGORO FOR A WALK.
UGH ...
!
PANT
PANT
HUFF
HUFF
HUFF
PANT

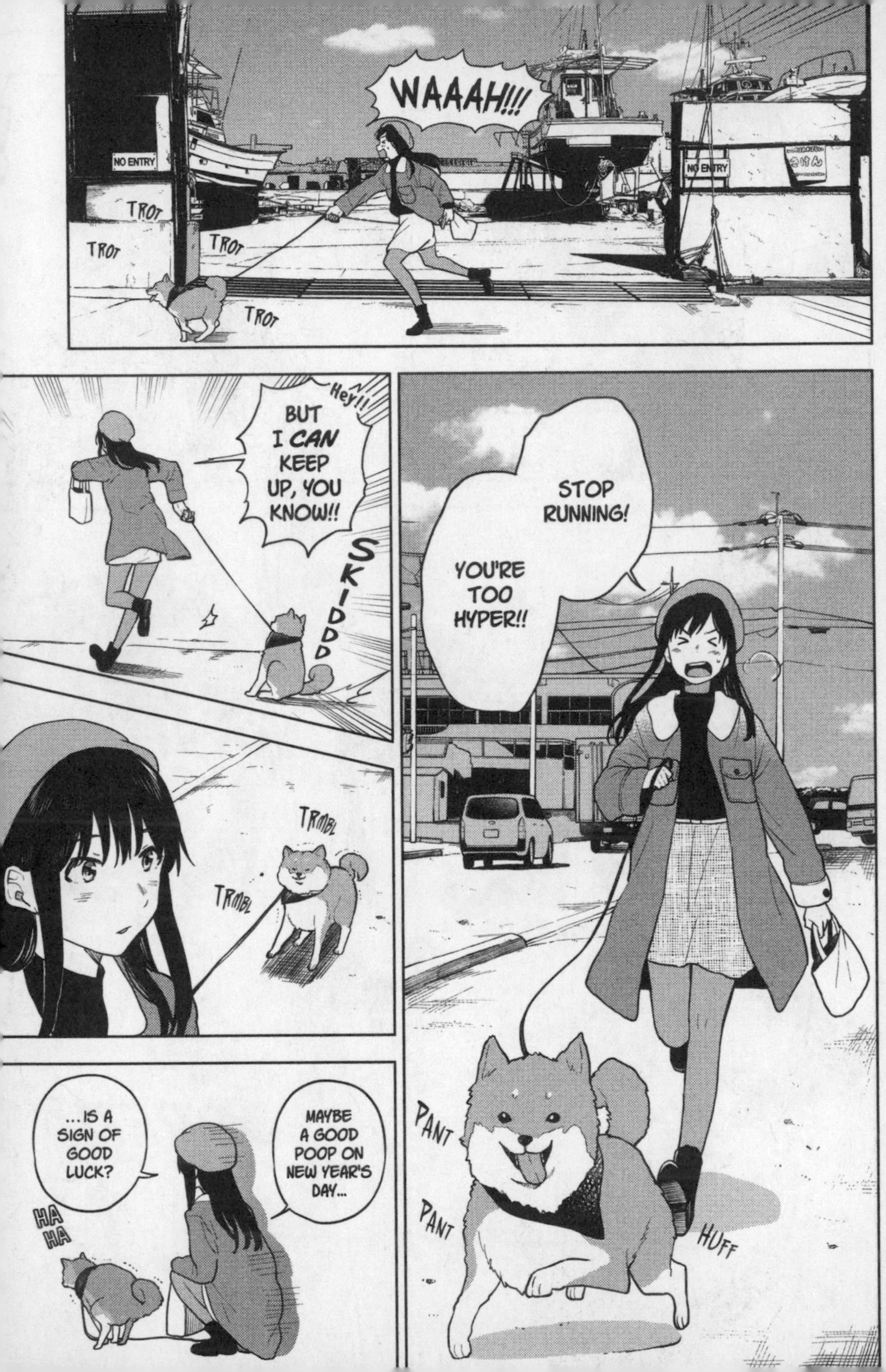
WAAAH!!!
NO ENTRY
NO ENTRY
TROT
TROT
TROT
TROT
STOP RUNNING!
YOU'RE TOO HYPER!!
PANT
PANT
HUFF
Hey!!
BUT I CAN KEEP UP, YOU KNOW!!
SKIDDD
TRMBL
TRMBL
MAYBE A GOOD POOP ON NEW YEAR'S DAY...
...IS A SIGN OF GOOD LUCK?
HA HA

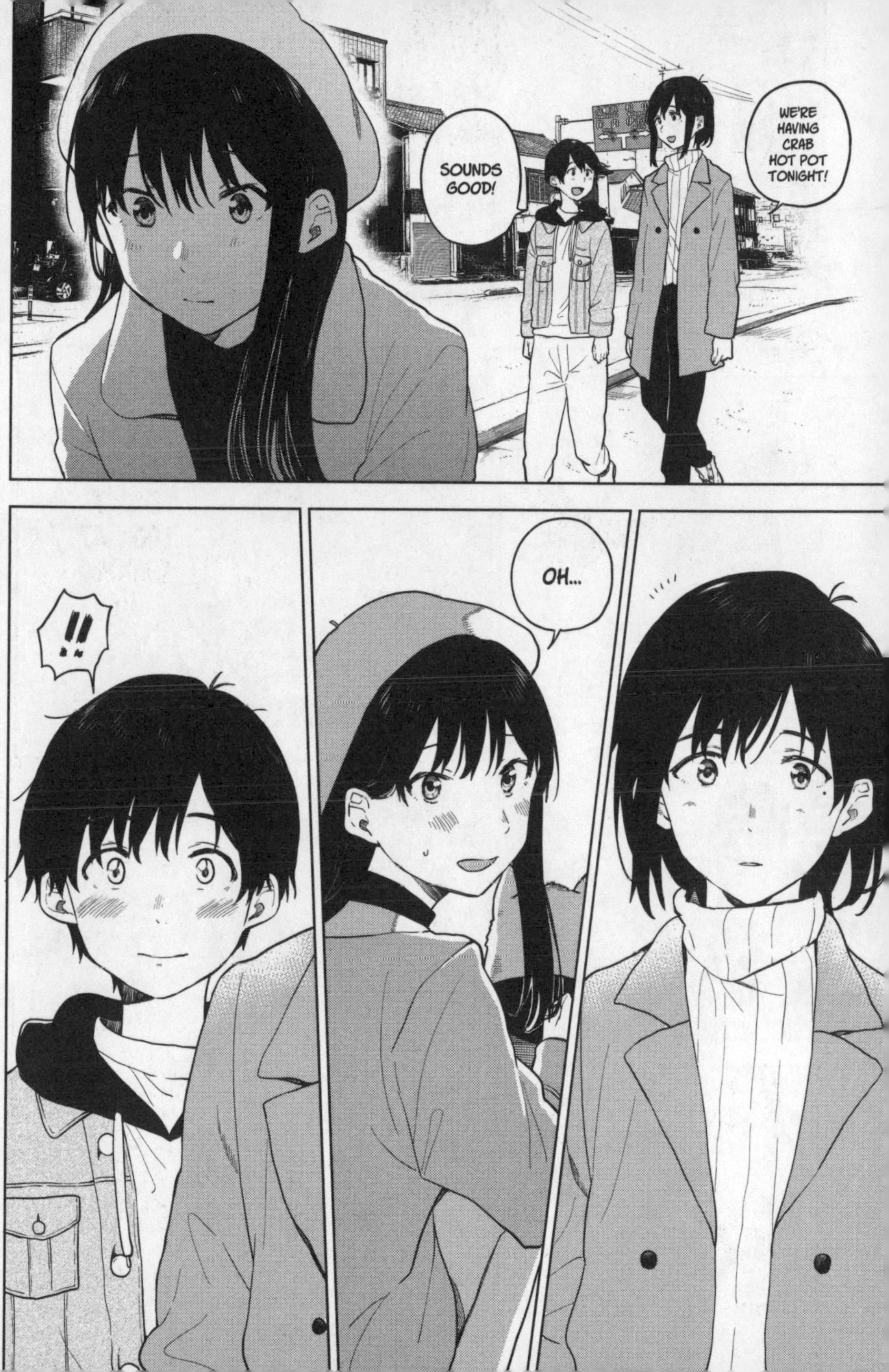
WE'RE HAVING CRAB HOT POT TONIGHT!
SOUNDS GOOD!
OH...
!!

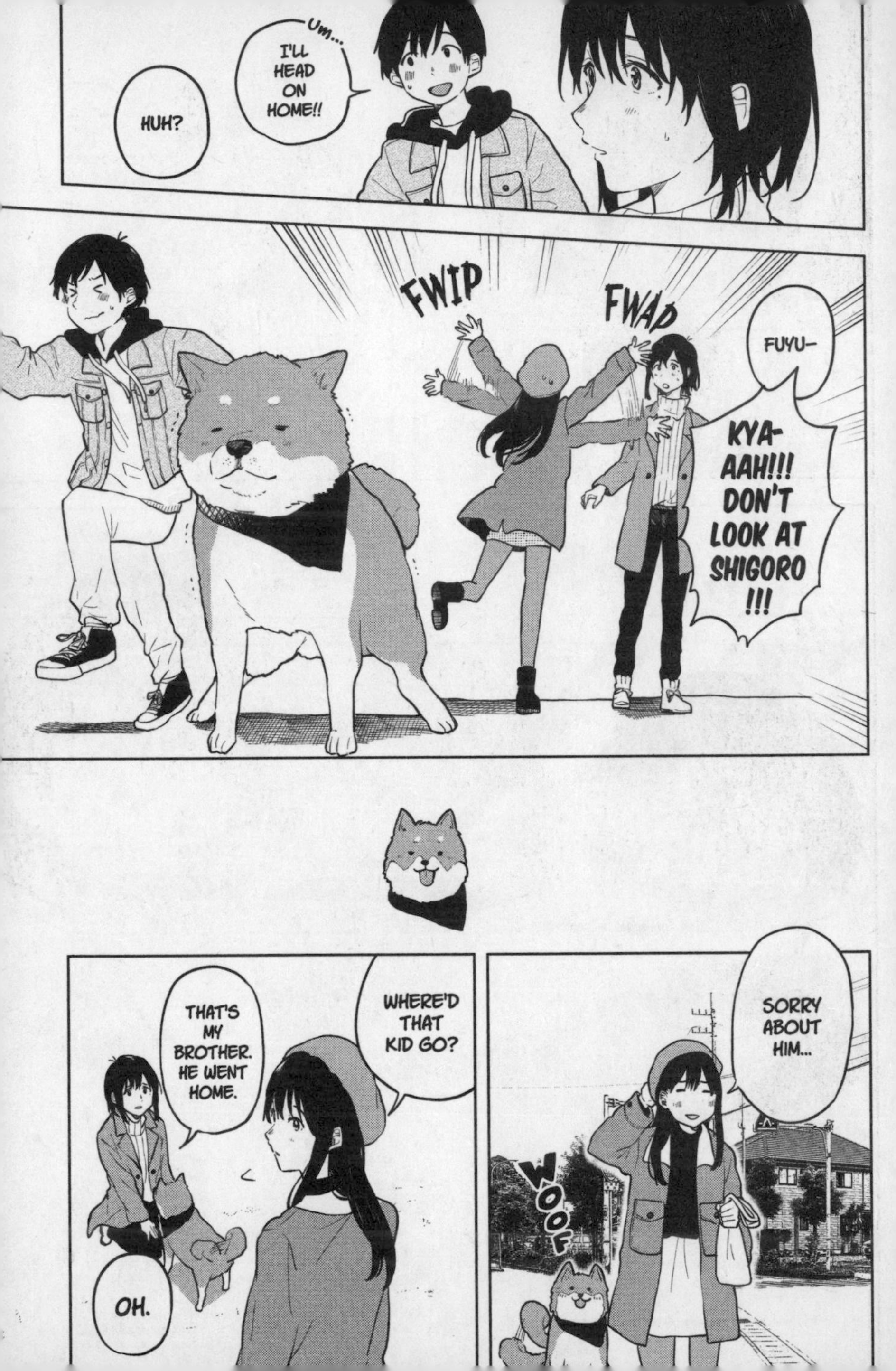
Um...
I'LL HEAD ON HOME!!
HUH?
FUYU-
KYA-AAH!!! DON'T LOOK AT SHIGORO!!!
FWAP
FWIP
SORRY ABOUT HIM...
WOOF
WHERE'D THAT KID GO?
THAT'S MY BROTHER. HE WENT HOME.
OH.

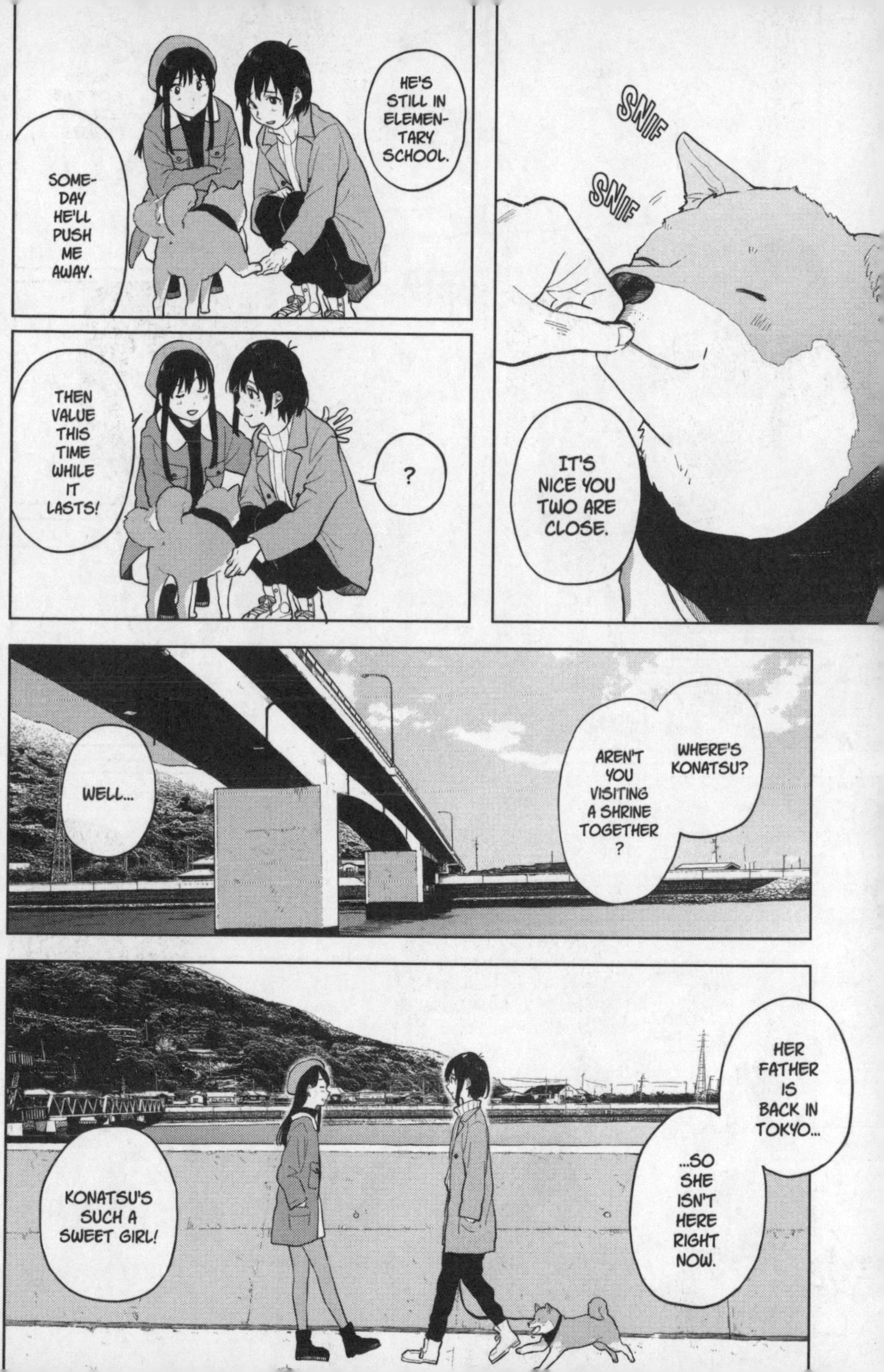
SNIF
SNIF
IT'S NICE YOU TWO ARE CLOSE.
HE'S STILL IN ELEMENTARY SCHOOL.
SOMEDAY HE'LL PUSH ME AWAY.
?
THEN VALUE THIS TIME WHILE IT LASTS!
WHERE'S KONATSU?
AREN'T YOU VISITING A SHRINE TOGETHER?
WELL...
HER FATHER IS BACK IN TOKYO...
...SO SHE ISN'T HERE RIGHT NOW.
KONATSU'S SUCH A SWEET GIRL!

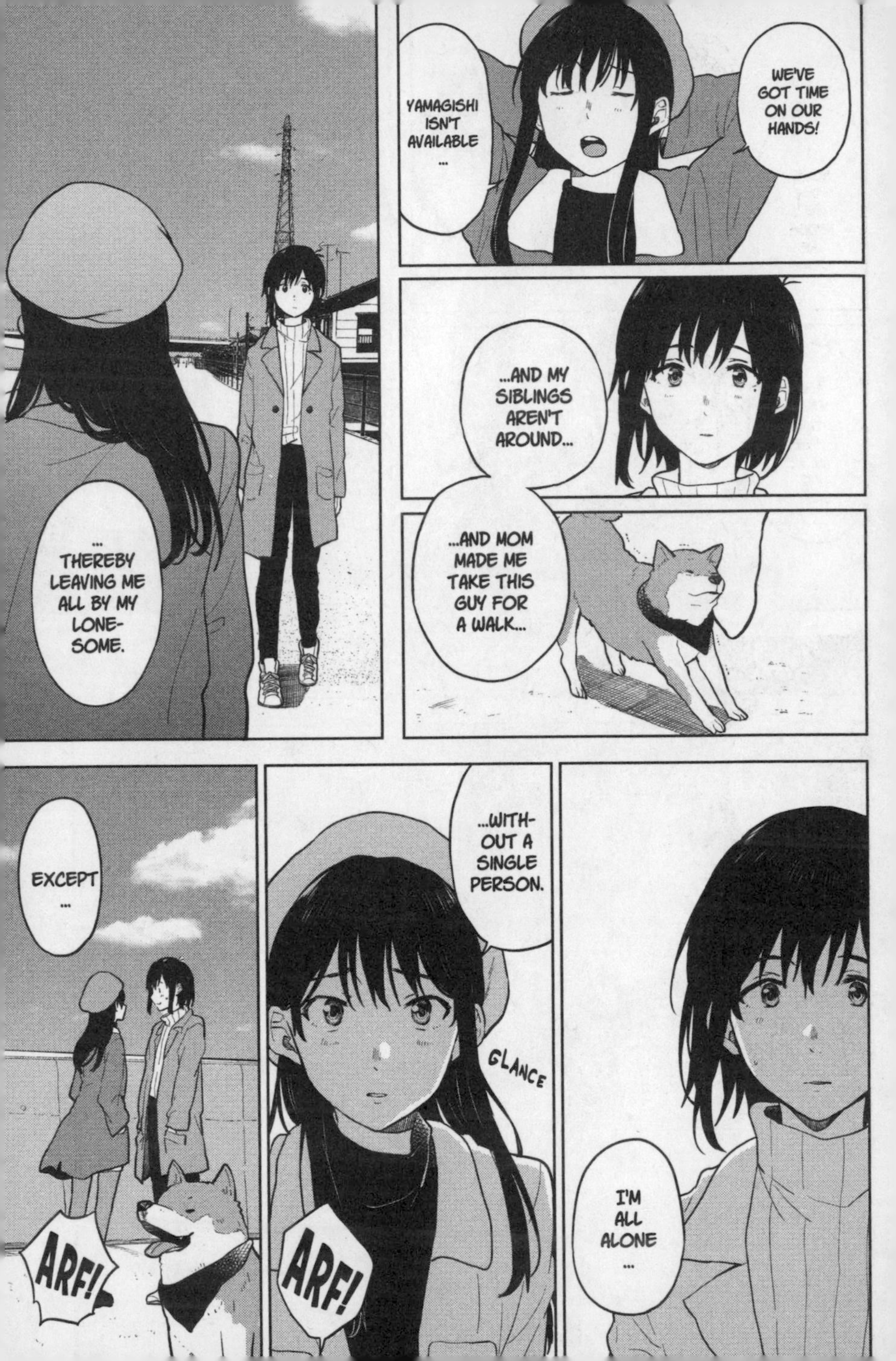
WE'VE GOT TIME ON OUR HANDS!
YAMAGISHI ISN'T AVAILABLE ...
...AND MY SIBLINGS AREN'T AROUND...
...AND MOM MADE ME TAKE THIS GUY FOR A WALK...
... THEREBY LEAVING ME ALL BY MY LONE-SOME.
I'M ALL ALONE ...
...WITH-OUT A SINGLE PERSON.
GLANCE
ARF!
EXCEPT ...
ARF!

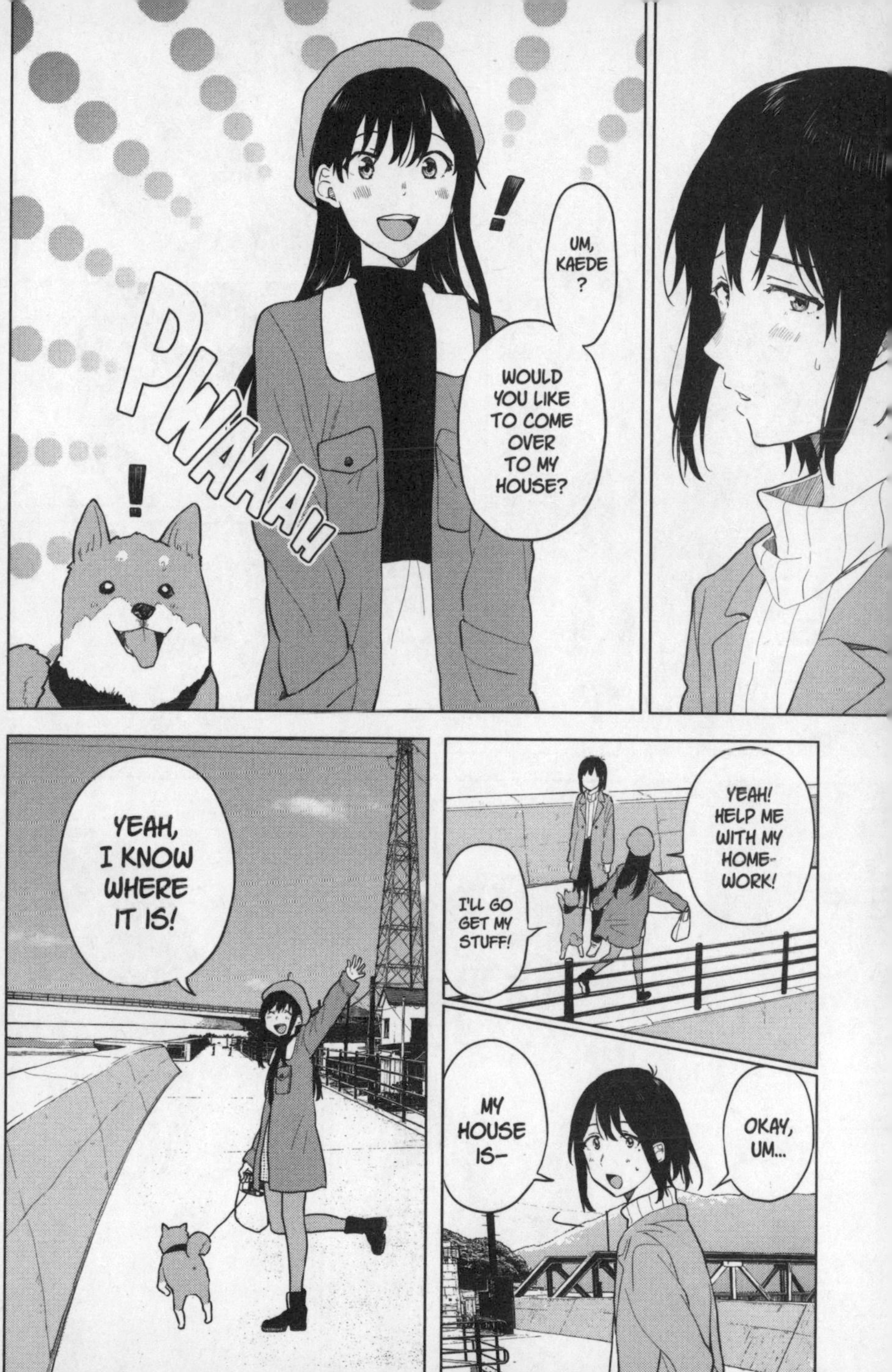
UM, KAEDE?
WOULD YOU LIKE TO COME OVER TO MY HOUSE?
!
PWAAAAH
!
YEAH! HELP ME WITH MY HOME-WORK!
I'LL GO GET MY STUFF!
OKAY, UM...
MY HOUSE IS-
YEAH, I KNOW WHERE IT IS!

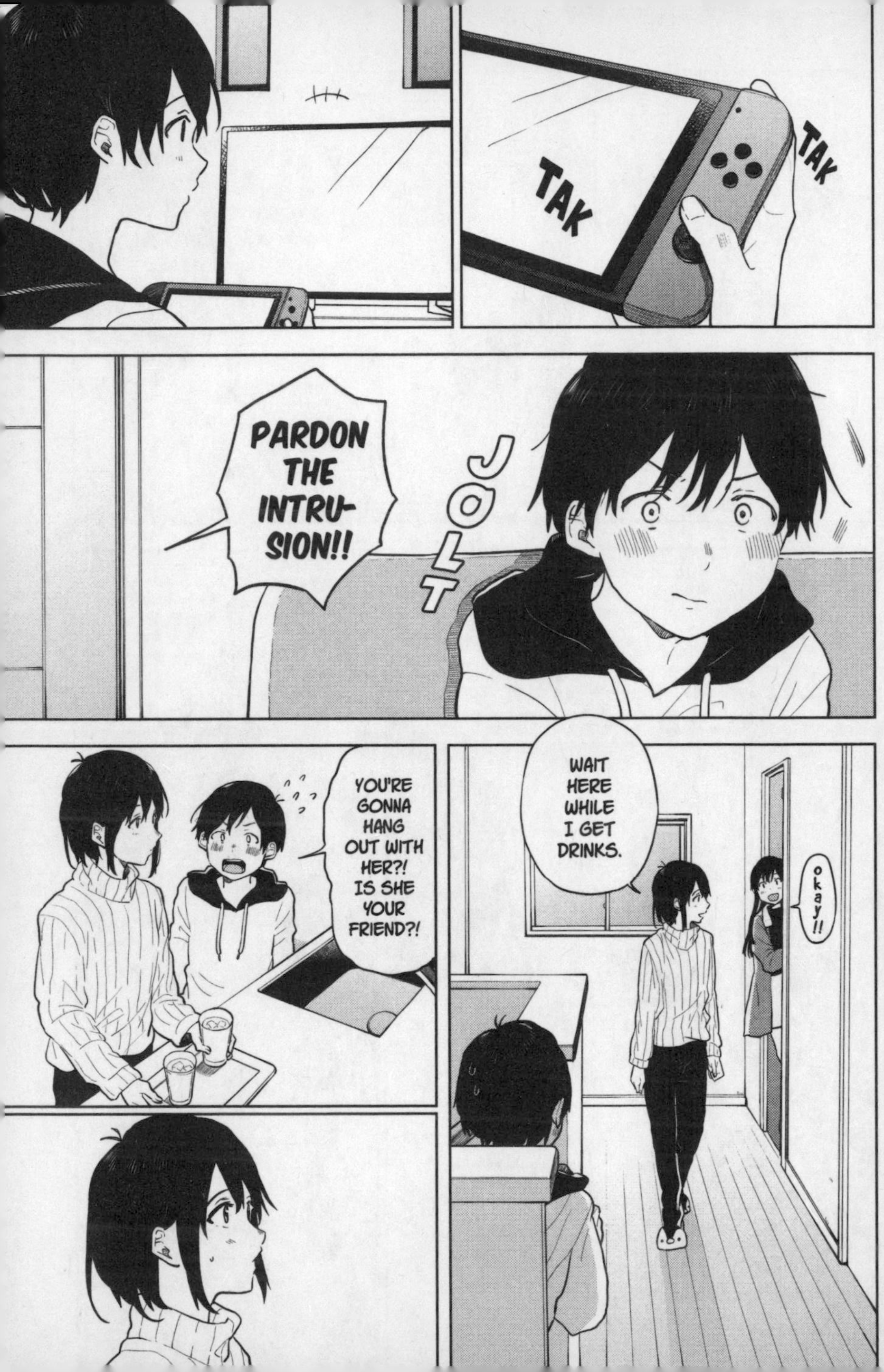
TAK
TAK
JOLT
PARDON THE INTRU-SION!!
WAIT HERE WHILE I GET DRINKS.
okay!!
YOU'RE GONNA HANG OUT WITH HER?! IS SHE YOUR FRIEND?!

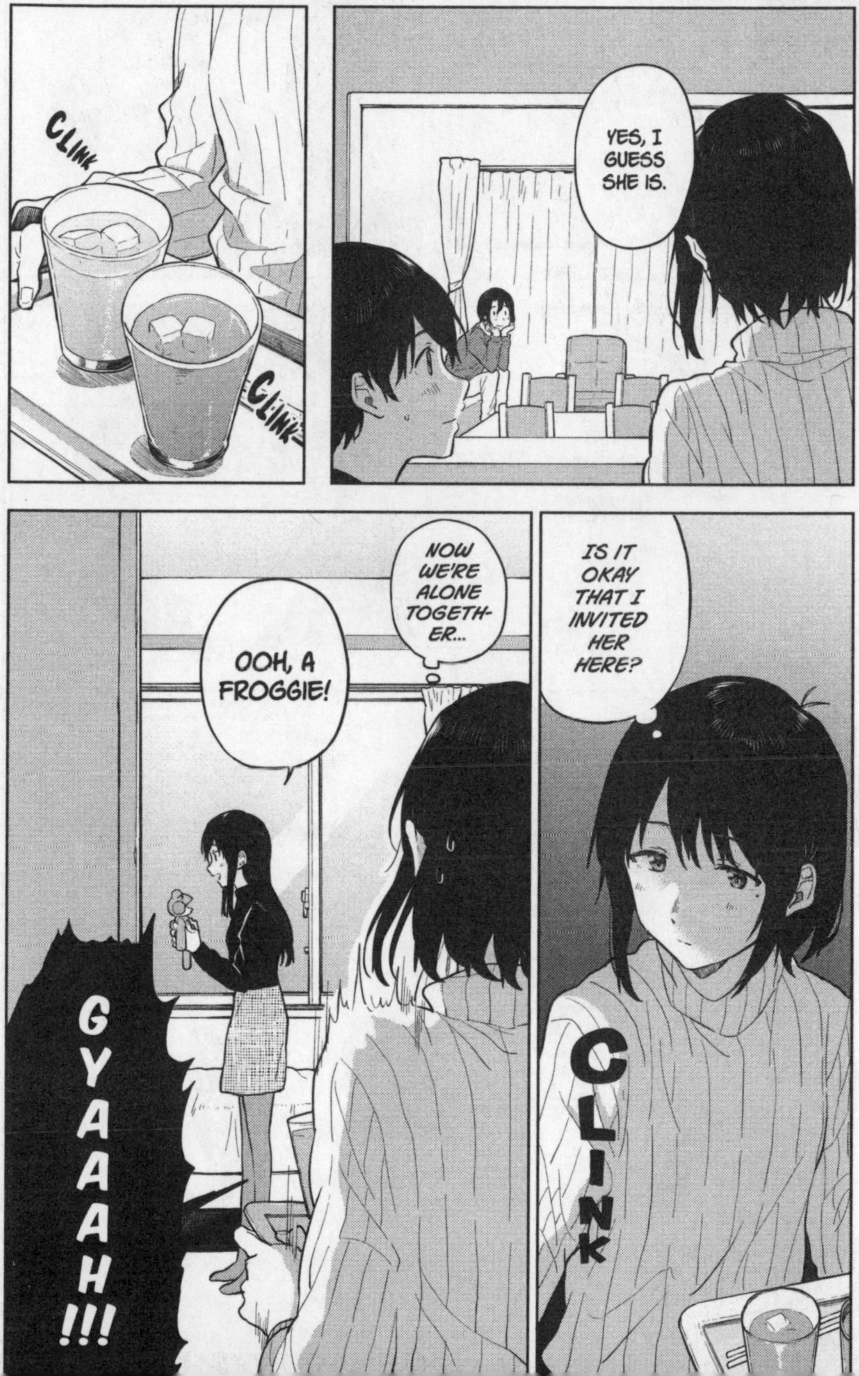
YES, I GUESS SHE IS.
CLINK
CLINK
IS IT OKAY THAT I INVITED HER HERE?
CLINK
NOW WE'RE ALONE TOGETH-ER...
OOH, A FROGGIE!
GYAAAAH!!!

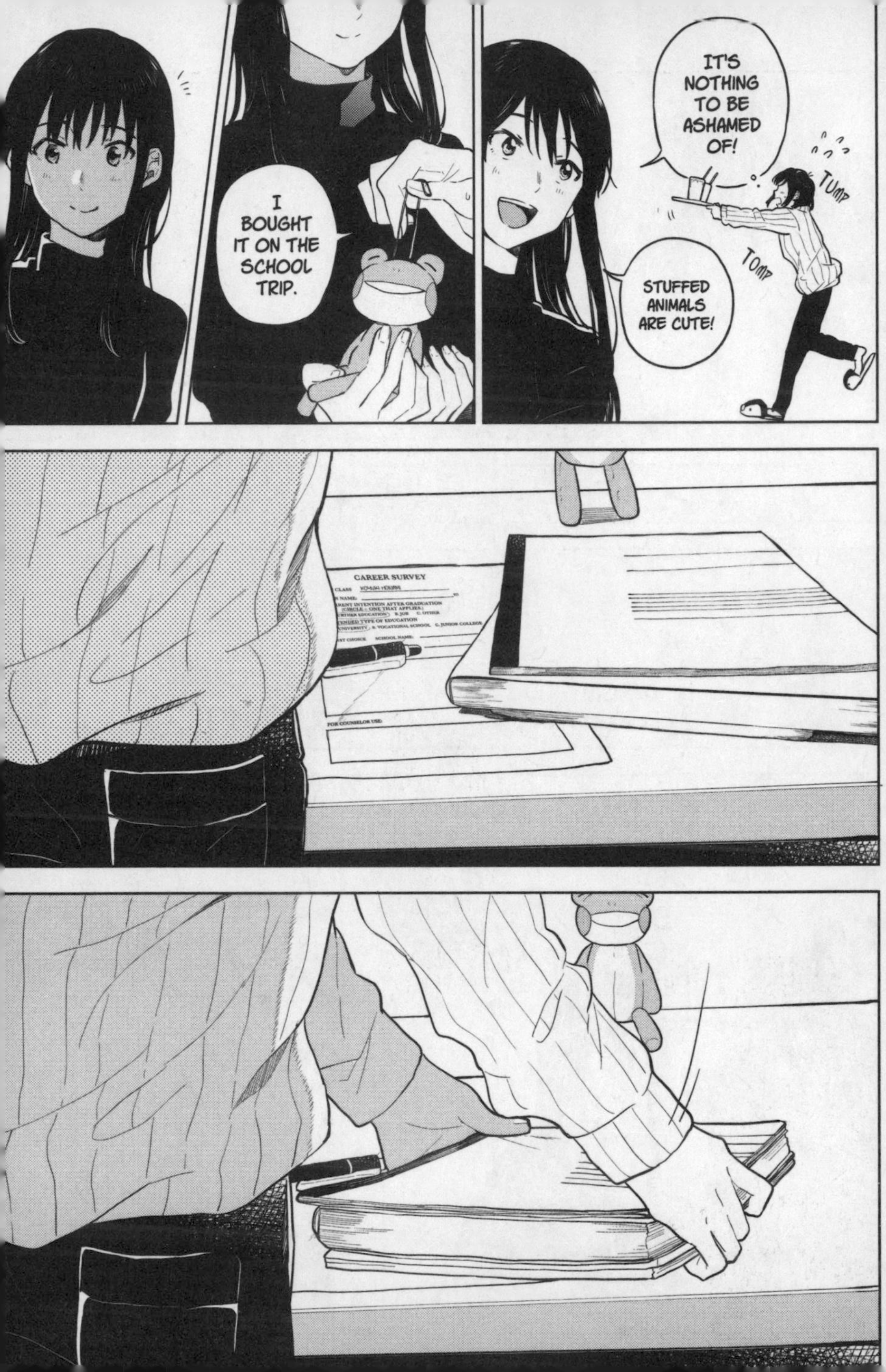
IT'S NOTHING TO BE ASHAMED OF!
TUMP
TOMP
STUFFED ANIMALS ARE CUTE!
I BOUGHT IT ON THE SCHOOL TRIP.
CAREER SURVEY
FOR COUNSELOR USE:

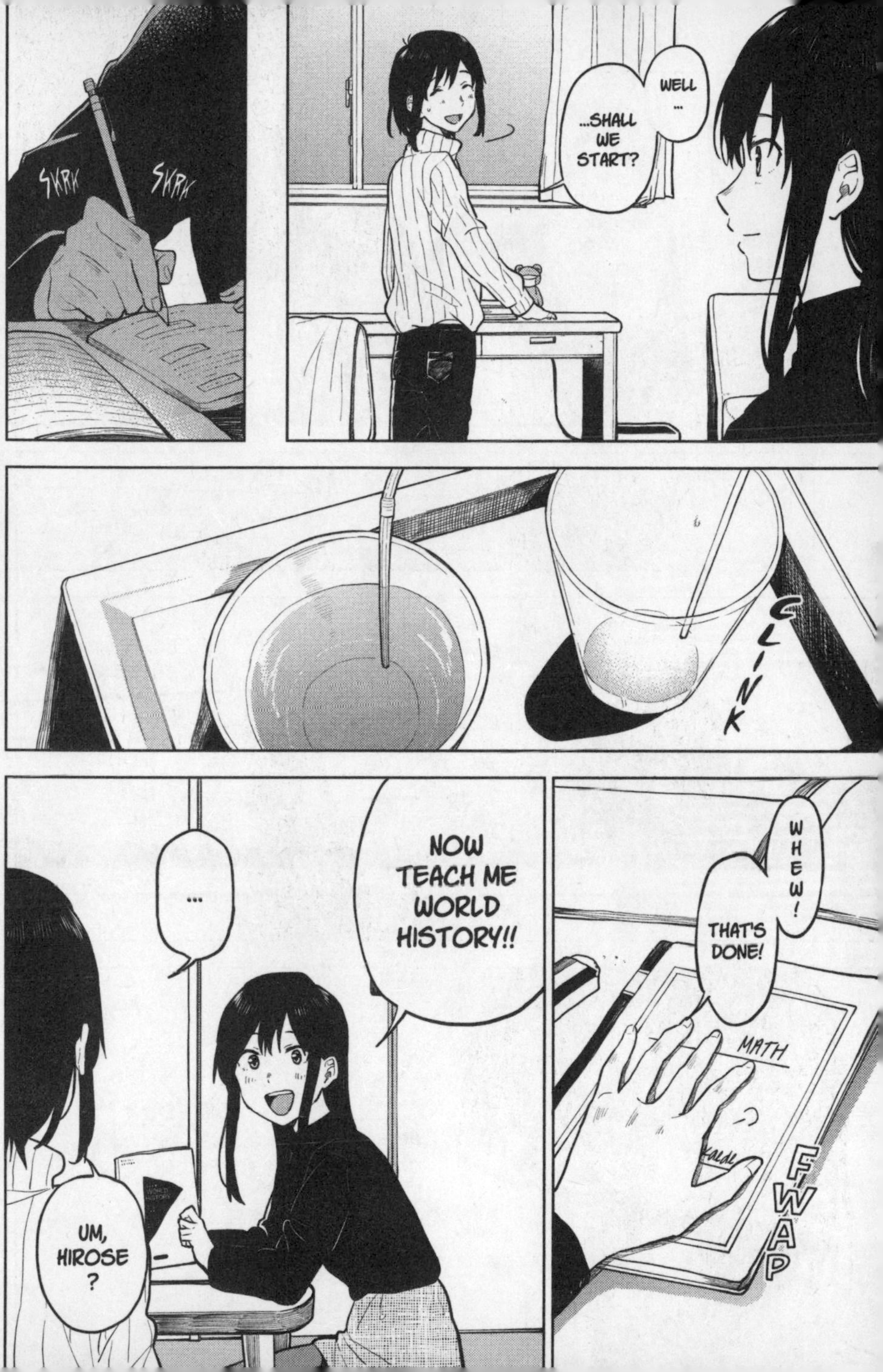
WELL ...
...SHALL WE START?
SKRK
SKRK
CLINK
WHEW!
THAT'S DONE!
MATH
FWAP
NOW TEACH ME WORLD HISTORY!!
...
UM, HIROSE?

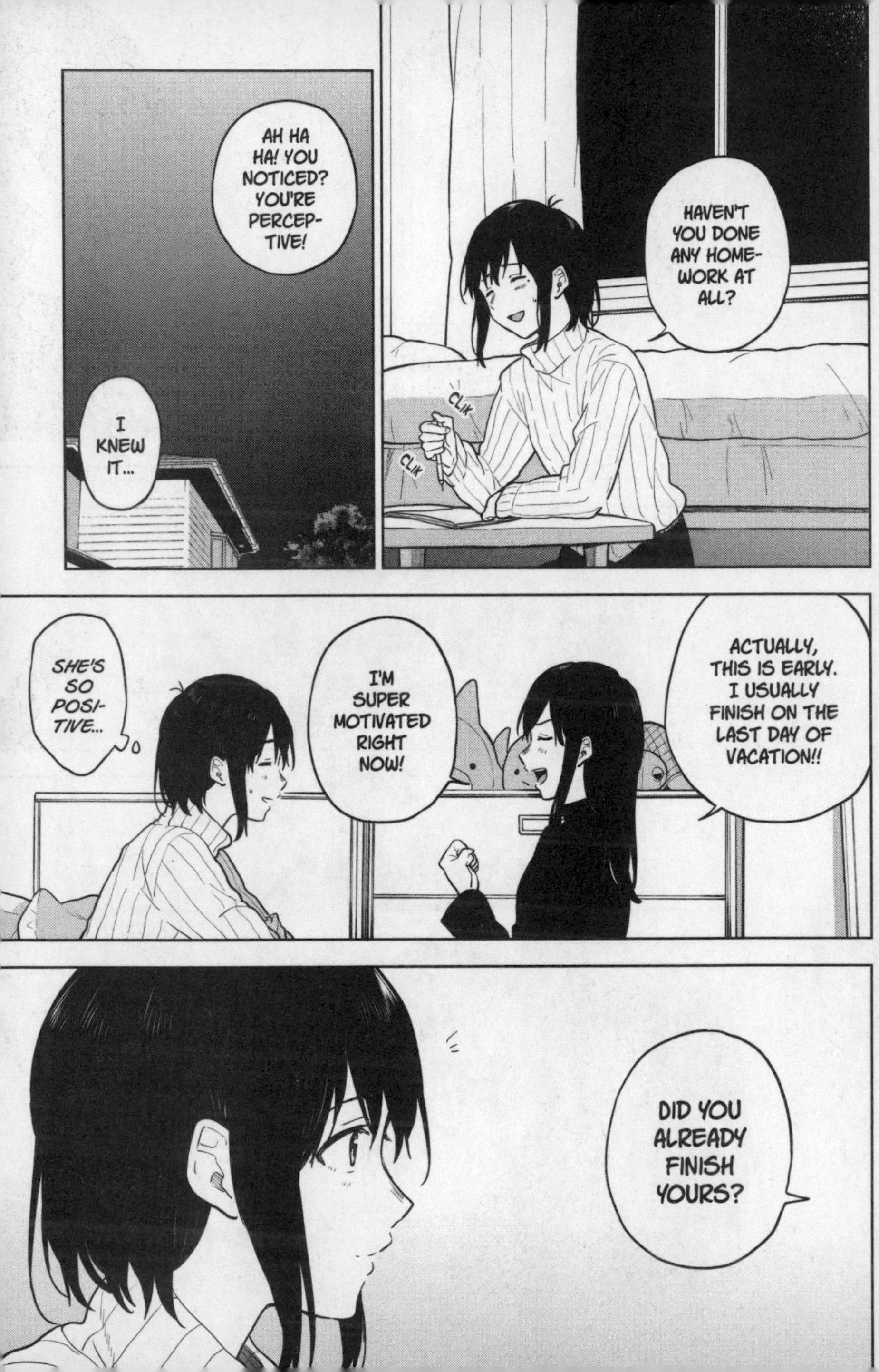
HAVEN'T YOU DONE ANY HOME-WORK AT ALL?
CLIK
CLIK
AH HA HA! YOU NOTICED? YOU'RE PERCEP-TIVE!
I KNEW IT...
ACTUALLY, THIS IS EARLY. I USUALLY FINISH ON THE LAST DAY OF VACATION!!
I'M SUPER MOTIVATED RIGHT NOW!
SHE'S SO POSI-TIVE...
DID YOU ALREADY FINISH YOURS?

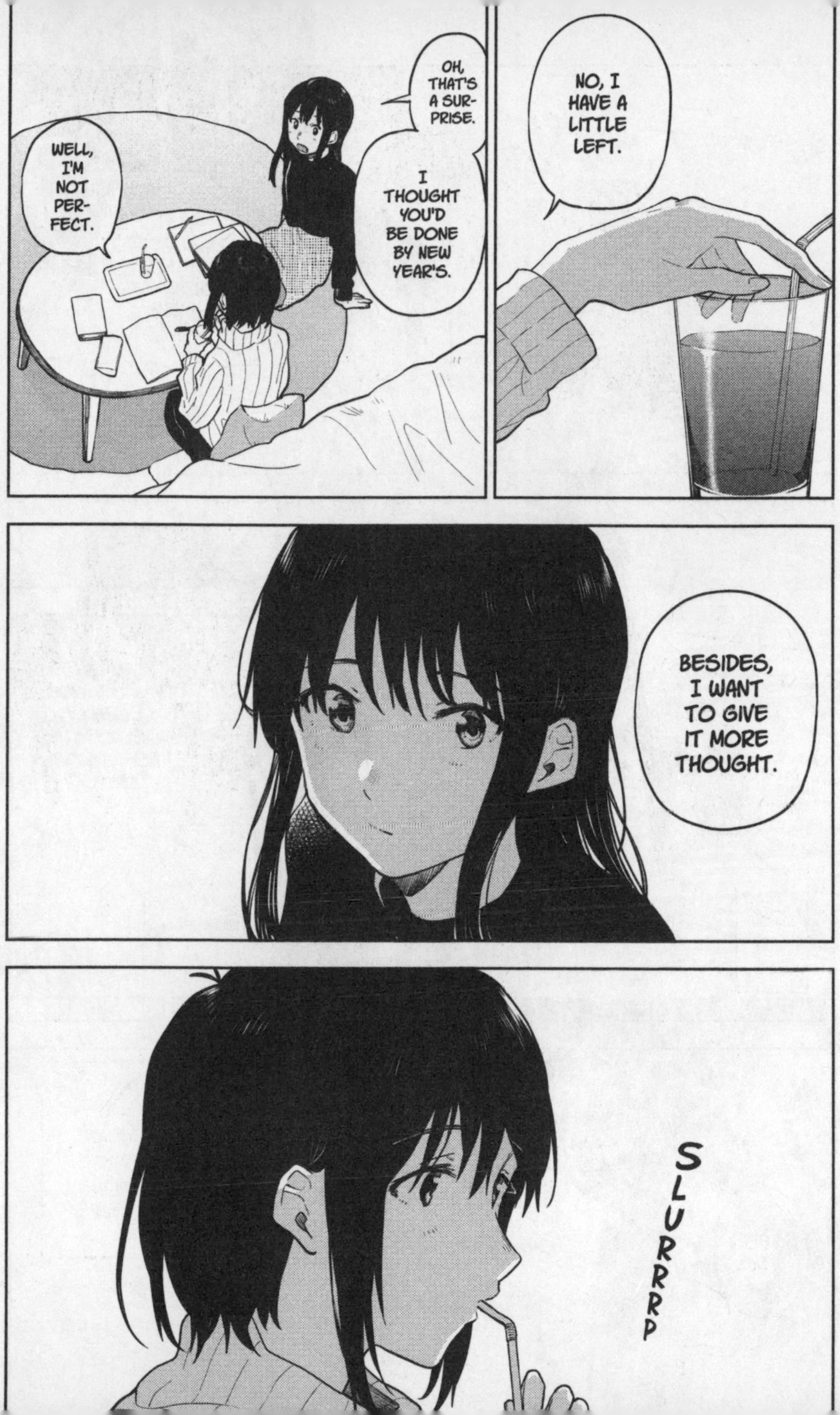
NO, I HAVE A LITTLE LEFT.
OH, THAT'S A SURPRISE.
I THOUGHT YOU'D BE DONE BY NEW YEAR'S.
WELL, I'M NOT PERFECT.
BESIDES, I WANT TO GIVE IT MORE THOUGHT.
SLURRRP

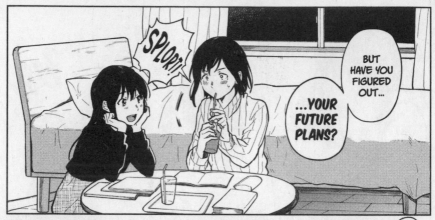

SPLORT!

BUT HAVE YOU FIGURED OUT...

...YOUR FUTURE PLANS?

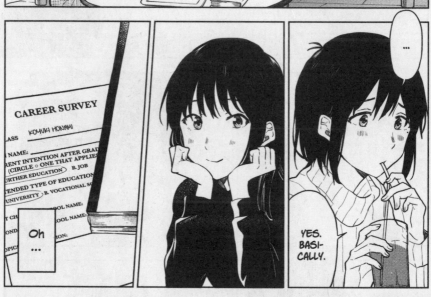

CAREER SURVEY

LASS KOYUKI HONAMI

A NAME:
RENT INTENTION AFTER GRAD
(CIRCLE ○ ONE THAT APPLIES
URTHER EDUCATION B. JOB
ENDED TYPE OF EDUCATION
UNIVERSITY B. VOCATIONAL SC

T CH   OOL NAME:
OND   OOL NAME:
OPIC   ON:

Oh
...

...

YES. BASI-CALLY.

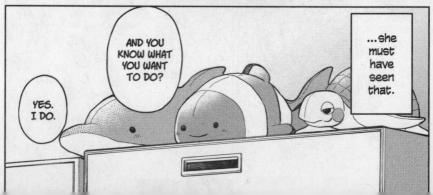

AND YOU KNOW WHAT YOU WANT TO DO?

YES. I DO.

...she must have seen that.

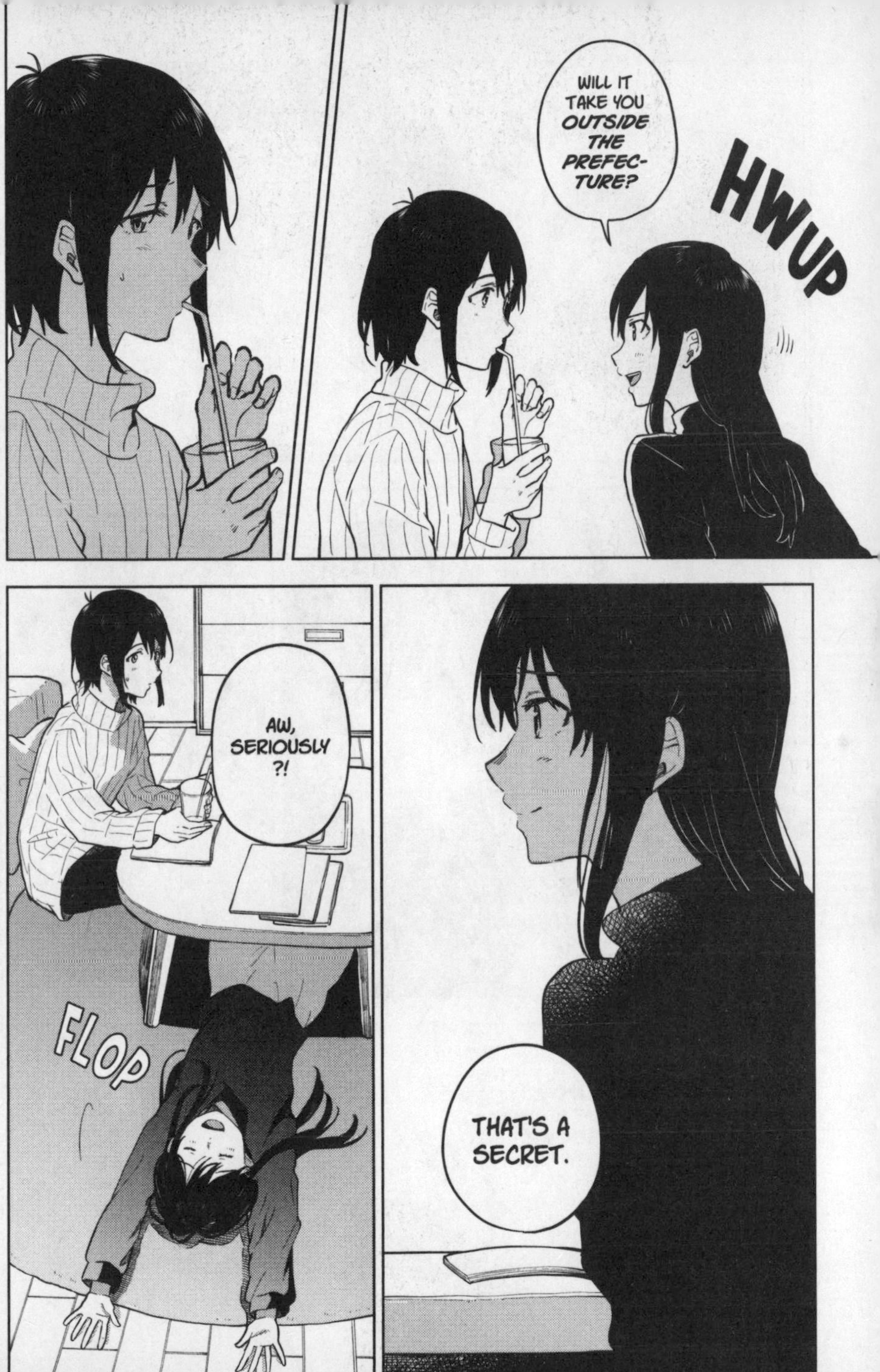
WILL IT TAKE YOU *OUTSIDE THE PREFEC-TURE?*
HWUP
THAT'S A SECRET.
AW, SERIOUSLY ?!
FLOP

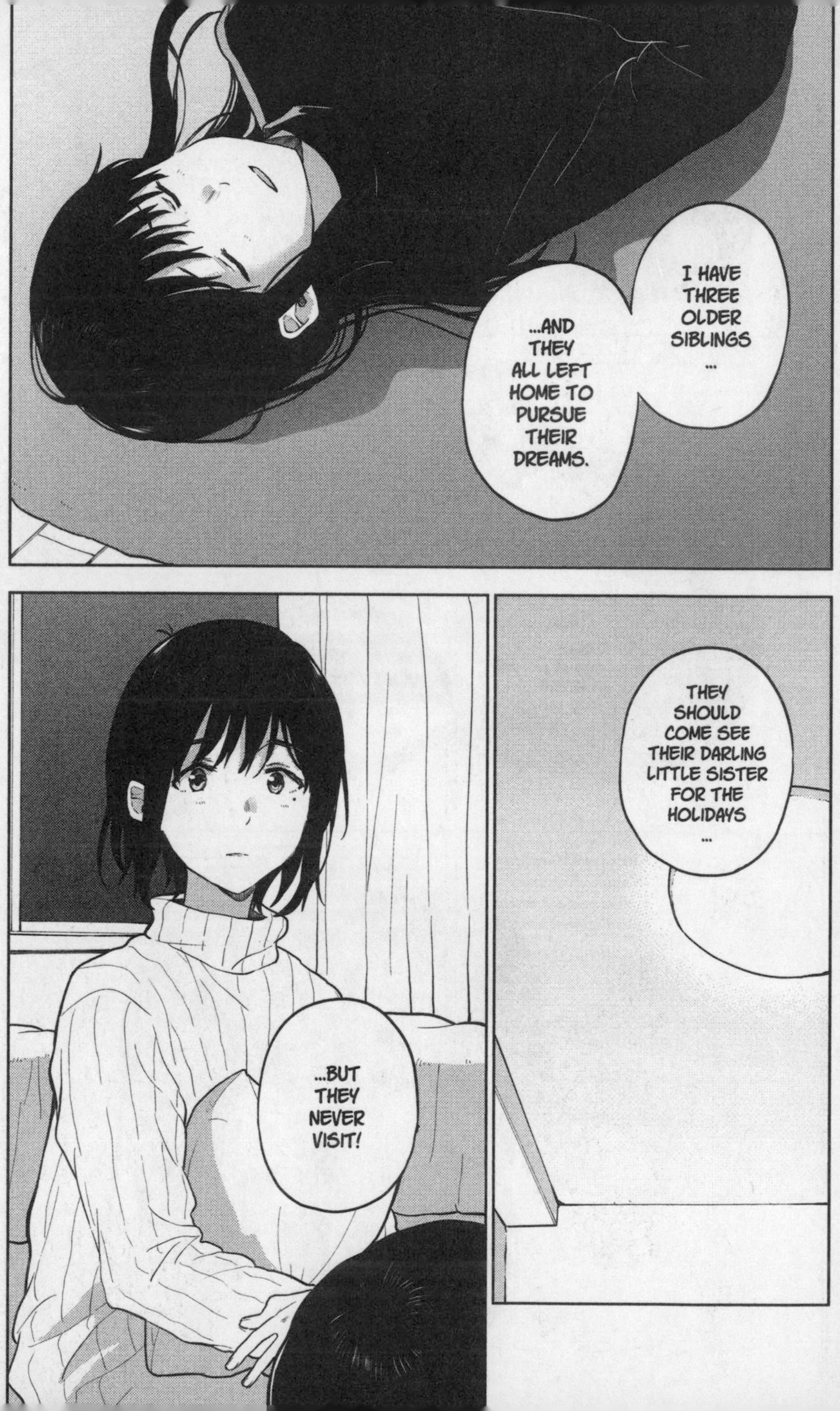
I HAVE THREE OLDER SIBLINGS ...
...AND THEY ALL LEFT HOME TO PURSUE THEIR DREAMS.
THEY SHOULD COME SEE THEIR DARLING LITTLE SISTER FOR THE HOLIDAYS ...
...BUT THEY NEVER VISIT!

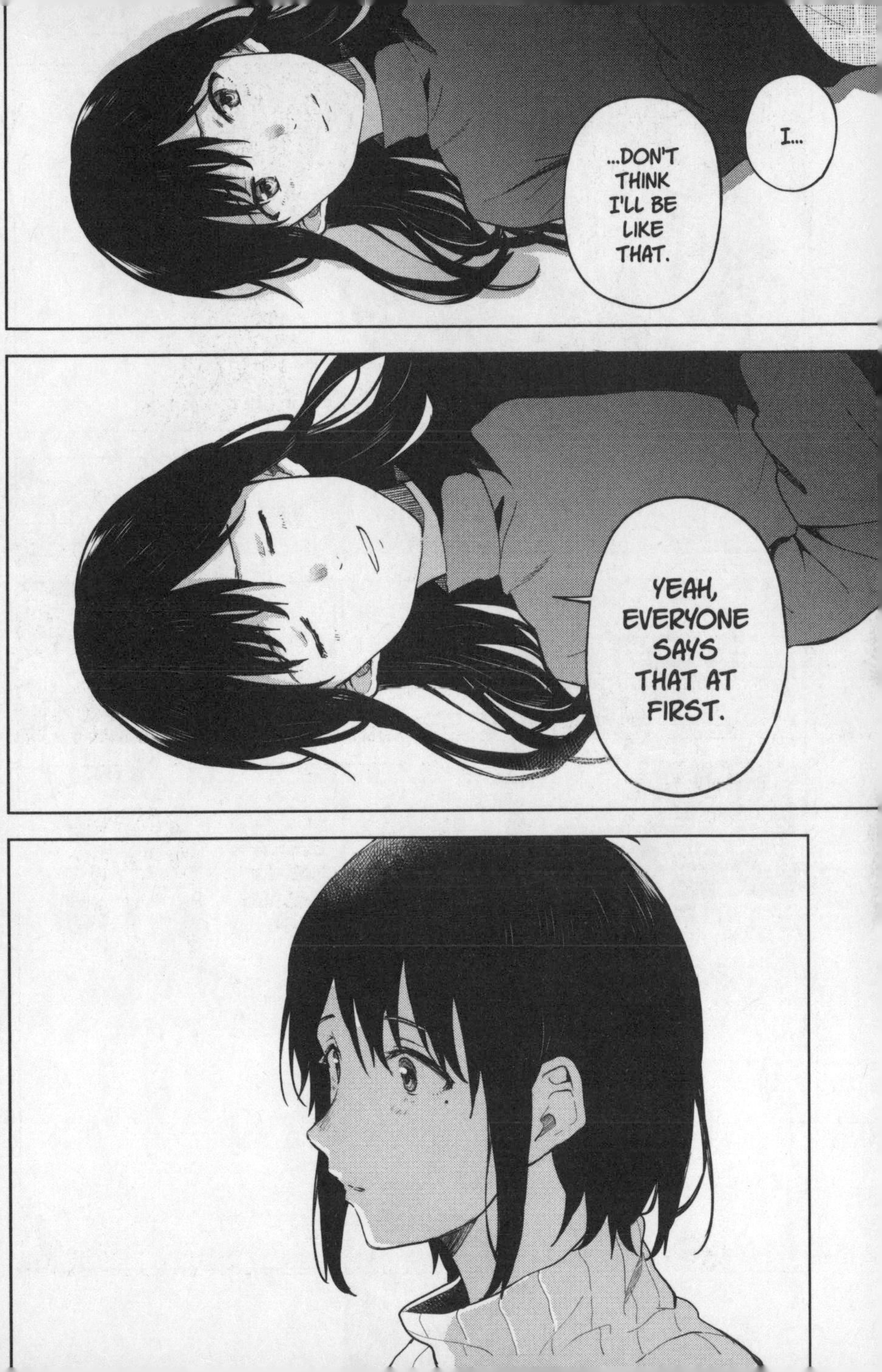
I...
...DON'T THINK I'LL BE LIKE THAT.
YEAH, EVERYONE SAYS THAT AT FIRST.

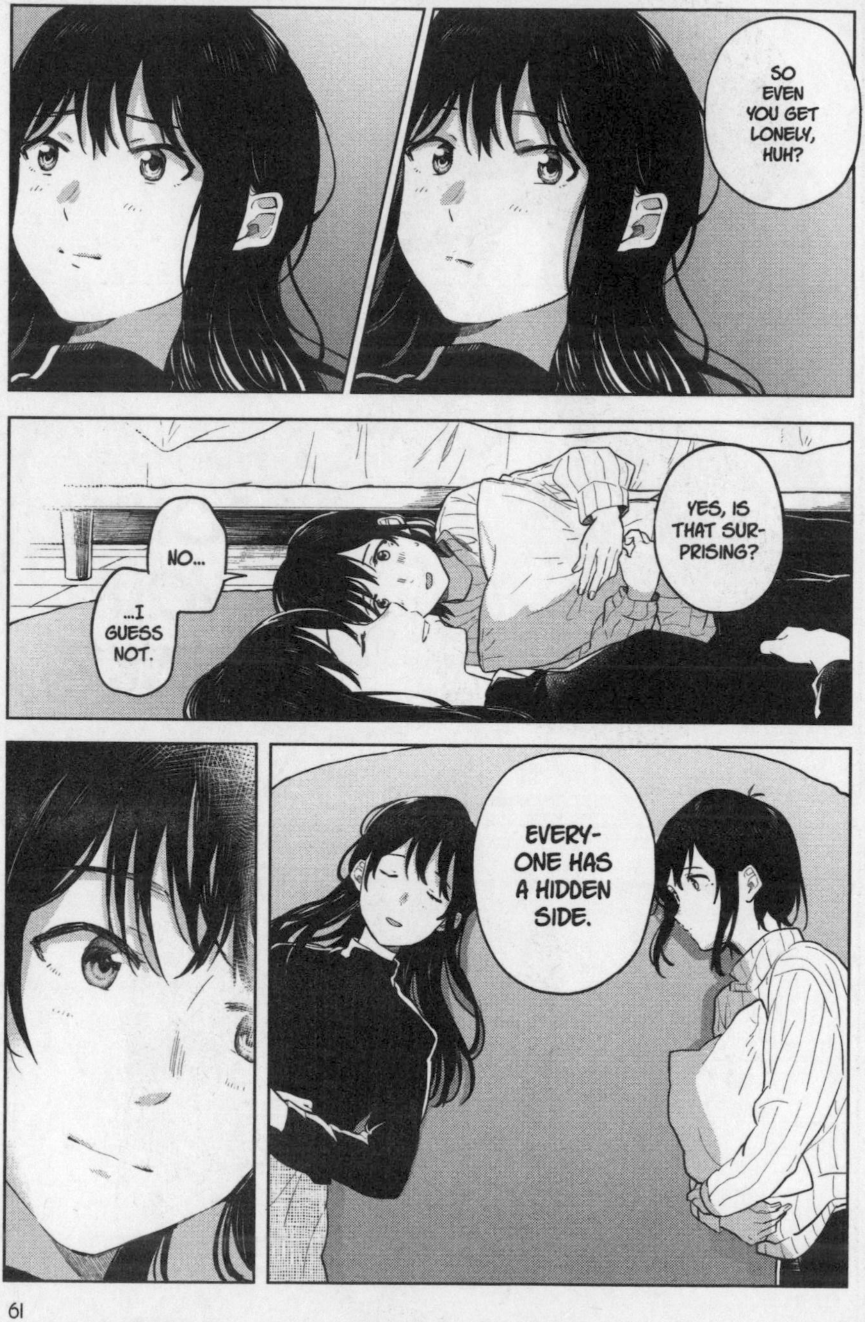
SO EVEN YOU GET LONELY, HUH?
YES, IS THAT SUR-PRISING?
NO...
...I GUESS NOT.
EVERY-ONE HAS A HIDDEN SIDE.

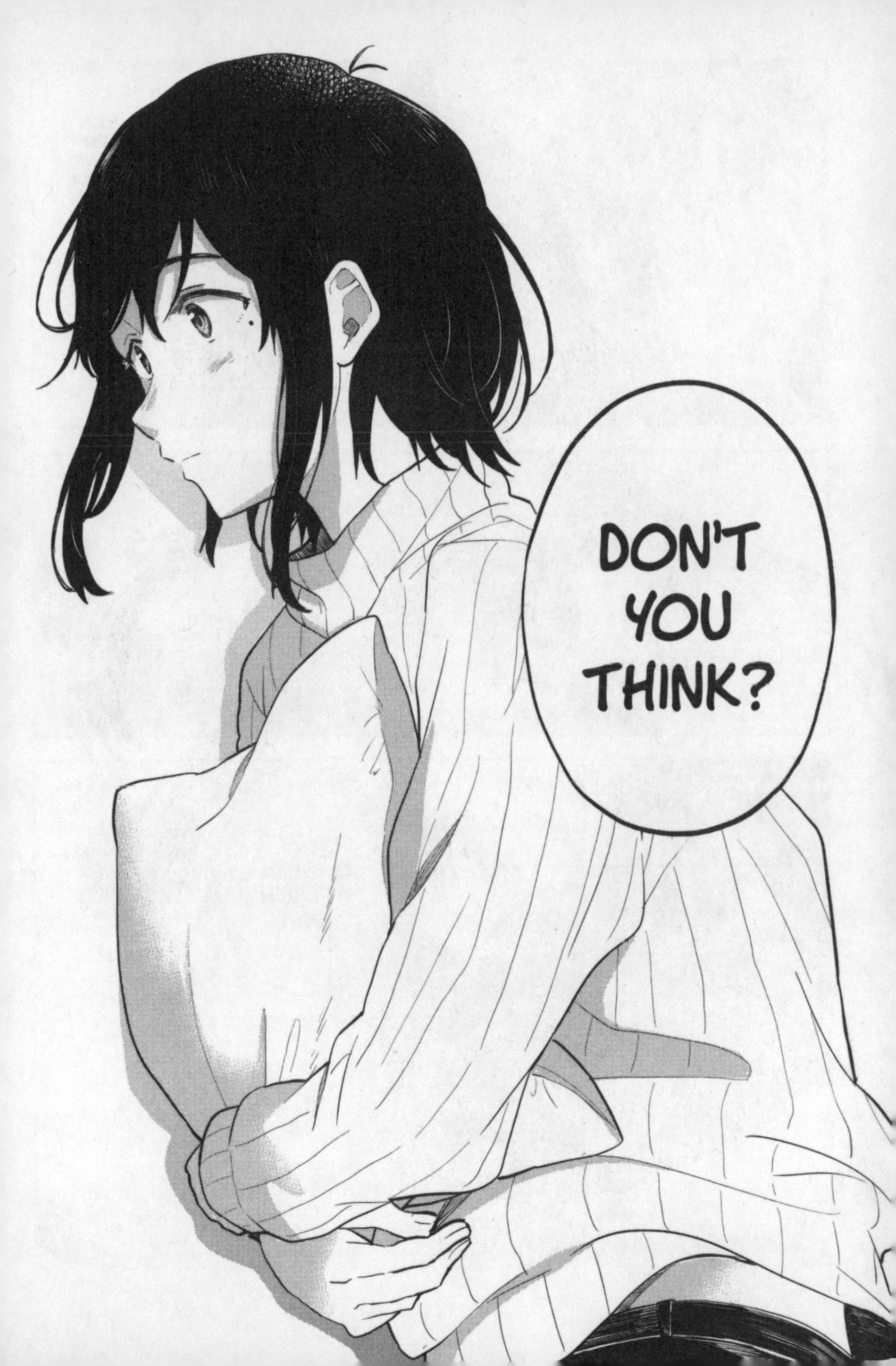
DON'T YOU THINK?

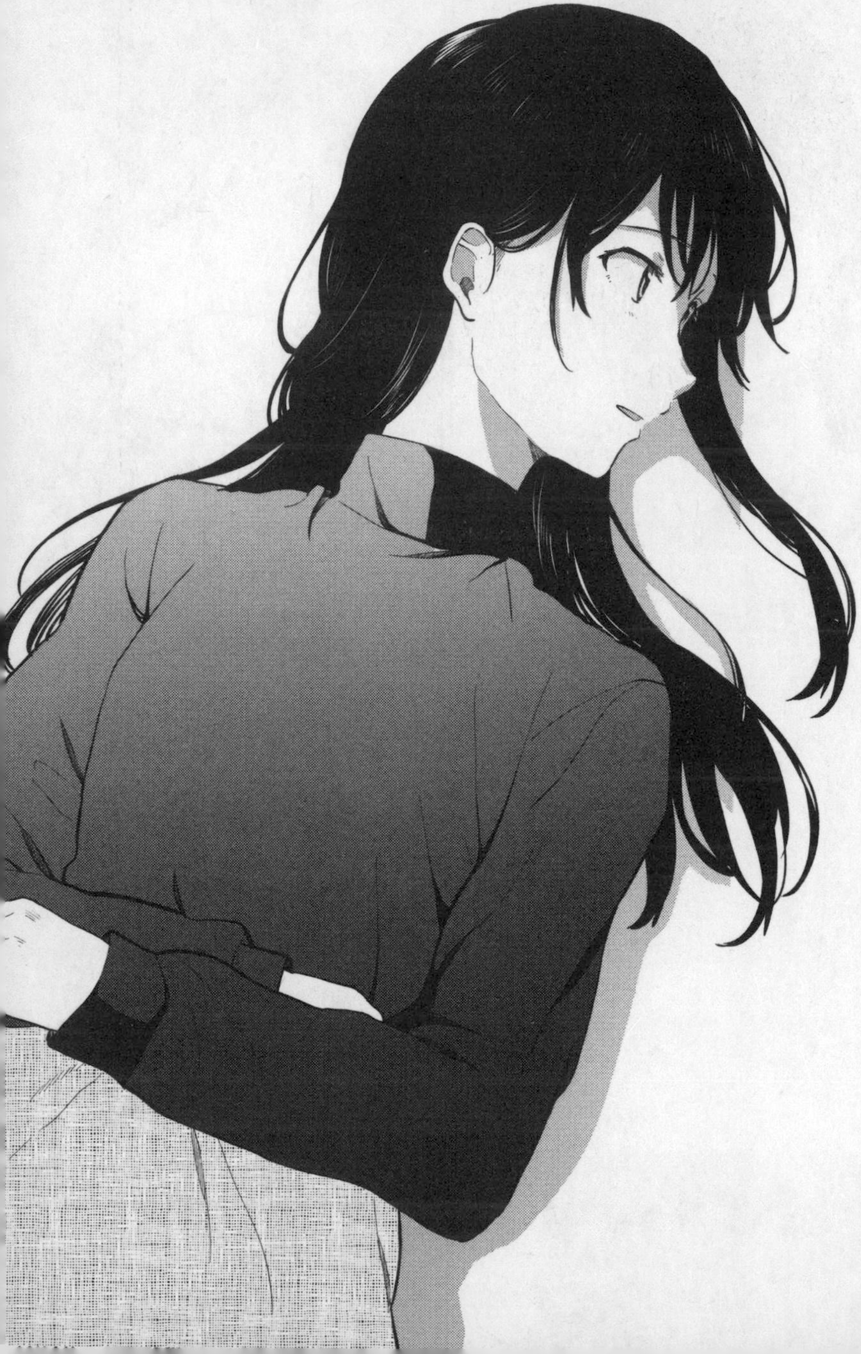

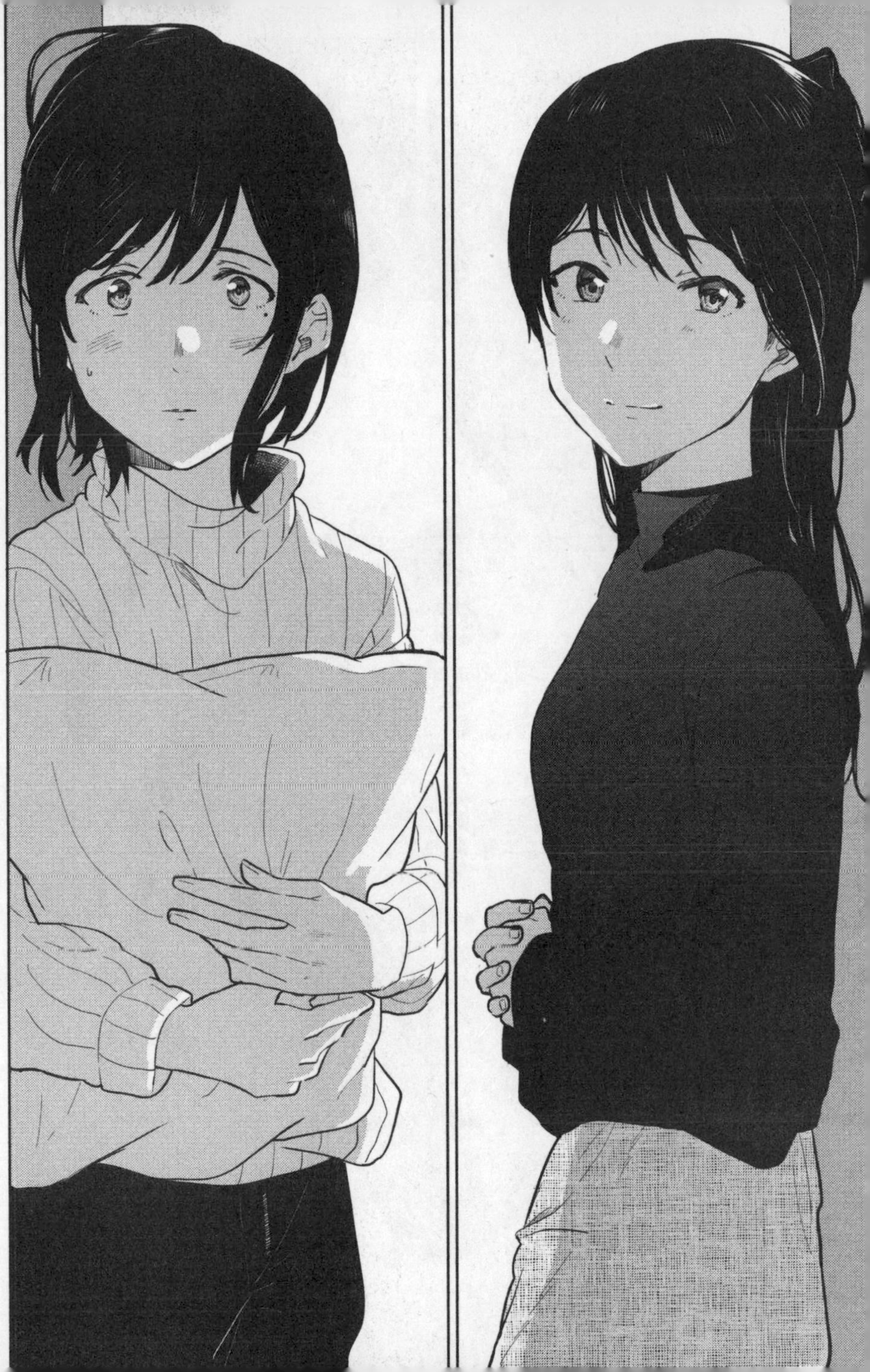

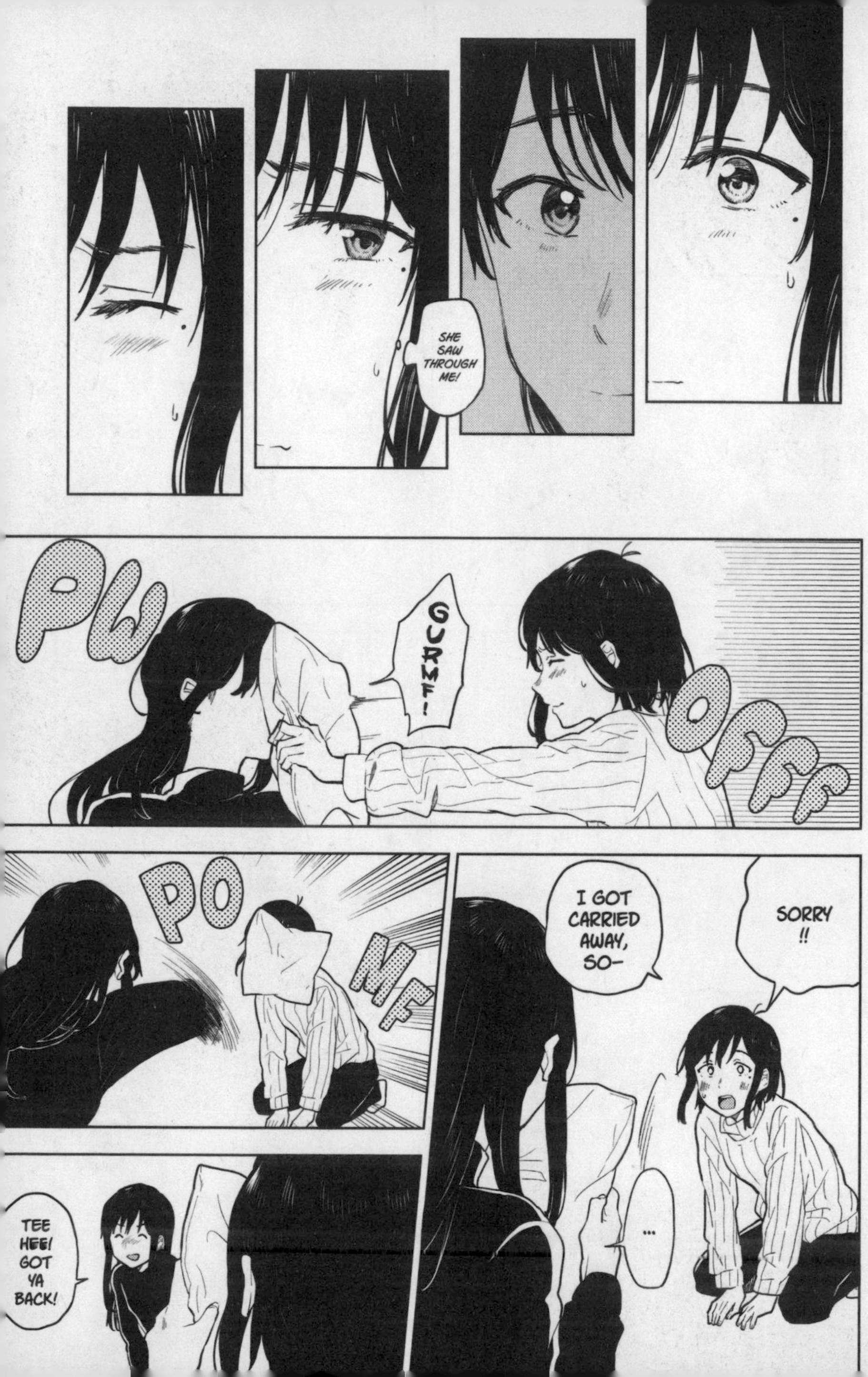
SHE SAW THROUGH ME!
GURMF!
PW
OFFF
SORRY!!
I GOT CARRIED AWAY, SO-
...
PO
MF
TEE HEE! GOT YA BACK!

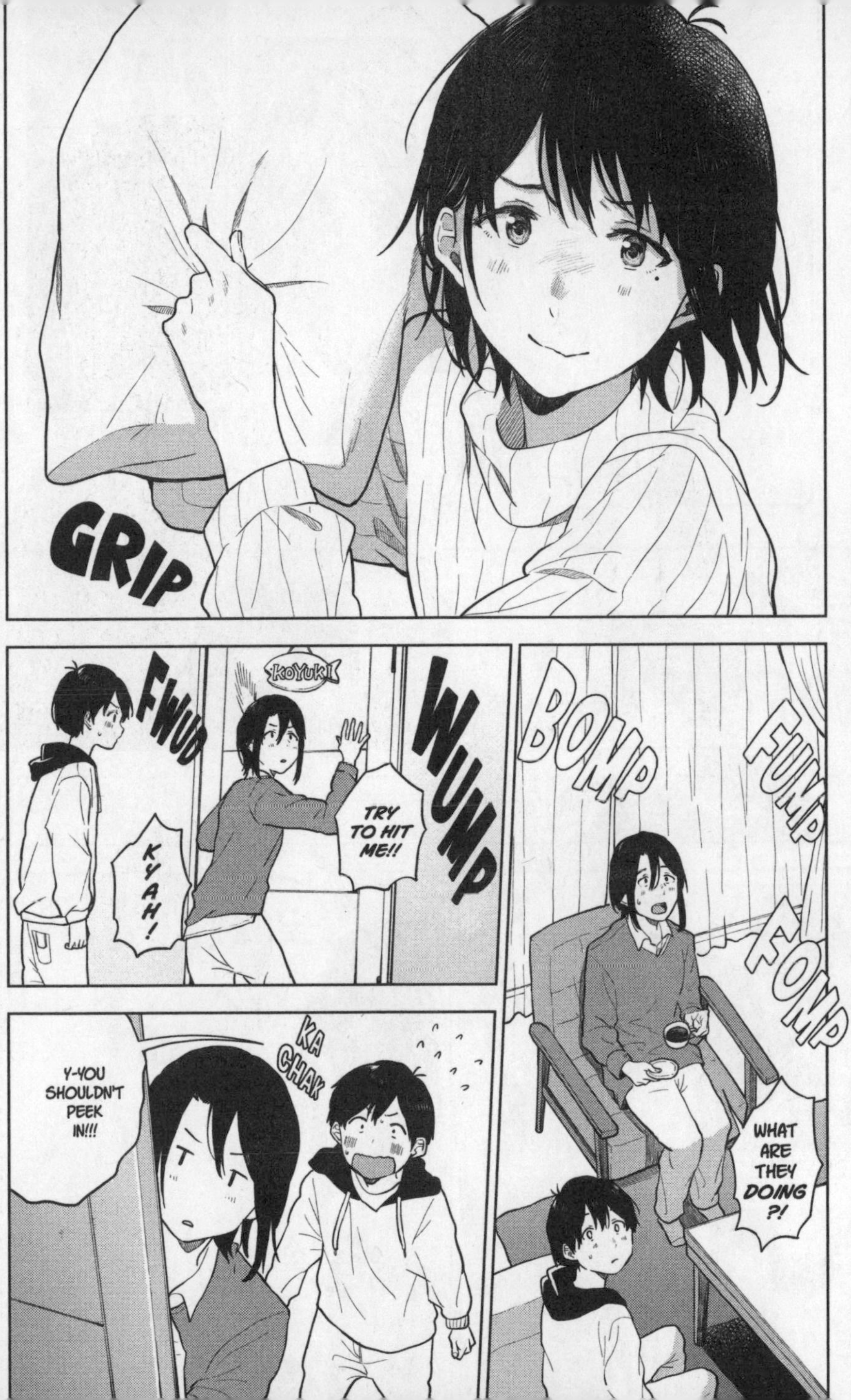
GRIP
FUMP
BOMP
FOMP
WHAT ARE THEY DOING?!
WUMP
KOYUKI
TRY TO HIT ME!!
FWUD
KYAH!
KA CHAK
Y-YOU SHOULDN'T PEEK IN!!!

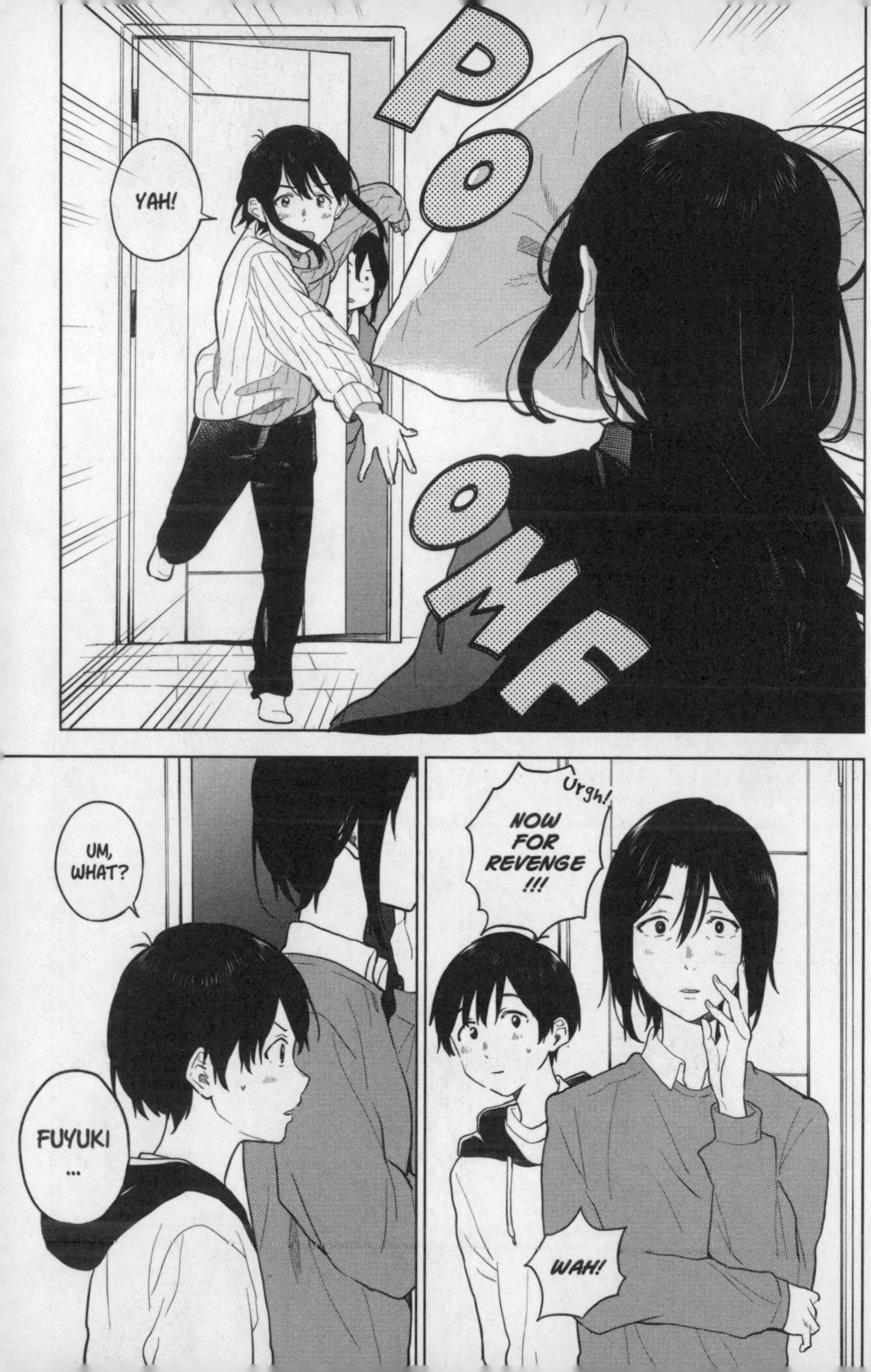
POMF
YAH!
Urgh!
NOW FOR REVENGE!!!
WAH!
UM, WHAT?
FUYUKI...

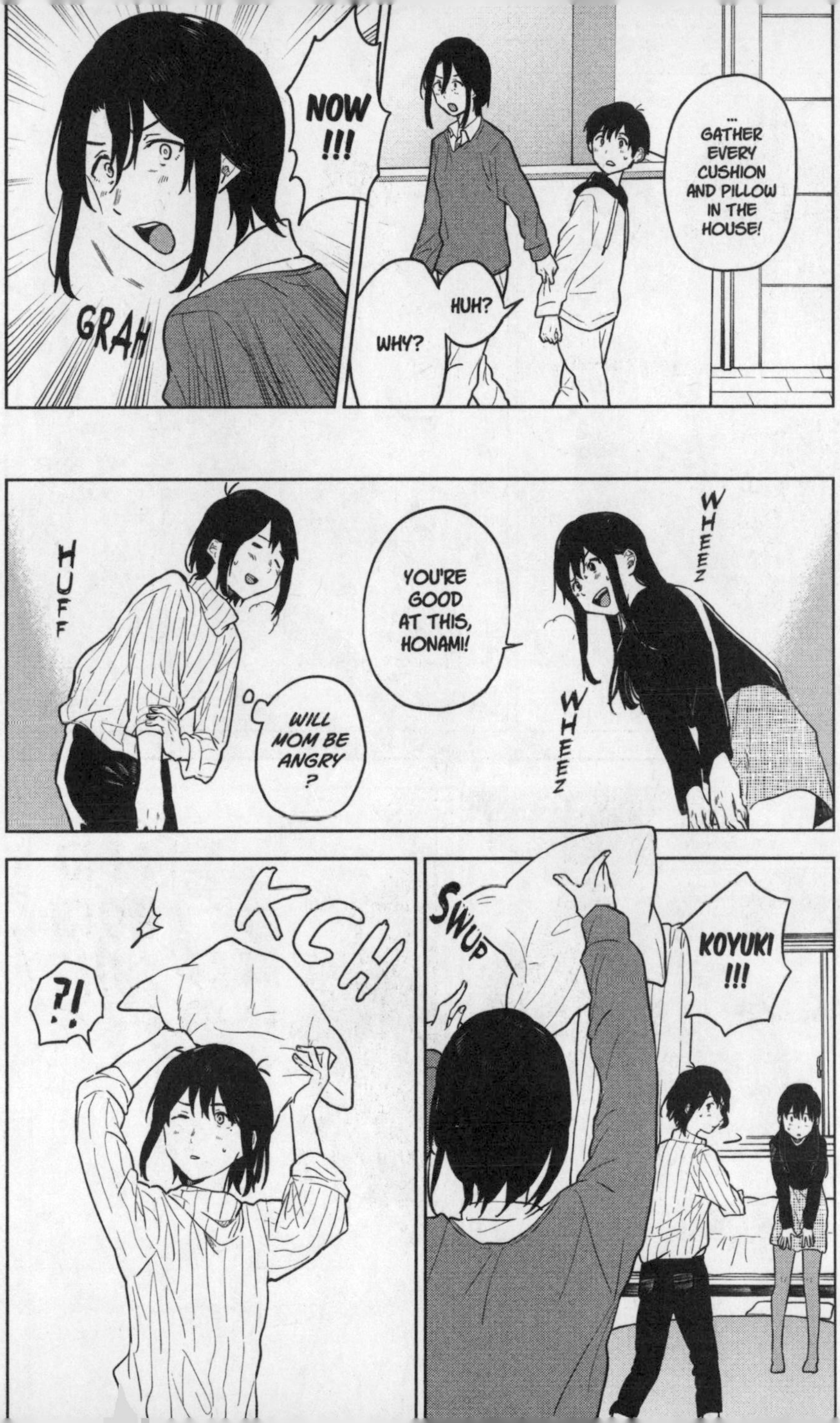
...GATHER EVERY CUSHION AND PILLOW IN THE HOUSE!
NOW!!!
HUH?
WHY?
GRAH
WHEEZ
WHEEZ
YOU'RE GOOD AT THIS, HONAMI!
HUFF
WILL MOM BE ANGRY?
KOYUKI!!!
SWUP
KCH
?!

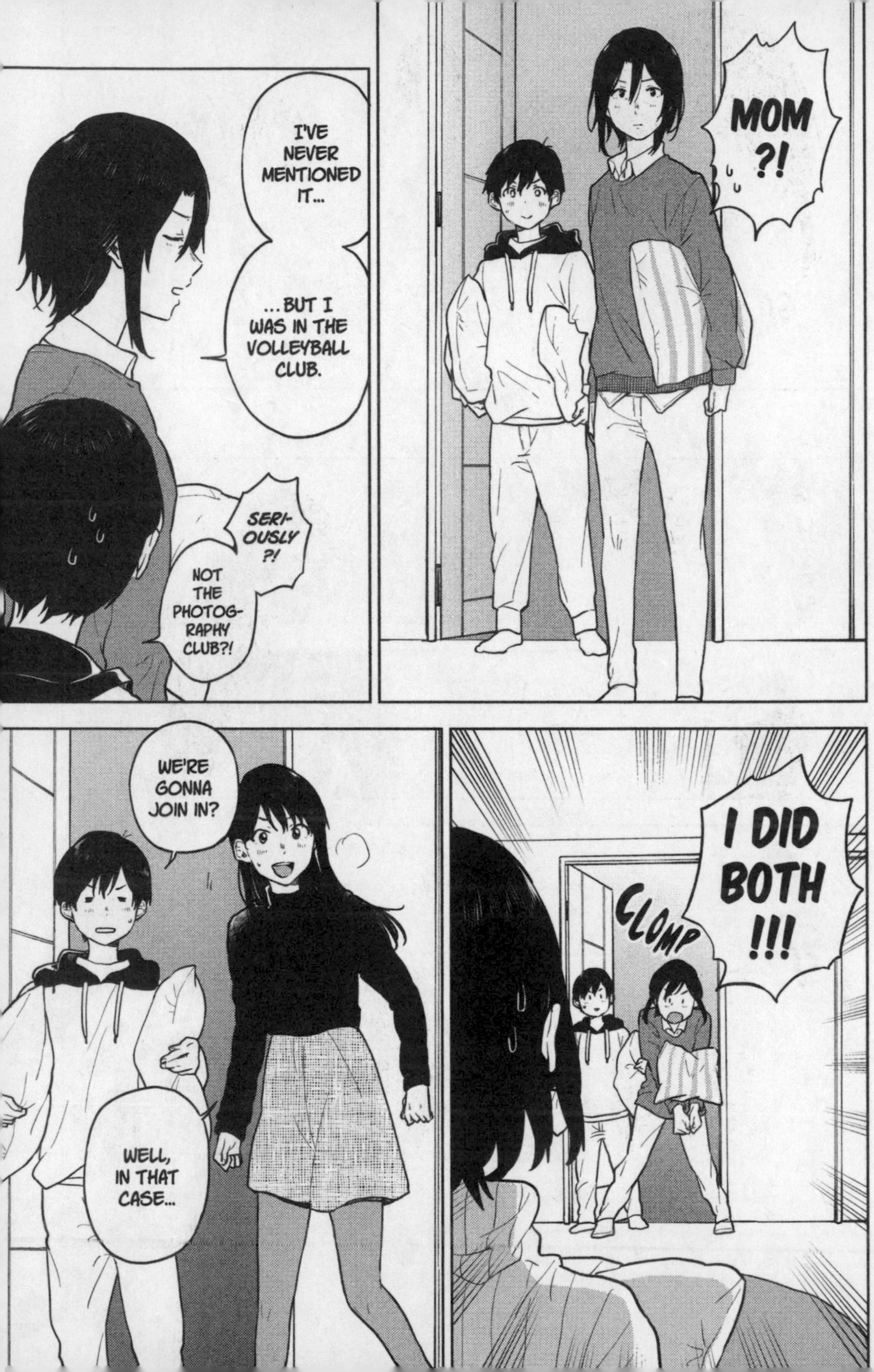
MOM ?!
I'VE NEVER MENTIONED IT... ...BUT I WAS IN THE VOLLEYBALL CLUB.
SERI-OUSLY ?!
NOT THE PHOTOG-RAPHY CLUB?!
CLOMP
I DID BOTH !!!
WE'RE GONNA JOIN IN?
WELL, IN THAT CASE...

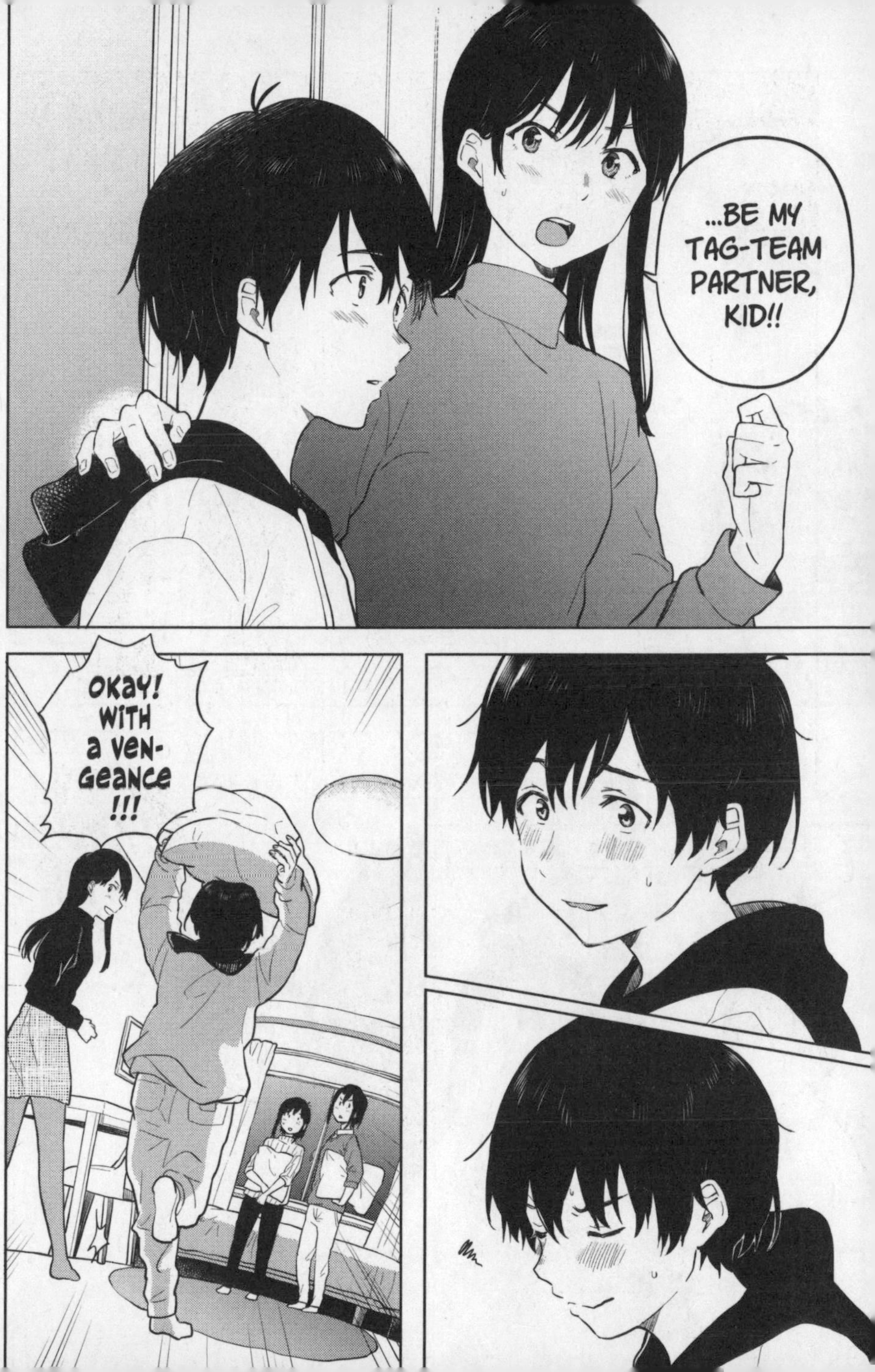
...BE MY TAG-TEAM PARTNER, KID!!
OKAY! WITH a VEN-GEANCE!!!

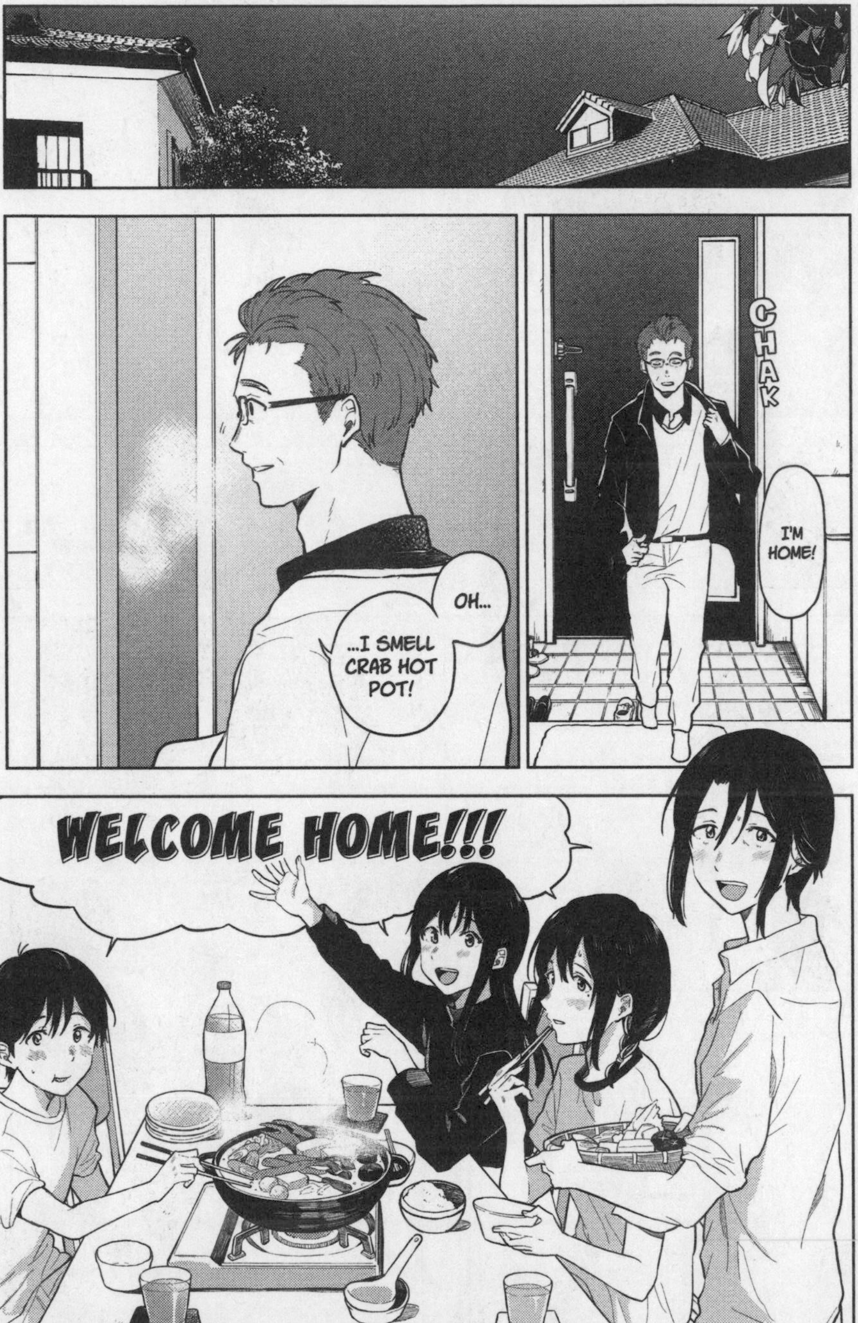
CHAK
I'M HOME!
OH...
...I SMELL CRAB HOT POT!
WELCOME HOME!!!

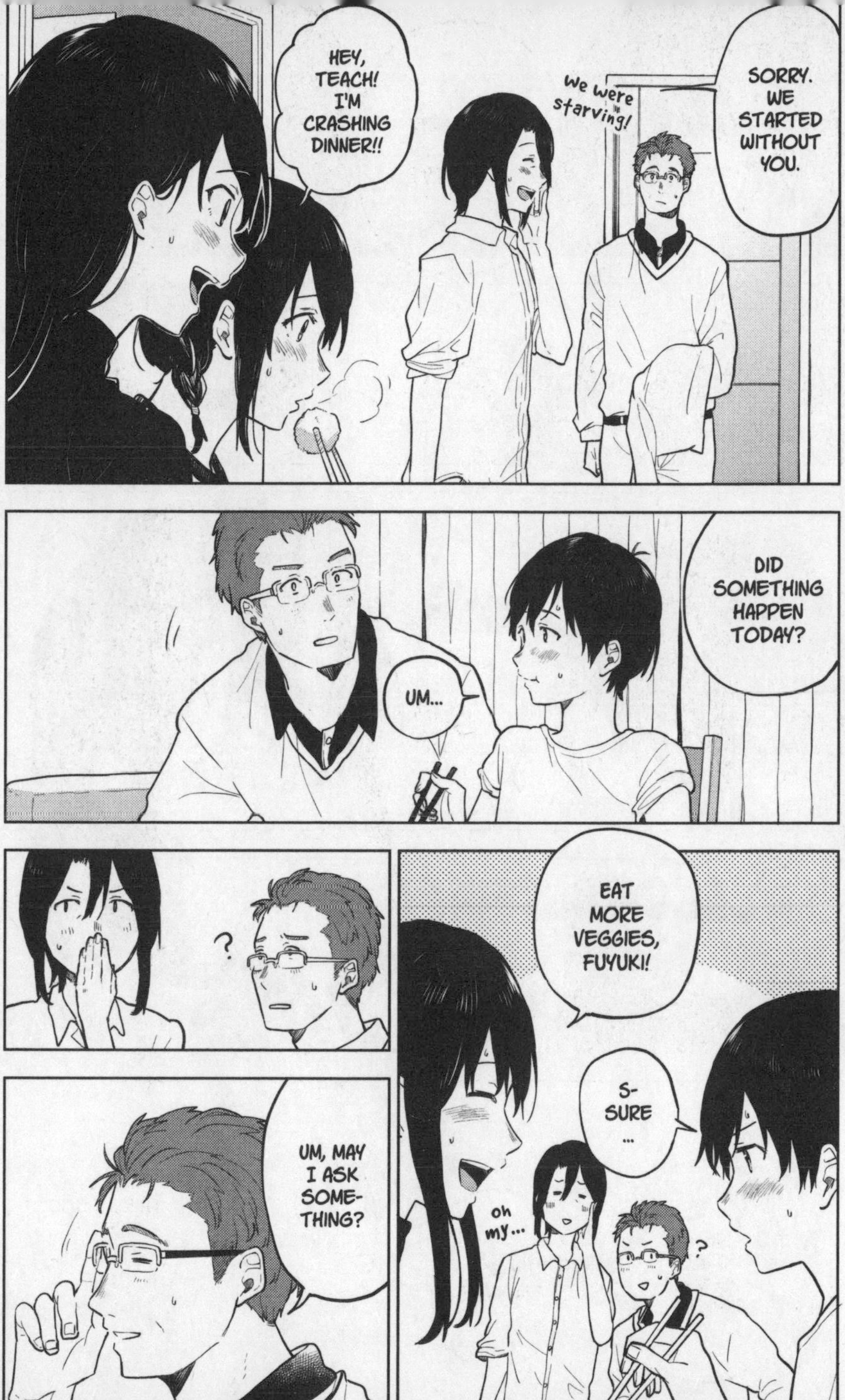
SORRY. WE STARTED WITHOUT YOU.
We were starving!
HEY, TEACH! I'M CRASHING DINNER!!
DID SOMETHING HAPPEN TODAY?
UM...
EAT MORE VEGGIES, FUYUKI!
S-SURE ...
?
oh my...
?
UM, MAY I ASK SOMETHING?

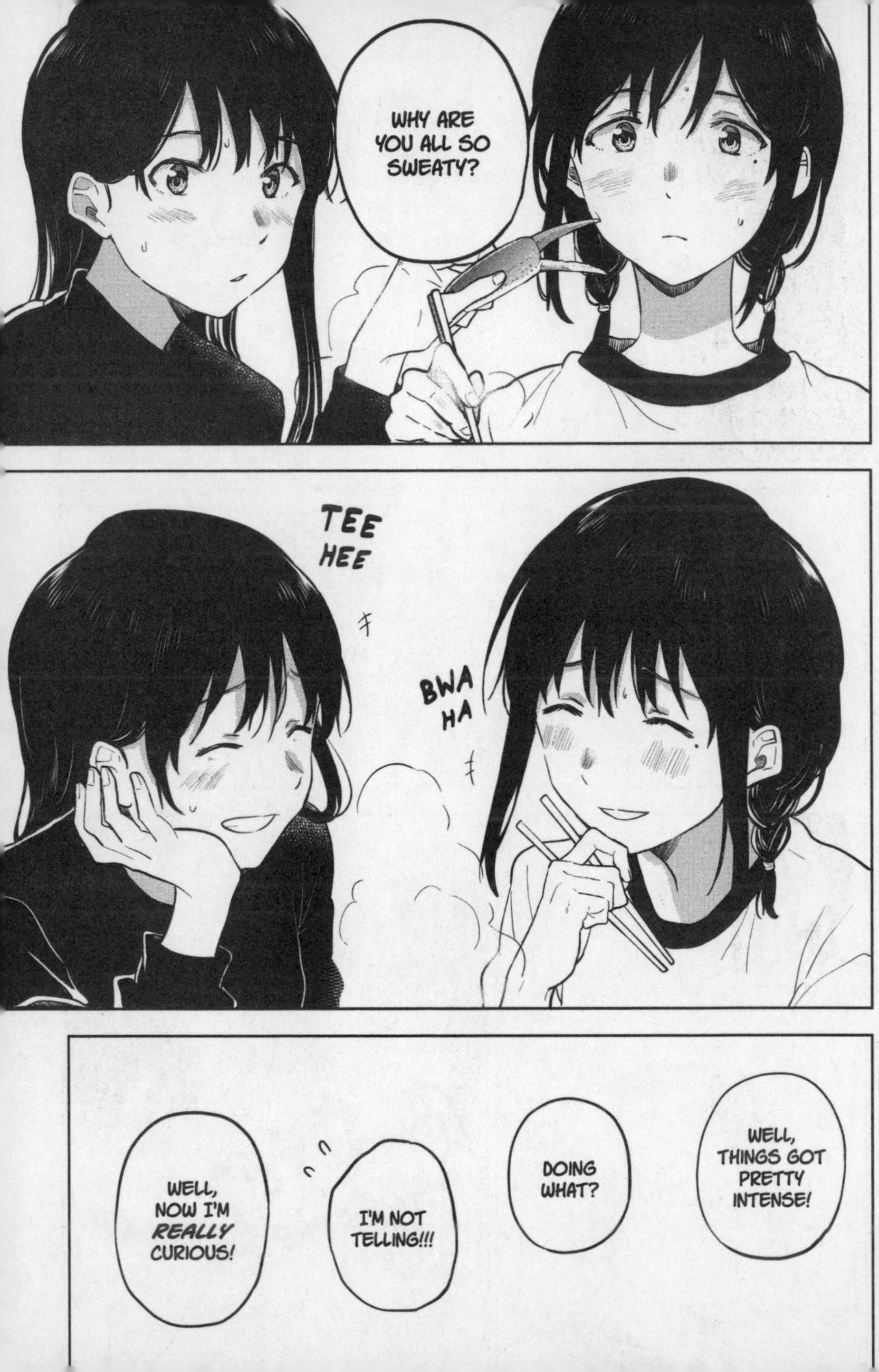
WHY ARE YOU ALL SO SWEATY?
TEE HEE
BWA HA
WELL, THINGS GOT PRETTY INTENSE!
DOING WHAT?
I'M NOT TELLING!!!
WELL, NOW I'M *REALLY* CURIOUS!

A Tropical Fish
Yearns for Snow

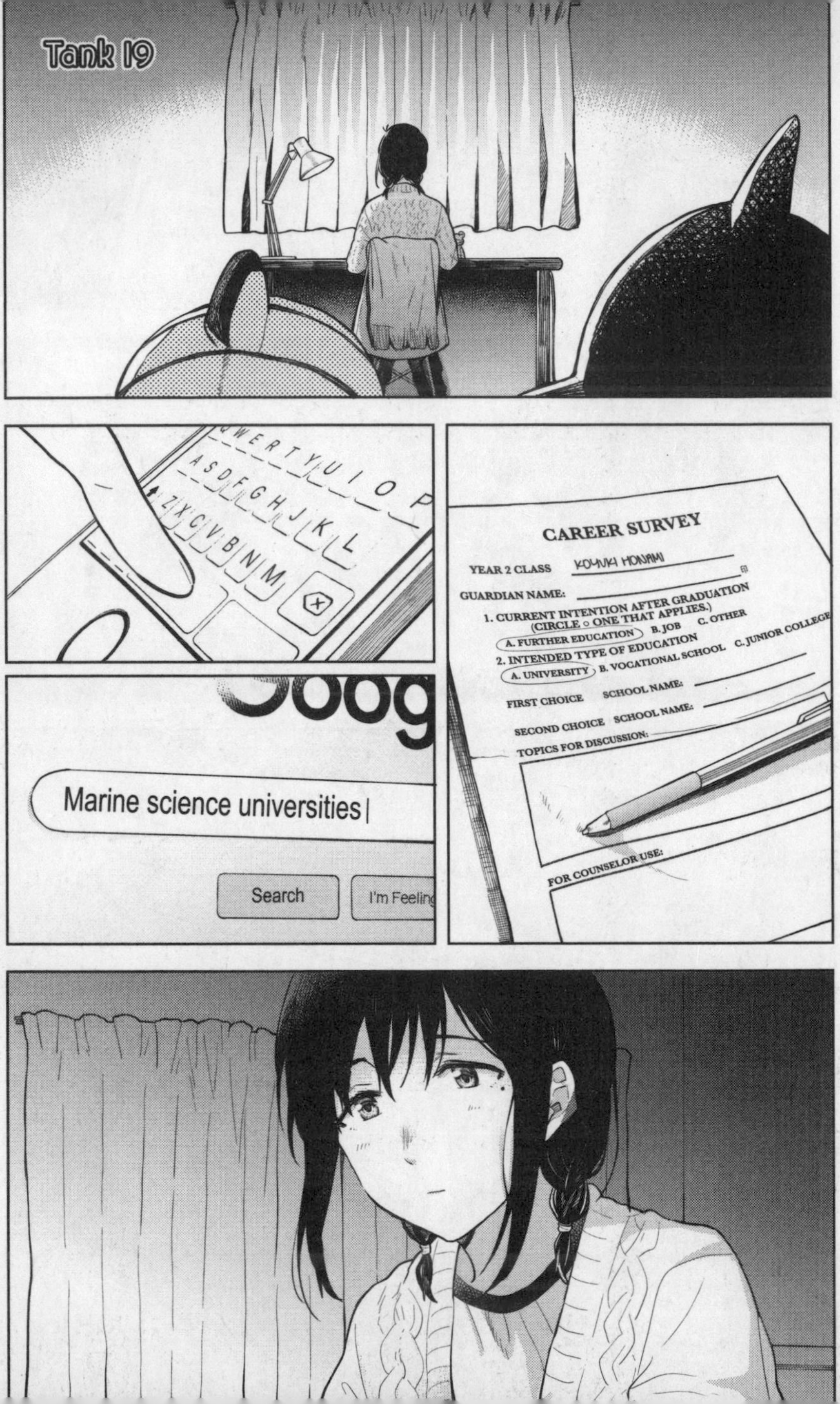
Tank 19
CAREER SURVEY
YEAR 2 CLASS
KOYUKI HONAMI
GUARDIAN NAME:
1. CURRENT INTENTION AFTER GRADUATION
(CIRCLE ○ ONE THAT APPLIES.)
A. FURTHER EDUCATION
B. JOB
C. OTHER
2. INTENDED TYPE OF EDUCATION
A. UNIVERSITY
B. VOCATIONAL SCHOOL
C. JUNIOR COLLEGE
FIRST CHOICE
SCHOOL NAME:
SECOND CHOICE
SCHOOL NAME:
TOPICS FOR DISCUSSION:
FOR COUNSELOR USE:
QWERTYUIOP
ASDFGHJKL
ZXCVBNM
Marine science universities
Search
I'm Feeling

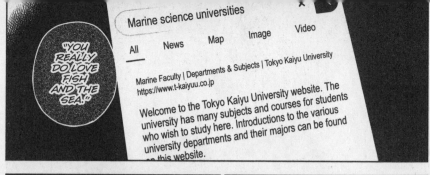

Marine science universities
All
News
Map
Image
Video
Marine Faculty | Departments & Subjects | Tokyo Kaiyu University
https://www.t-kaiyuu.co.jp
Welcome to the Tokyo Kaiyu University website. The university has many subjects and courses for students who wish to study here. Introductions to the various university departments and their majors can be found on this website.
"YOU REALLY DO LOVE FISH AND THE SEA!"
"WELL, THAT CAME NATURALLY."
"SOME INTERESTS JUST COME NATURALLY."
A. FURTHER EDUCATION
2. INTENDED TYPE OF EDUCATION
A. UNIVERSITY
B. VOCATIONAL SCHOOL
FIRST CHOICE
SCHOOL NAME:
TOKYO KAIYU UNIVERSITY
SECOND CHOICE
SCHOOL NAME:
TOPICS FOR DISCUSSION:

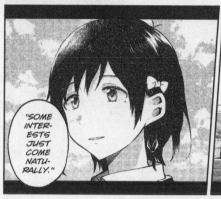

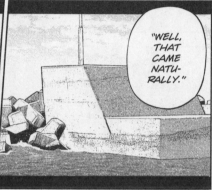

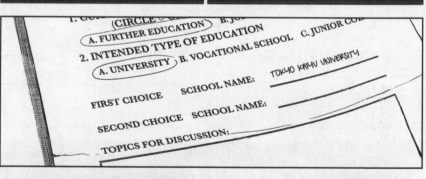

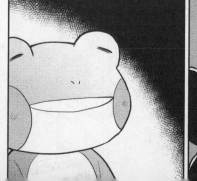

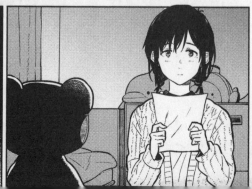

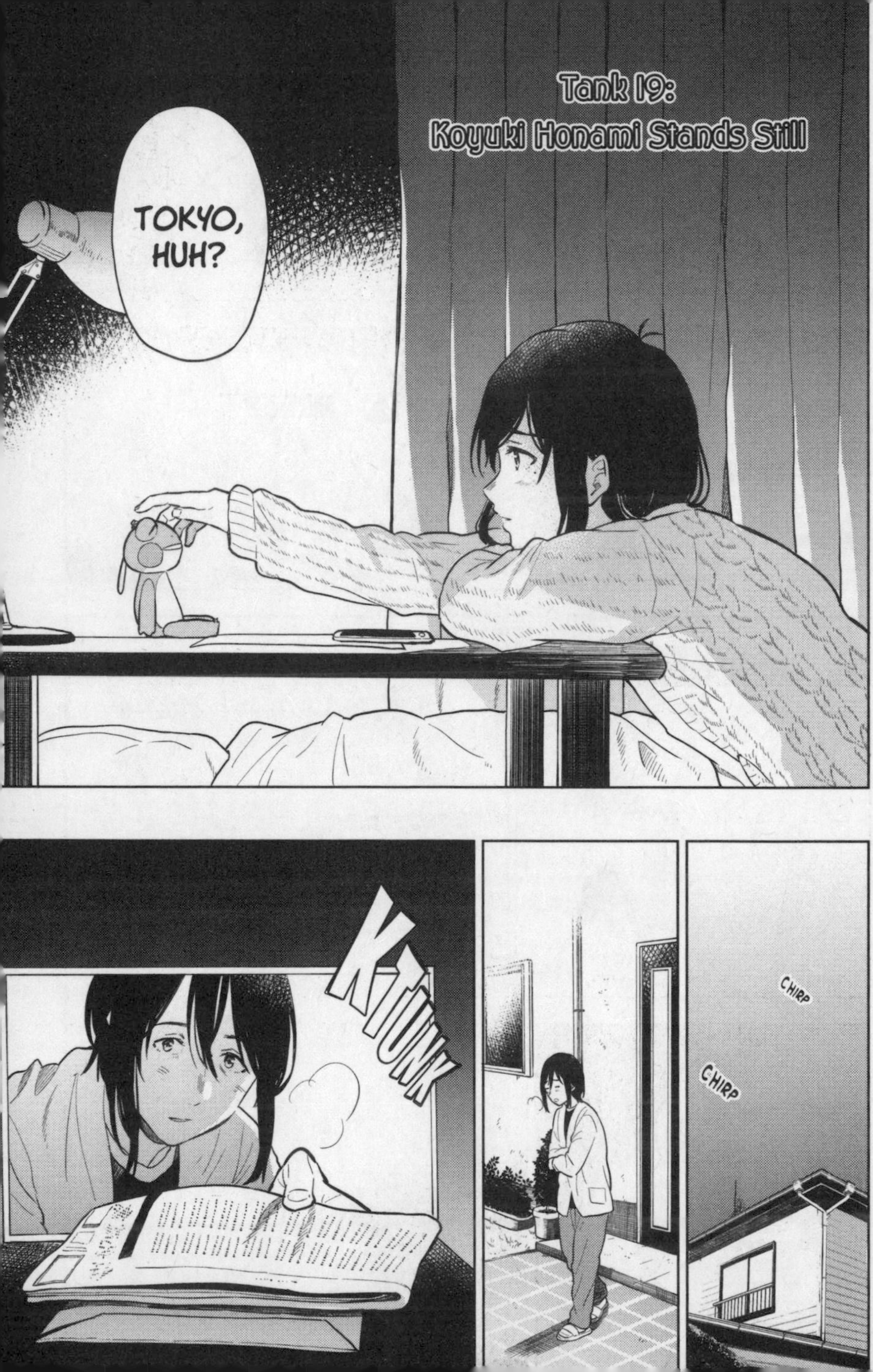
Tank 19:
Koyuki Honami Stands Still
TOKYO, HUH?
CHIRP
CHIRP
K-TUNK

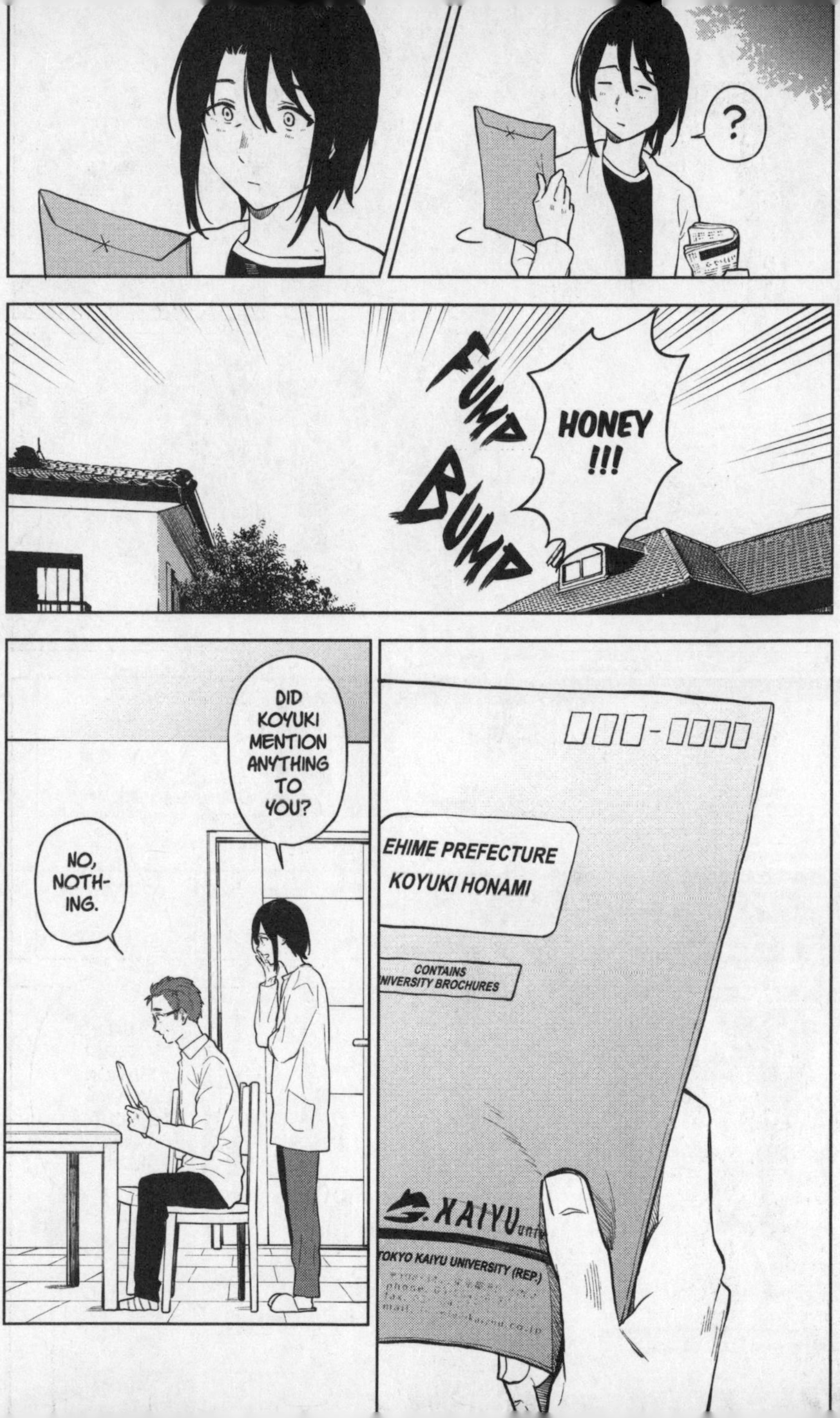
?
HONEY !!!
FUMP BUMP
EHIME PREFECTURE
KOYUKI HONAMI
CONTAINS UNIVERSITY BROCHURES
XAIYU
TOKYO KAIYU UNIVERSITY (REP.)
DID KOYUKI MENTION ANYTHING TO YOU?
NO, NOTHING.

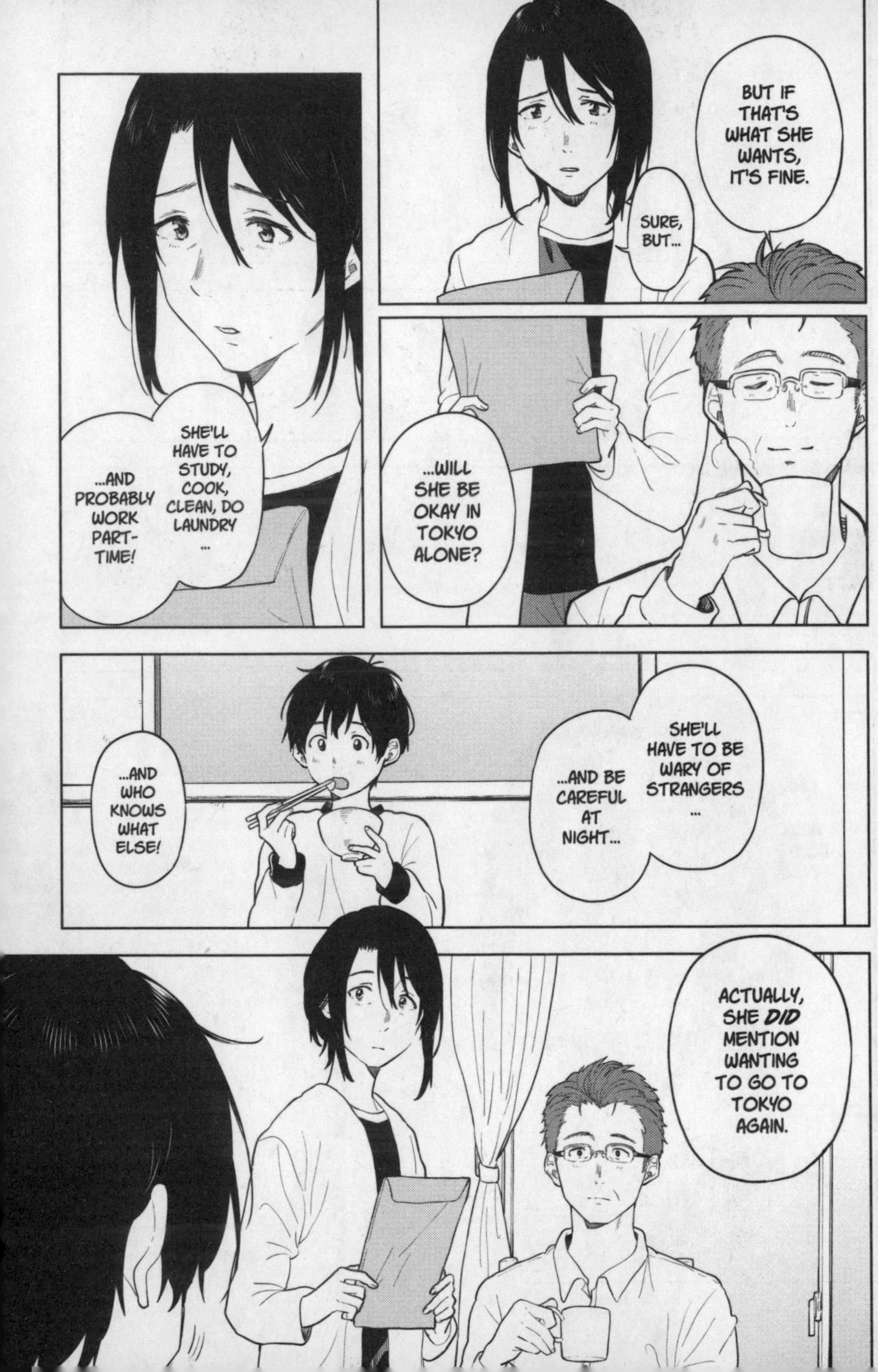
BUT IF THAT'S WHAT SHE WANTS, IT'S FINE.
SURE, BUT...
...WILL SHE BE OKAY IN TOKYO ALONE?
SHE'LL HAVE TO STUDY, COOK, CLEAN, DO LAUNDRY...
...AND PROBABLY WORK PART-TIME!
SHE'LL HAVE TO BE WARY OF STRANGERS...
...AND BE CAREFUL AT NIGHT...
...AND WHO KNOWS WHAT ELSE!
ACTUALLY, SHE *DID* MENTION WANTING TO GO TO TOKYO AGAIN.

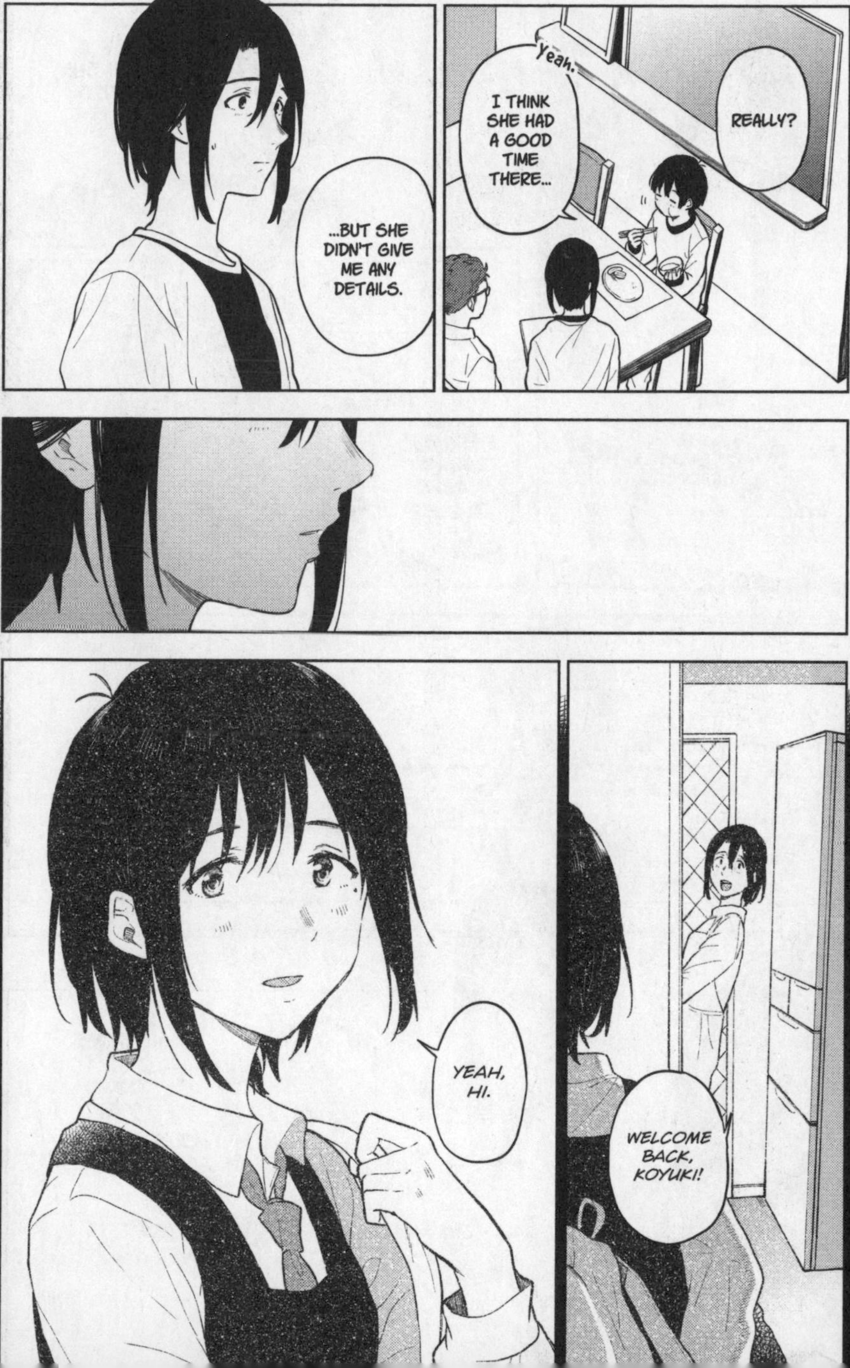
REALLY?
Yeah.
I THINK SHE HAD A GOOD TIME THERE...
...BUT SHE DIDN'T GIVE ME ANY DETAILS.
WELCOME BACK, KOYUKI!
YEAH, HI.

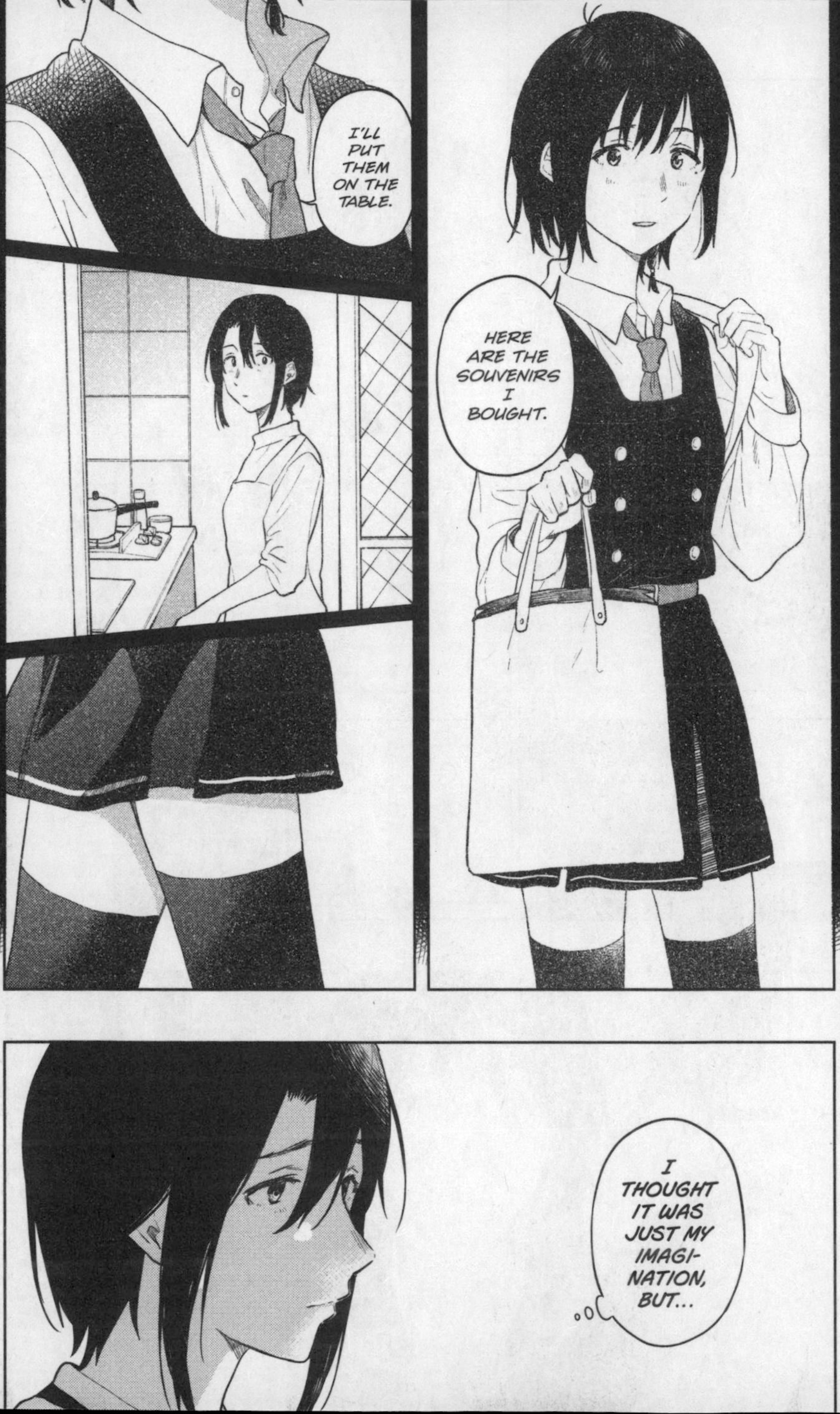
HERE ARE THE SOUVENIRS I BOUGHT.
I'LL PUT THEM ON THE TABLE.
I THOUGHT IT WAS JUST MY IMAGI-NATION, BUT...

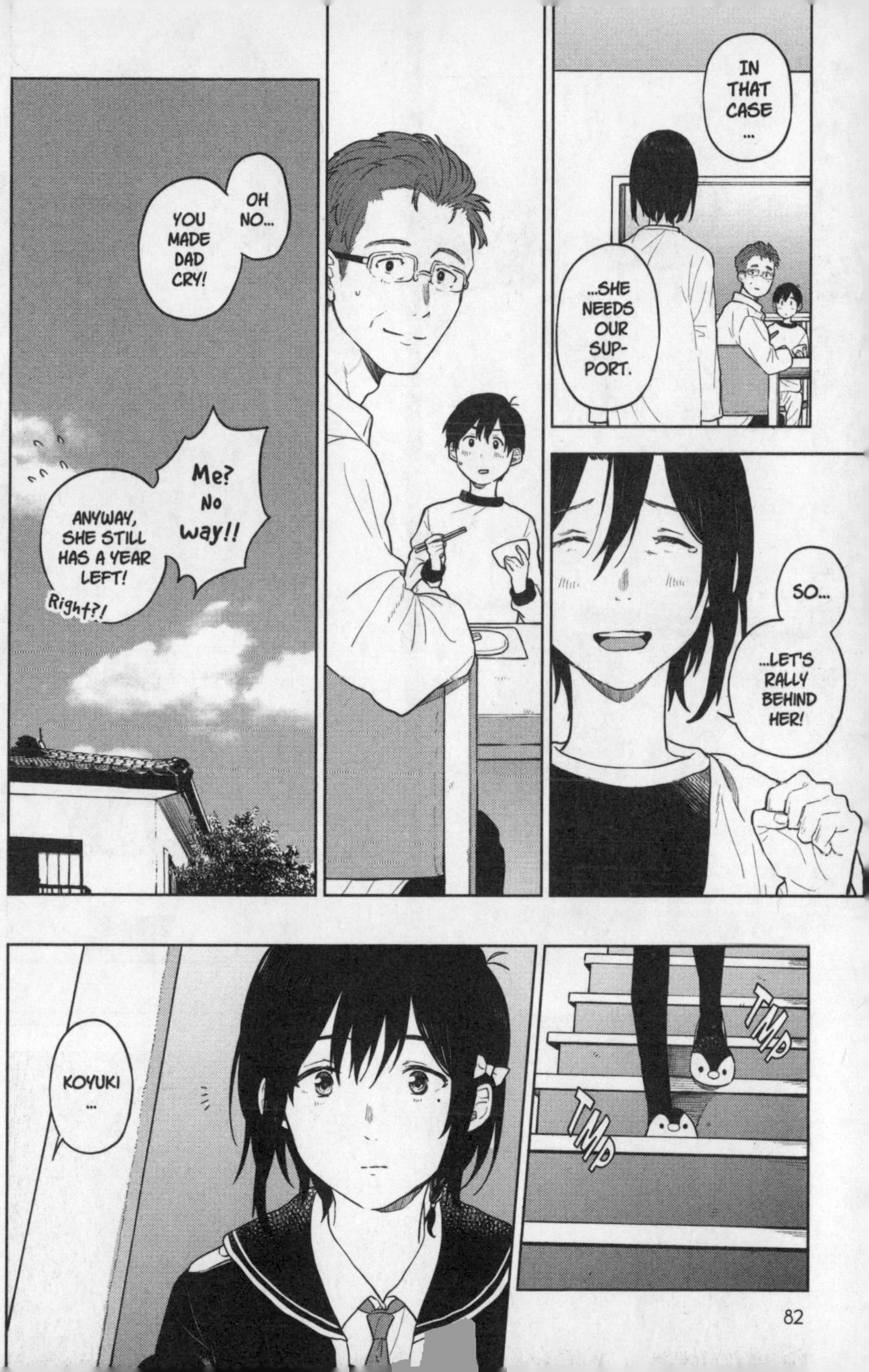

IN THAT CASE ...
...SHE NEEDS OUR SUPPORT.
SO...
...LET'S RALLY BEHIND HER!
OH NO...
YOU MADE DAD CRY!
Me? No way!!
ANYWAY, SHE STILL HAS A YEAR LEFT!
Right?!
TMP
TMP
KOYUKI ...

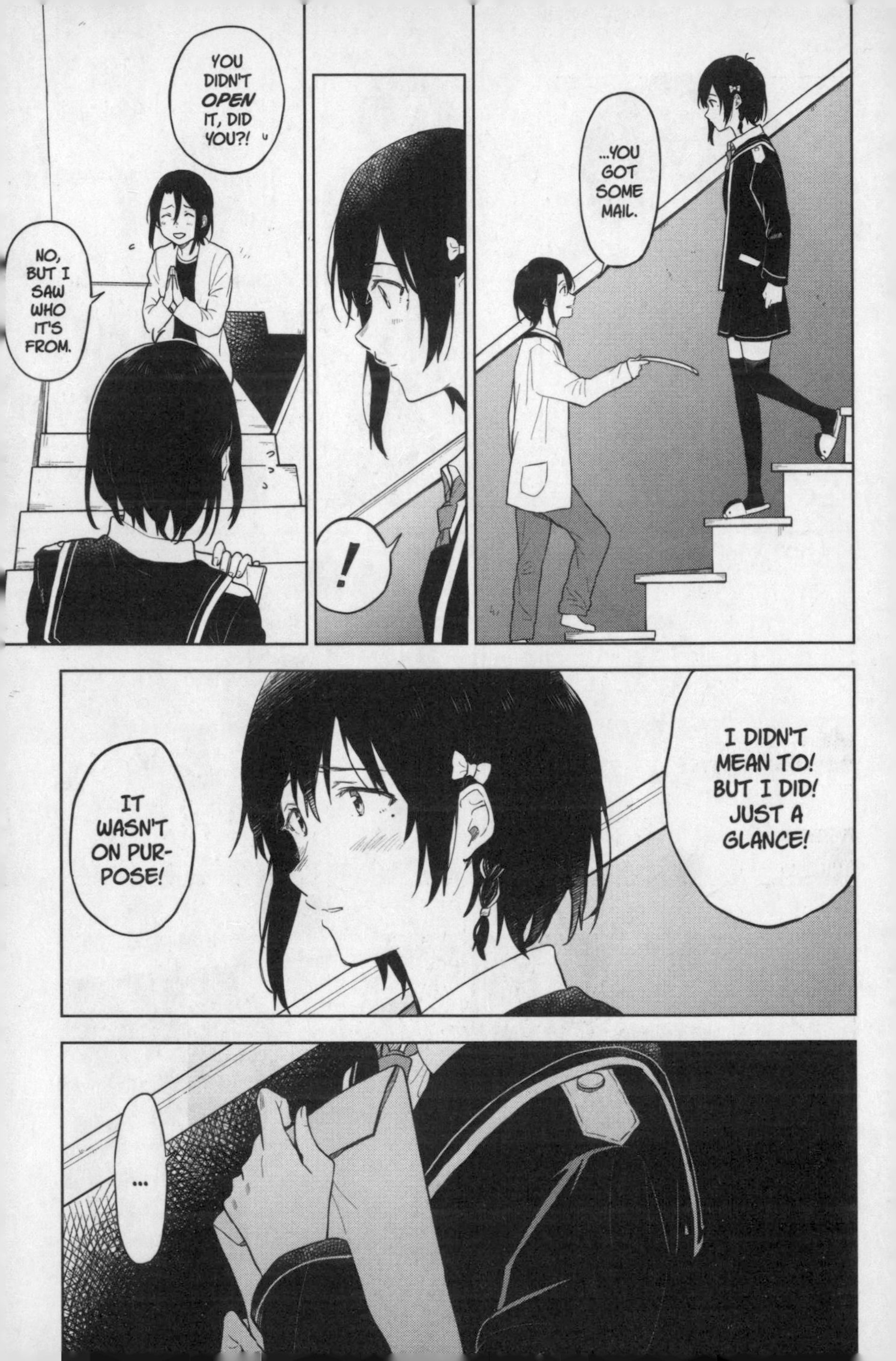
...YOU GOT SOME MAIL.
!
YOU DIDN'T *OPEN* IT, DID YOU?!
NO, BUT I SAW WHO IT'S FROM.
I DIDN'T MEAN TO! BUT I DID! JUST A GLANCE!
IT WASN'T ON PURPOSE!
...

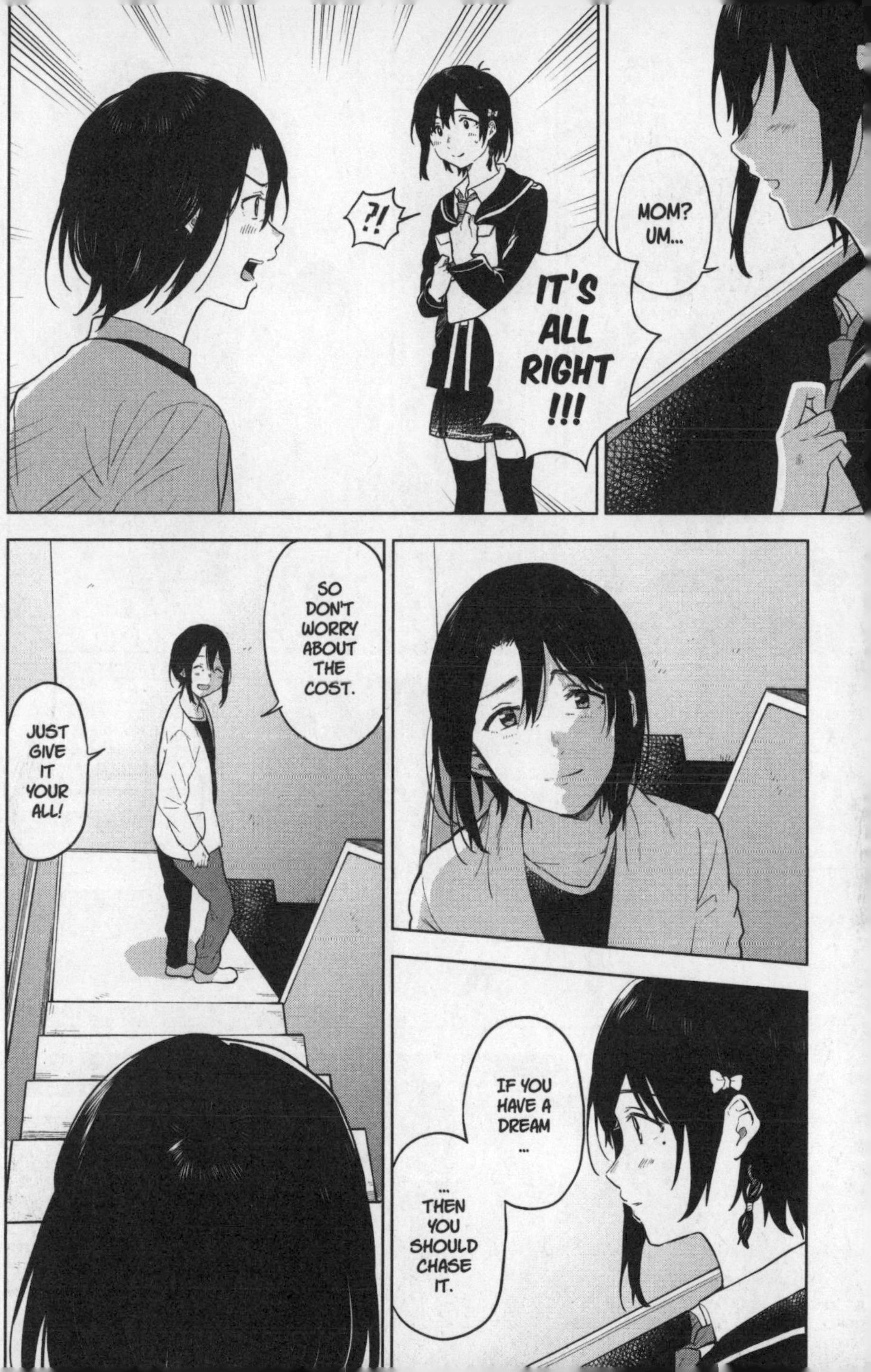
MOM? UM...
IT'S ALL RIGHT!!!
?!
IF YOU HAVE A DREAM...
...THEN YOU SHOULD CHASE IT.
SO DON'T WORRY ABOUT THE COST.
JUST GIVE IT YOUR ALL!

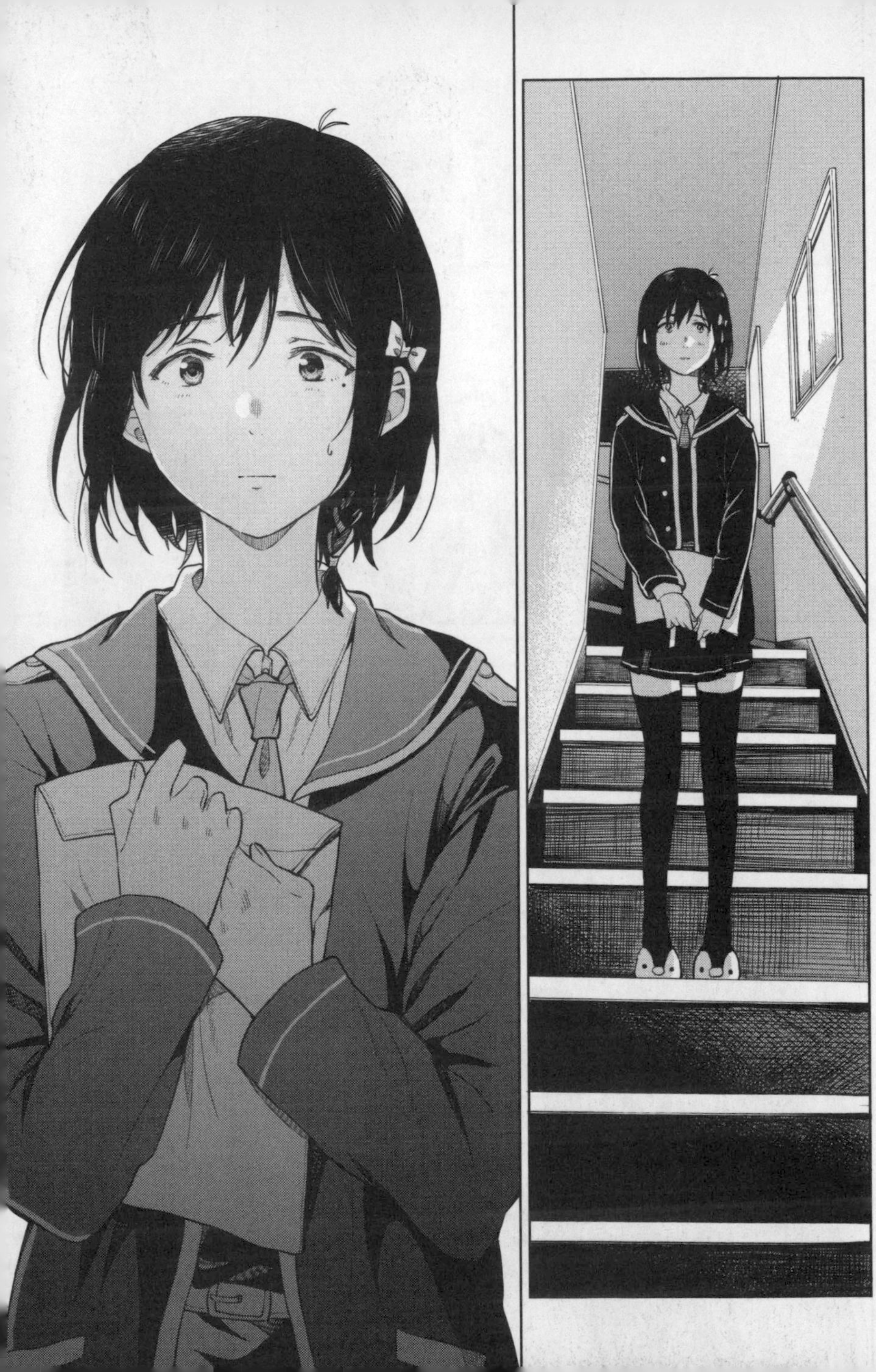

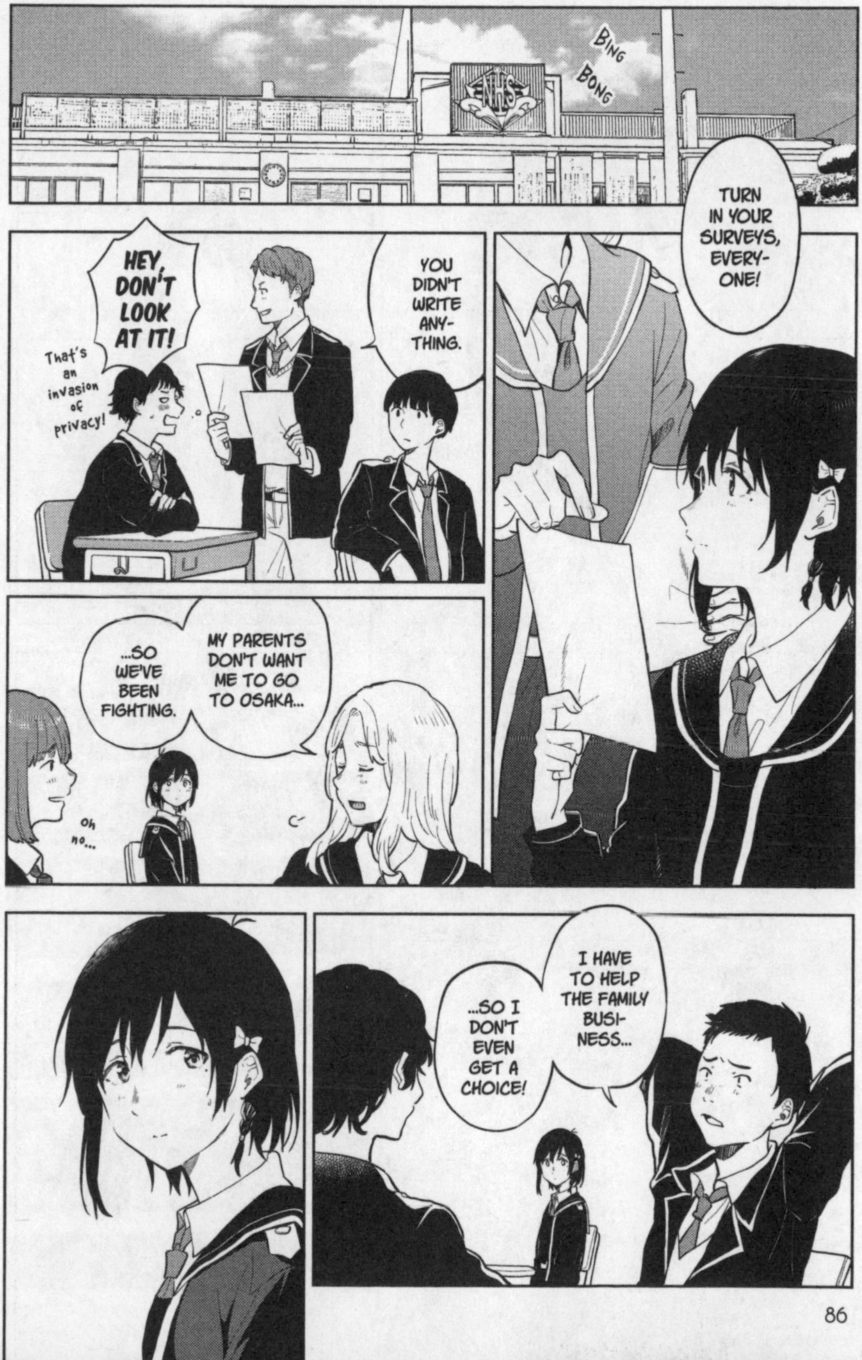
BING BONG
TURN IN YOUR SURVEYS, EVERYONE!
YOU DIDN'T WRITE ANYTHING.
HEY, DON'T LOOK AT IT!
That's an invasion of privacy!
MY PARENTS DON'T WANT ME TO GO TO OSAKA...
...SO WE'VE BEEN FIGHTING.
Oh no...
I HAVE TO HELP THE FAMILY BUSINESS...
...SO I DON'T EVEN GET A CHOICE!

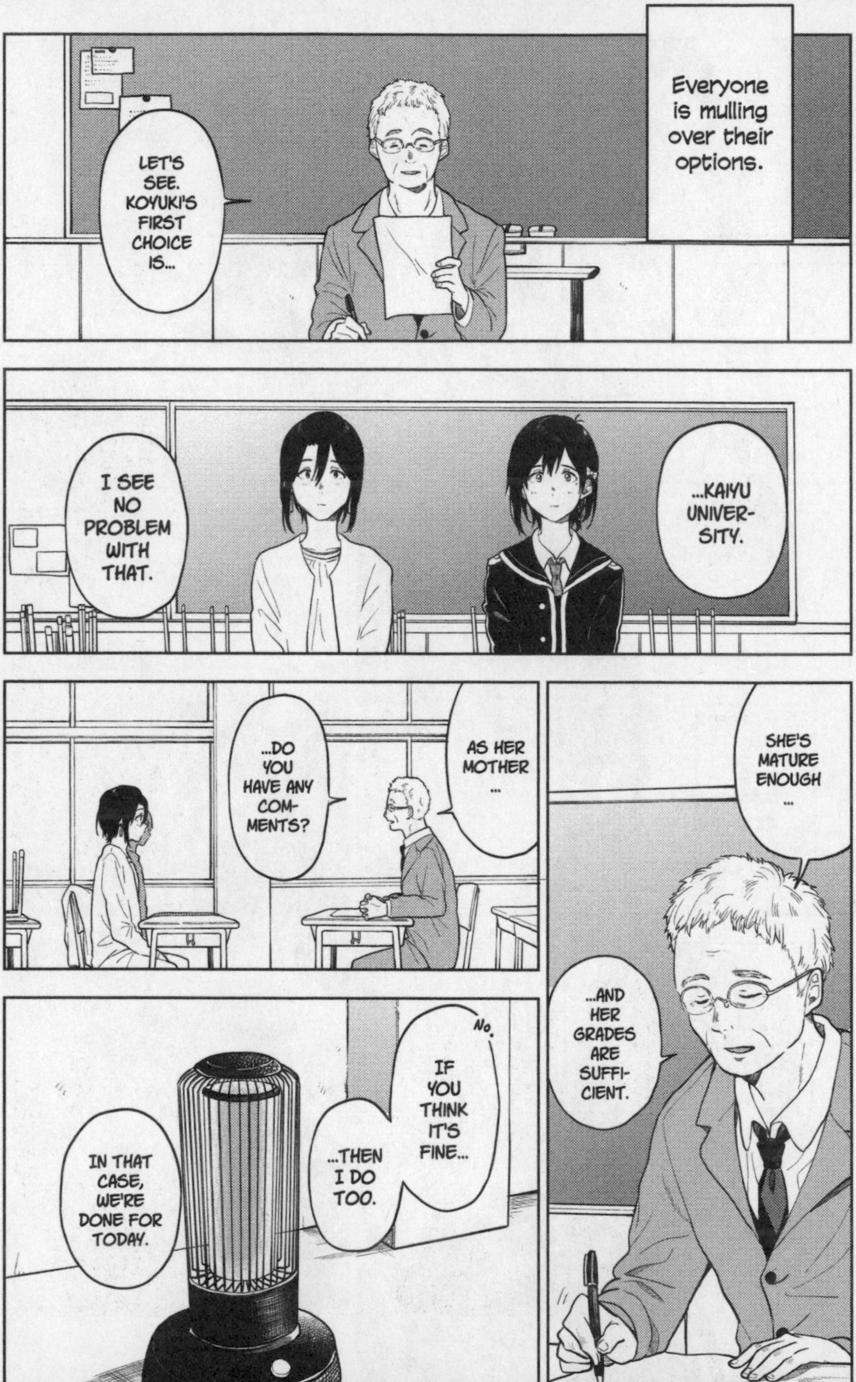
Everyone is mulling over their options.
LET'S SEE. KOYUKI'S FIRST CHOICE IS...
...KAIYU UNIVERSITY.
I SEE NO PROBLEM WITH THAT.
SHE'S MATURE ENOUGH...
...AND HER GRADES ARE SUFFICIENT.
AS HER MOTHER...
...DO YOU HAVE ANY COMMENTS?
No.
IF YOU THINK IT'S FINE...
...THEN I DO TOO.
IN THAT CASE, WE'RE DONE FOR TODAY.

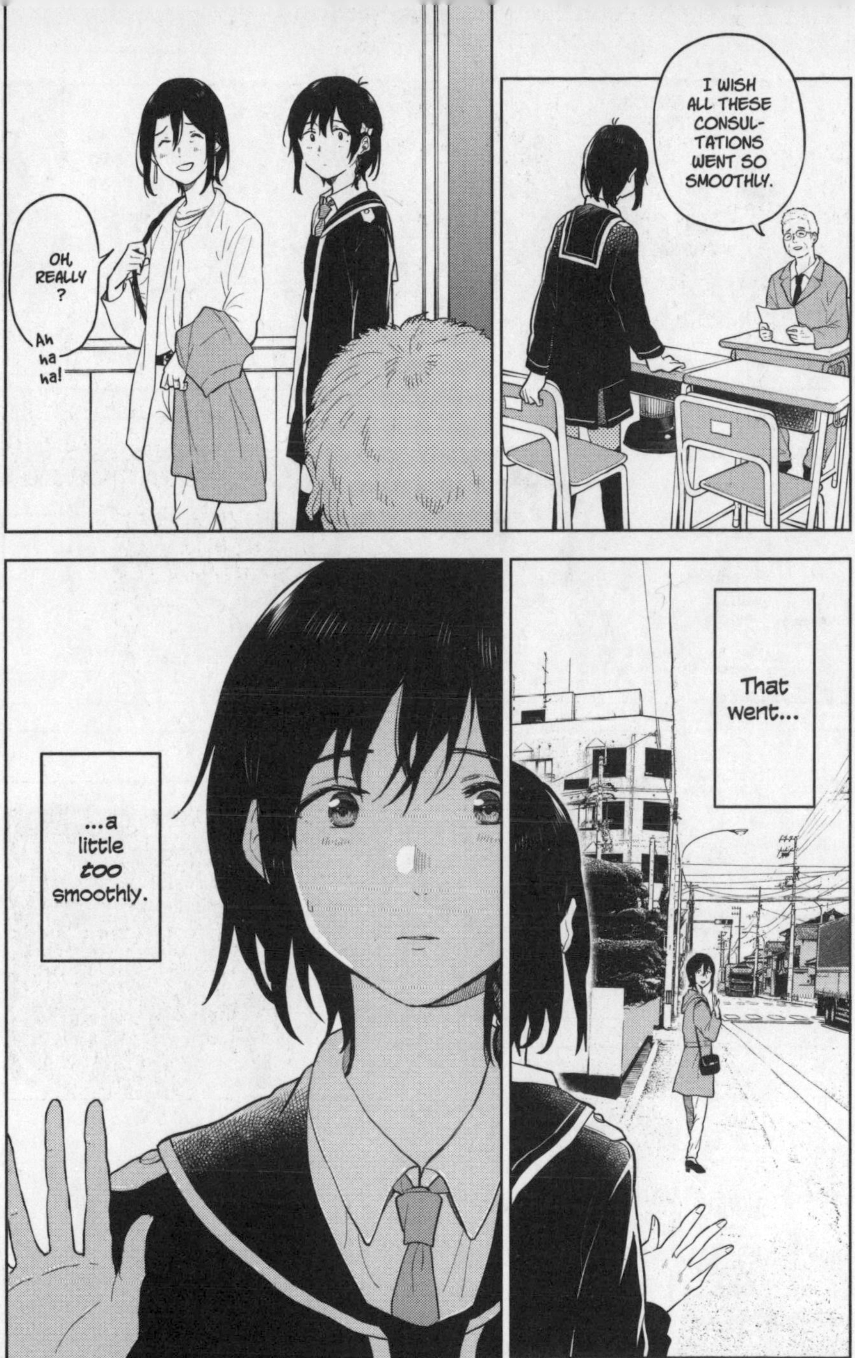
I WISH ALL THESE CONSUL-TATIONS WENT SO SMOOTHLY.
OH, REALLY?
Ah ha ha!
That went...
...a little *too* smoothly.

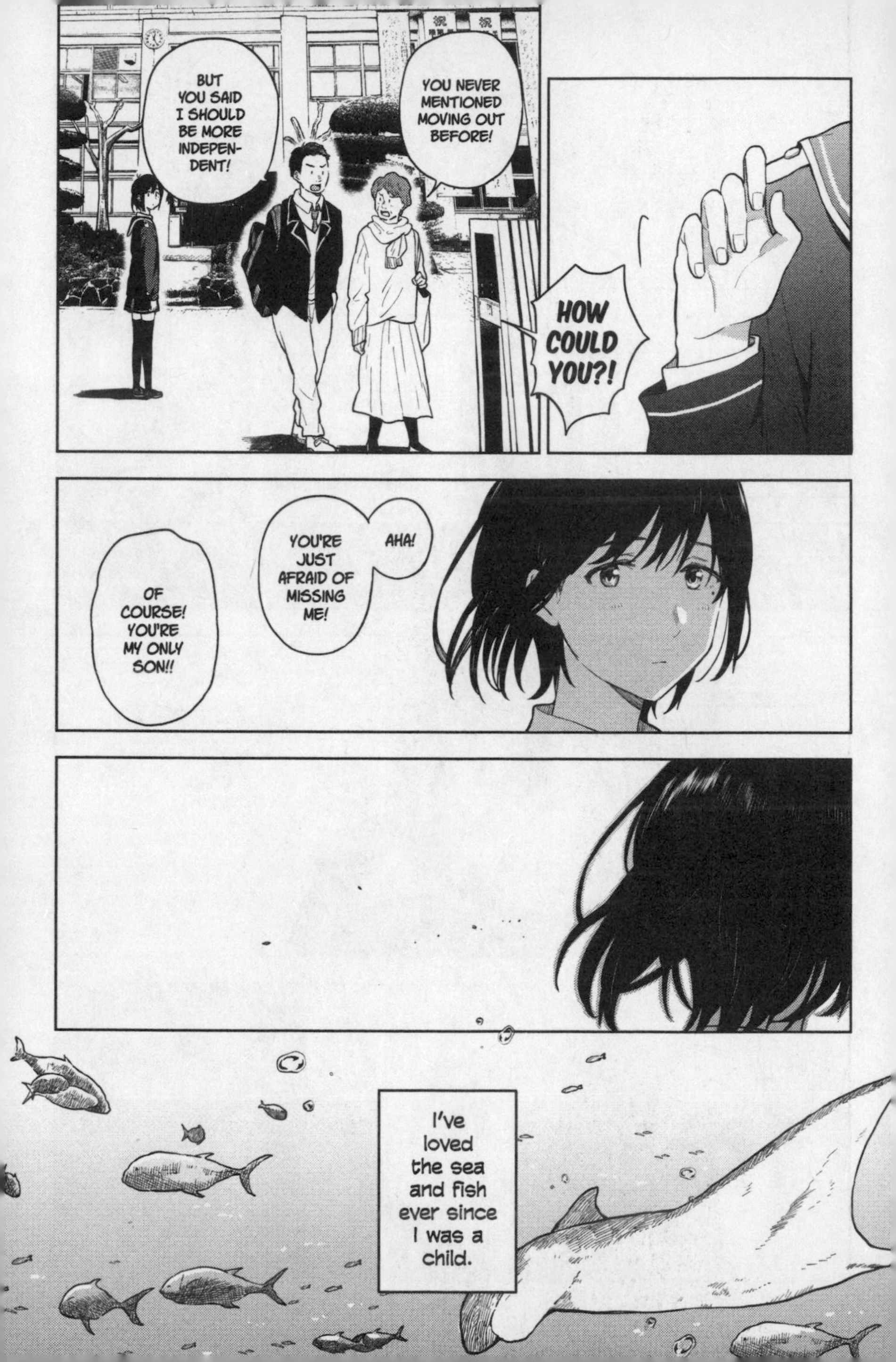
HOW COULD YOU?!
YOU NEVER MENTIONED MOVING OUT BEFORE!
BUT YOU SAID I SHOULD BE MORE INDEPENDENT!
AHA!
YOU'RE JUST AFRAID OF MISSING ME!
OF COURSE! YOU'RE MY ONLY SON!!
I've loved the sea and fish ever since I was a child.

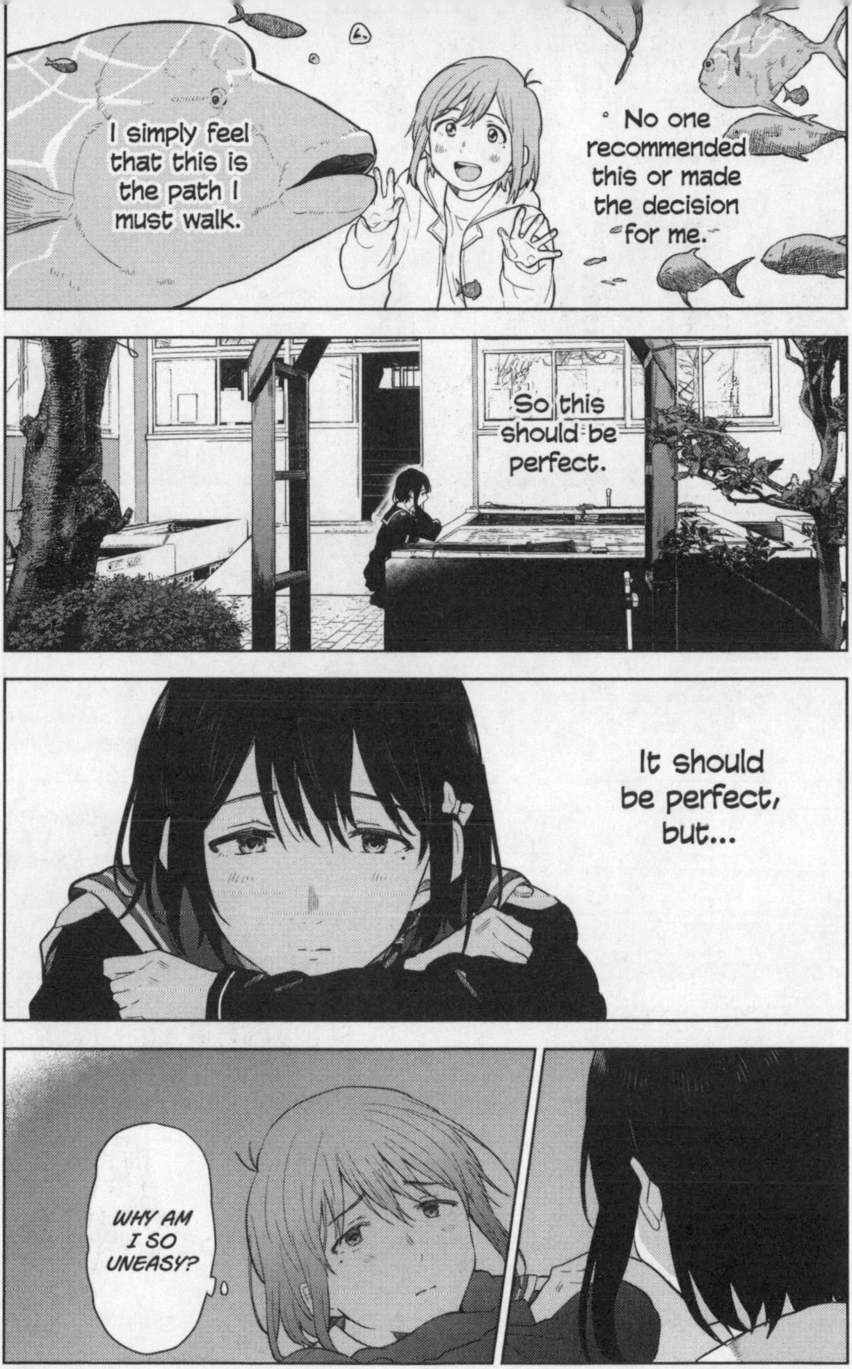
No one recommended this or made the decision for me.
I simply feel that this is the path I must walk.
So this should be perfect.
It should be perfect, but...
WHY AM I SO UNEASY?

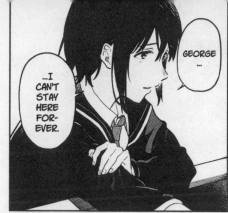

GEORGE
...

...I CAN'T STAY HERE FOR- EVER.

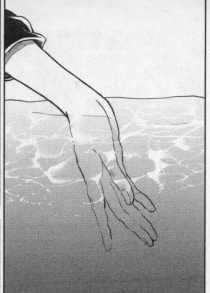

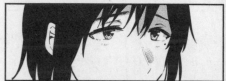

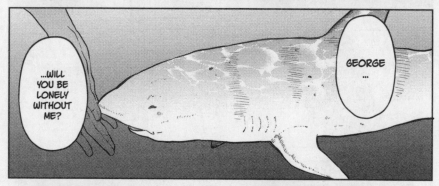

...WILL YOU BE LONELY WITHOUT ME?

GEORGE
...

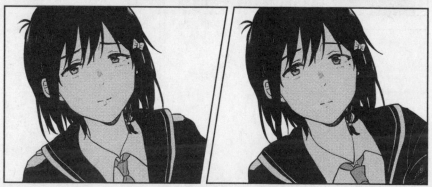

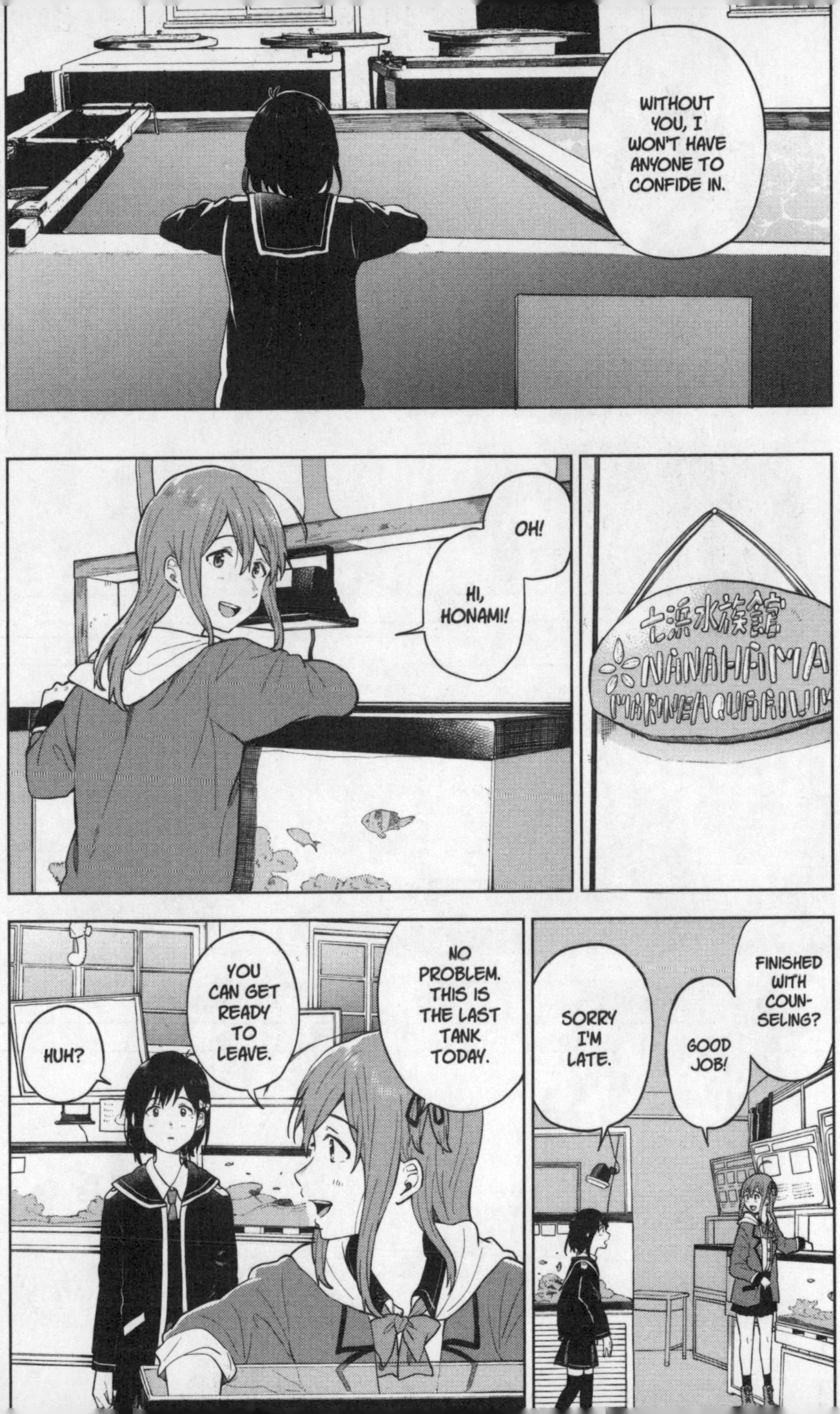
WITHOUT YOU, I WON'T HAVE ANYONE TO CONFIDE IN.
七浜水族館
OH!
HI, HONAMI!
FINISHED WITH COUN-SELING?
GOOD JOB!
SORRY I'M LATE.
NO PROBLEM. THIS IS THE LAST TANK TODAY.
YOU CAN GET READY TO LEAVE.
HUH?

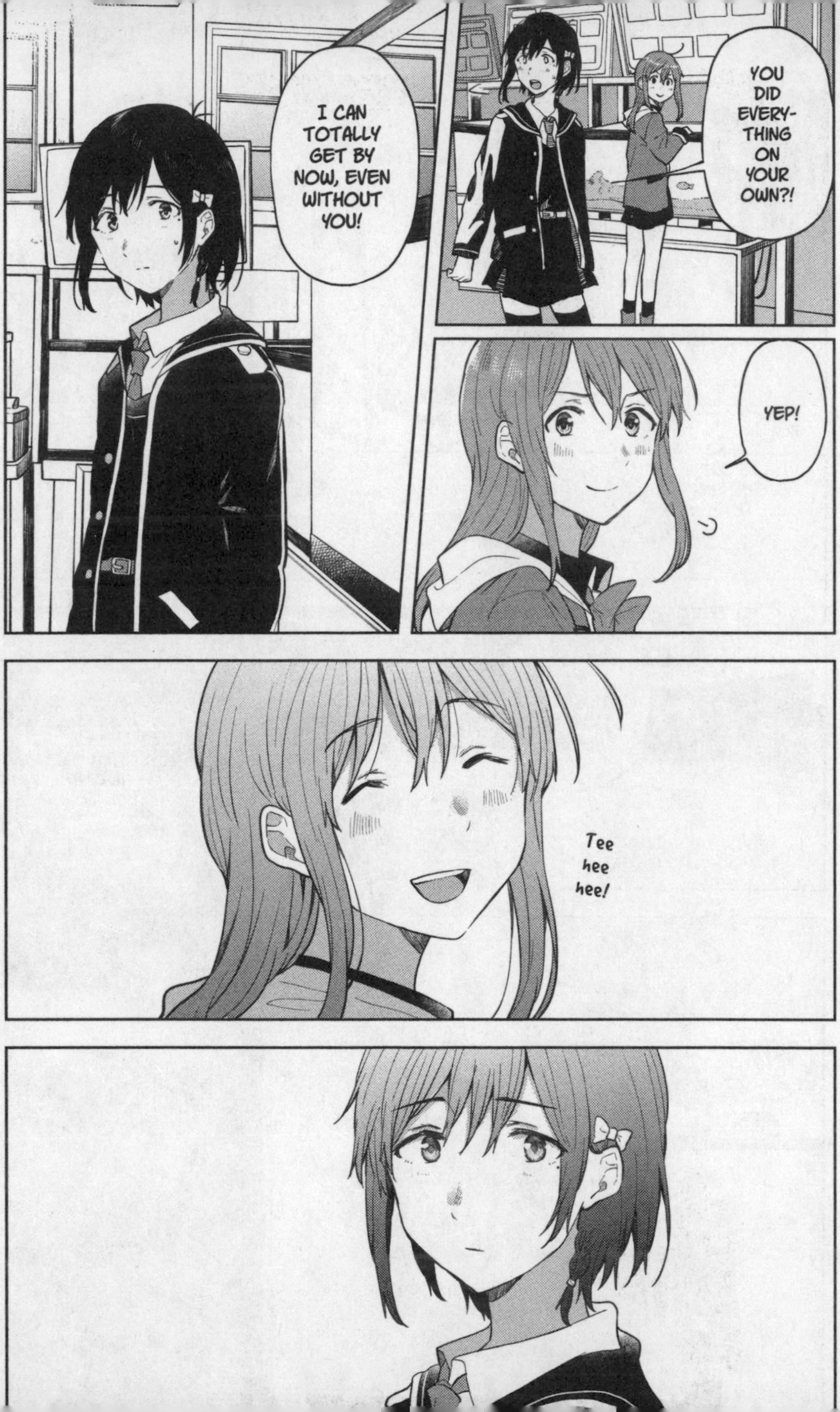

YOU DID EVERY-THING ON YOUR OWN?!
YEP!
I CAN TOTALLY GET BY NOW, EVEN WITHOUT YOU!
Tee hee hee!

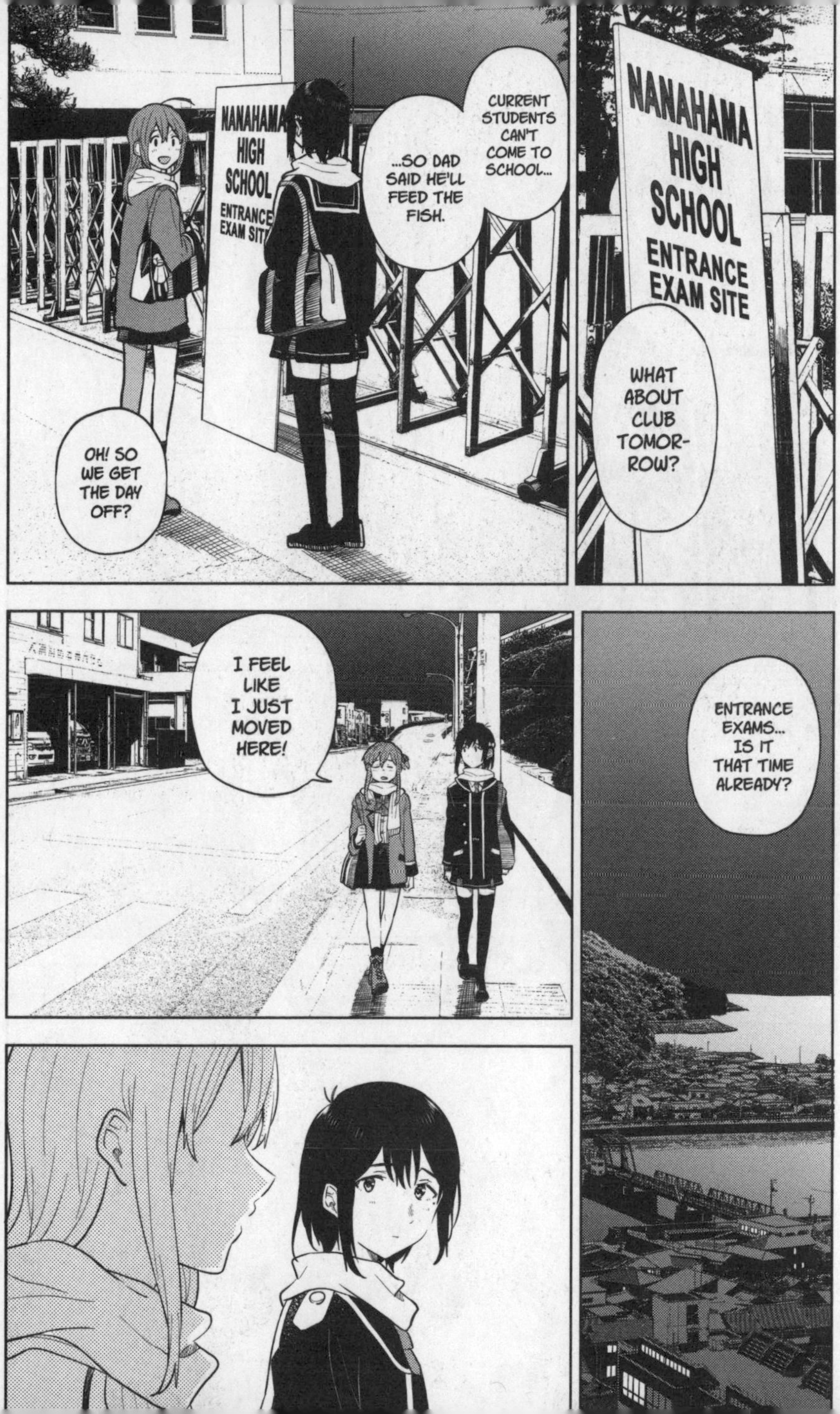
NANAHAMA HIGH SCHOOL
ENTRANCE EXAM SITE
WHAT ABOUT CLUB TOMORROW?
NANAHAMA HIGH SCHOOL
ENTRANCE EXAM SITE
CURRENT STUDENTS CAN'T COME TO SCHOOL...
...SO DAD SAID HE'LL FEED THE FISH.
OH! SO WE GET THE DAY OFF?
ENTRANCE EXAMS... IS IT THAT TIME ALREADY?
I FEEL LIKE I JUST MOVED HERE!

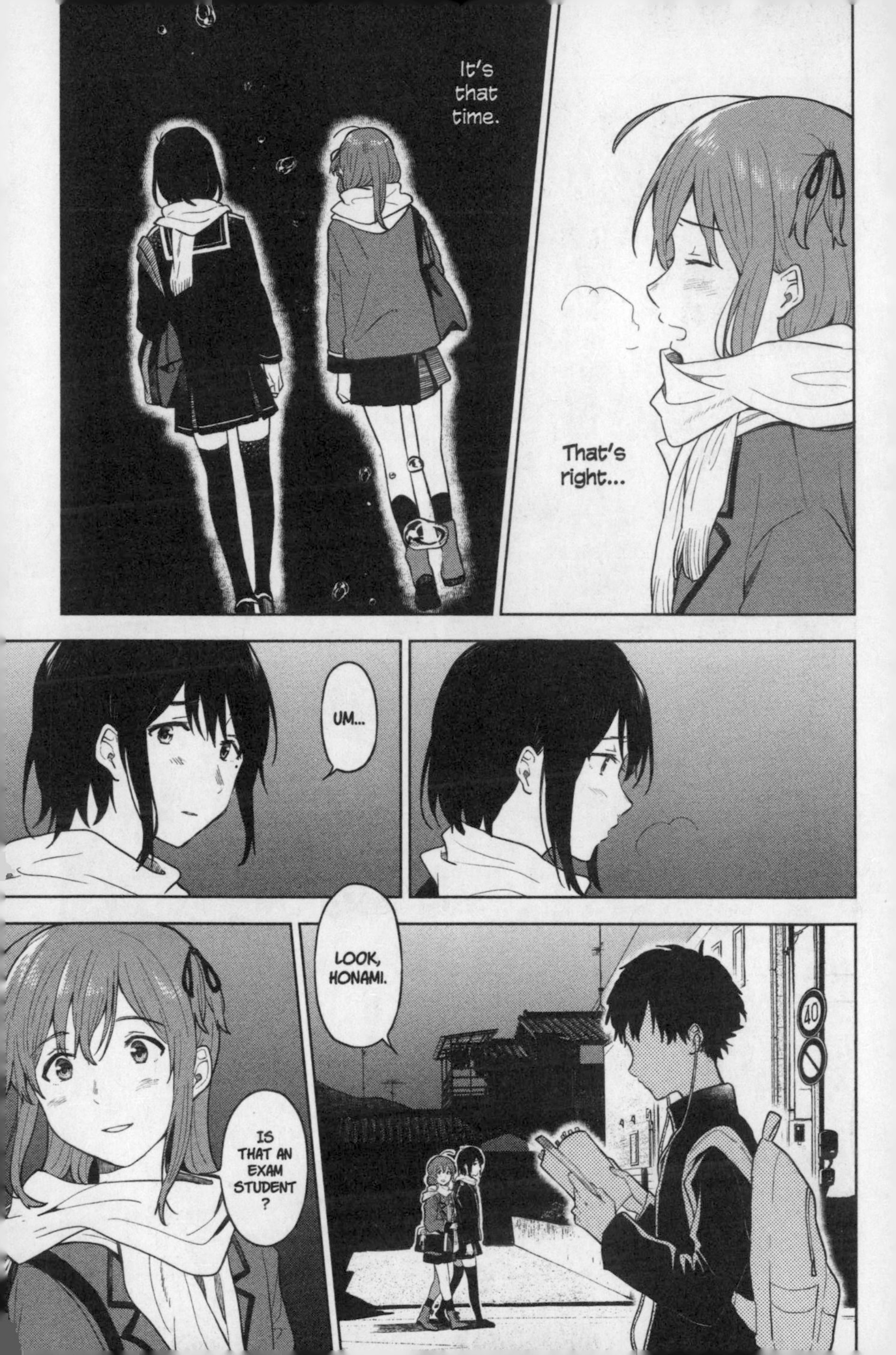
That's right...
It's that time.
UM...
LOOK, HONAMI.
IS THAT AN EXAM STUDENT?

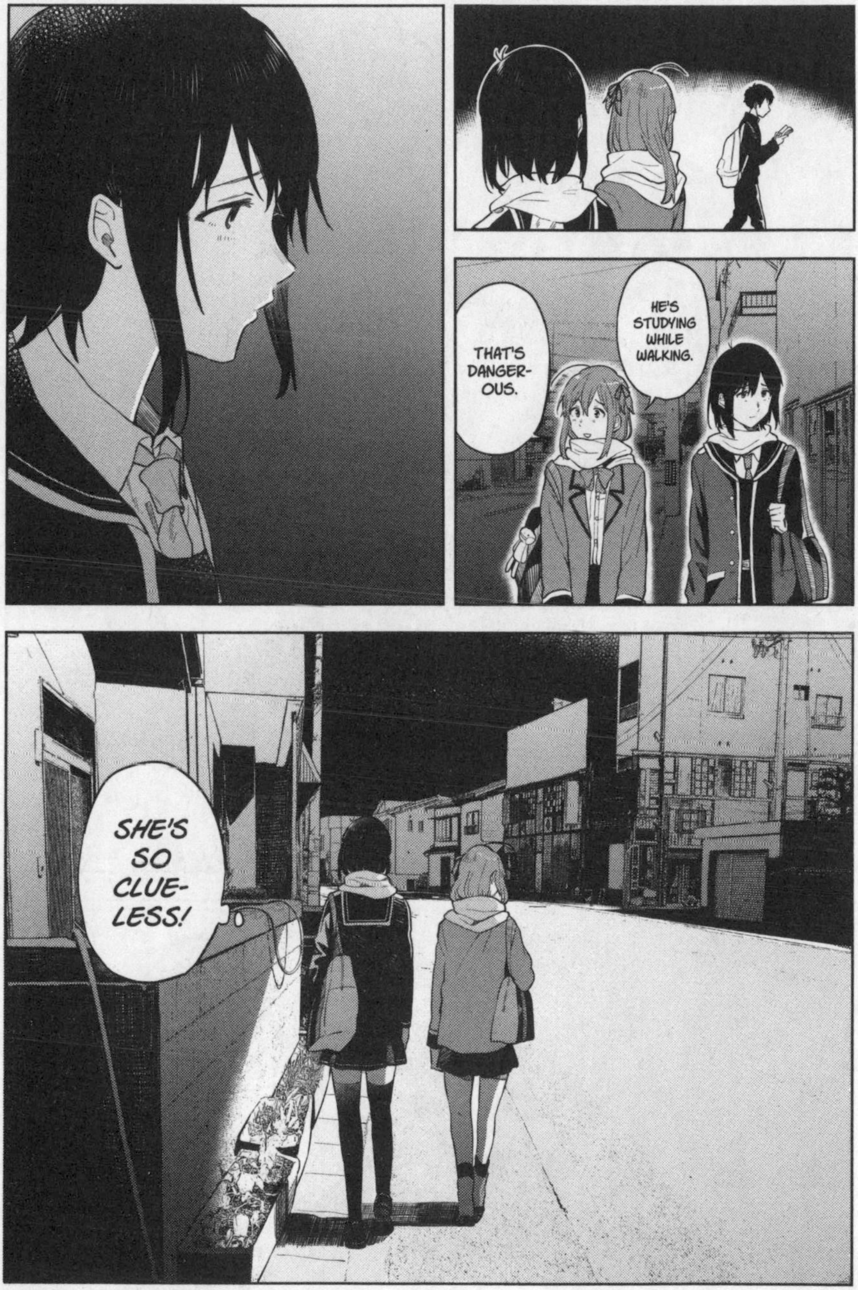
HE'S STUDYING WHILE WALKING.
THAT'S DANGER-OUS.
SHE'S SO CLUE-LESS!

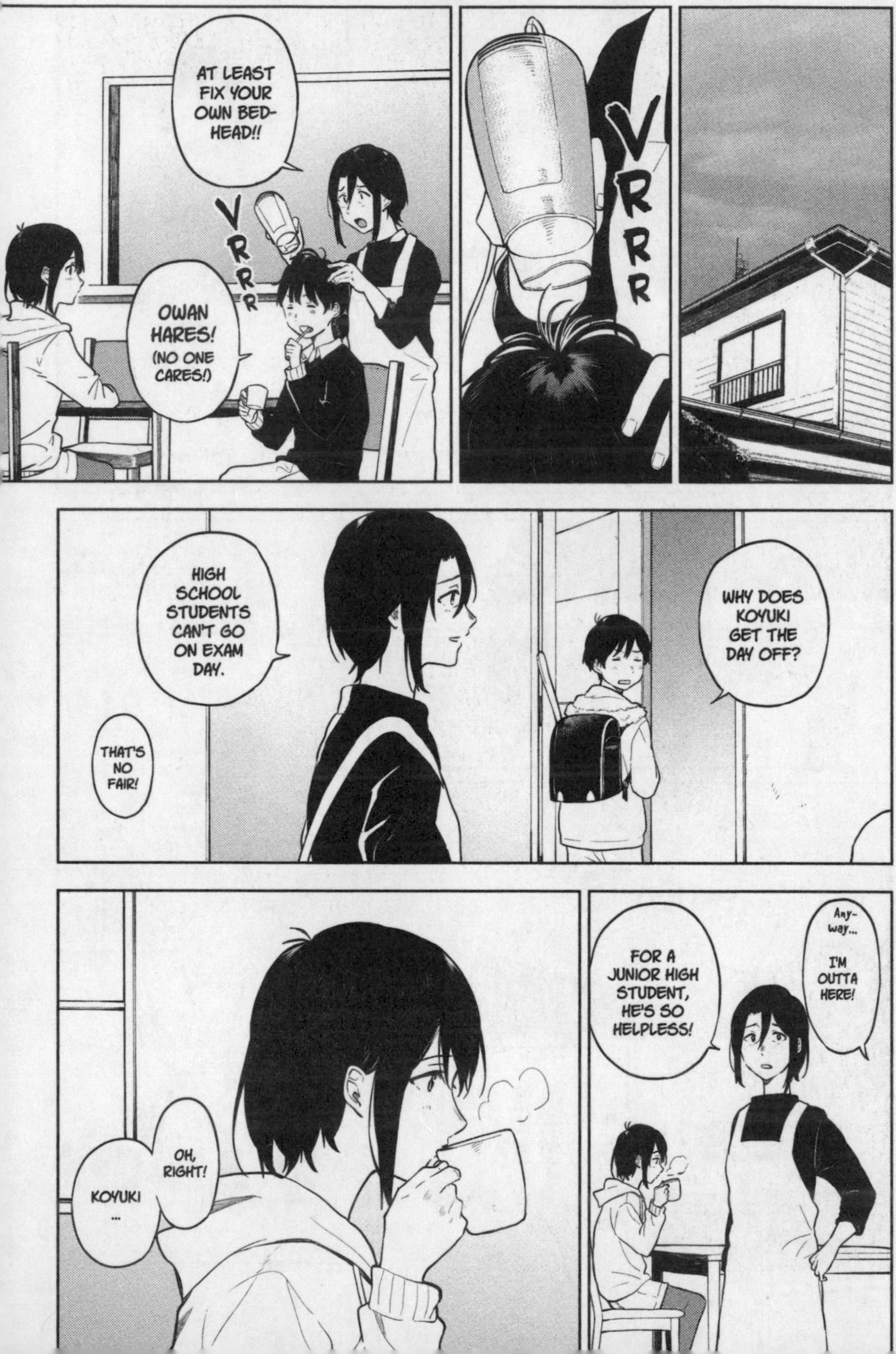
VRRR
AT LEAST FIX YOUR OWN BED-HEAD!!
VRRR
OWAN HARES! (NO ONE CARES!)
WHY DOES KOYUKI GET THE DAY OFF?
HIGH SCHOOL STUDENTS CAN'T GO ON EXAM DAY.
THAT'S NO FAIR!
Any-way... I'M OUTTA HERE!
FOR A JUNIOR HIGH STUDENT, HE'S SO HELPLESS!
OH, RIGHT!
KOYUKI...

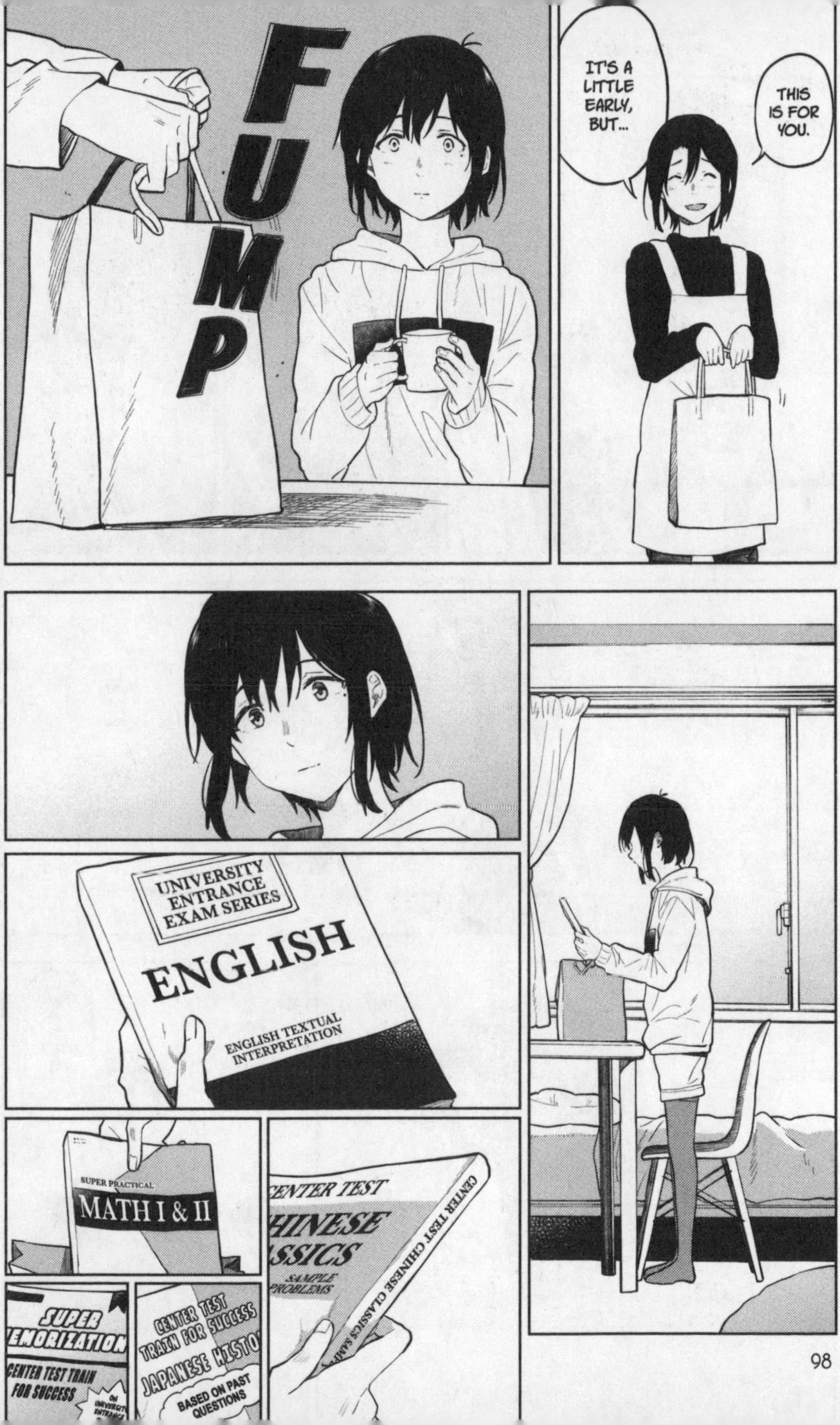
IT'S A LITTLE EARLY, BUT...
THIS IS FOR YOU.
FUMP
UNIVERSITY ENTRANCE EXAM SERIES
ENGLISH
ENGLISH TEXTUAL INTERPRETATION
CENTER TEST
CENTER TEST CHINESE CLASSICS
SAMPLE PROBLEMS
SUPER PRACTICAL
MATH I & II
CENTER TEST TRAIN FOR SUCCESS
BASED ON PAST QUESTIONS
CENTER TEST TRAIN FOR SUCCESS

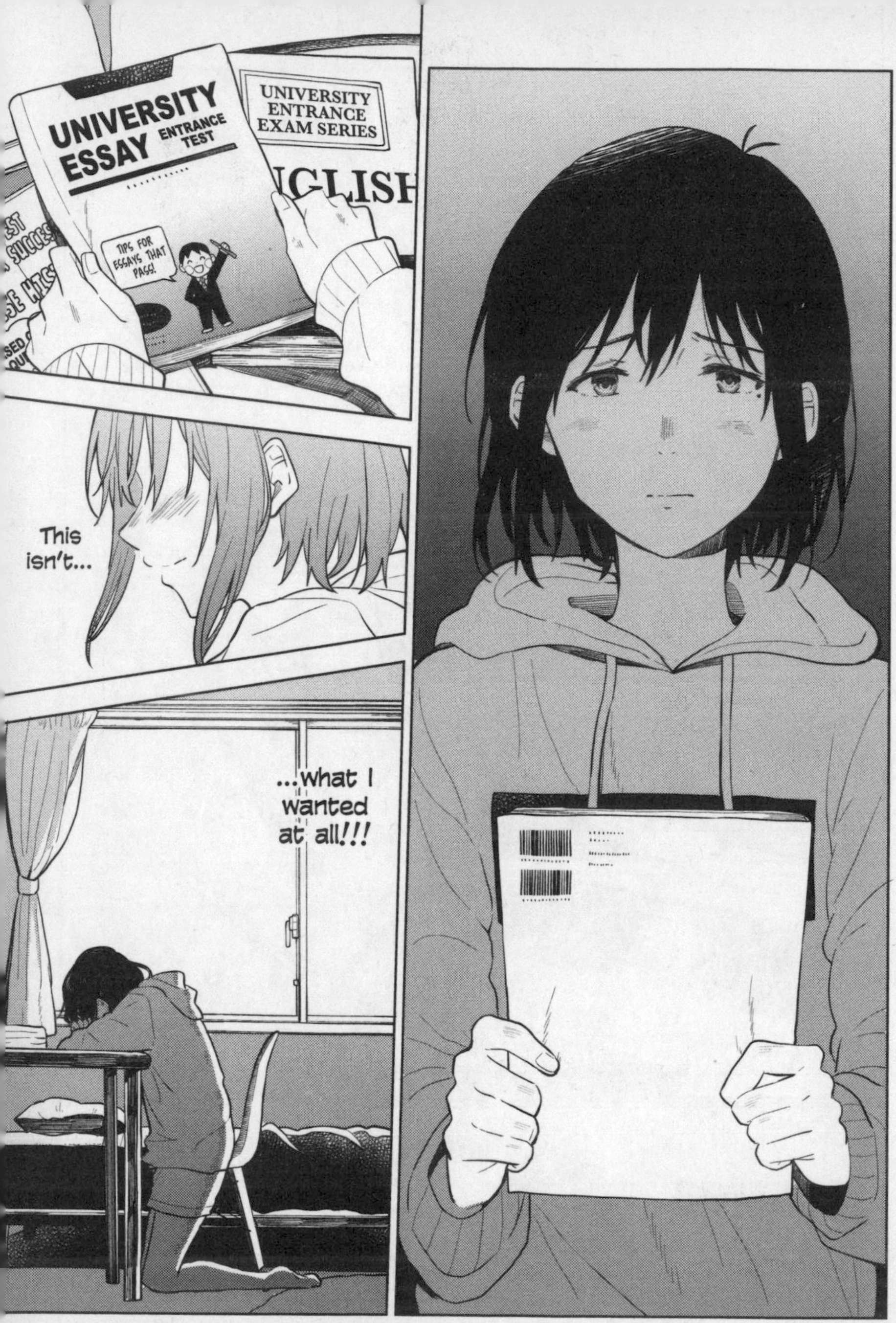
UNIVERSITY ESSAY ENTRANCE TEST
TIPS FOR ESSAYS THAT PASS!
UNIVERSITY ENTRANCE EXAM SERIES
This isn't...
...what I wanted at all!!!

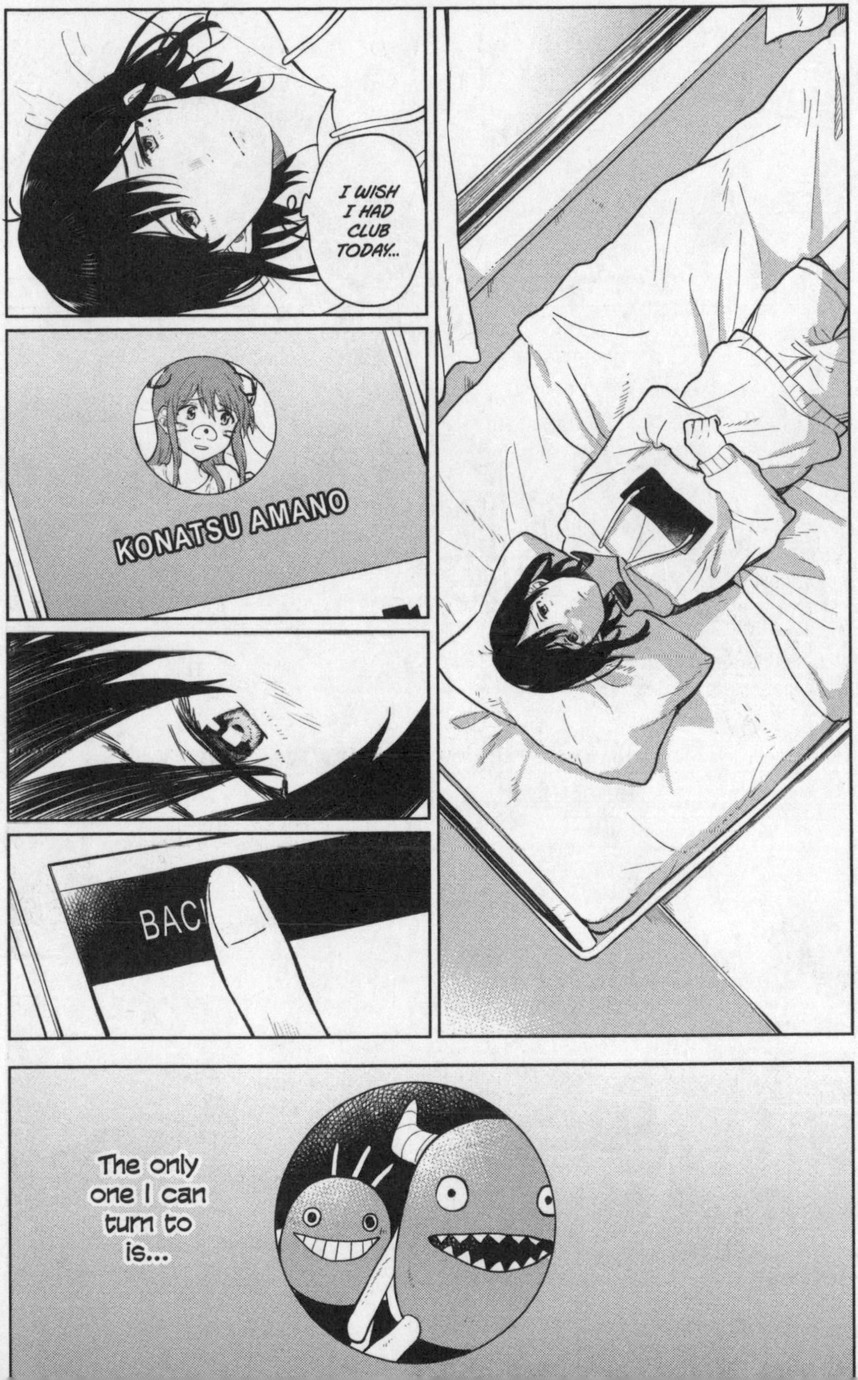
I WISH I HAD CLUB TODAY...
KONATSU AMANO
BAC
The only one I can turn to is...

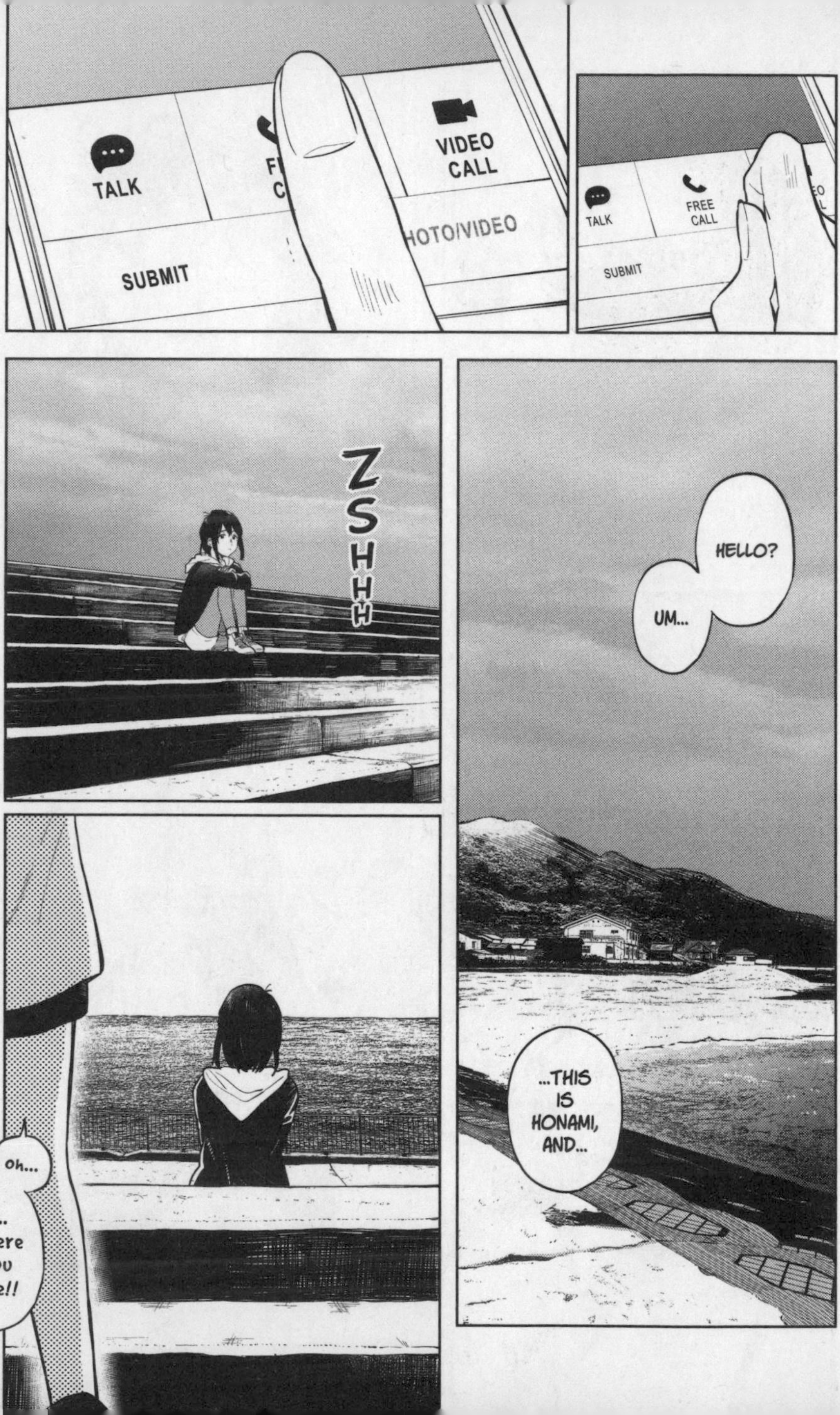
TALK
FREE CALL
SUBMIT
VIDEO CALL
TALK
HOTO/VIDEO
SUBMIT
HELLO?
UM...
...THIS IS HONAMI, AND...
ZSHHH
oh...
...there you are!!

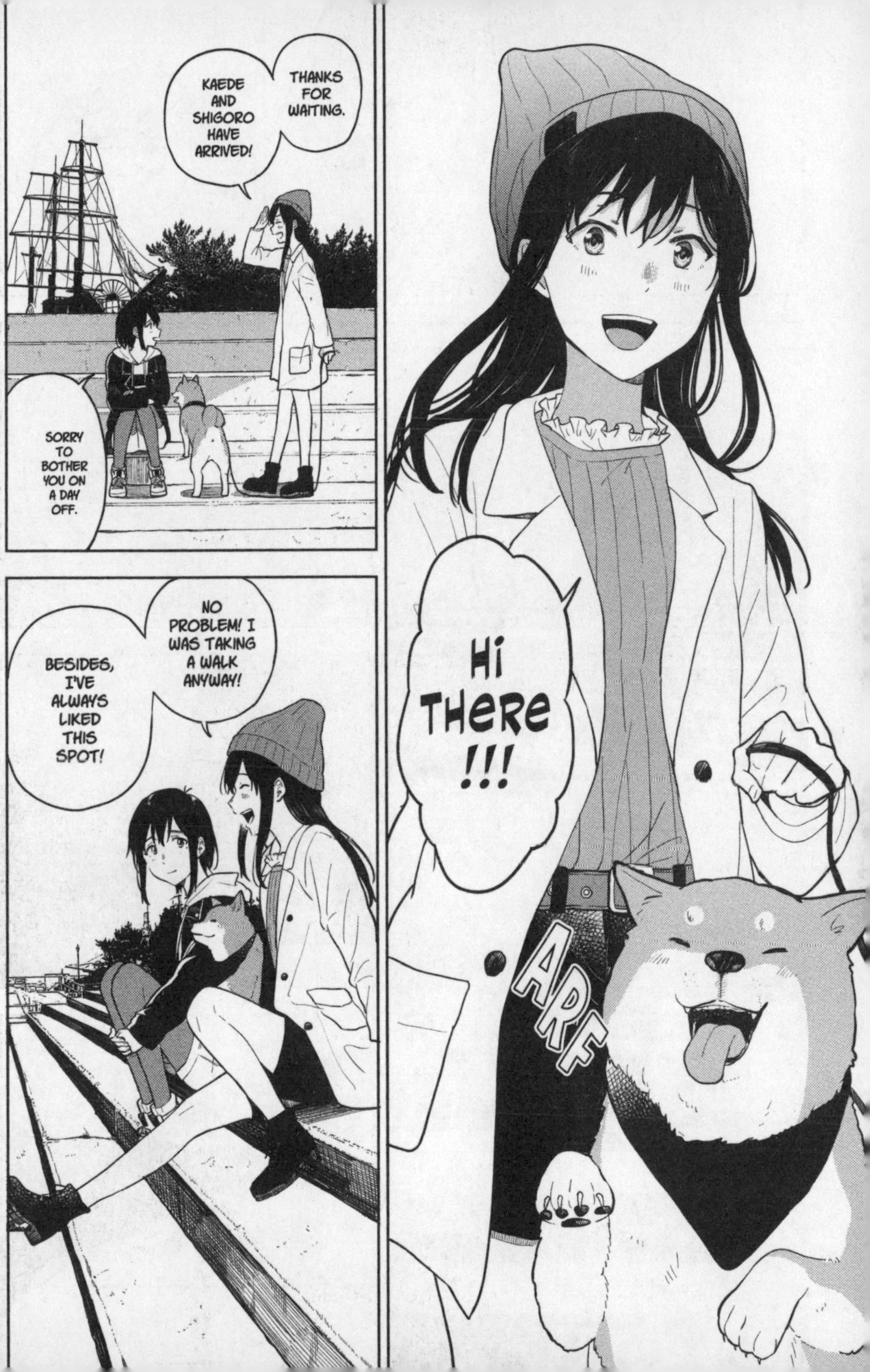
Hi THERE!!!
ARF
THANKS FOR WAITING.
KAEDE AND SHIGORO HAVE ARRIVED!
SORRY TO BOTHER YOU ON A DAY OFF.
NO PROBLEM! I WAS TAKING A WALK ANYWAY!
BESIDES, I'VE ALWAYS LIKED THIS SPOT!

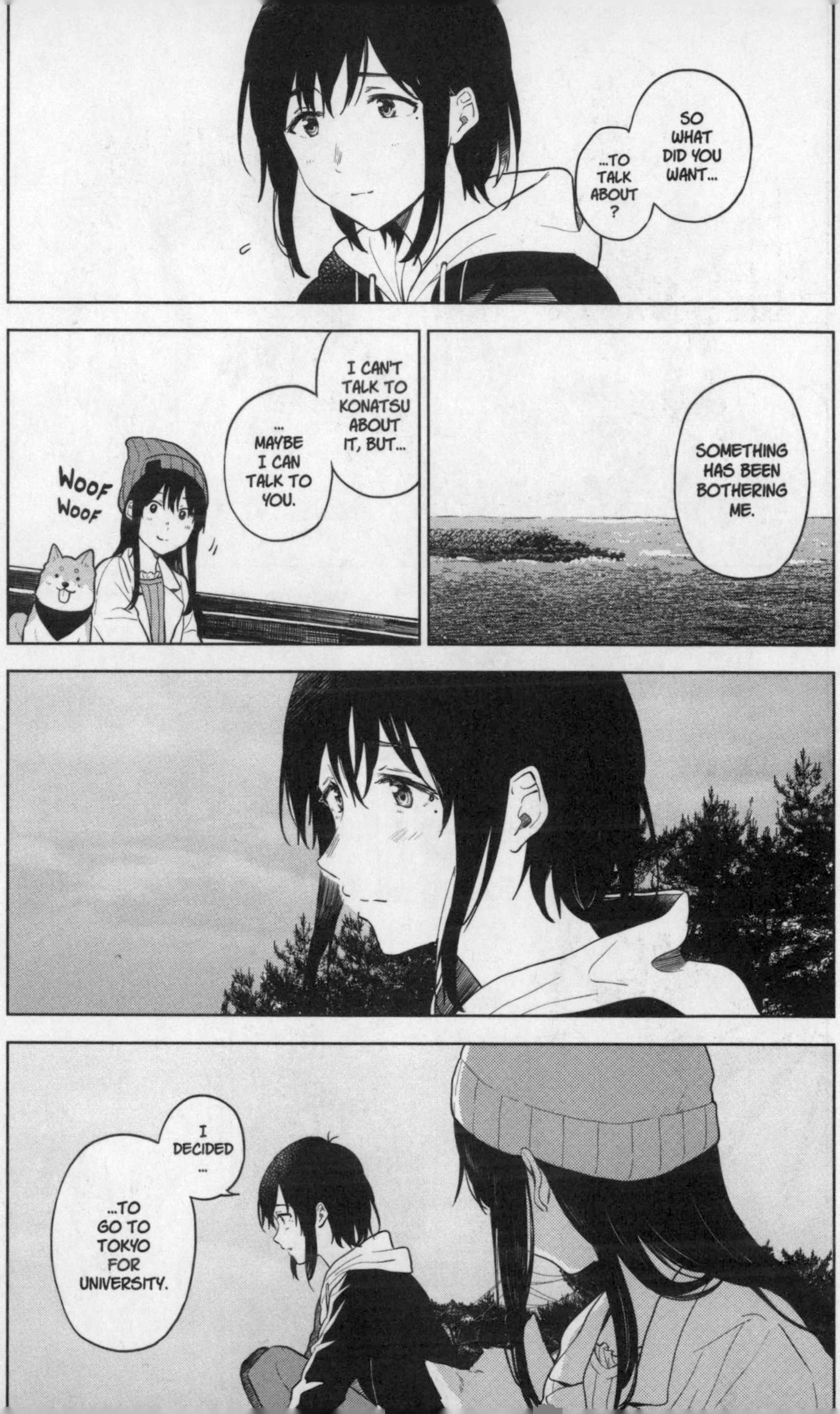
SO WHAT DID YOU WANT...
...TO TALK ABOUT?
SOMETHING HAS BEEN BOTHERING ME.
I CAN'T TALK TO KONATSU ABOUT IT, BUT...
...MAYBE I CAN TALK TO YOU.
WOOF WOOF
I DECIDED...
...TO GO TO TOKYO FOR UNIVERSITY.

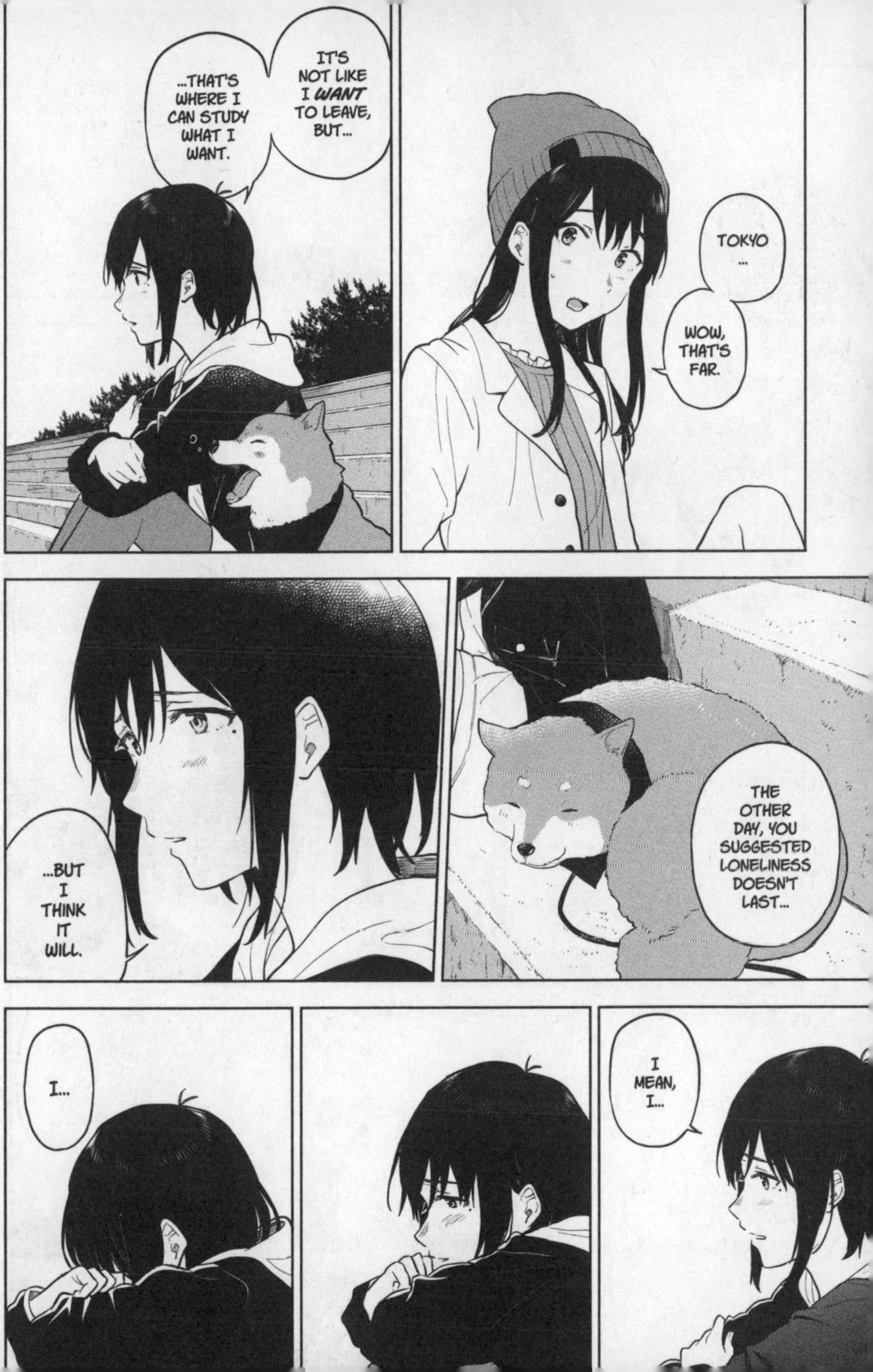
TOKYO ...
WOW, THAT'S FAR.
IT'S NOT LIKE I *WANT* TO LEAVE, BUT...
...THAT'S WHERE I CAN STUDY WHAT I WANT.
THE OTHER DAY, YOU SUGGESTED LONELINESS DOESN'T LAST...
...BUT I THINK IT WILL.
I MEAN, I...
I...

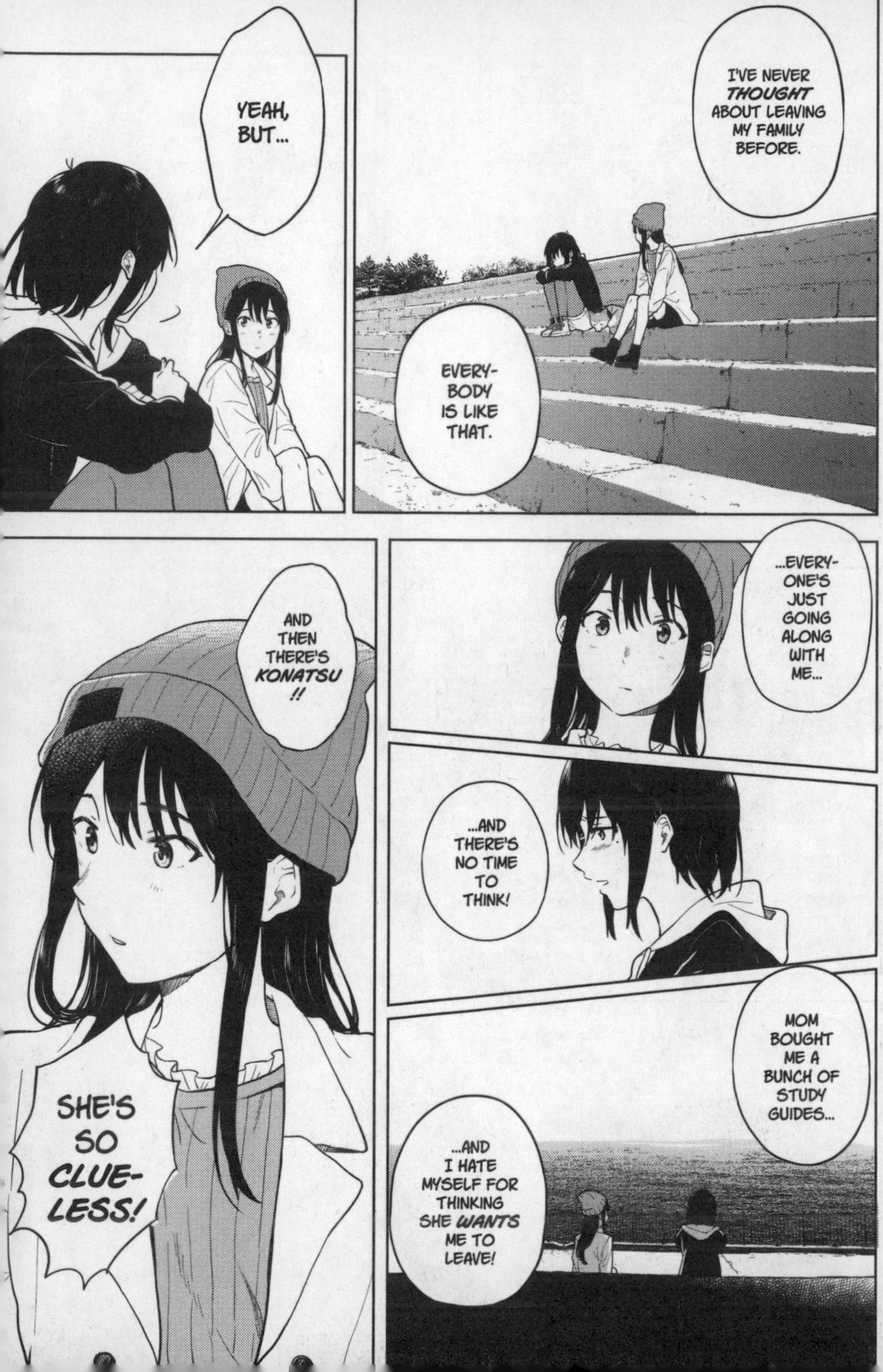
I'VE NEVER *THOUGHT* ABOUT LEAVING MY FAMILY BEFORE.
EVERY-BODY IS LIKE THAT.
YEAH, BUT...
...EVERY-ONE'S JUST GOING ALONG WITH ME...
...AND THERE'S NO TIME TO THINK!
MOM BOUGHT ME A BUNCH OF STUDY GUIDES...
...AND I HATE MYSELF FOR THINKING SHE *WANTS* ME TO LEAVE!
AND THEN THERE'S *KONATSU* !!
SHE'S SO *CLUE-LESS!*

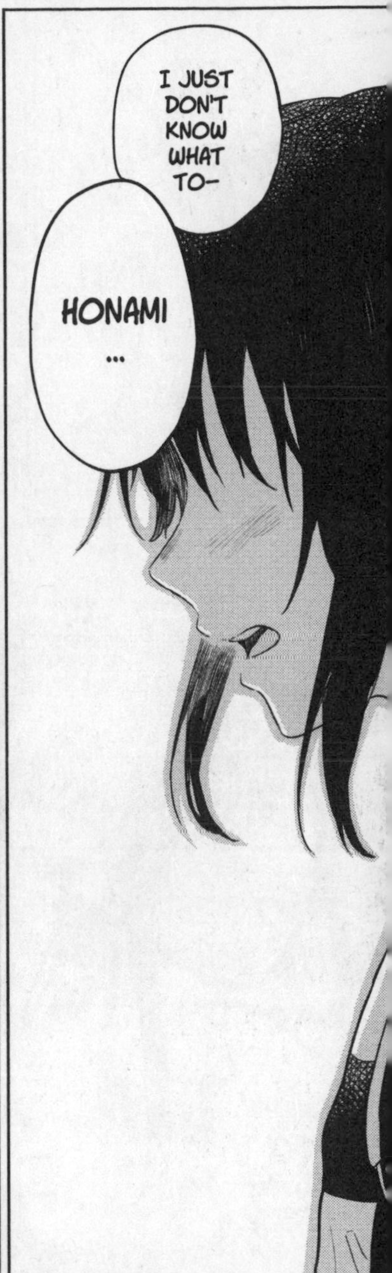
I JUST DON'T KNOW WHAT TO-
HONAMI ...

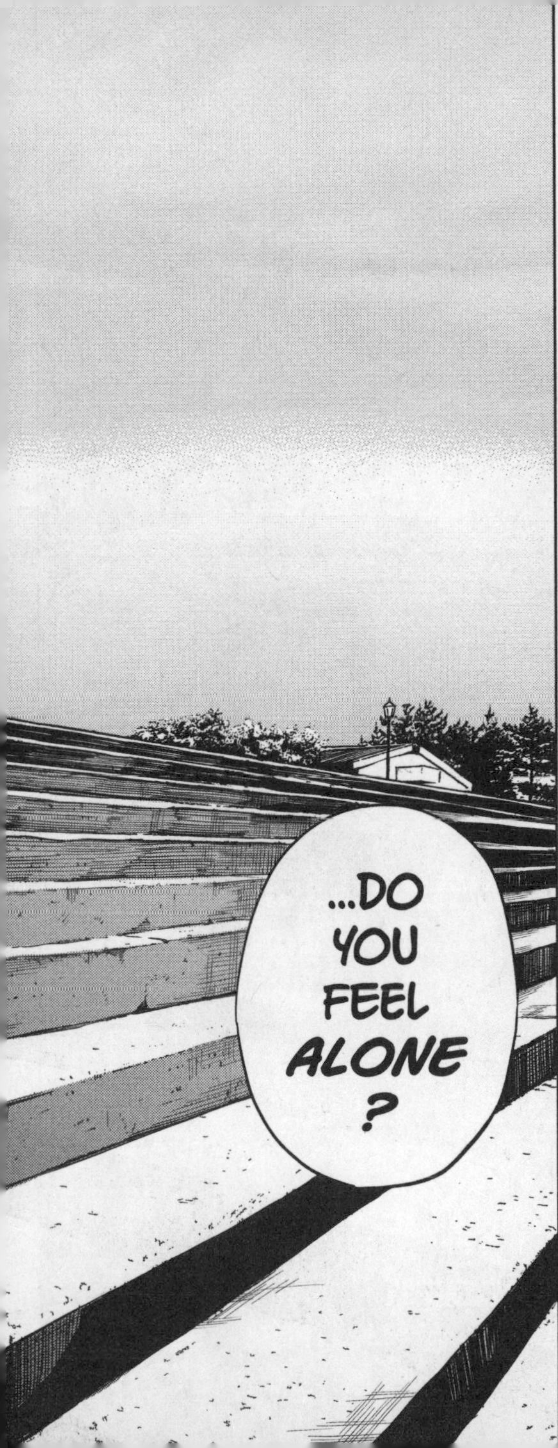
...DO YOU FEEL ALONE ?

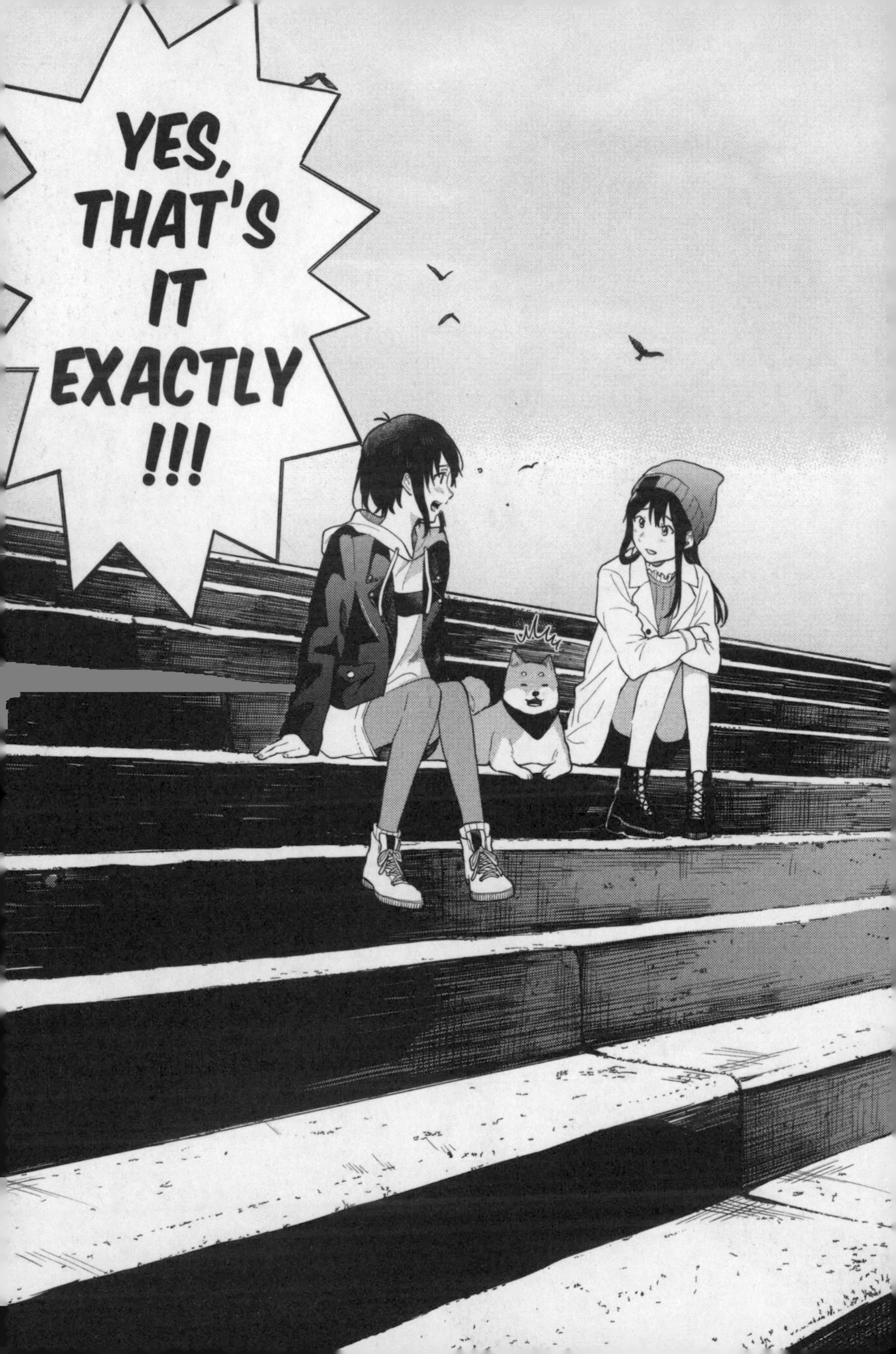
YES, THAT'S IT EXACTLY !!!

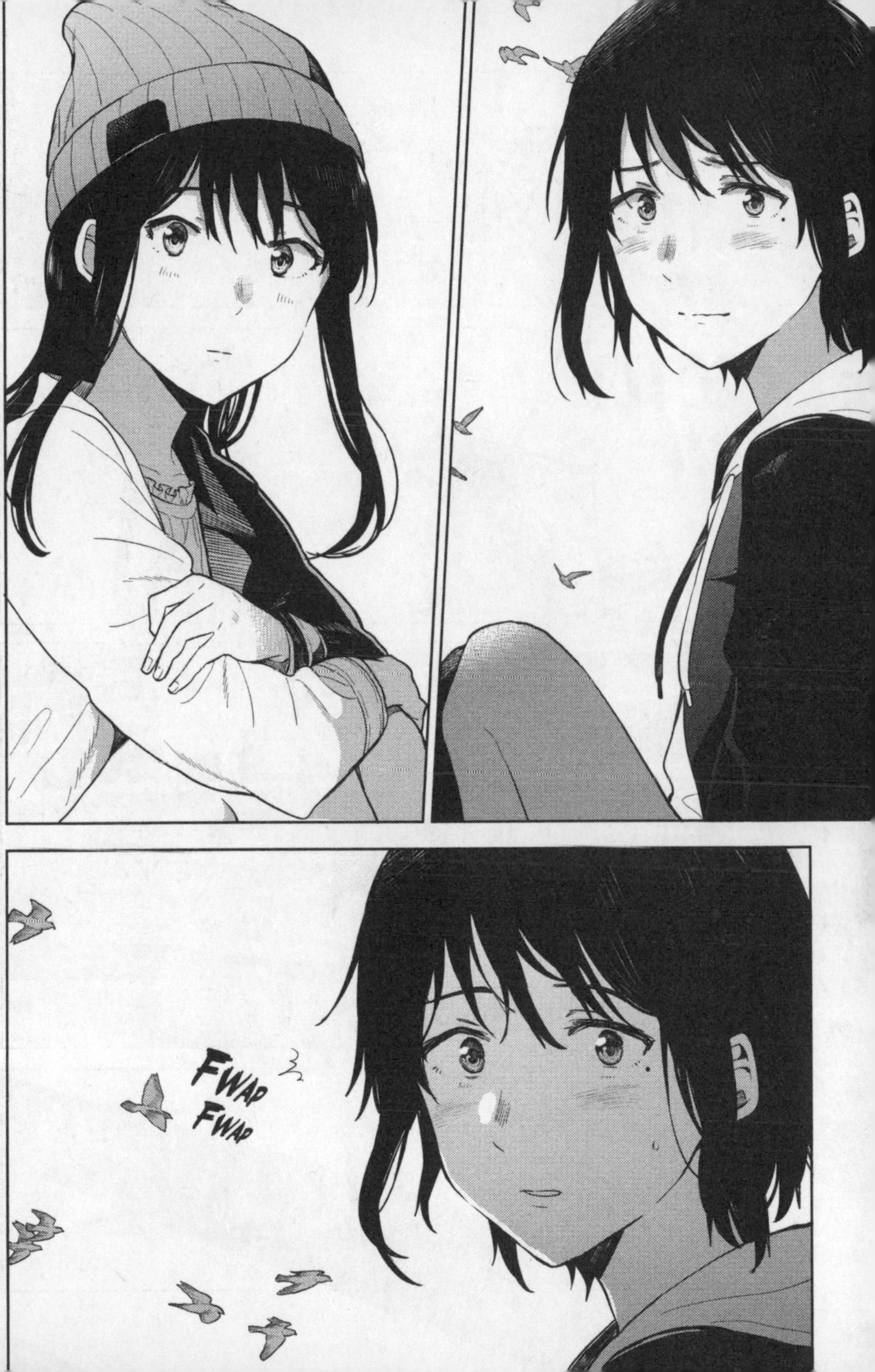
FWAP
FWAP

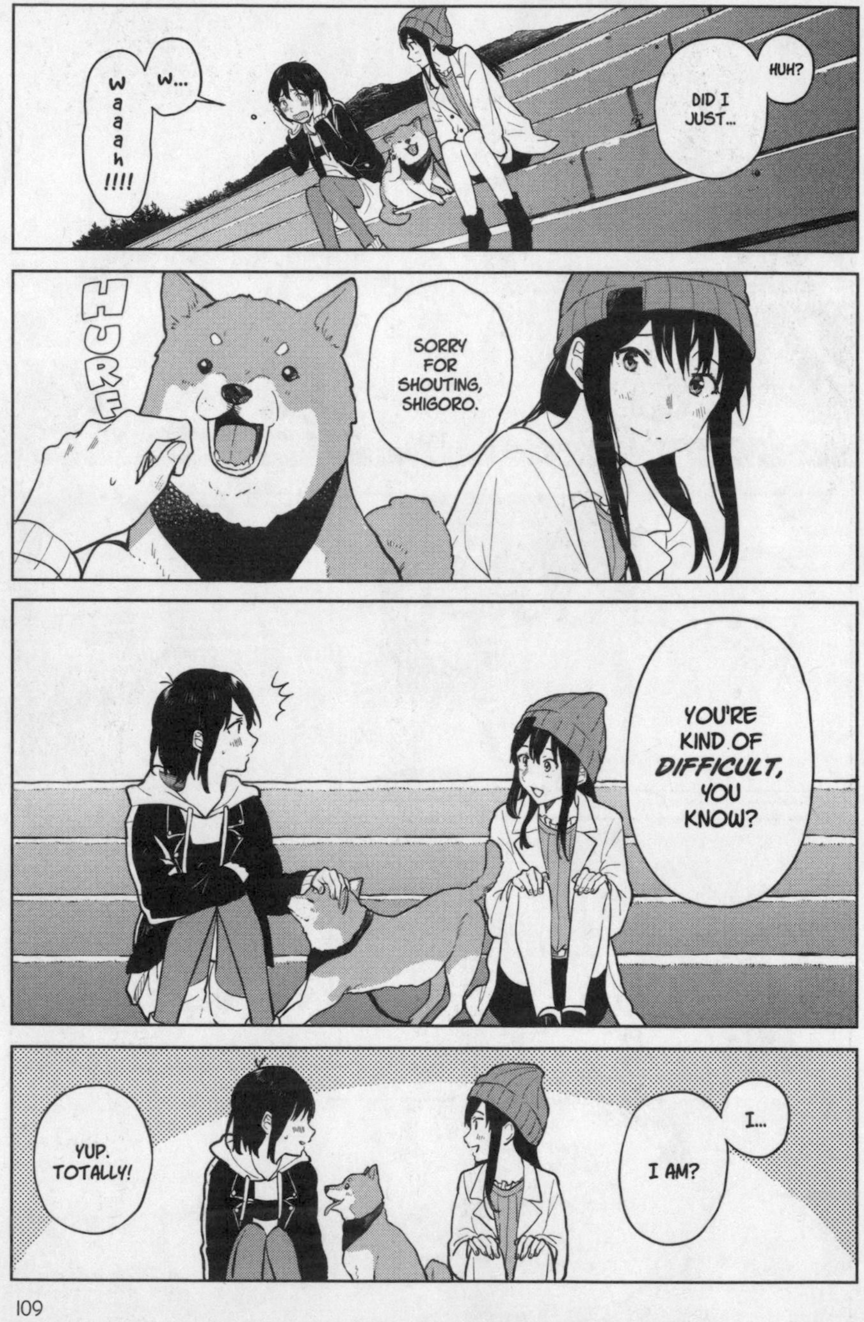
HUH?
DID I JUST...
W... Waaah!!!!
SORRY FOR SHOUTING, SHIGORO.
HURF
YOU'RE KIND OF *DIFFICULT,* YOU KNOW?
I...
I AM?
YUP. TOTALLY!

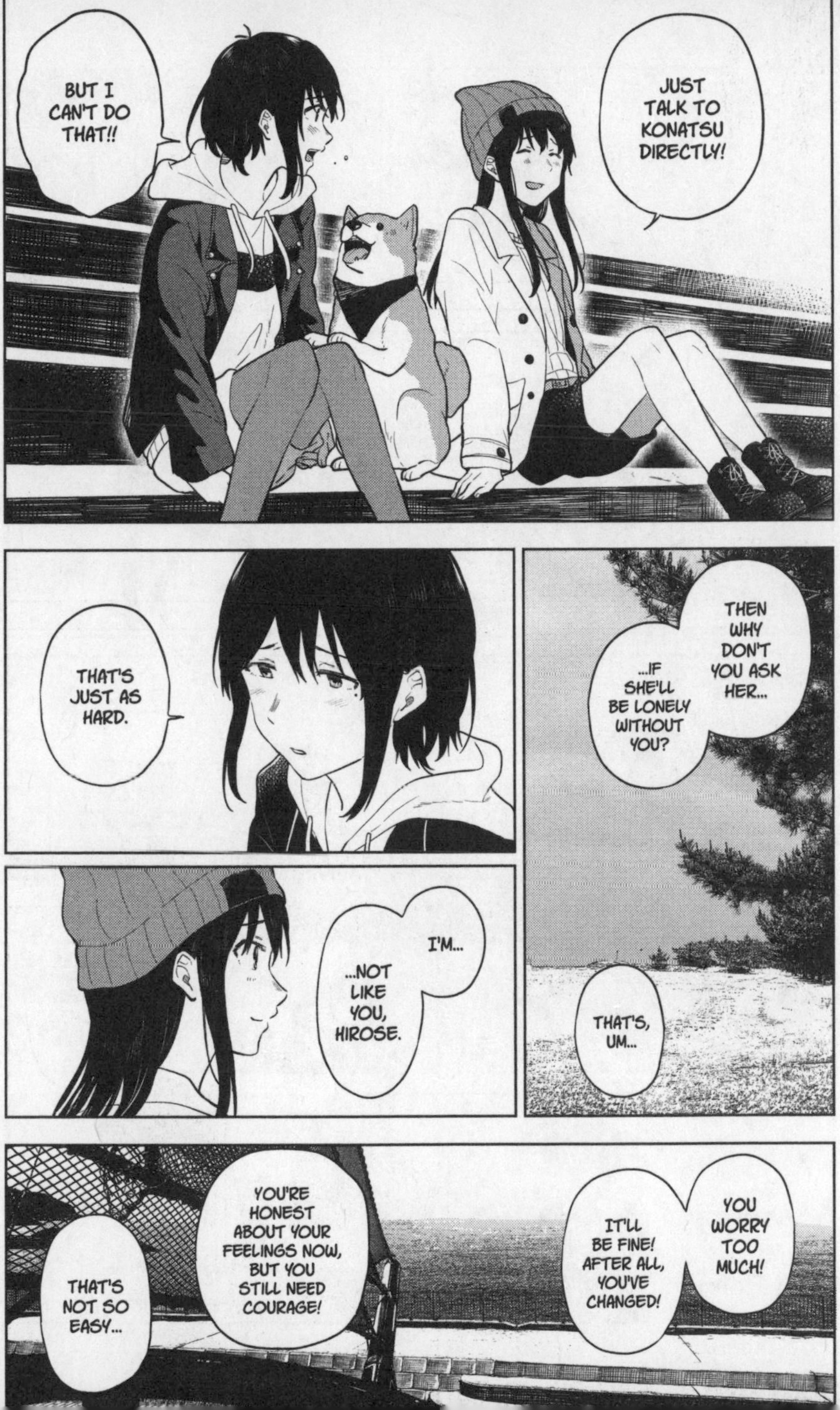
JUST TALK TO KONATSU DIRECTLY!
BUT I CAN'T DO THAT!!
THEN WHY DON'T YOU ASK HER...
...IF SHE'LL BE LONELY WITHOUT YOU?
THAT'S, UM...
THAT'S JUST AS HARD.
I'M...
...NOT LIKE YOU, HIROSE.
YOU WORRY TOO MUCH!
IT'LL BE FINE! AFTER ALL, YOU'VE CHANGED!
YOU'RE HONEST ABOUT YOUR FEELINGS NOW, BUT YOU STILL NEED COURAGE!
THAT'S NOT SO EASY...

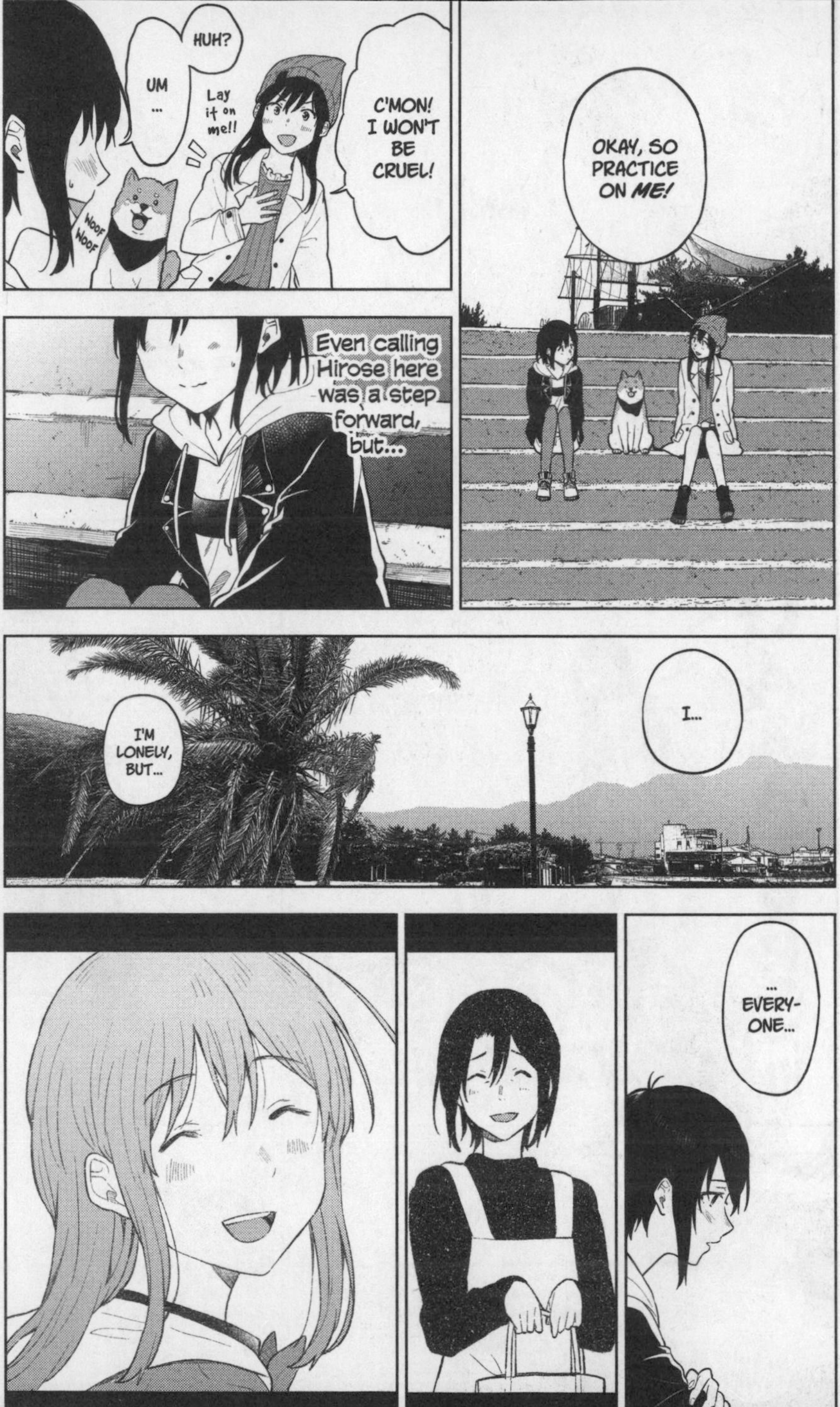
OKAY, SO PRACTICE ON ME!
C'MON! I WON'T BE CRUEL!
HUH?
Lay it on me!!
UM ...
WOOF WOOF
Even calling Hirose here was a step forward, but...
I...
I'M LONELY, BUT...
... EVERY-ONE...

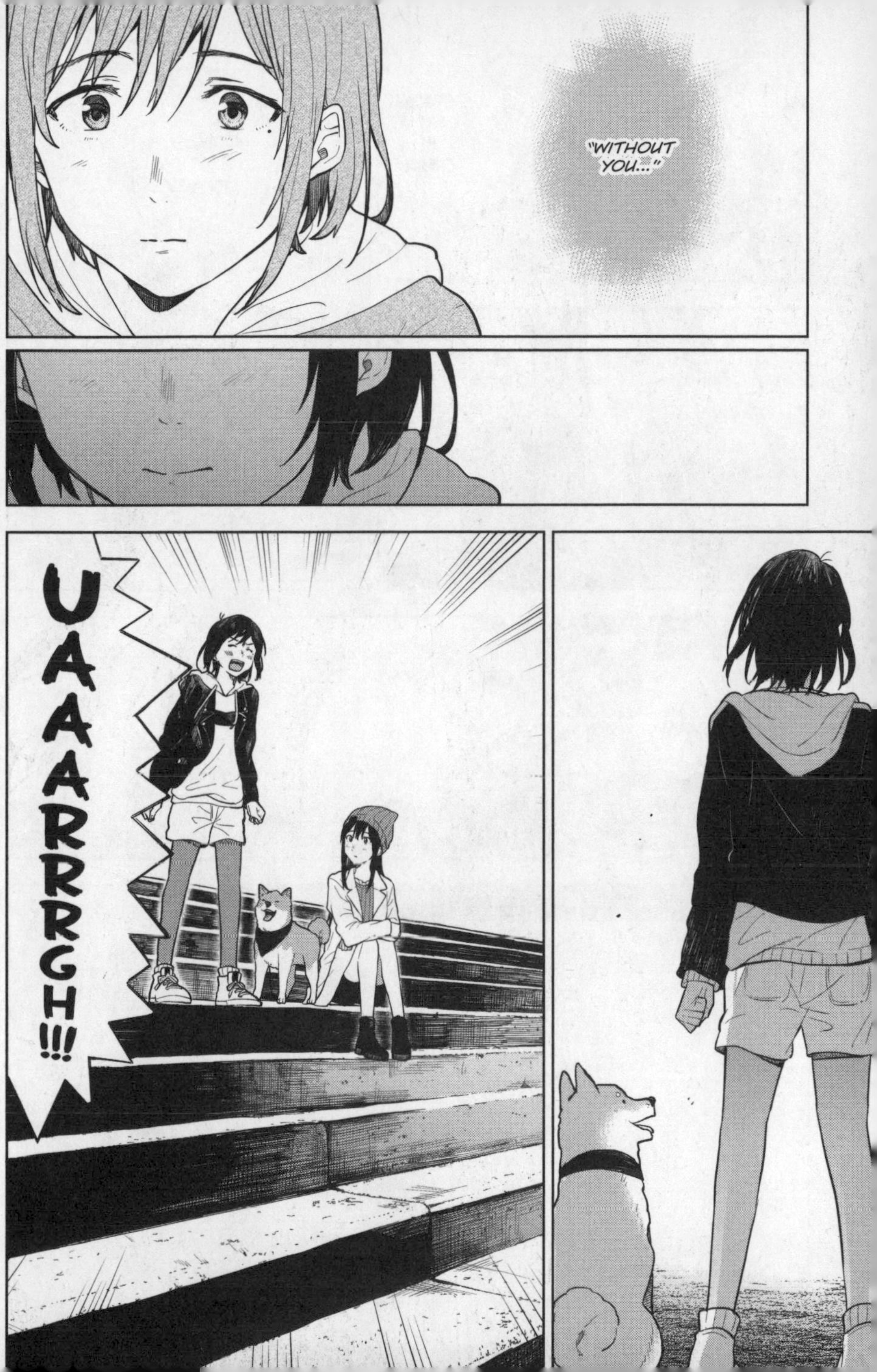
"WITHOUT YOU..."
UAAARRRGH!!!

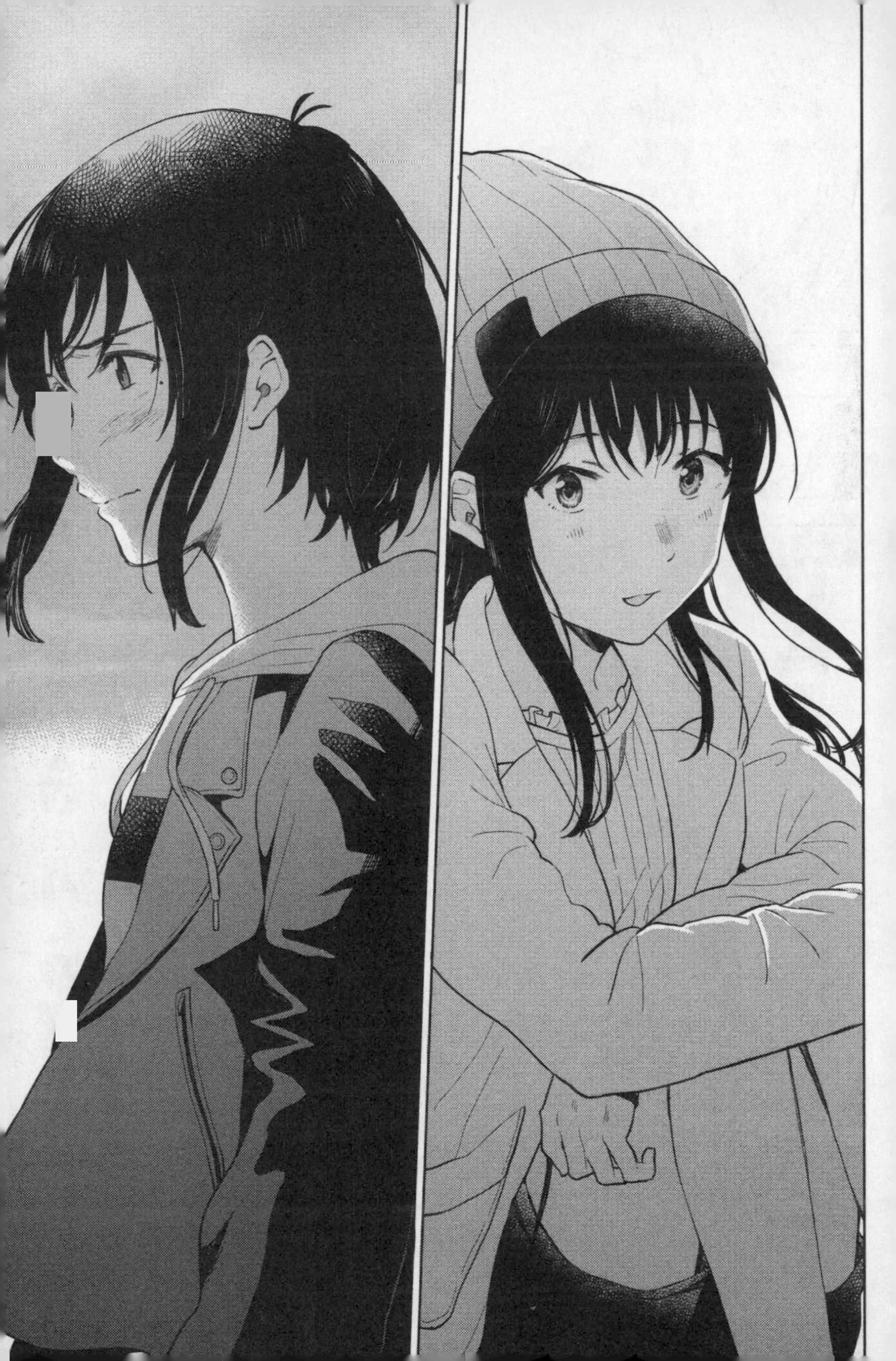

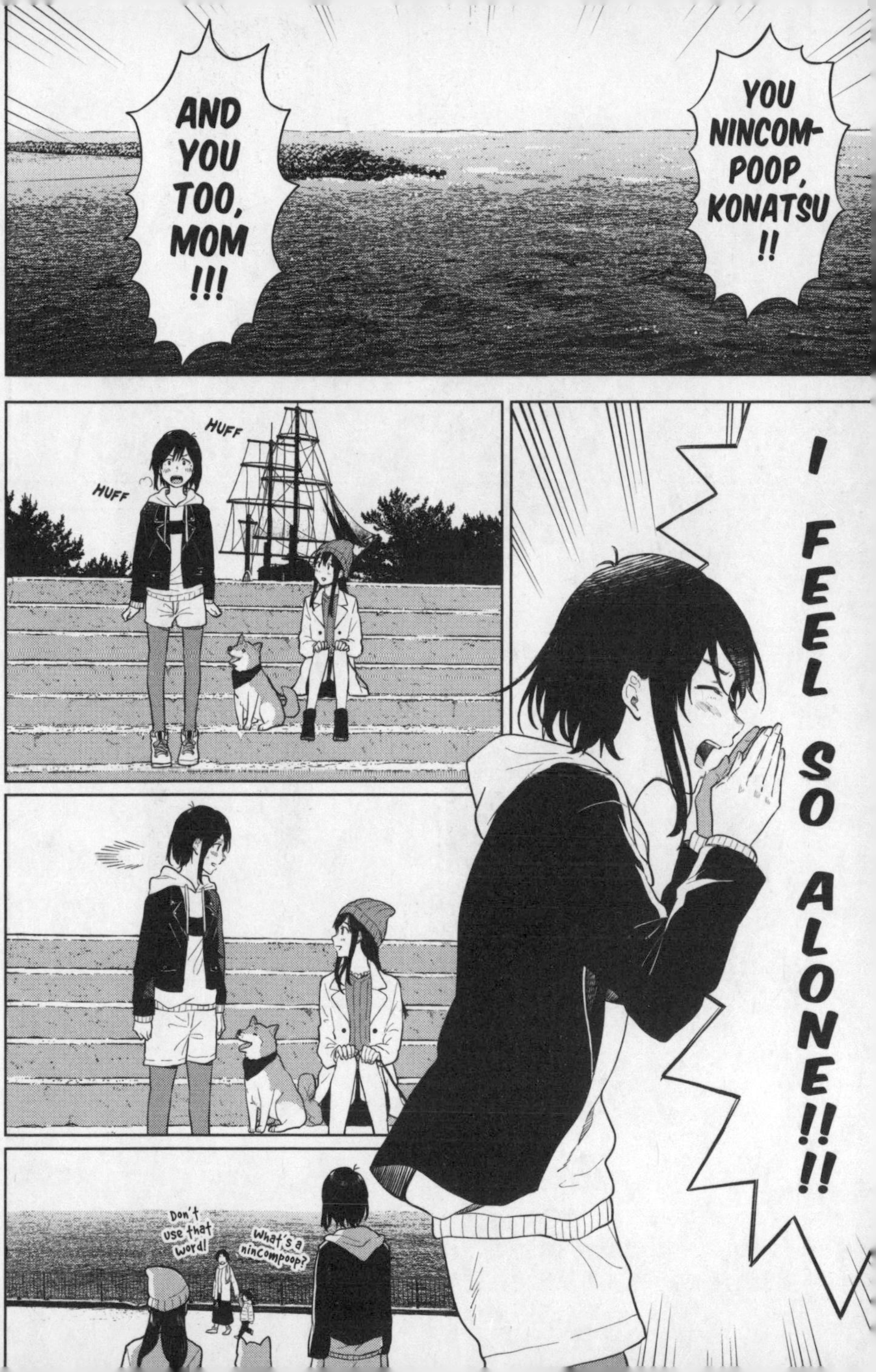
YOU NINCOM-POOP, KONATSU !!
AND YOU TOO, MOM !!!
I FEEL SO ALONE!!!!
HUFF
HUFF
What's a nincompoop?
Don't use that word!

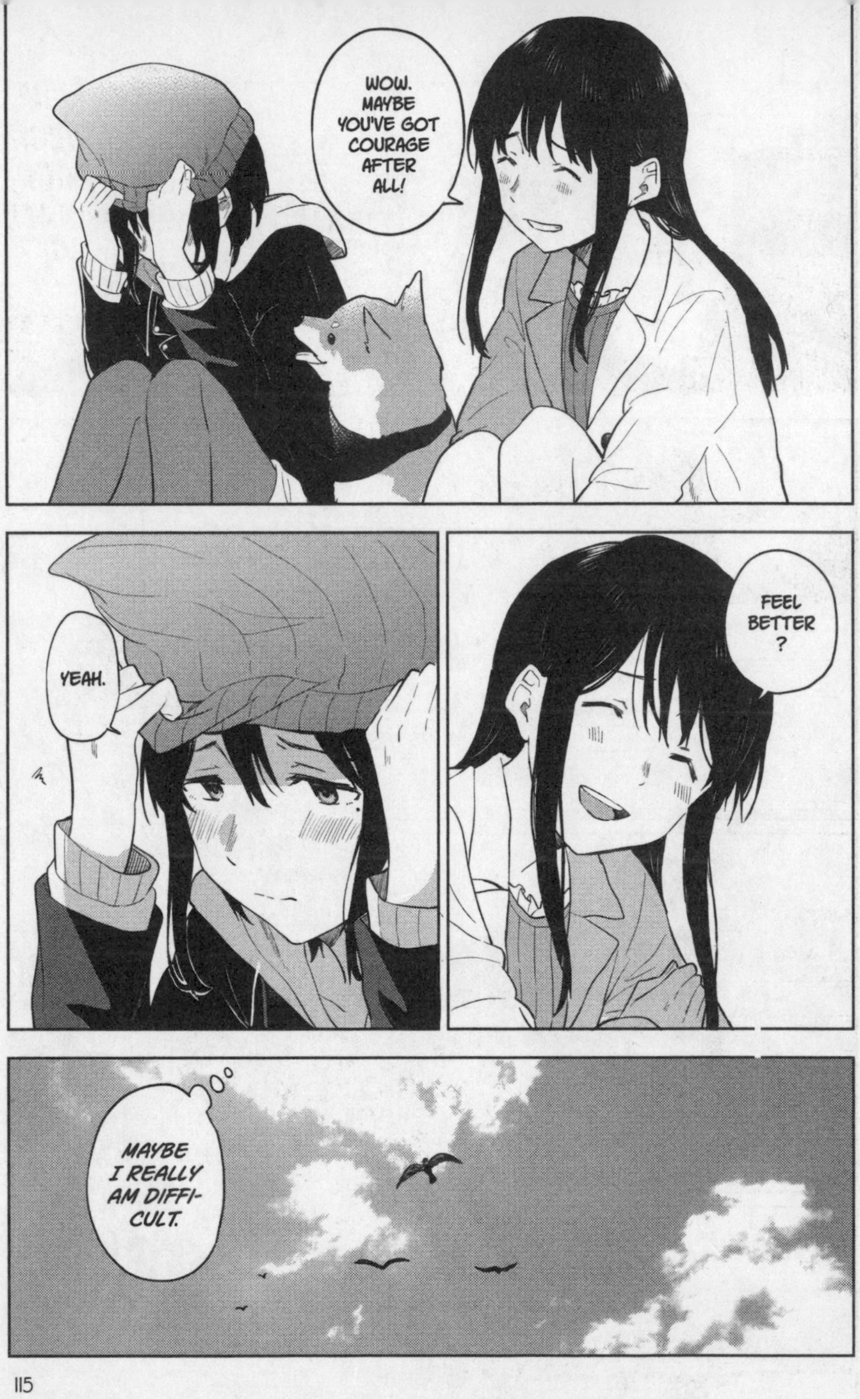
WOW. MAYBE YOU'VE GOT COURAGE AFTER ALL!
FEEL BETTER ?
YEAH.
MAYBE I REALLY AM DIFFI-CULT.

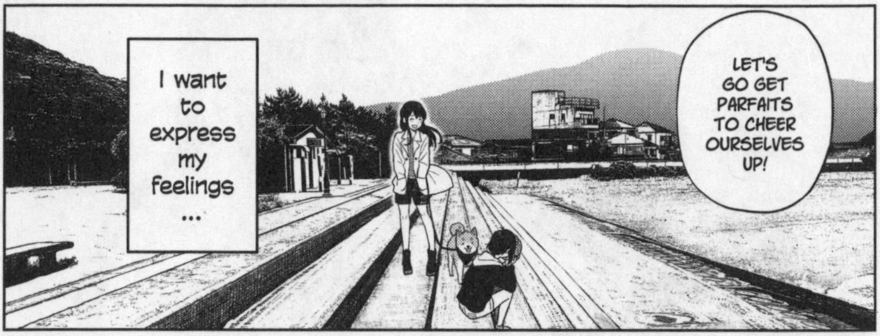
LET'S GO GET PARFAITS TO CHEER OURSELVES UP!
I want to express my feelings ...

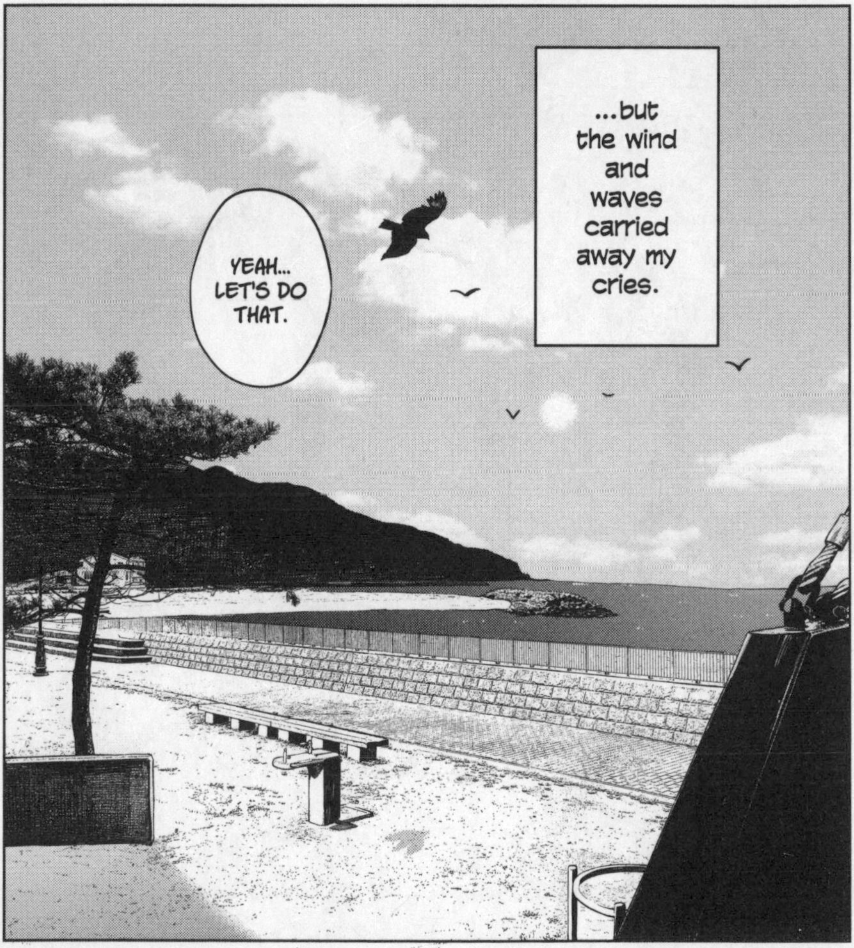
...but the wind and waves carried away my cries.
YEAH... LET'S DO THAT.

A Tropical Fish
Yearns for Snow

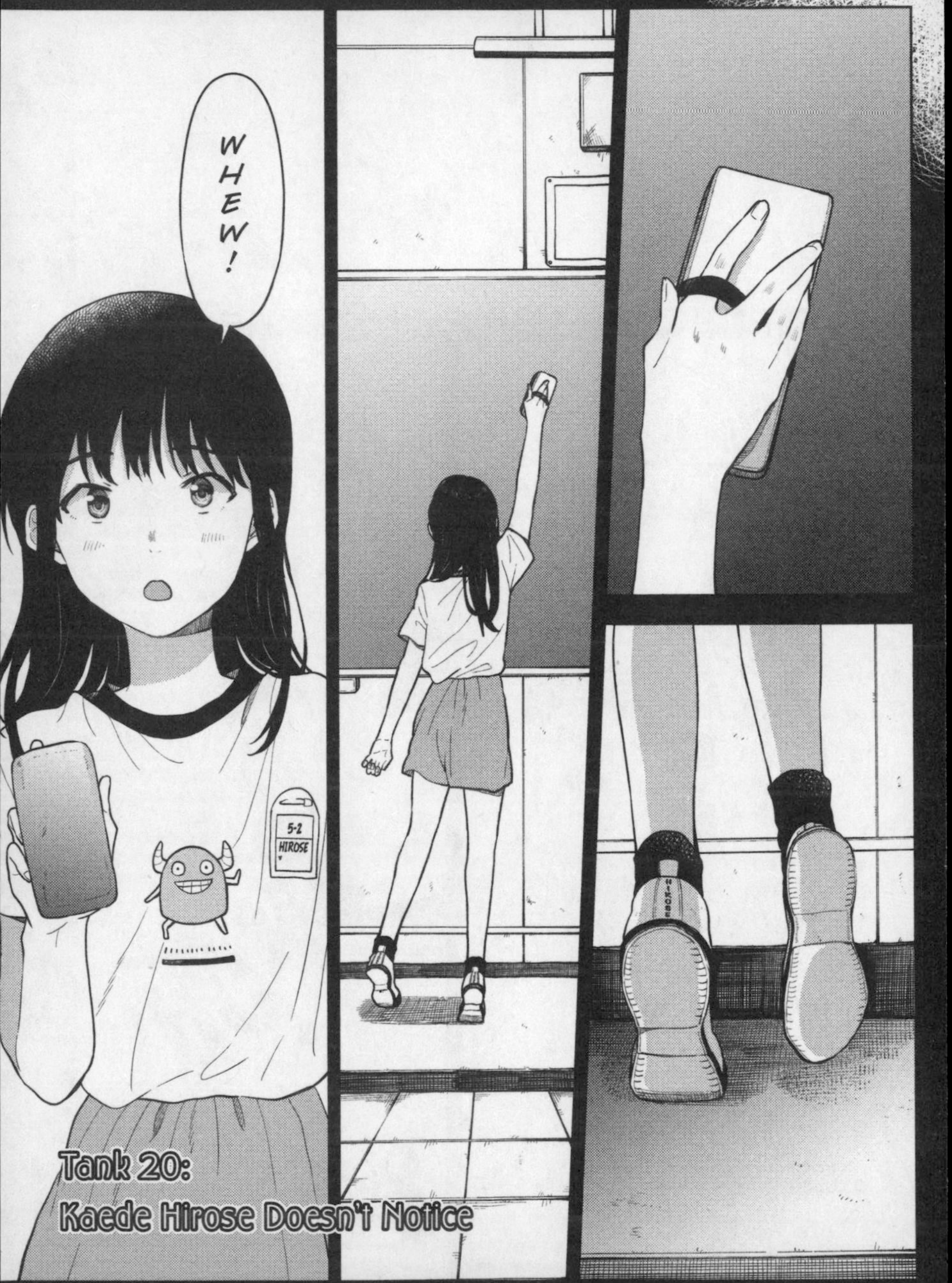
WHEW!
5-2 HIROSE
Tank 20:
Kaede Hirose Doesn't Notice

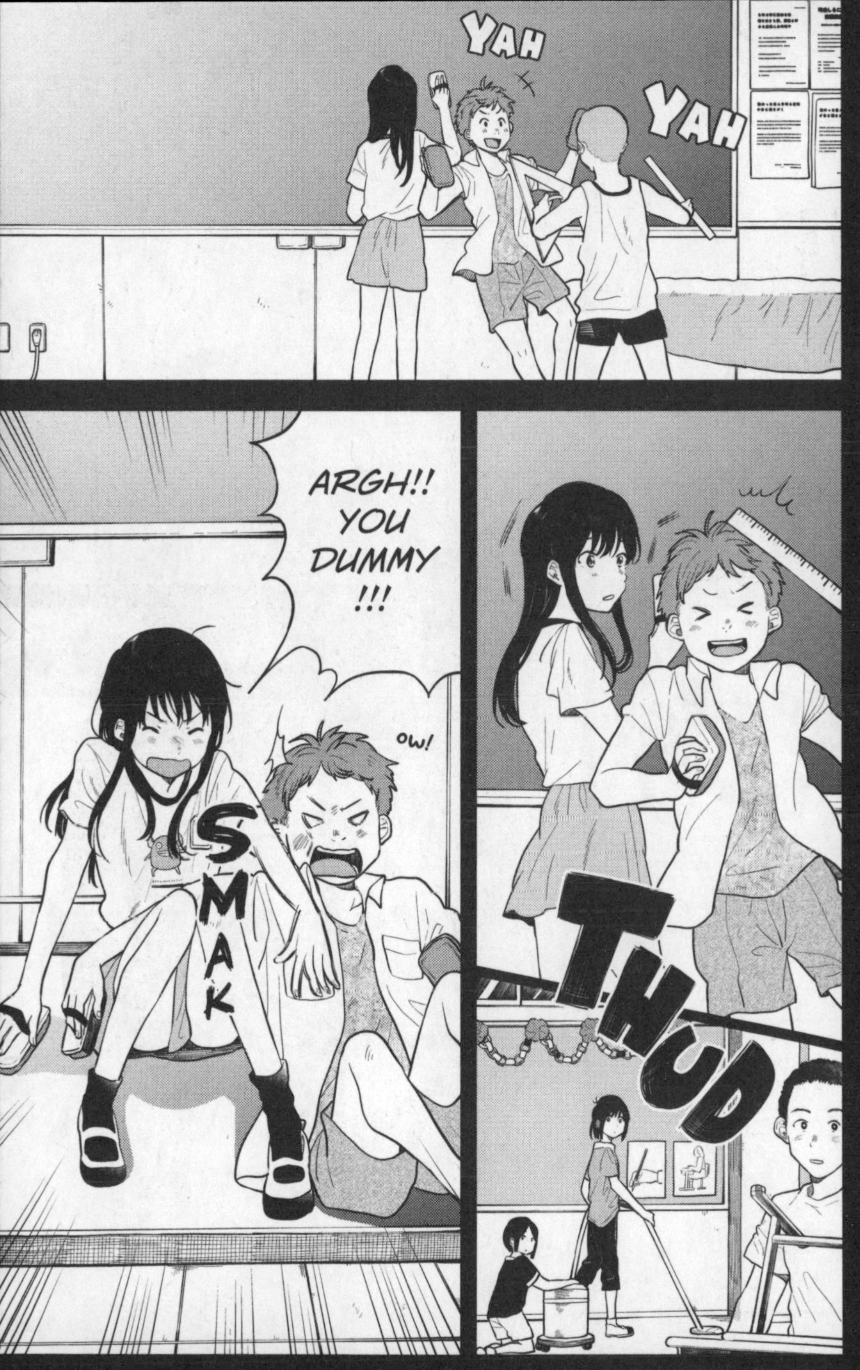
YAH
YAH
THUD
ARGH!! YOU DUMMY!!!
OW!
SMAK

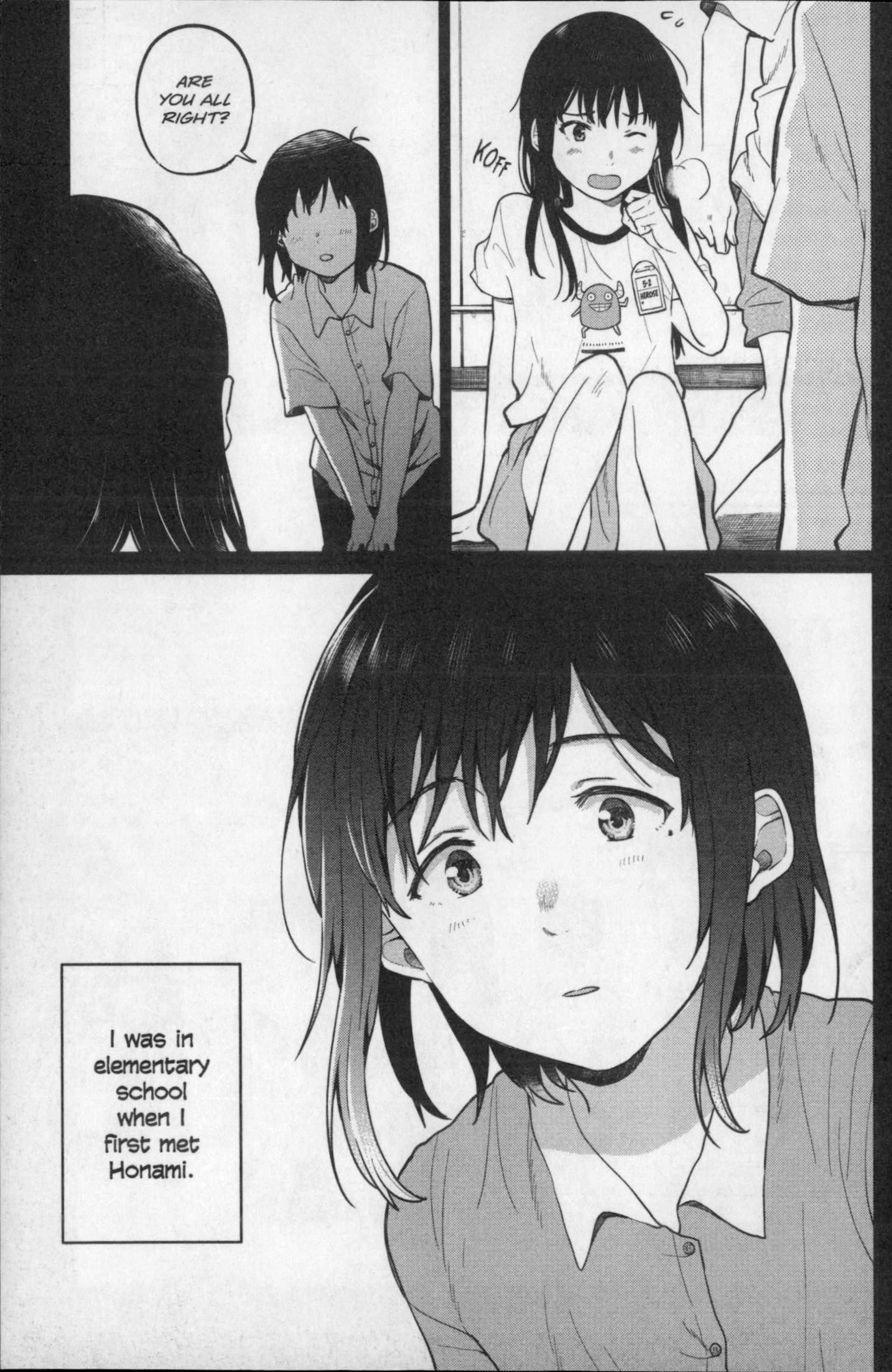
KOFF
5-2
HIROSE
ARE YOU ALL RIGHT?
I was in elementary school when I first met Honami.

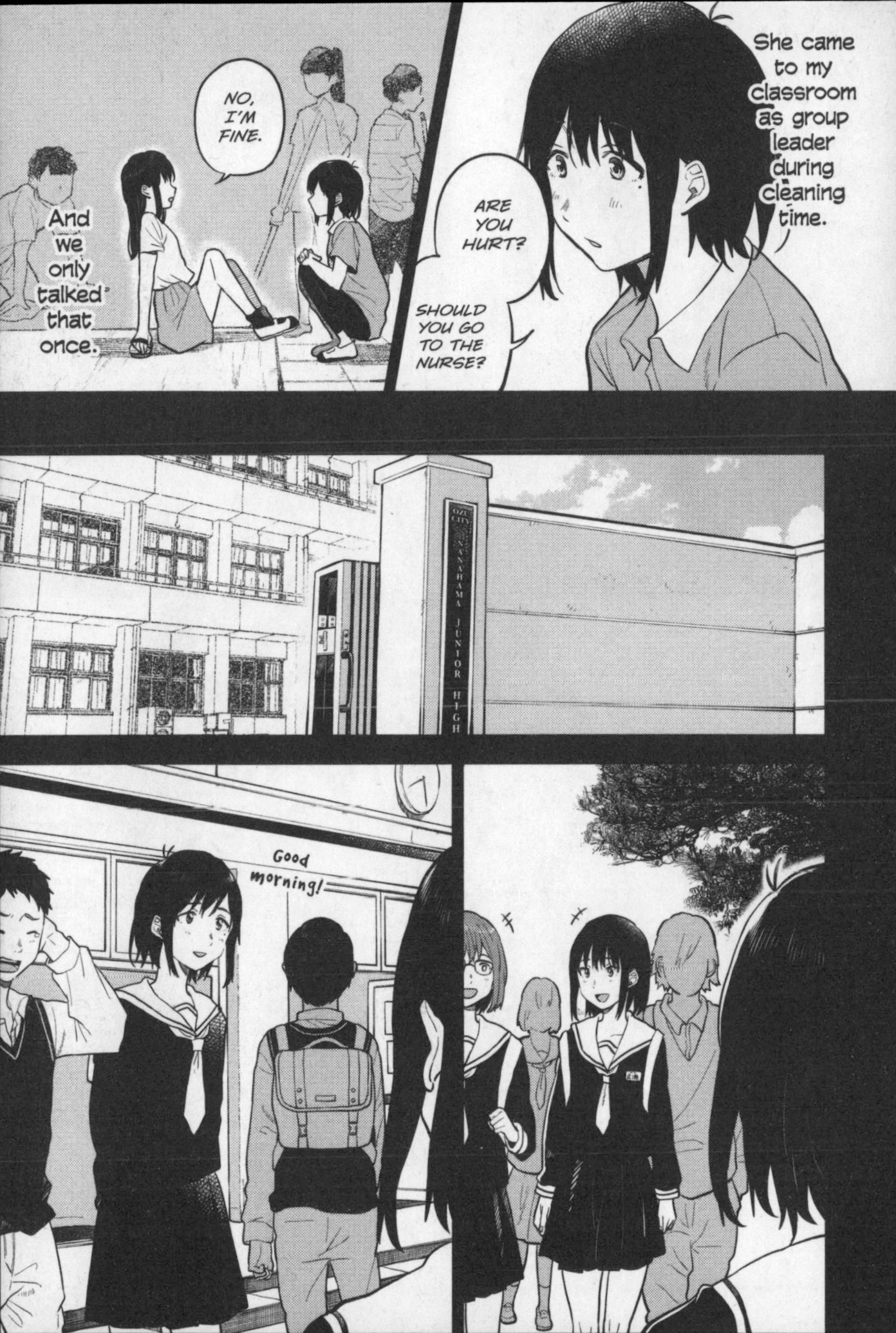
She came to my classroom as group leader during cleaning time.
ARE YOU HURT?
SHOULD YOU GO TO THE NURSE?
NO, I'M FINE.
And we only talked that once.
OZU CITY NANAHAMA JUNIOR HIGH
Good morning!

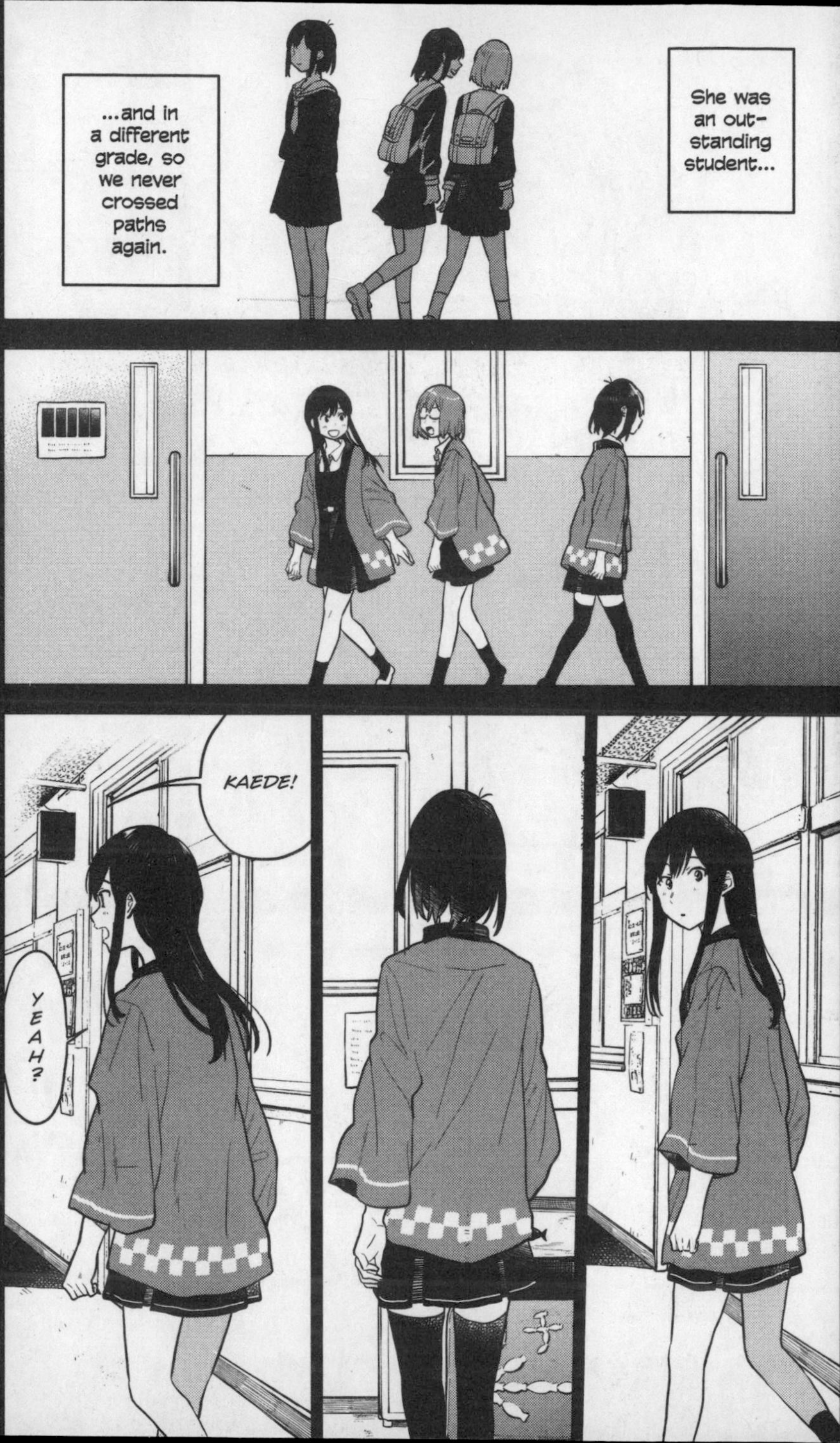
She was an out-standing student...
...and in a different grade, so we never crossed paths again.
KAEDE!
YEAH?

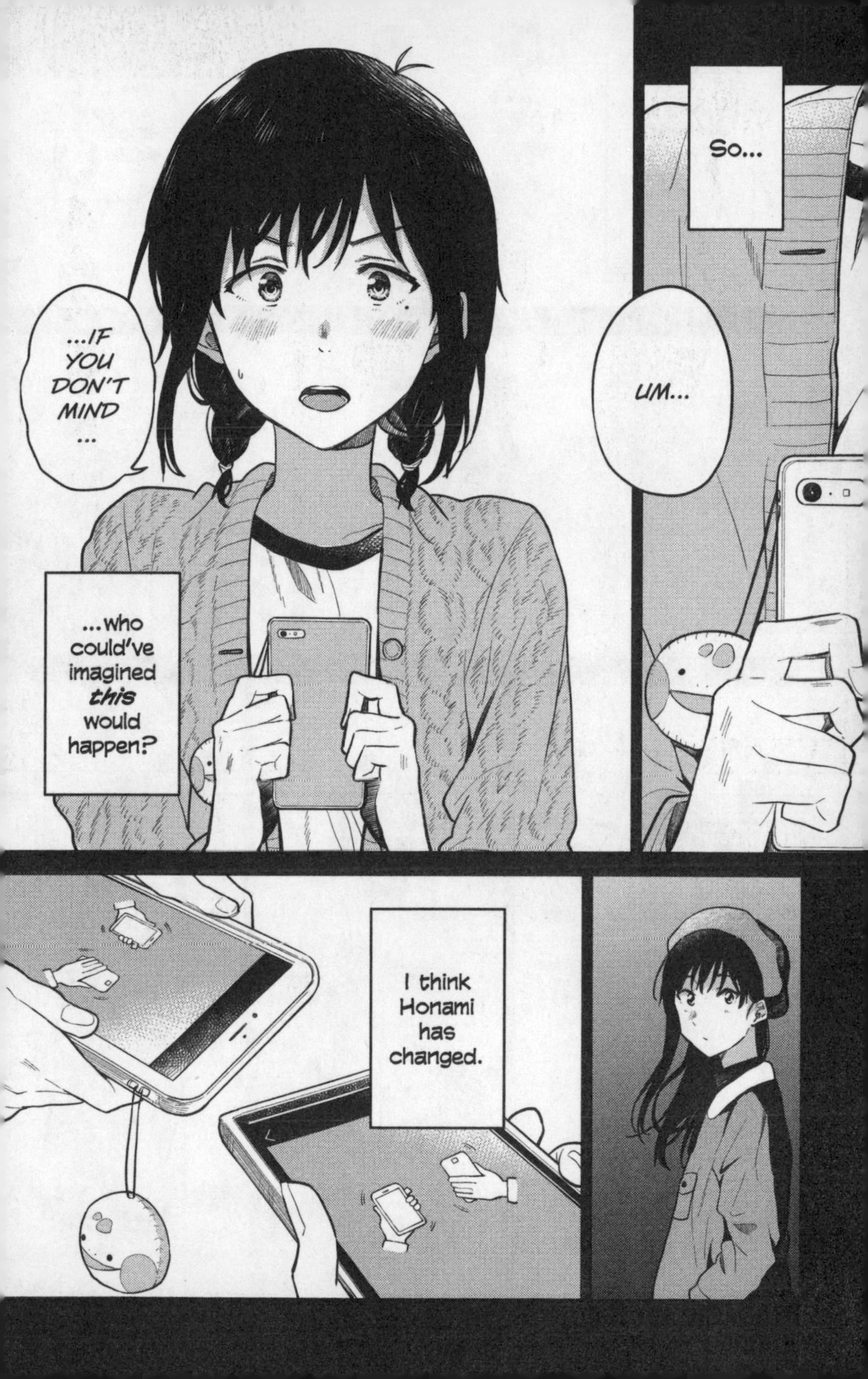
So...
UM...
...IF YOU DON'T MIND ...
...who could've imagined *this* would happen?
I think Honami has changed.

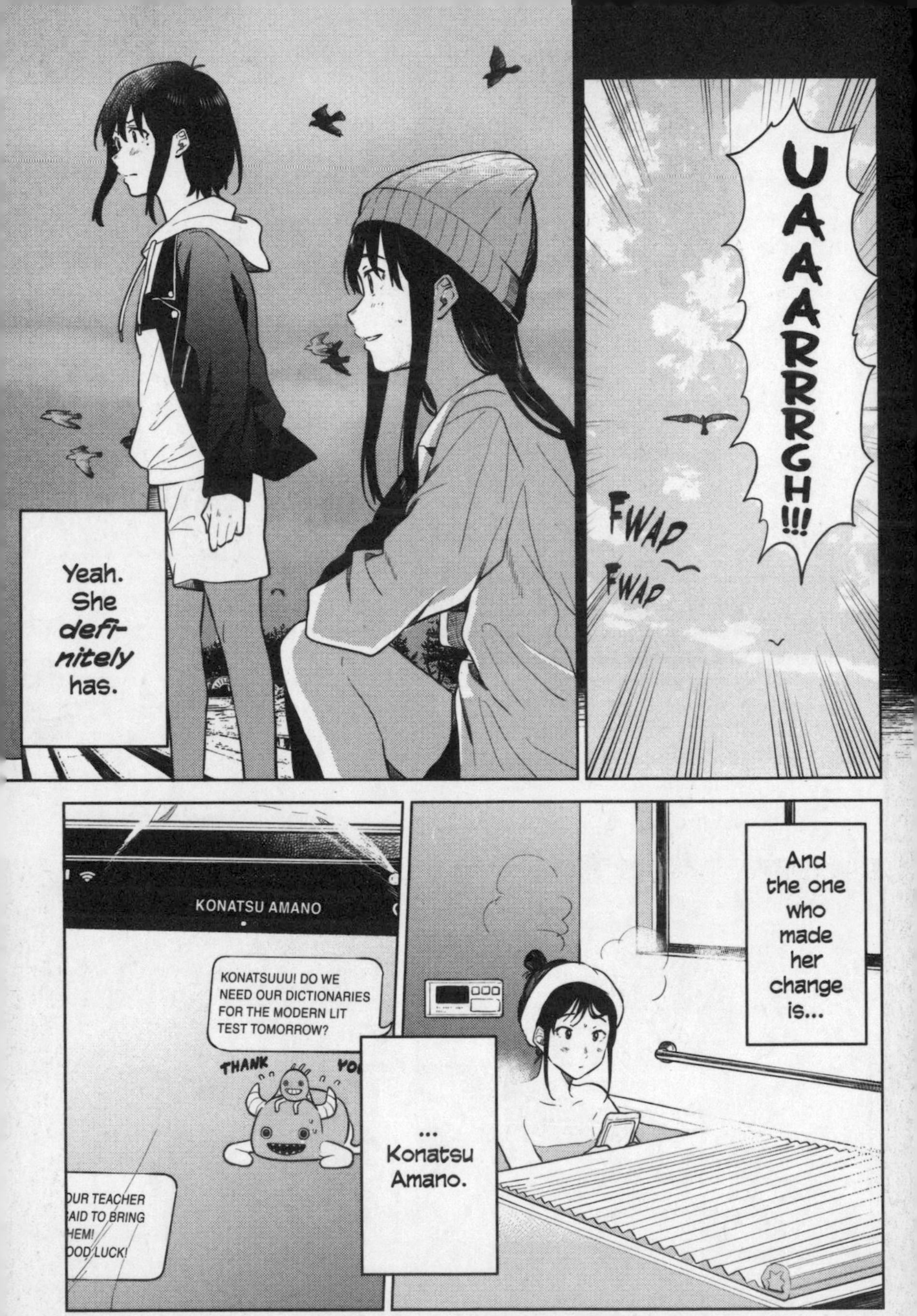
UAAAARRRGH!!!
FWAP
FWAP
Yeah. She definitely has.
And the one who made her change is...
... Konatsu Amano.
KONATSU AMANO
KONATSUUU! DO WE NEED OUR DICTIONARIES FOR THE MODERN LIT TEST TOMORROW?
THANK
OUR TEACHER
AID TO BRING
HEM!
OOD LUCK!

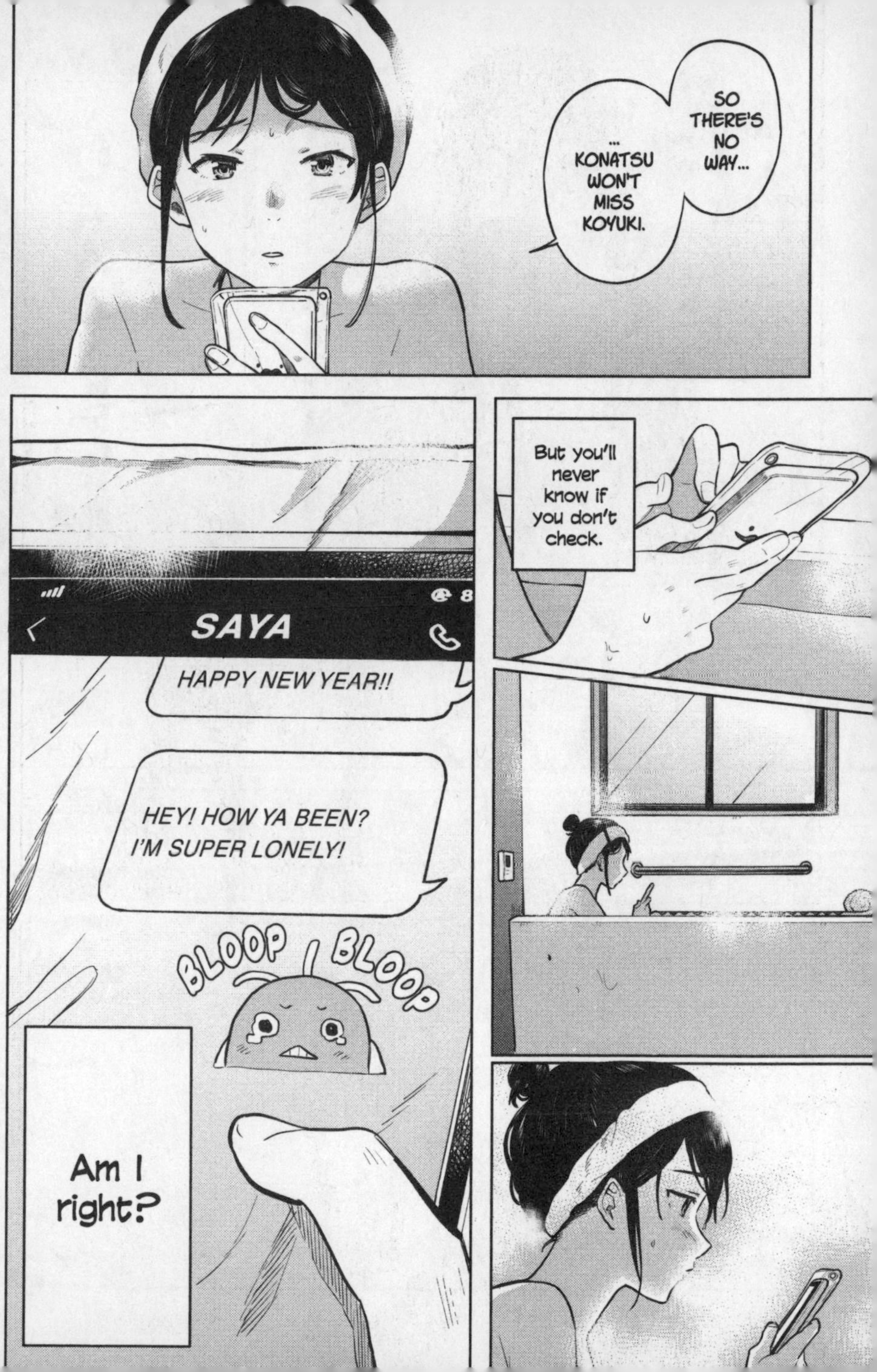
SO THERE'S NO WAY...
...KONATSU WON'T MISS KOYUKI.
But you'll never know if you don't check.
SAYA
HAPPY NEW YEAR!!
HEY! HOW YA BEEN? I'M SUPER LONELY!
BLOOP BLOOP
Am I right?

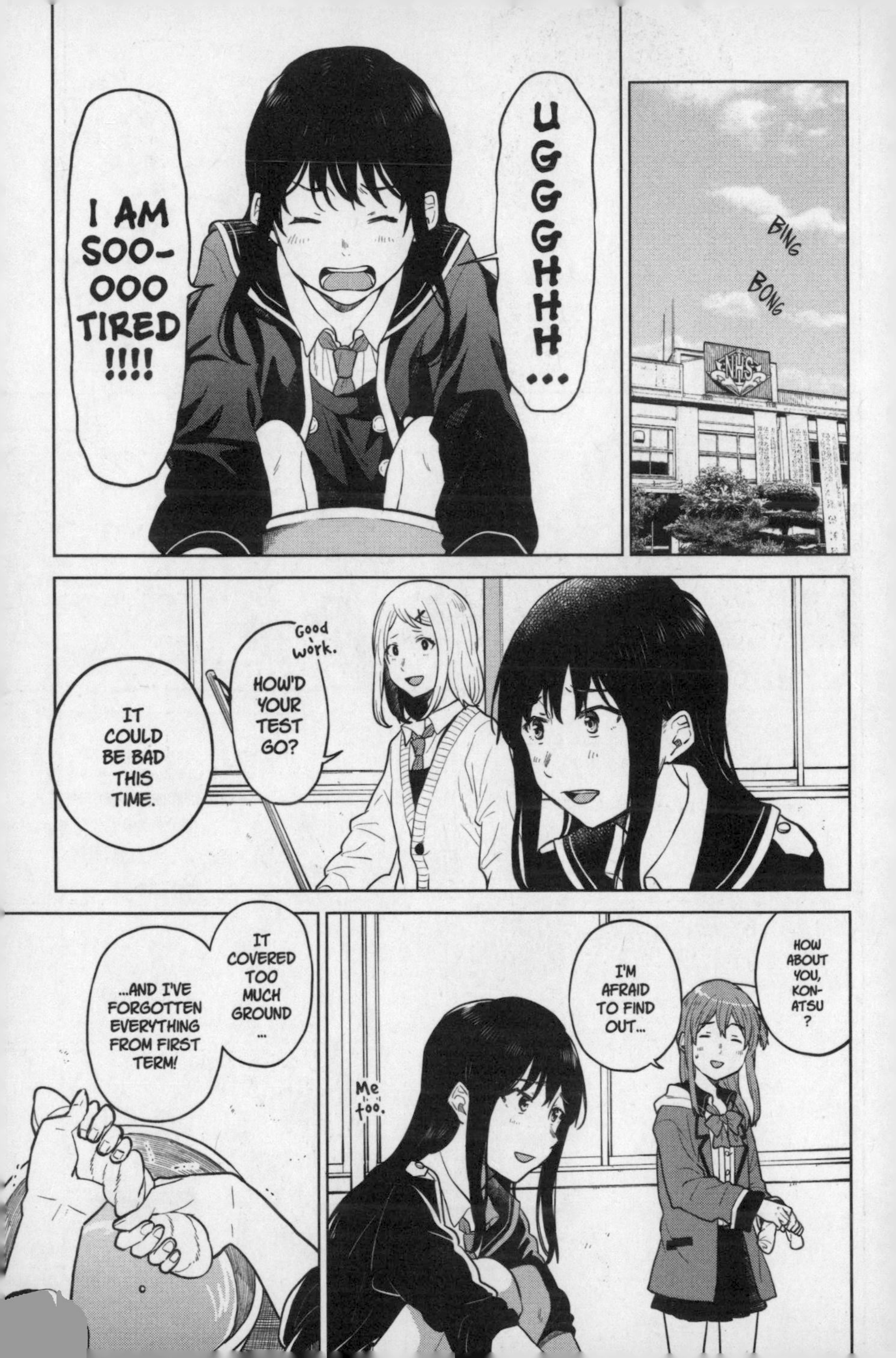
BING
BONG
UGGGHHH...
I AM SOOOOO TIRED!!!!
Good work.
HOW'D YOUR TEST GO?
IT COULD BE BAD THIS TIME.
HOW ABOUT YOU, KONATSU?
I'M AFRAID TO FIND OUT...
Me too.
IT COVERED TOO MUCH GROUND...
...AND I'VE FORGOTTEN EVERYTHING FROM FIRST TERM!

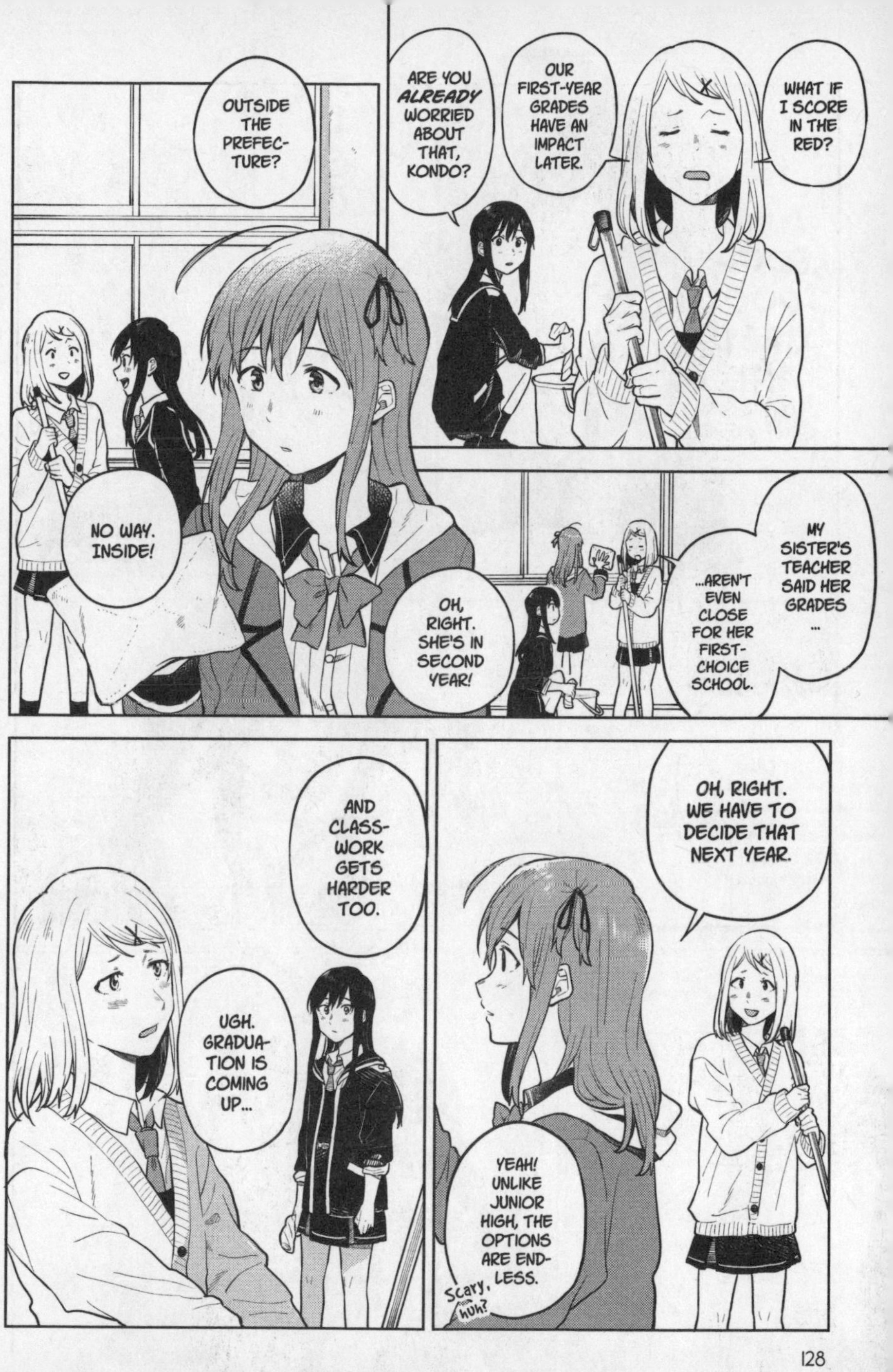
WHAT IF I SCORE IN THE RED?
OUR FIRST-YEAR GRADES HAVE AN IMPACT LATER.
ARE YOU *ALREADY* WORRIED ABOUT THAT, KONDO?
MY SISTER'S TEACHER SAID HER GRADES ...
...AREN'T EVEN CLOSE FOR HER FIRST-CHOICE SCHOOL.
OH, RIGHT. SHE'S IN SECOND YEAR!
OUTSIDE THE PREFEC-TURE?
NO WAY. INSIDE!
OH, RIGHT. WE HAVE TO DECIDE THAT NEXT YEAR.
YEAH! UNLIKE JUNIOR HIGH, THE OPTIONS ARE END-LESS.
Scary, huh?
AND CLASS-WORK GETS HARDER TOO.
UGH. GRADUA-TION IS COMING UP...

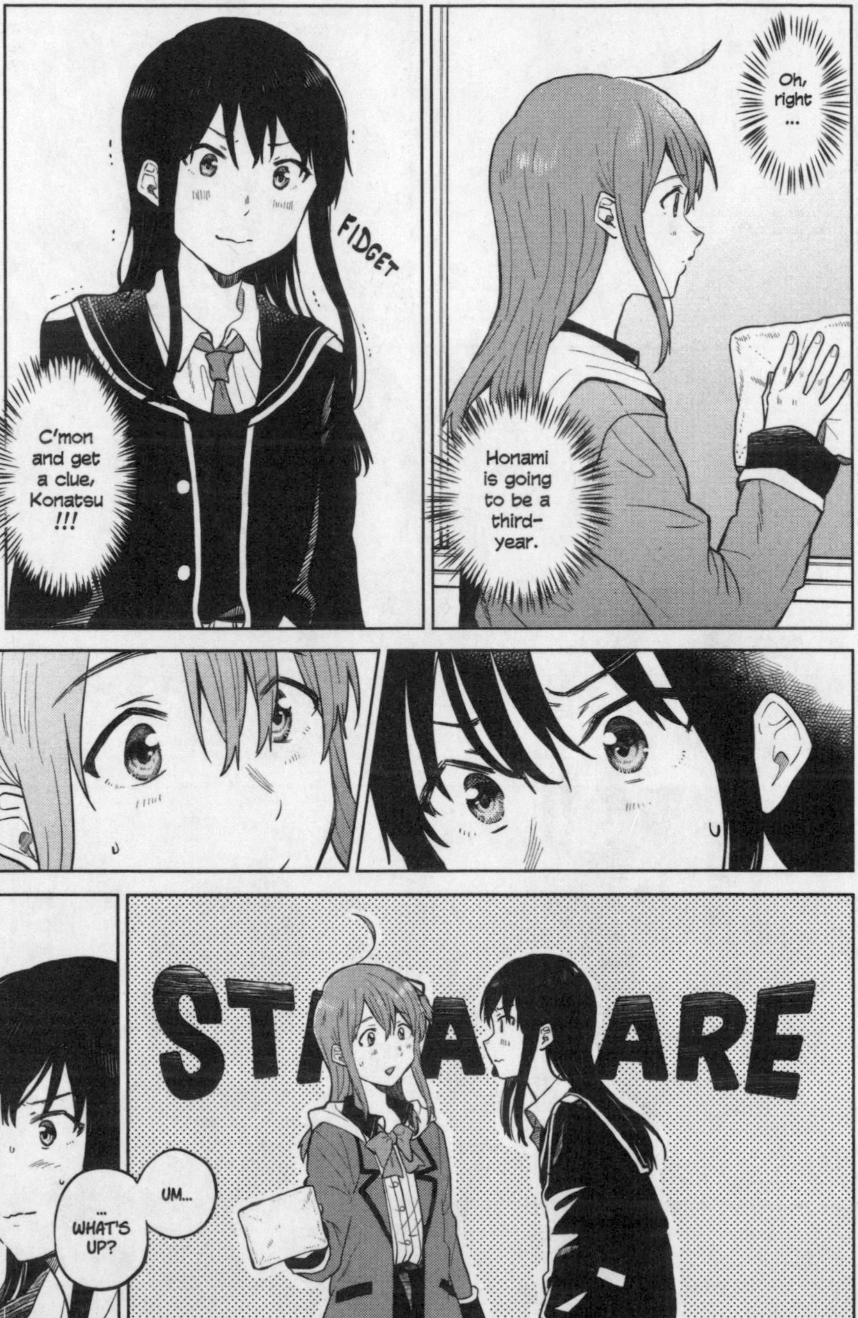
Oh, right ...
Honami is going to be a third-year.
FIDGET
C'mon and get a clue, Konatsu !!!
ST A ARE
UM...
... WHAT'S UP?

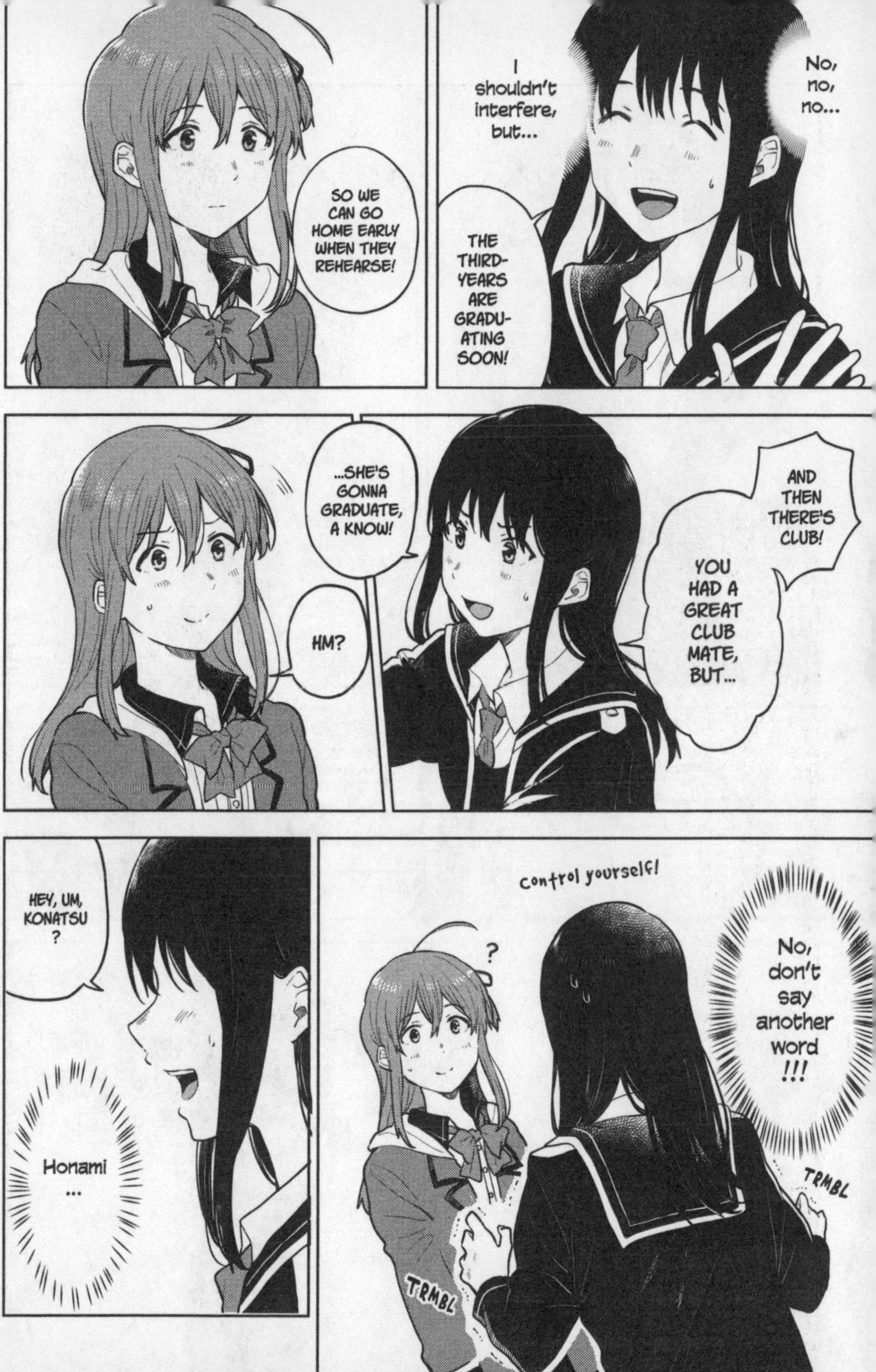
No, no, no...
I shouldn't interfere, but...
THE THIRD-YEARS ARE GRADUATING SOON!
SO WE CAN GO HOME EARLY WHEN THEY REHEARSE!
AND THEN THERE'S CLUB!
YOU HAD A GREAT CLUB MATE, BUT...
...SHE'S GONNA GRADUATE, A KNOW!
HM?
control yourself!
No, don't say another word!!!
?
TRMBL
TRMBL
HEY, UM, KONATSU?
Honami...

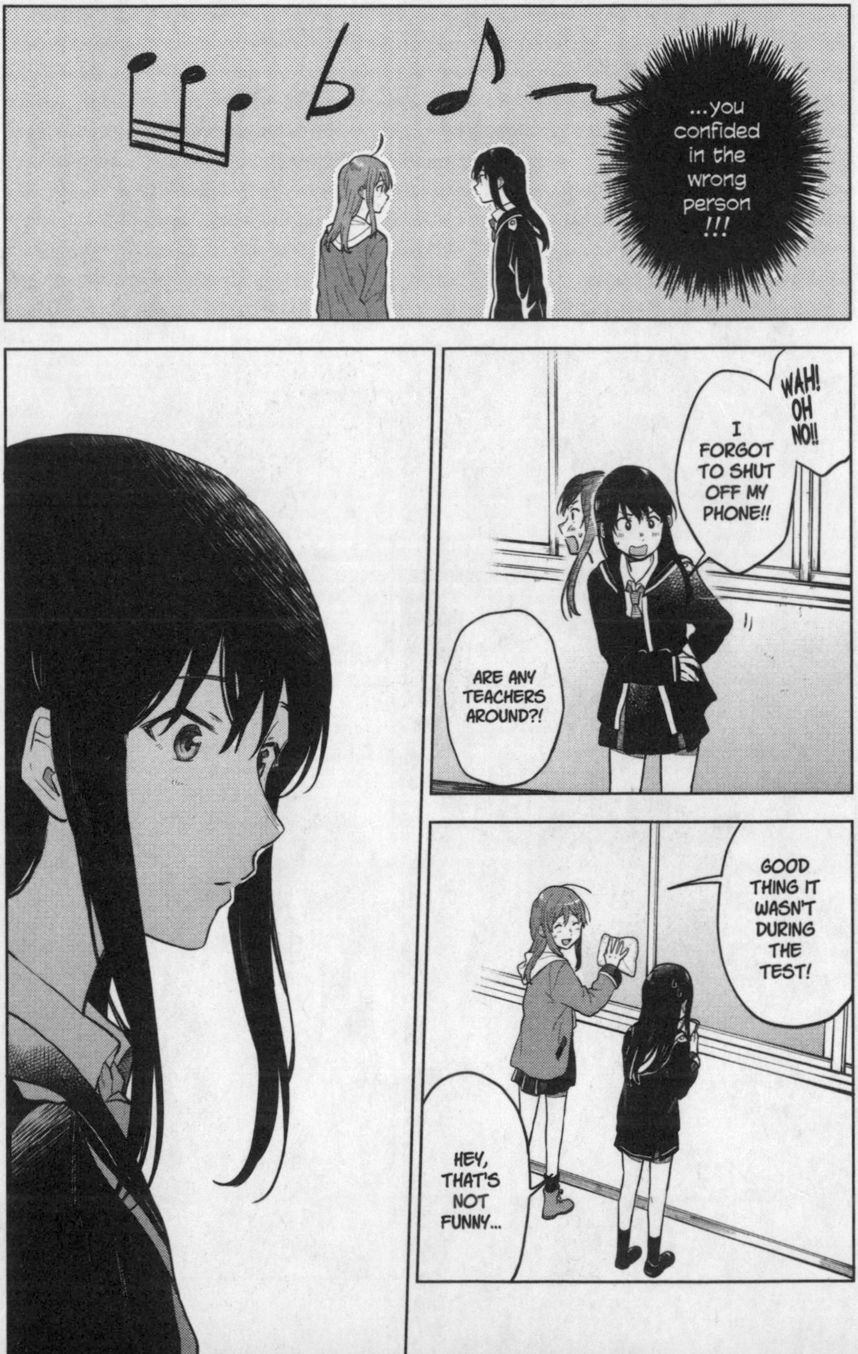
...you confided in the wrong person!!!
WAH! OH NO!!
I FORGOT TO SHUT OFF MY PHONE!!
ARE ANY TEACHERS AROUND?!
GOOD THING IT WASN'T DURING THE TEST!
HEY, THAT'S NOT FUNNY...

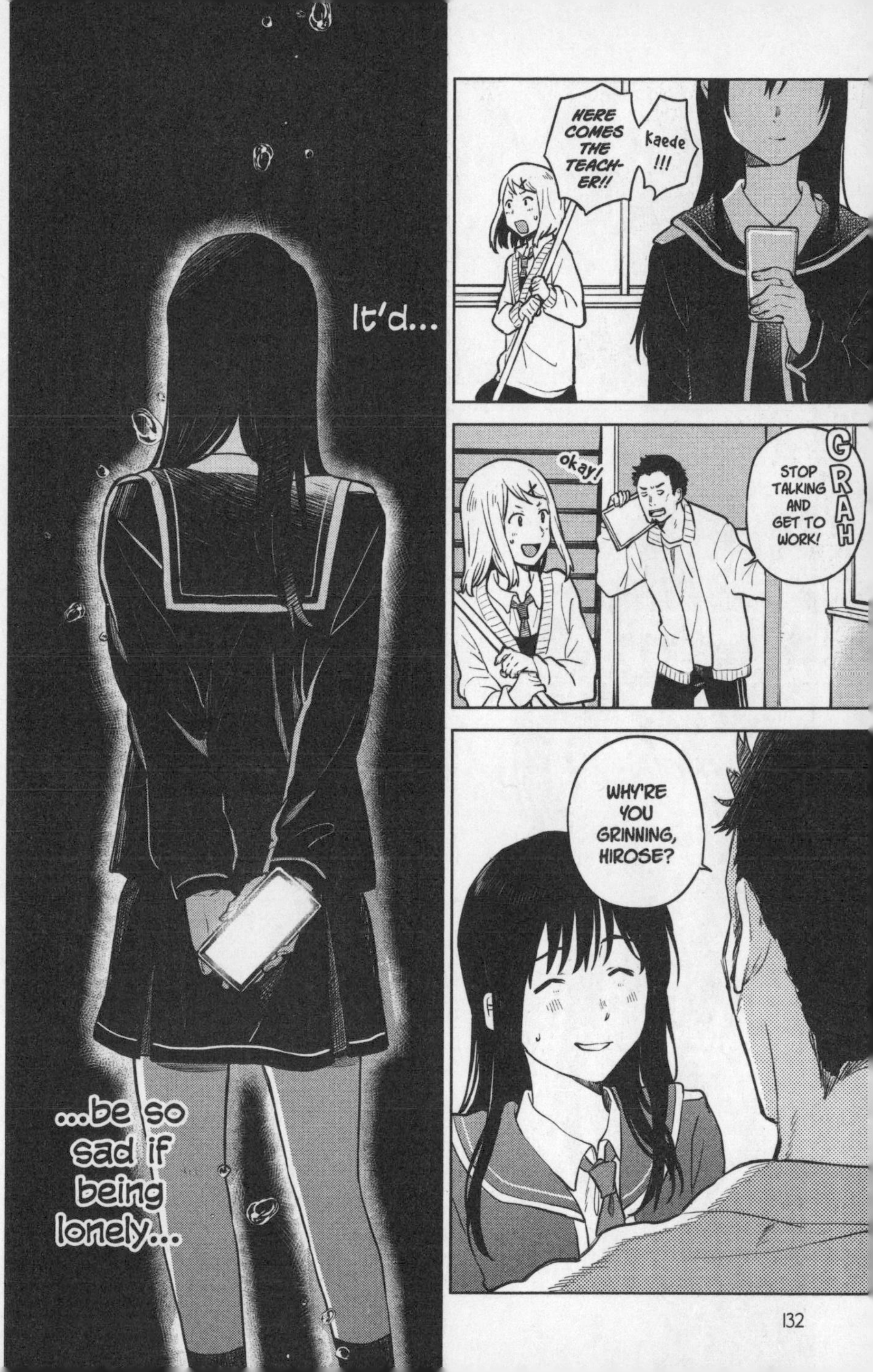

HERE COMES THE TEACHER!!
Kaede!!!
GRAH
STOP TALKING AND GET TO WORK!
okay!
WHY'RE YOU GRINNING, HIROSE?
It'd...
...be so sad if being lonely...

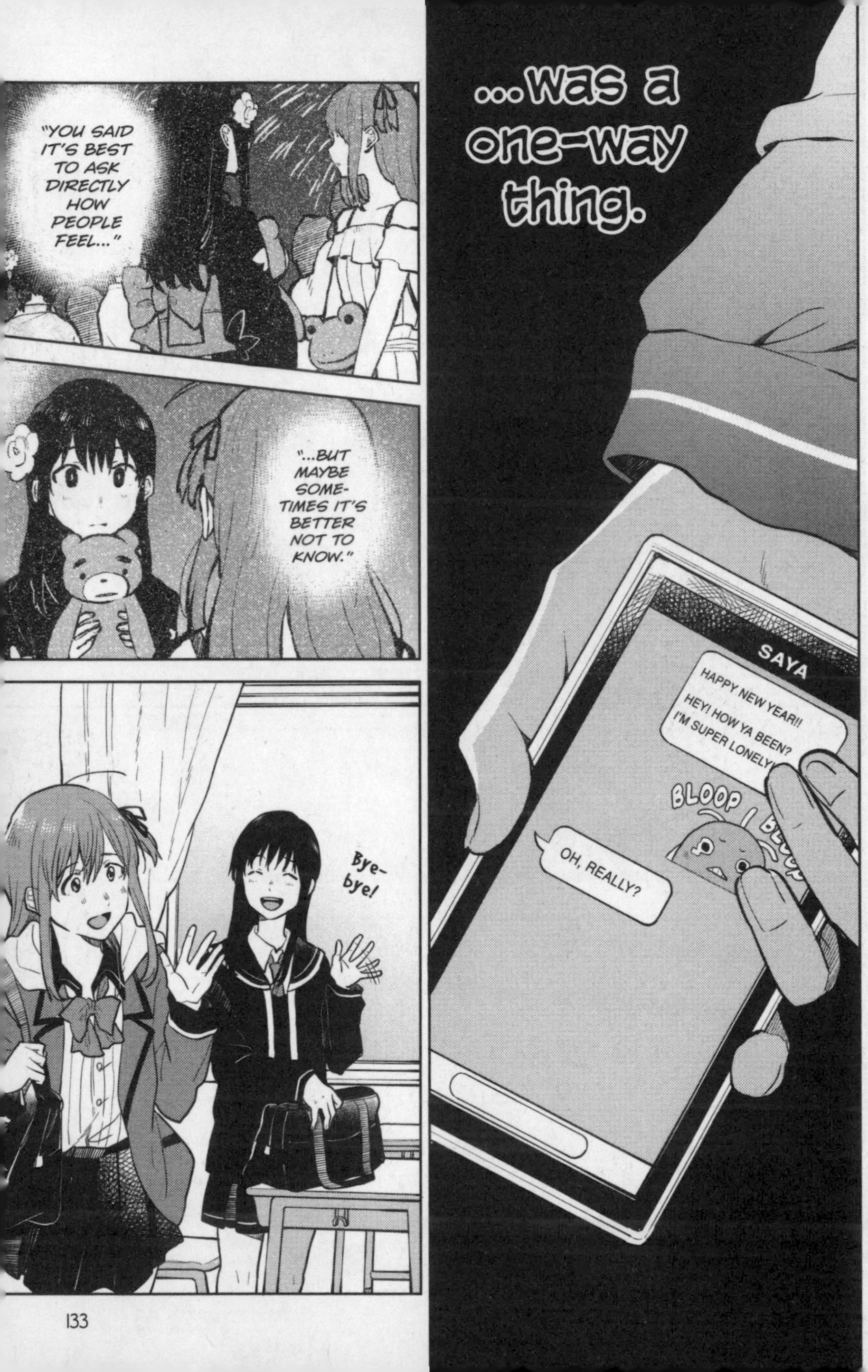
...was a one-way thing.
SAYA
HAPPY NEW YEAR!!
HEY! HOW YA BEEN? I'M SUPER LONELY!
BLOOP
OH, REALLY?
"YOU SAID IT'S BEST TO ASK DIRECTLY HOW PEOPLE FEEL..."
"...BUT MAYBE SOMETIMES IT'S BETTER NOT TO KNOW."
Bye-bye!

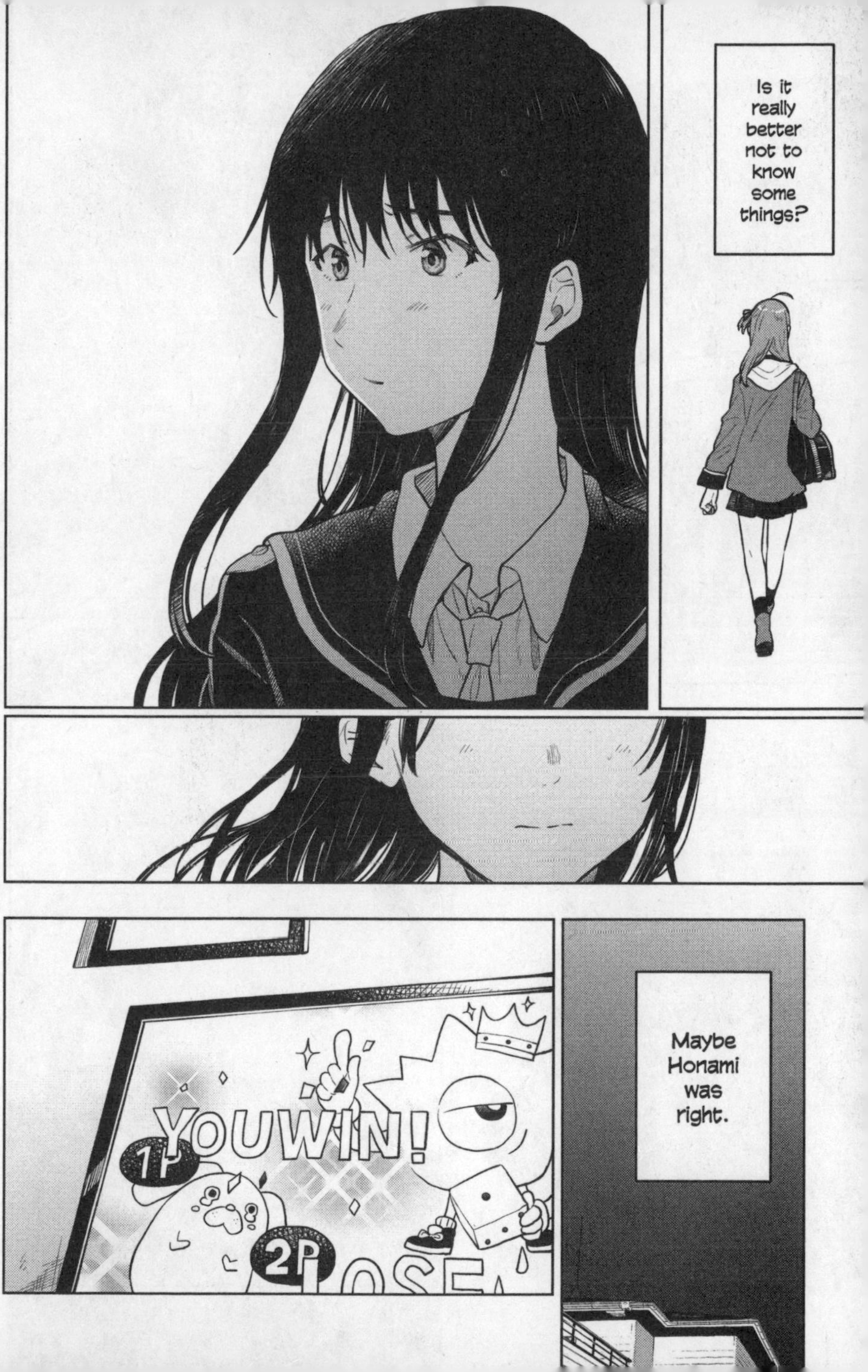
Is it really better not to know some things?
Maybe Honami was right.
YOUWIN!
1P
2P

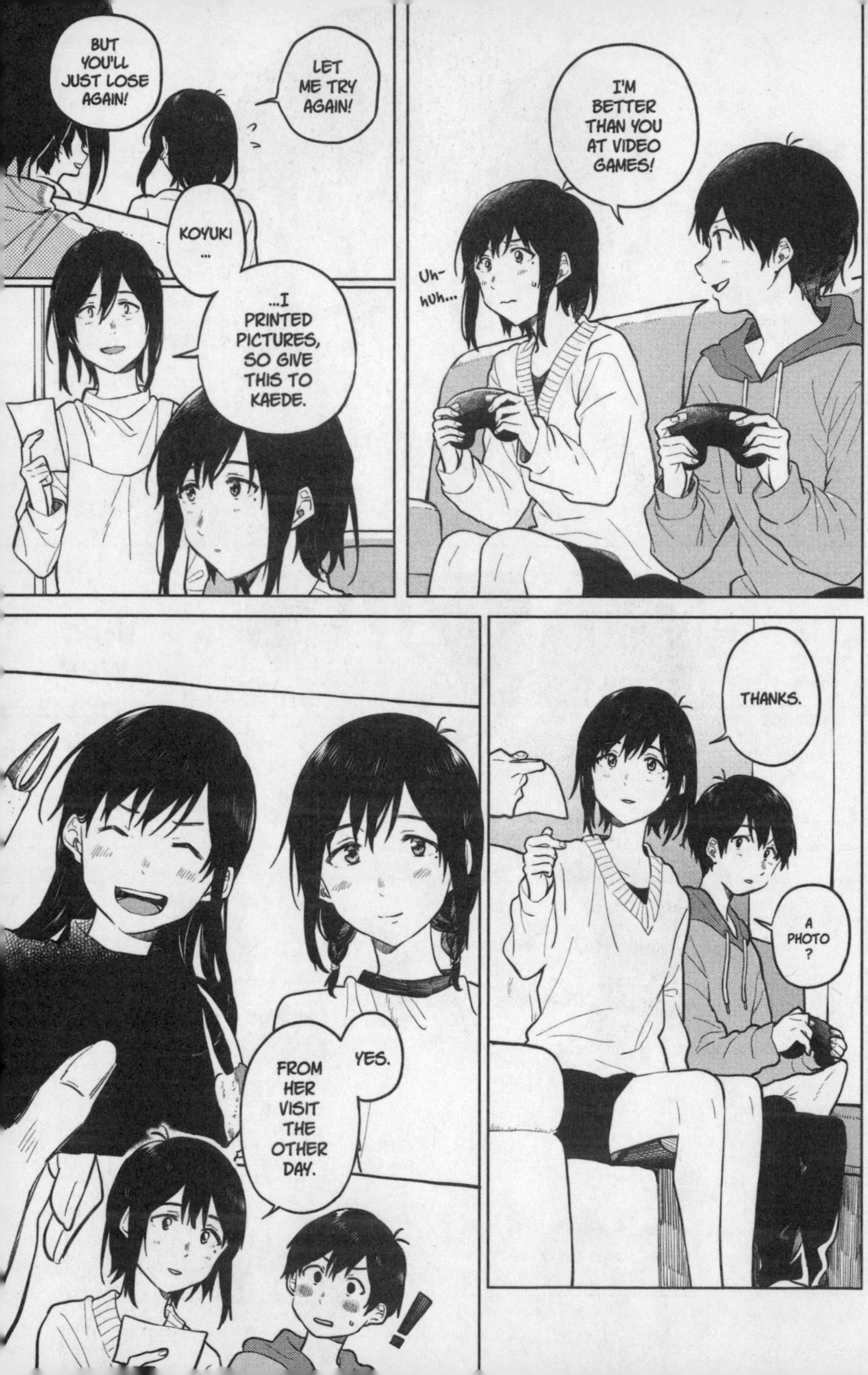
I'M BETTER THAN YOU AT VIDEO GAMES!
Uh-huh...
LET ME TRY AGAIN!
BUT YOU'LL JUST LOSE AGAIN!
KOYUKI ...
...I PRINTED PICTURES, SO GIVE THIS TO KAEDE.
THANKS.
A PHOTO ?
YES.
FROM HER VISIT THE OTHER DAY.

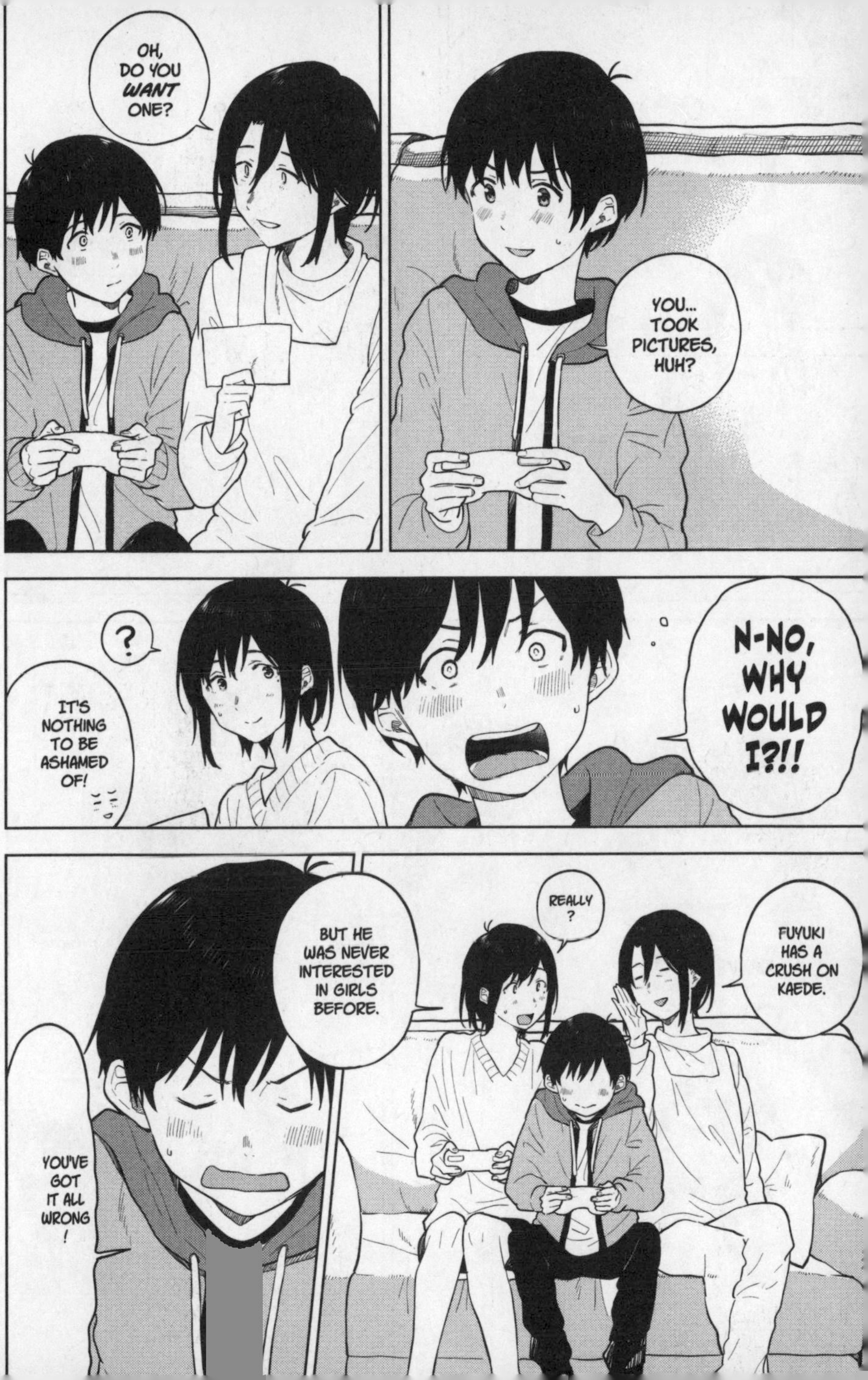
YOU... TOOK PICTURES, HUH?
OH, DO YOU *WANT* ONE?
N-NO, WHY WOULD I?!!
?
IT'S NOTHING TO BE ASHAMED OF!
FUYUKI HAS A CRUSH ON KAEDE.
REALLY?
BUT HE WAS NEVER INTERESTED IN GIRLS BEFORE.
YOU'VE GOT IT ALL WRONG!

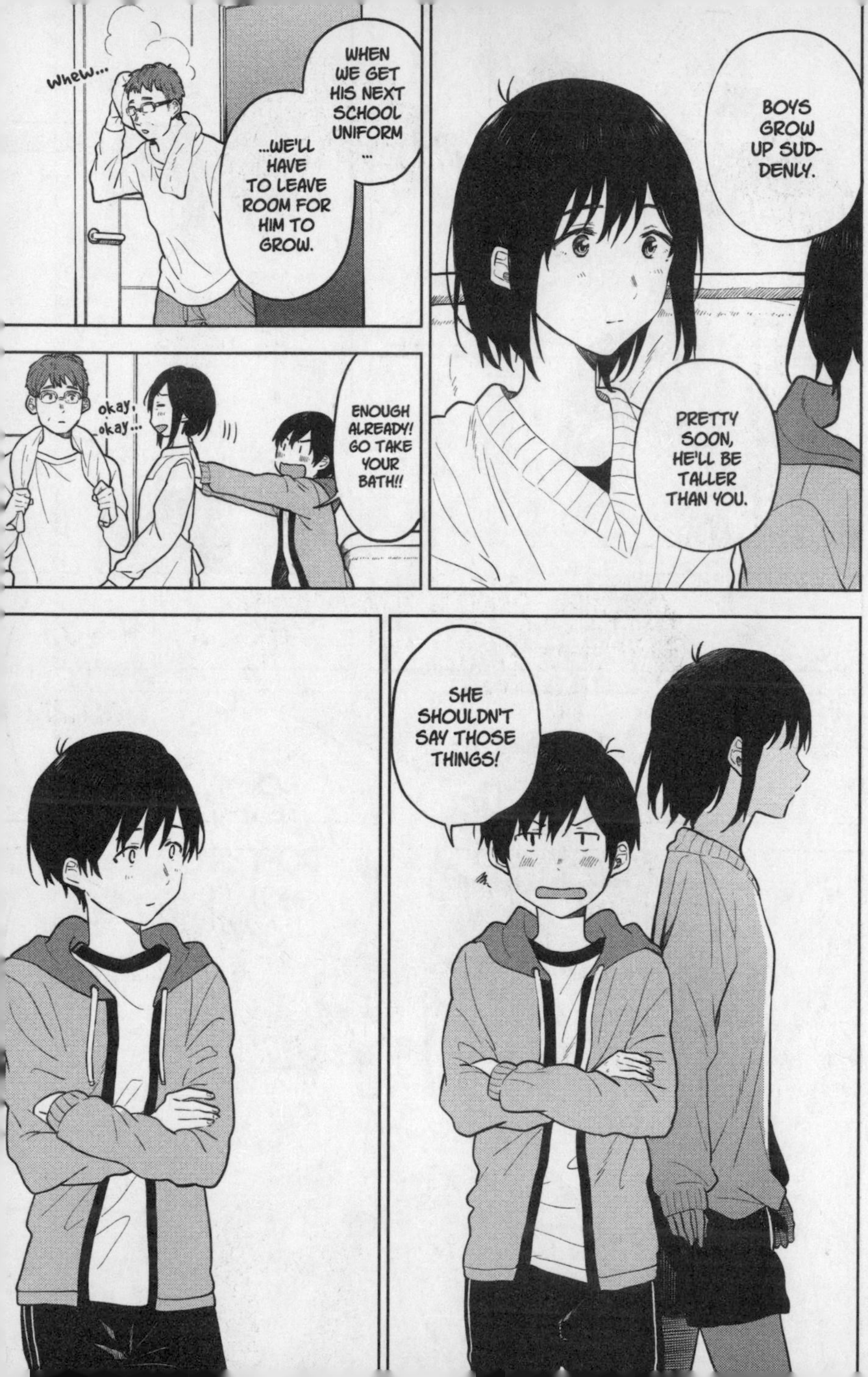
BOYS GROW UP SUDDENLY.
PRETTY SOON, HE'LL BE TALLER THAN YOU.
WHEN WE GET HIS NEXT SCHOOL UNIFORM ...
...WE'LL HAVE TO LEAVE ROOM FOR HIM TO GROW.
Whew...
ENOUGH ALREADY! GO TAKE YOUR BATH!!
okay, okay...
SHE SHOULDN'T SAY THOSE THINGS!

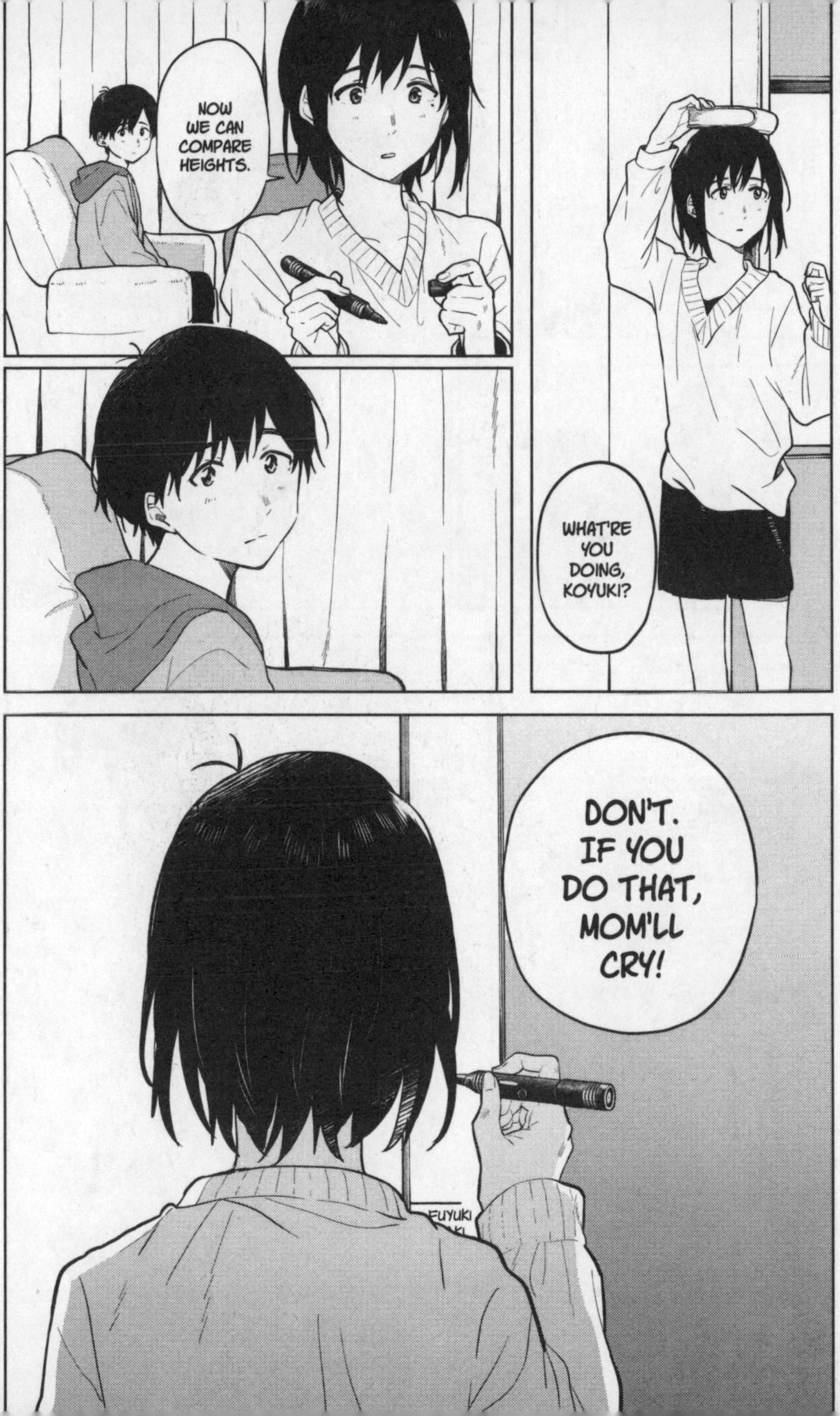
WHAT'RE YOU DOING, KOYUKI?
NOW WE CAN COMPARE HEIGHTS.
DON'T. IF YOU DO THAT, MOM'LL CRY!
FUYUKI

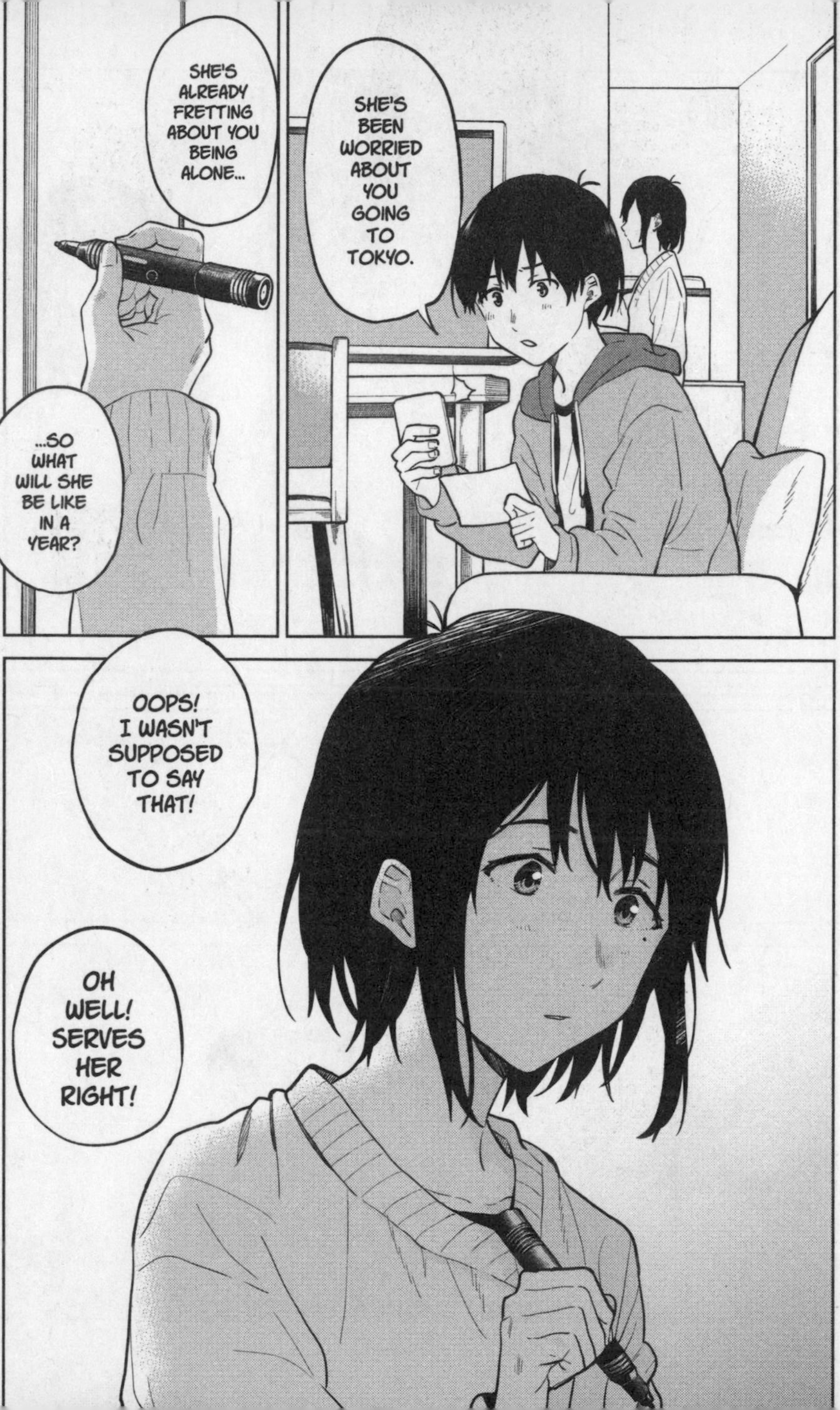
SHE'S BEEN WORRIED ABOUT YOU GOING TO TOKYO.
SHE'S ALREADY FRETTING ABOUT YOU BEING ALONE...
...SO WHAT WILL SHE BE LIKE IN A YEAR?
OOPS! I WASN'T SUPPOSED TO SAY THAT!
OH WELL! SERVES HER RIGHT!

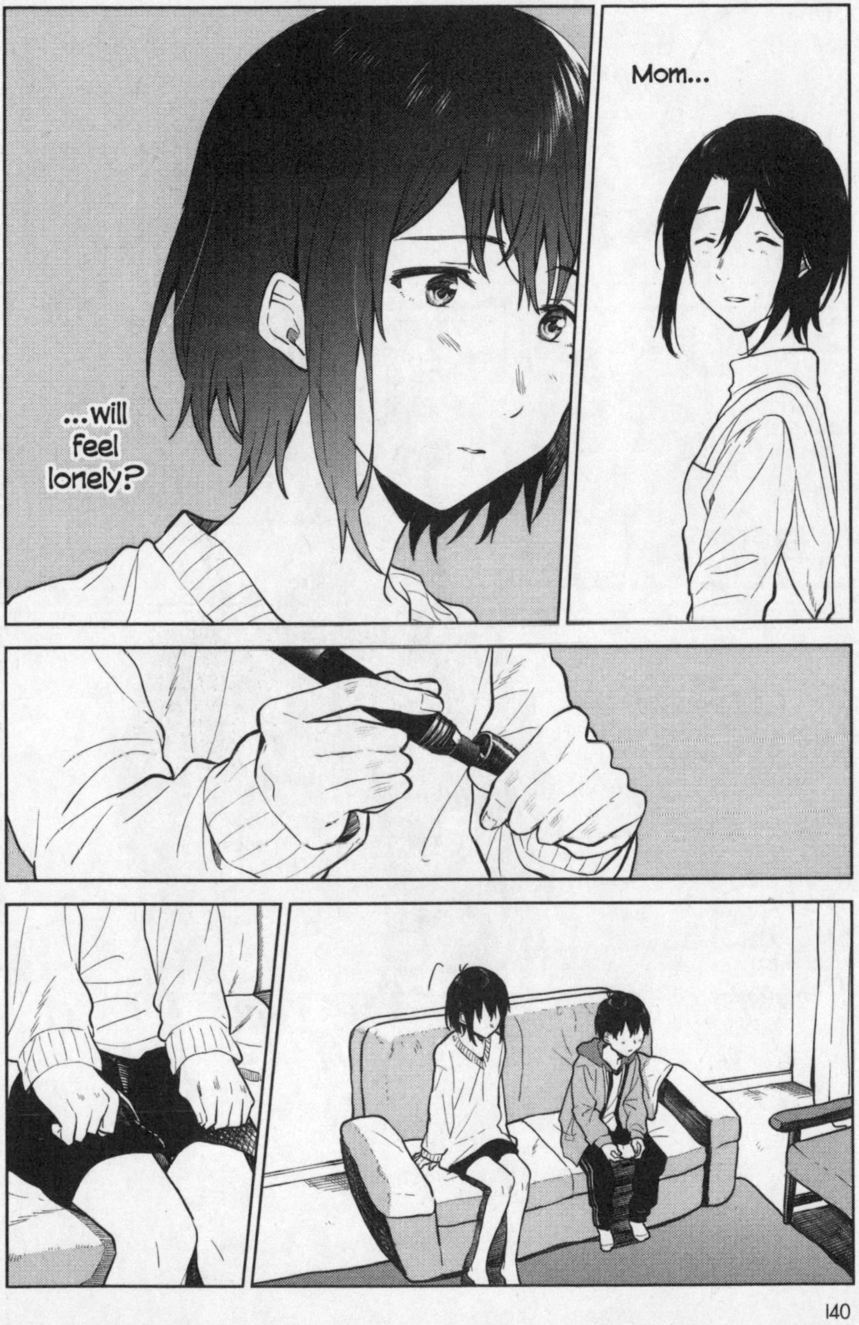
Mom...
...will feel lonely?

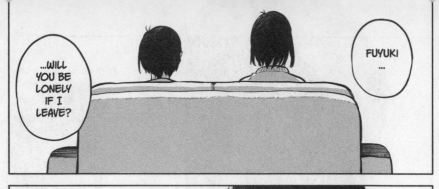

...WILL YOU BE LONELY IF I LEAVE?

FUYUKI
...

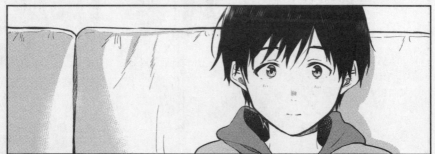

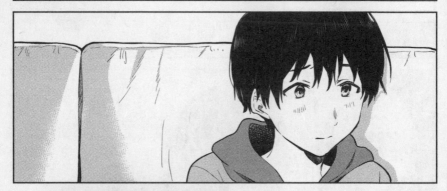

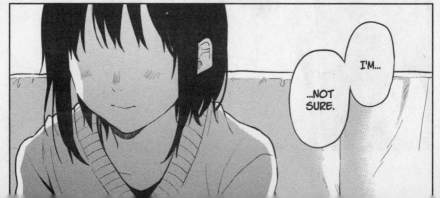

I'M...

...NOT SURE.

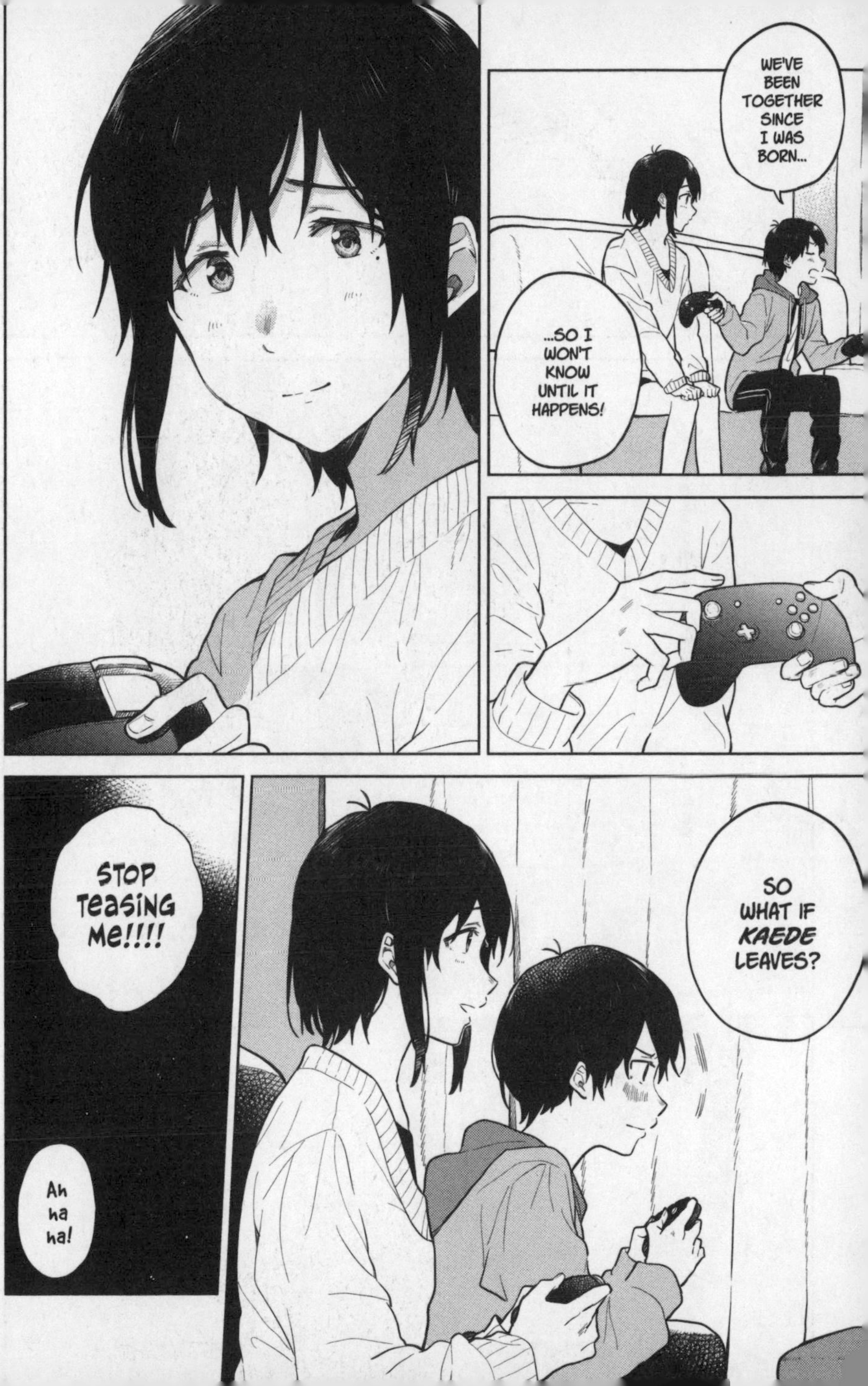
WE'VE BEEN TOGETHER SINCE I WAS BORN...
...SO I WON'T KNOW UNTIL IT HAPPENS!
SO WHAT IF KAEDE LEAVES?
STOP TEASING ME!!!!
Ah ha ha!

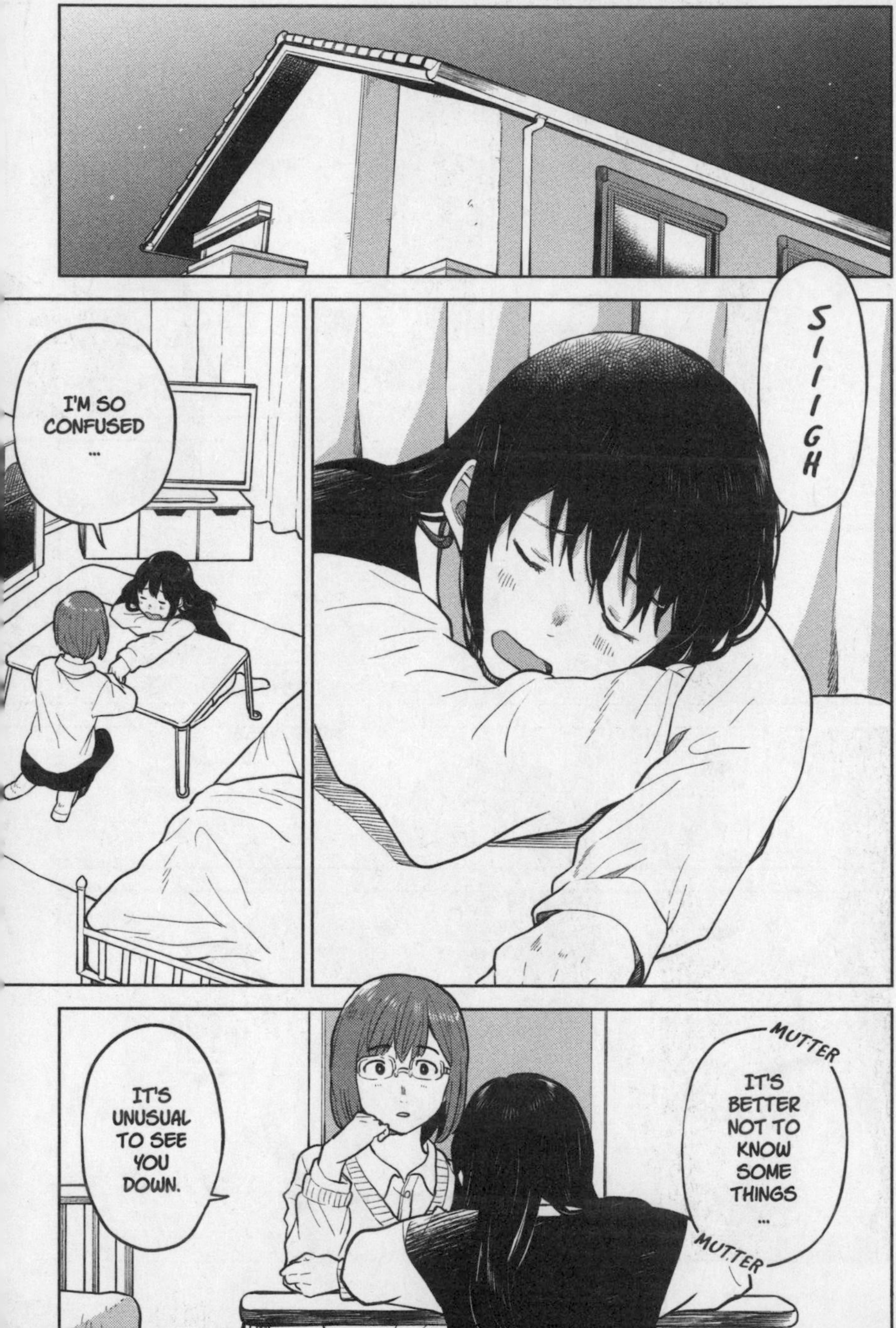
SIIIGH
I'M SO CONFUSED ...
MUTTER
IT'S BETTER NOT TO KNOW SOME THINGS ...
MUTTER
IT'S UNUSUAL TO SEE YOU DOWN.

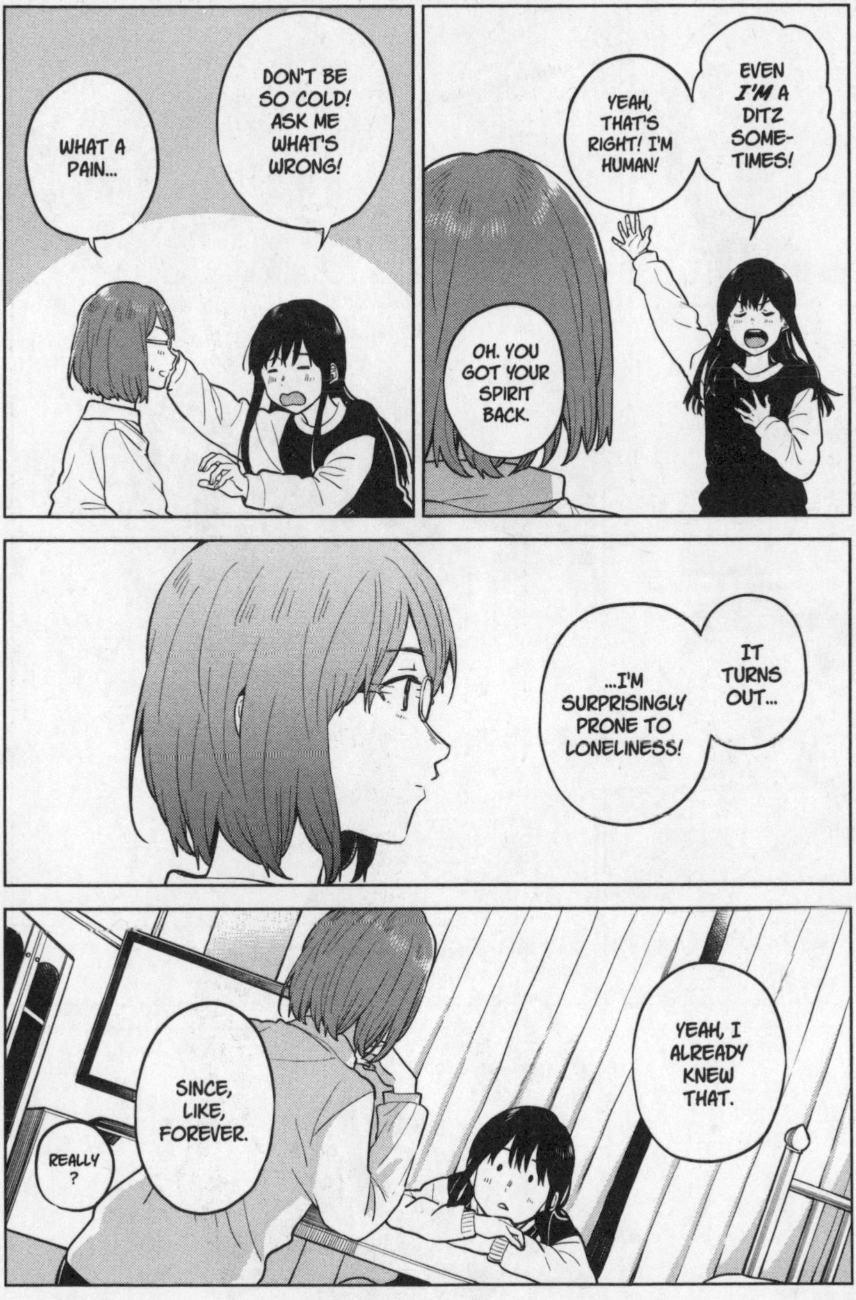
EVEN *I'M* A DITZ SOME-TIMES!
YEAH, THAT'S RIGHT! I'M HUMAN!
OH. YOU GOT YOUR SPIRIT BACK.
DON'T BE SO COLD! ASK ME WHAT'S WRONG!
WHAT A PAIN...
IT TURNS OUT...
...I'M SURPRISINGLY PRONE TO LONELINESS!
YEAH, I ALREADY KNEW THAT.
SINCE, LIKE, FOREVER.
REALLY?

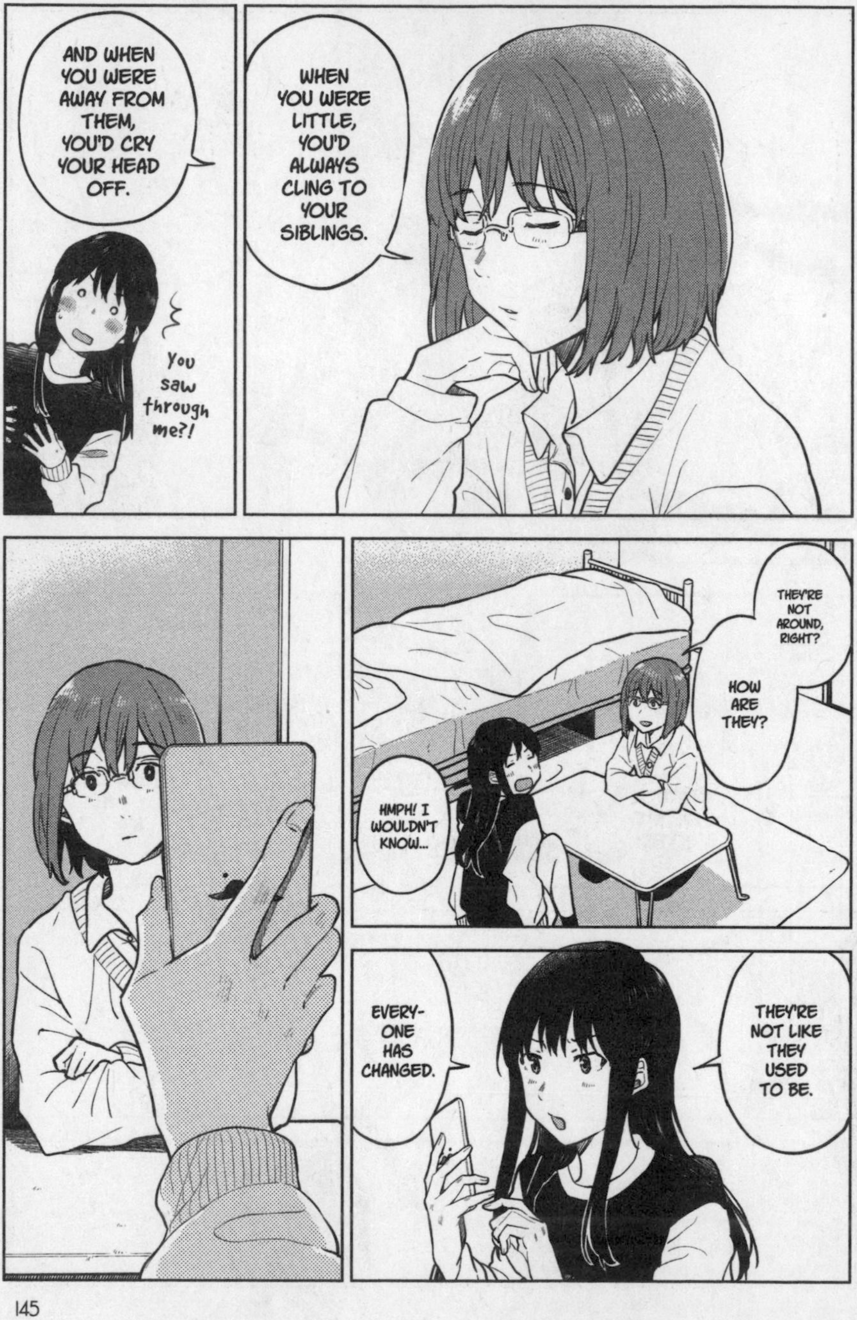
WHEN YOU WERE LITTLE, YOU'D ALWAYS CLING TO YOUR SIBLINGS.
AND WHEN YOU WERE AWAY FROM THEM, YOU'D CRY YOUR HEAD OFF.
You saw through me?!
THEY'RE NOT AROUND, RIGHT?
HOW ARE THEY?
HMPH! I WOULDN'T KNOW...
THEY'RE NOT LIKE THEY USED TO BE.
EVERY-ONE HAS CHANGED.

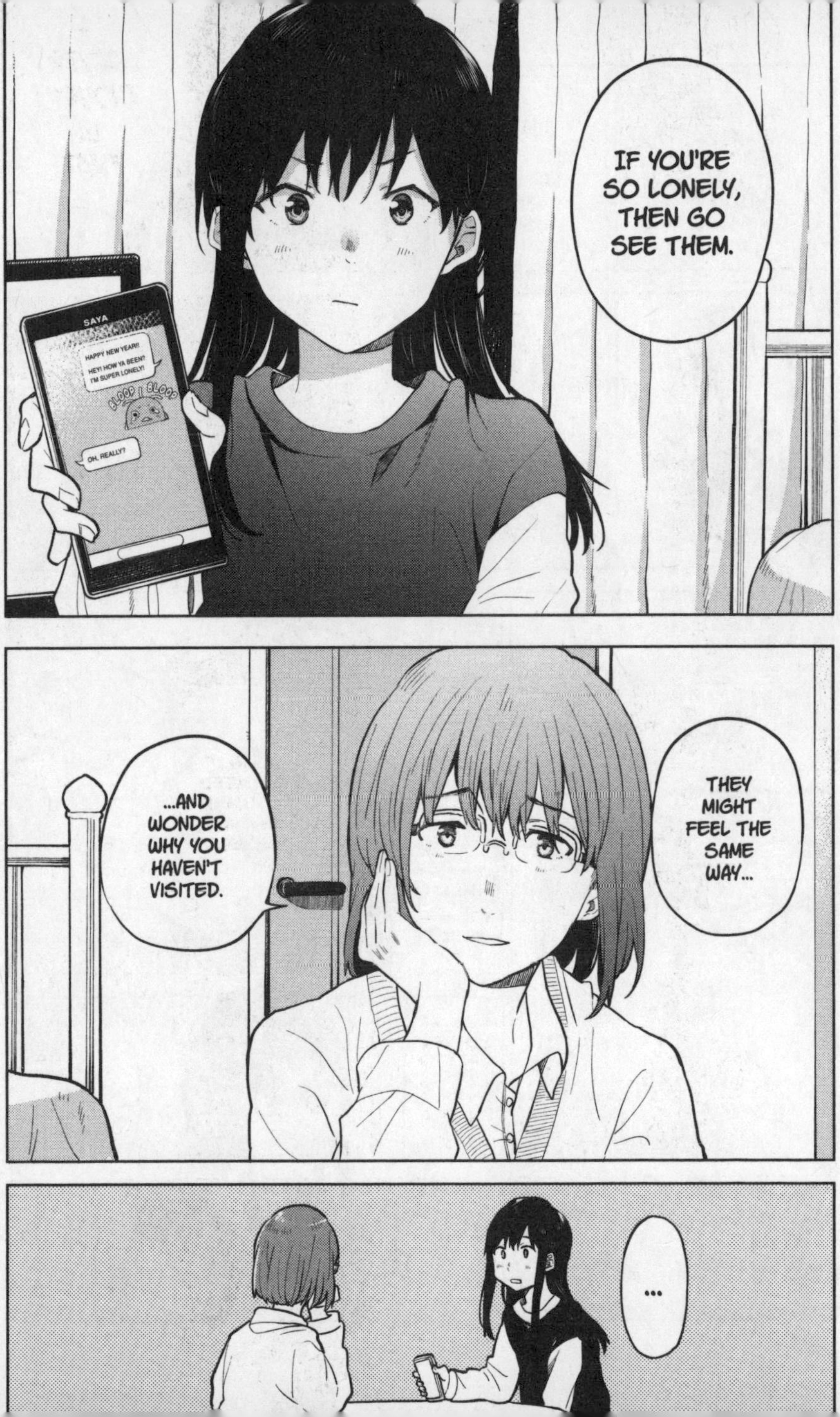
IF YOU'RE SO LONELY, THEN GO SEE THEM.
SAYA
HAPPY NEW YEAR!!
HEY! HOW YA BEEN? I'M SUPER LONELY!
BLOOP! BLOOP!
OH, REALLY?
THEY MIGHT FEEL THE SAME WAY...
...AND WONDER WHY YOU HAVEN'T VISITED.
...

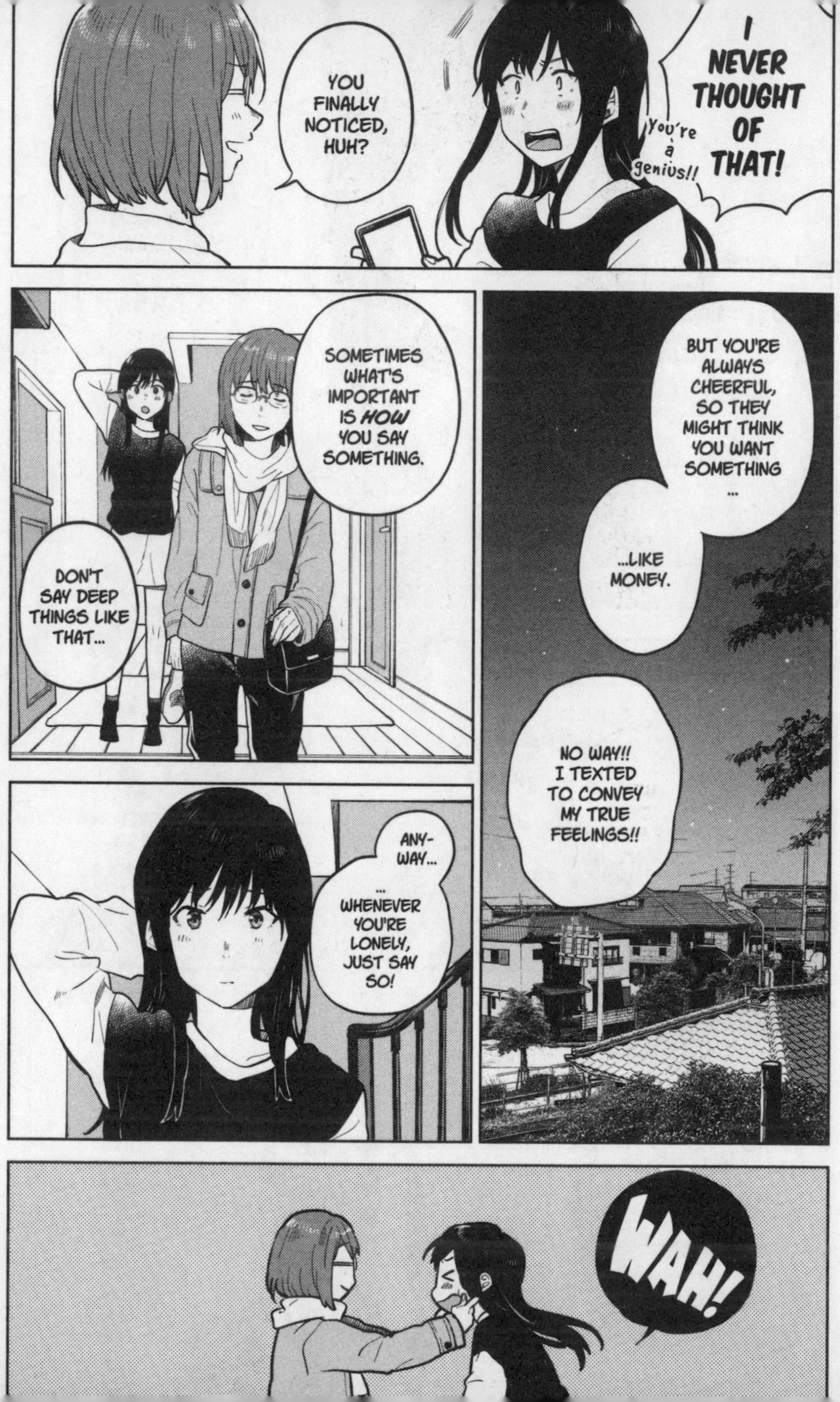
I NEVER THOUGHT OF THAT!
You're a genius!!
YOU FINALLY NOTICED, HUH?
BUT YOU'RE ALWAYS CHEERFUL, SO THEY MIGHT THINK YOU WANT SOMETHING ...
...LIKE MONEY.
NO WAY!! I TEXTED TO CONVEY MY TRUE FEELINGS!!
SOMETIMES WHAT'S IMPORTANT IS *HOW* YOU SAY SOMETHING.
DON'T SAY DEEP THINGS LIKE THAT...
ANY-WAY...
... WHENEVER YOU'RE LONELY, JUST SAY SO!
WAH!

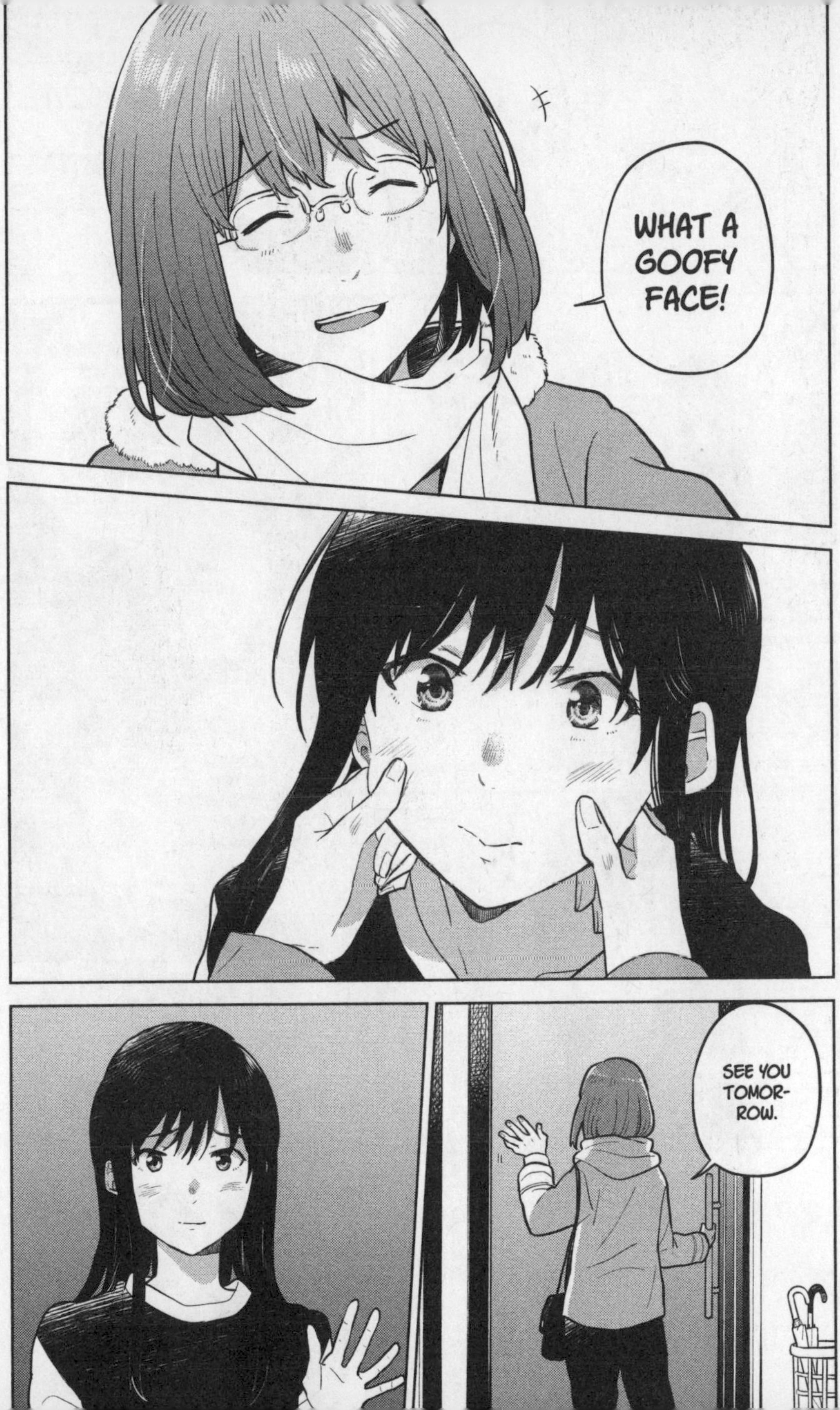
WHAT A GOOFY FACE!
SEE YOU TOMOR-ROW.

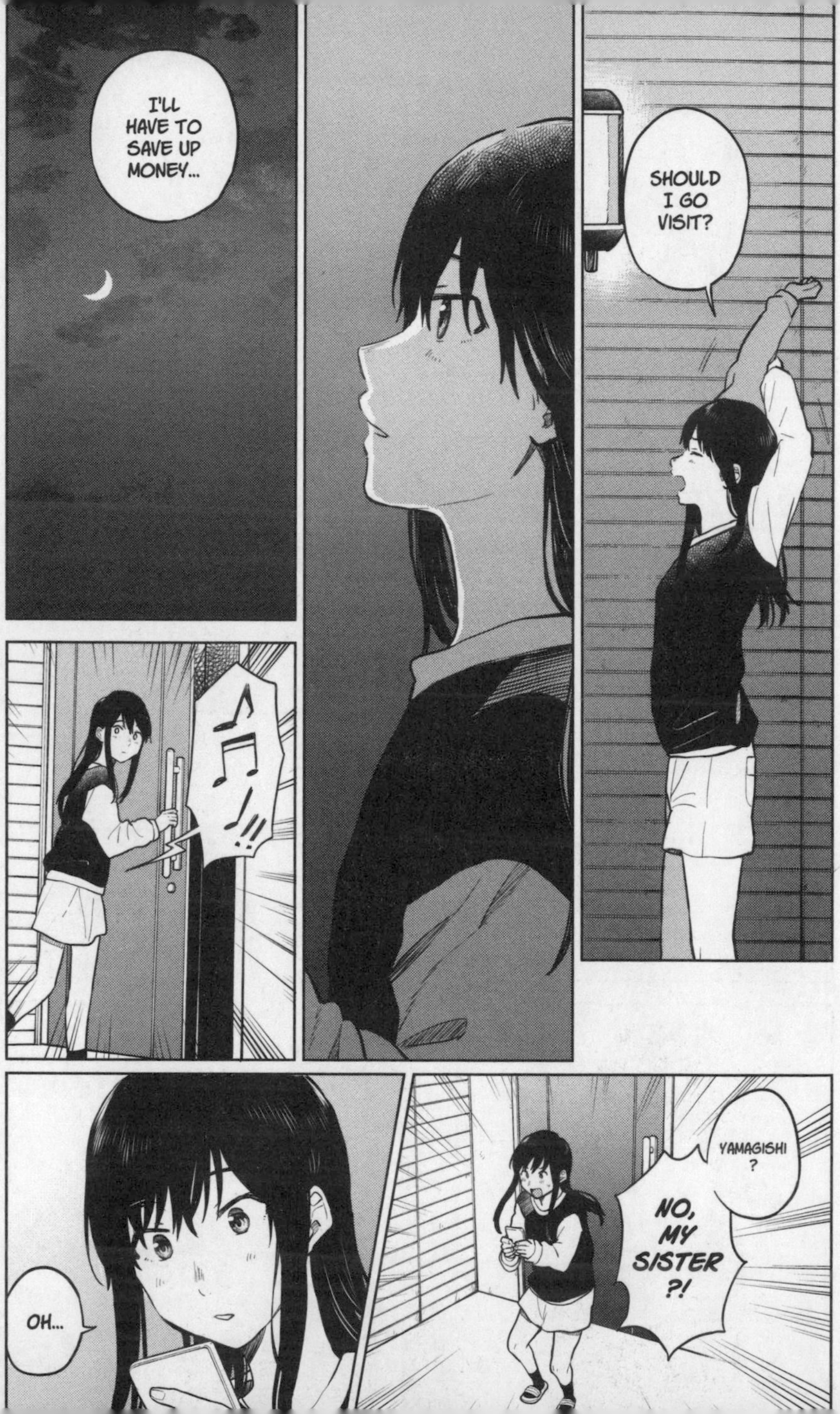
SHOULD I GO VISIT?
I'LL HAVE TO SAVE UP MONEY...
!!
YAMAGISHI?
NO, MY SISTER?!
OH...

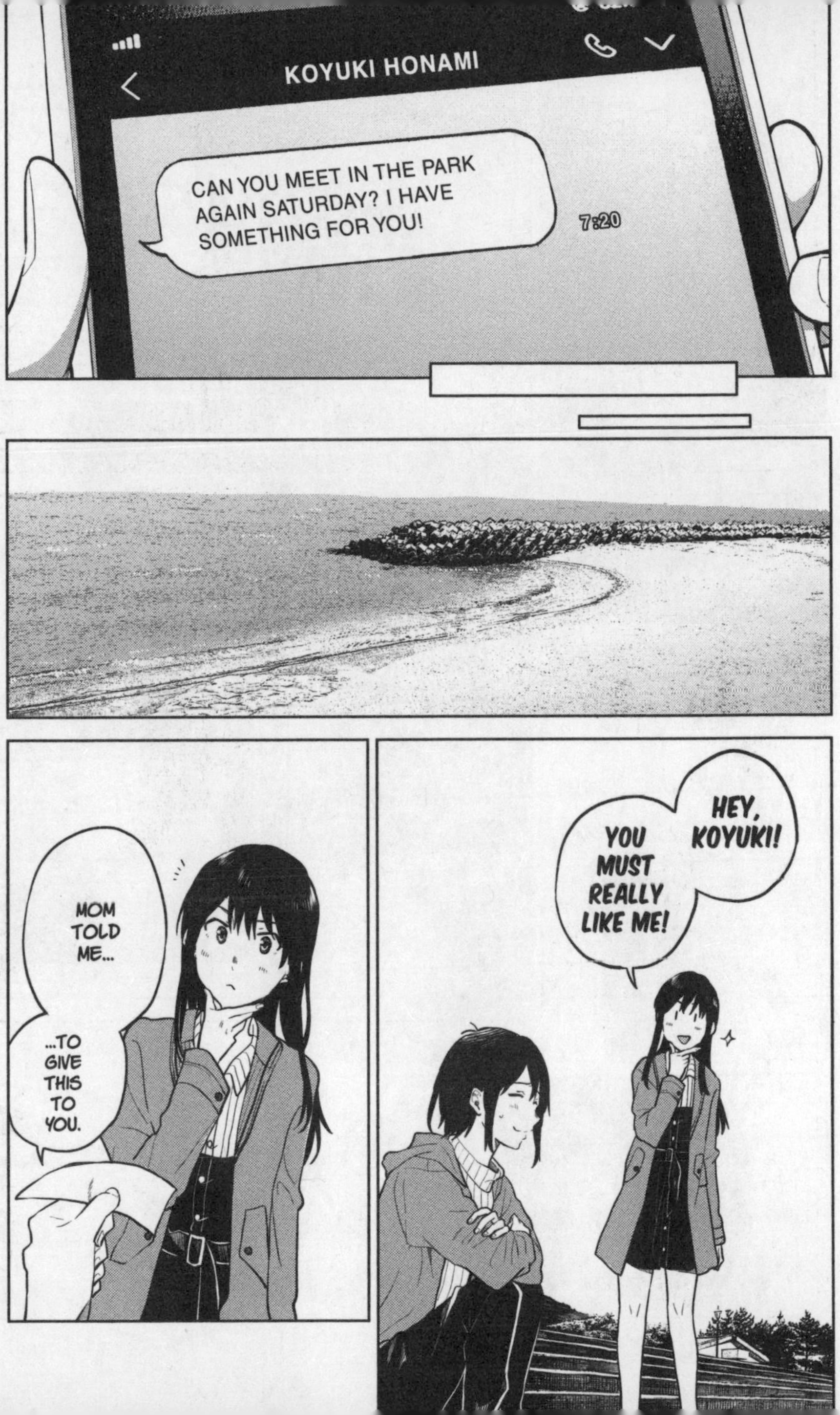
KOYUKI HONAMI
CAN YOU MEET IN THE PARK AGAIN SATURDAY? I HAVE SOMETHING FOR YOU!
7:20
HEY, KOYUKI!
YOU MUST REALLY LIKE ME!
MOM TOLD ME...
...TO GIVE THIS TO YOU.

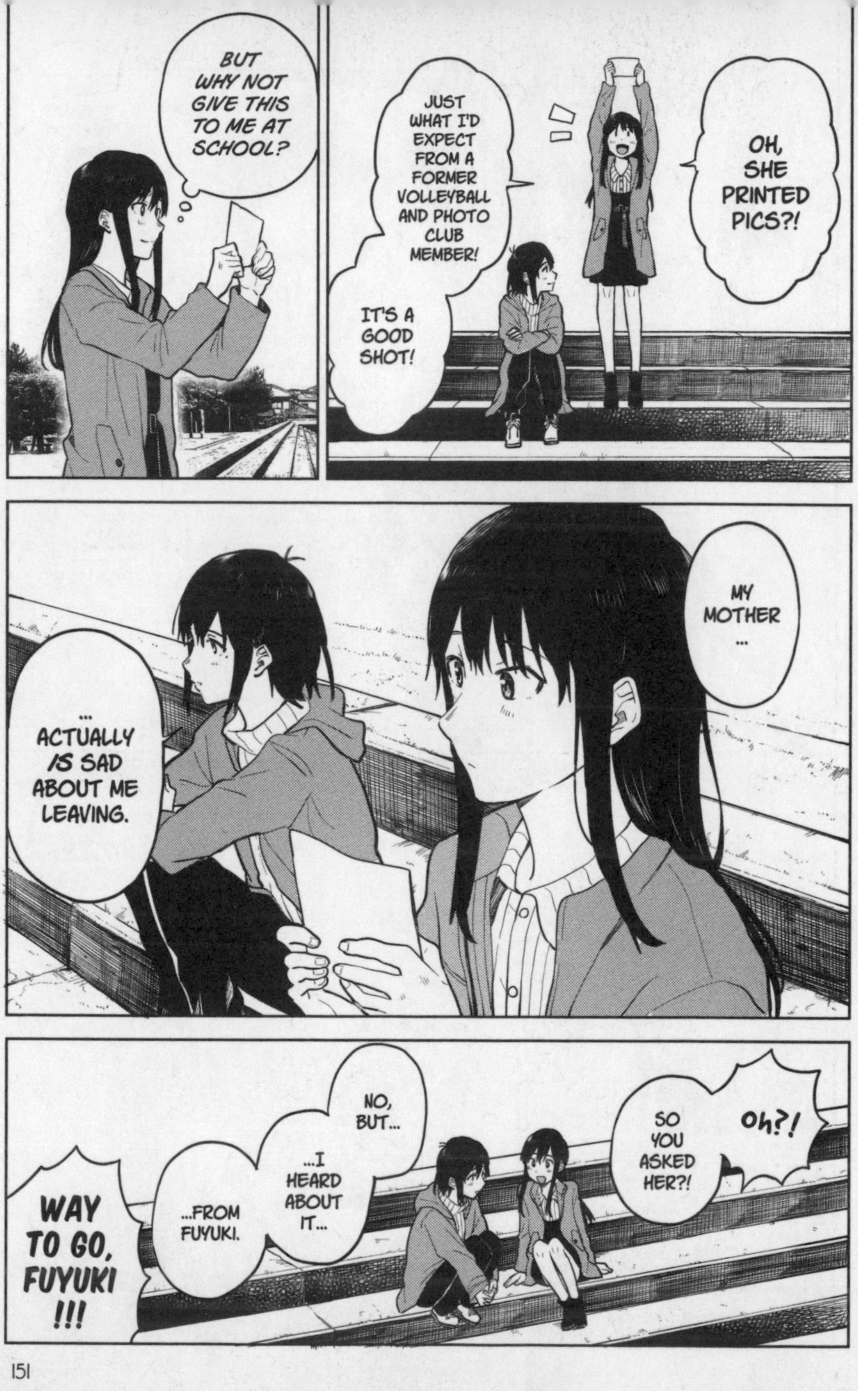
OH, SHE PRINTED PICS?!
JUST WHAT I'D EXPECT FROM A FORMER VOLLEYBALL AND PHOTO CLUB MEMBER!
IT'S A GOOD SHOT!
BUT WHY NOT GIVE THIS TO ME AT SCHOOL?
MY MOTHER...
...ACTUALLY IS SAD ABOUT ME LEAVING.
Oh?!
SO YOU ASKED HER?!
NO, BUT...
...I HEARD ABOUT IT...
...FROM FUYUKI.
WAY TO GO, FUYUKI!!!

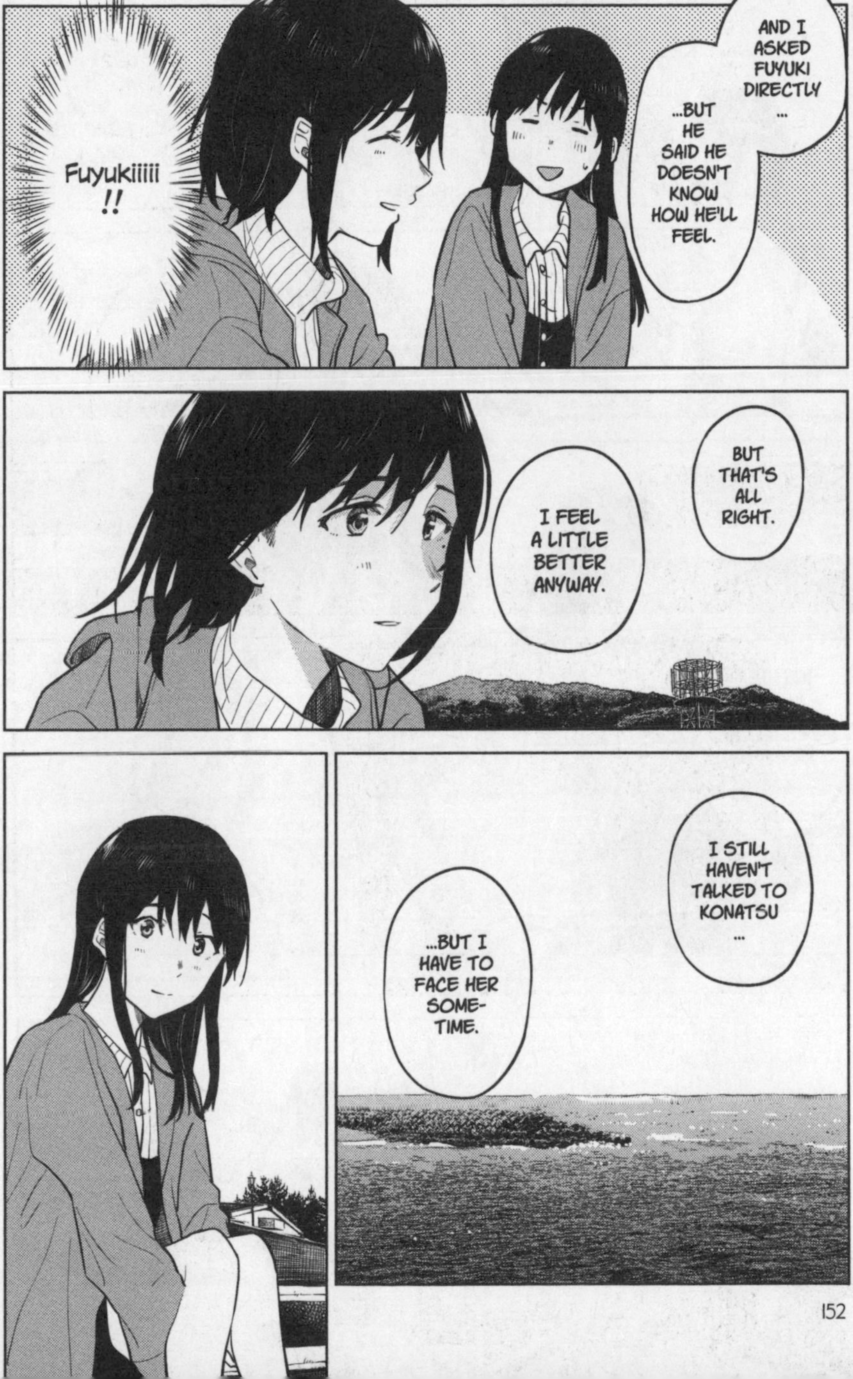
AND I ASKED FUYUKI DIRECTLY ...
...BUT HE SAID HE DOESN'T KNOW HOW HE'LL FEEL.
Fuyukiiiii !!
BUT THAT'S ALL RIGHT.
I FEEL A LITTLE BETTER ANYWAY.
I STILL HAVEN'T TALKED TO KONATSU ...
...BUT I HAVE TO FACE HER SOME-TIME.

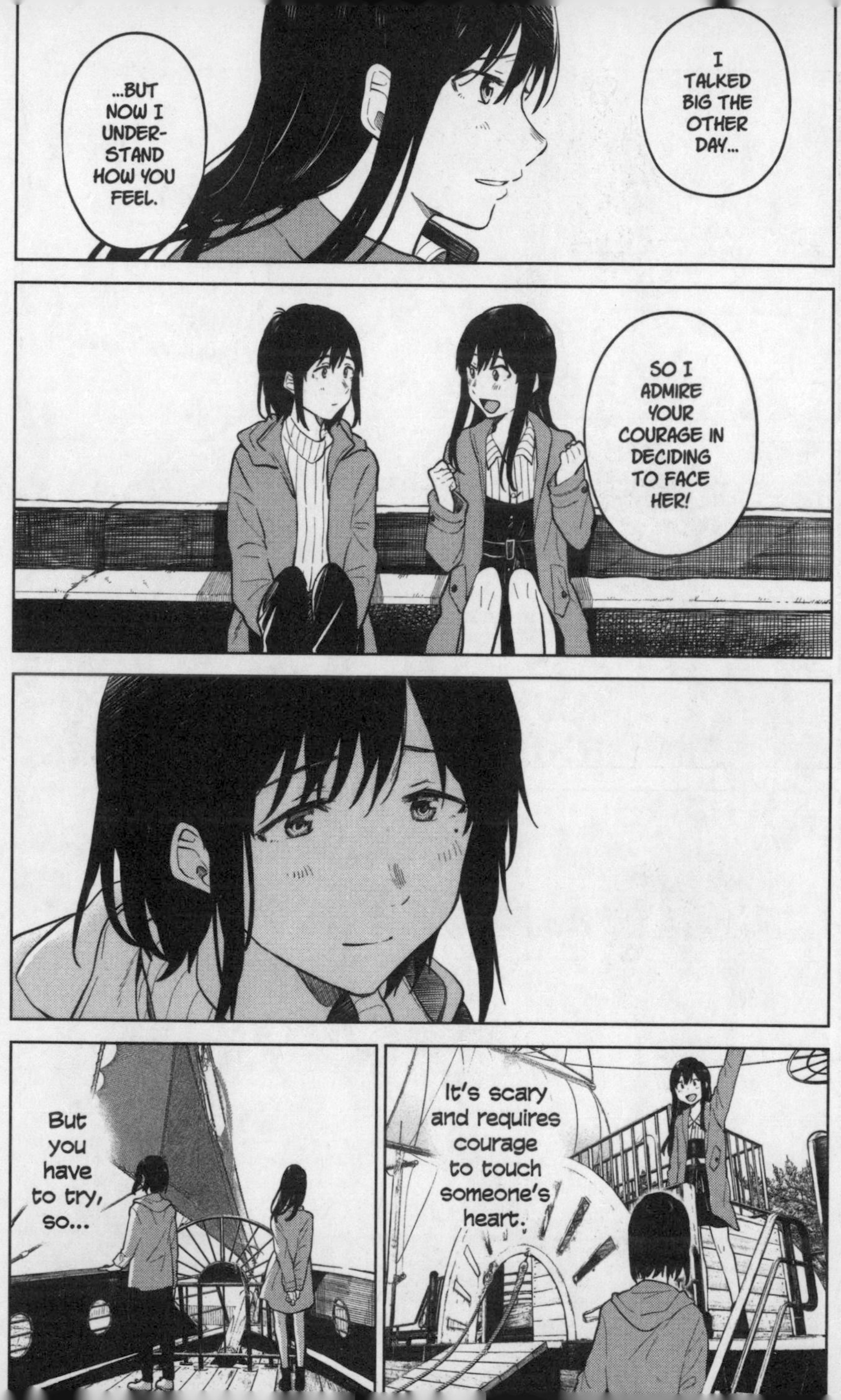
I TALKED BIG THE OTHER DAY...
...BUT NOW I UNDER-STAND HOW YOU FEEL.
SO I ADMIRE YOUR COURAGE IN DECIDING TO FACE HER!
It's scary and requires courage to touch someone's heart.
But you have to try, so...

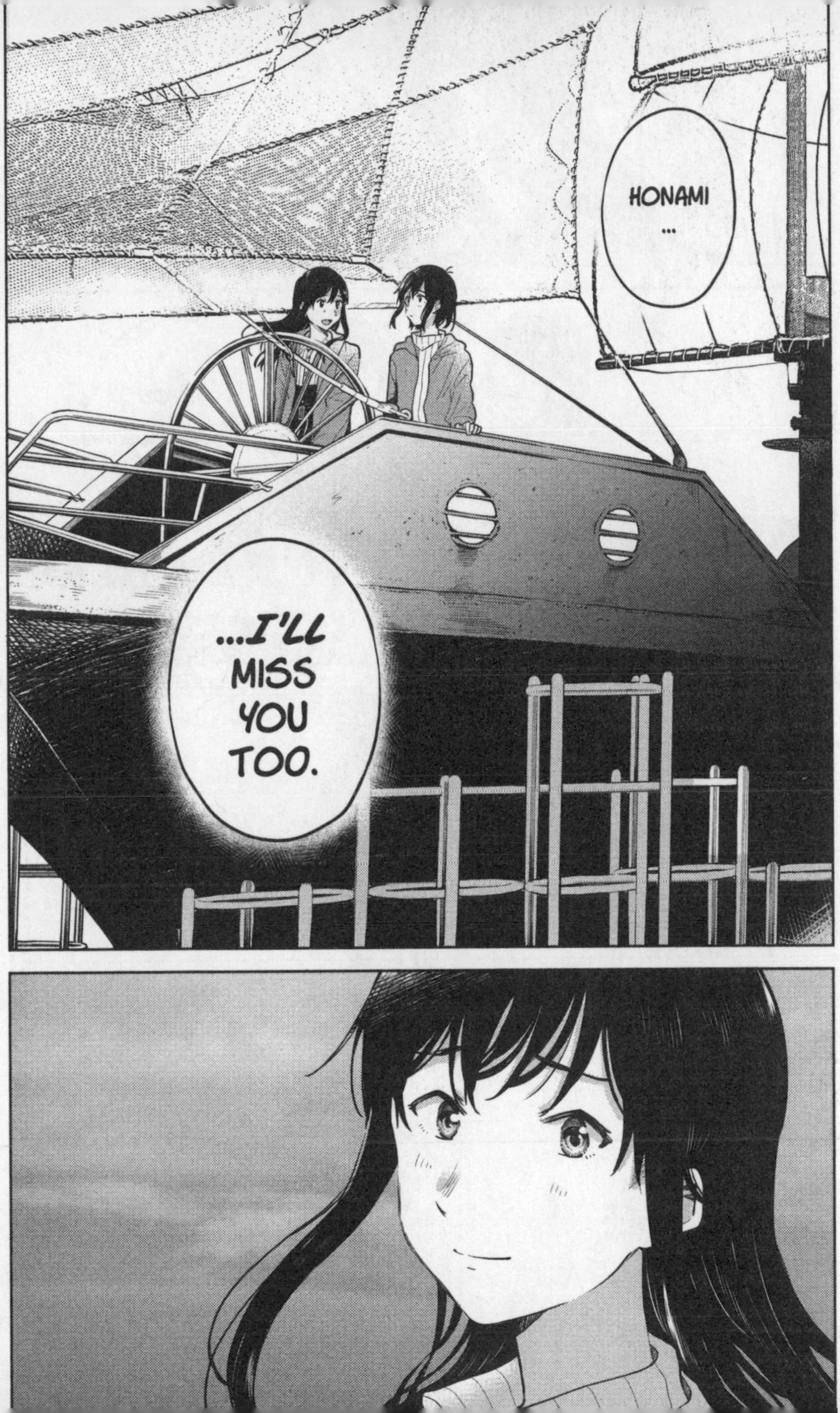
HONAMI
...
...I'LL MISS YOU TOO.

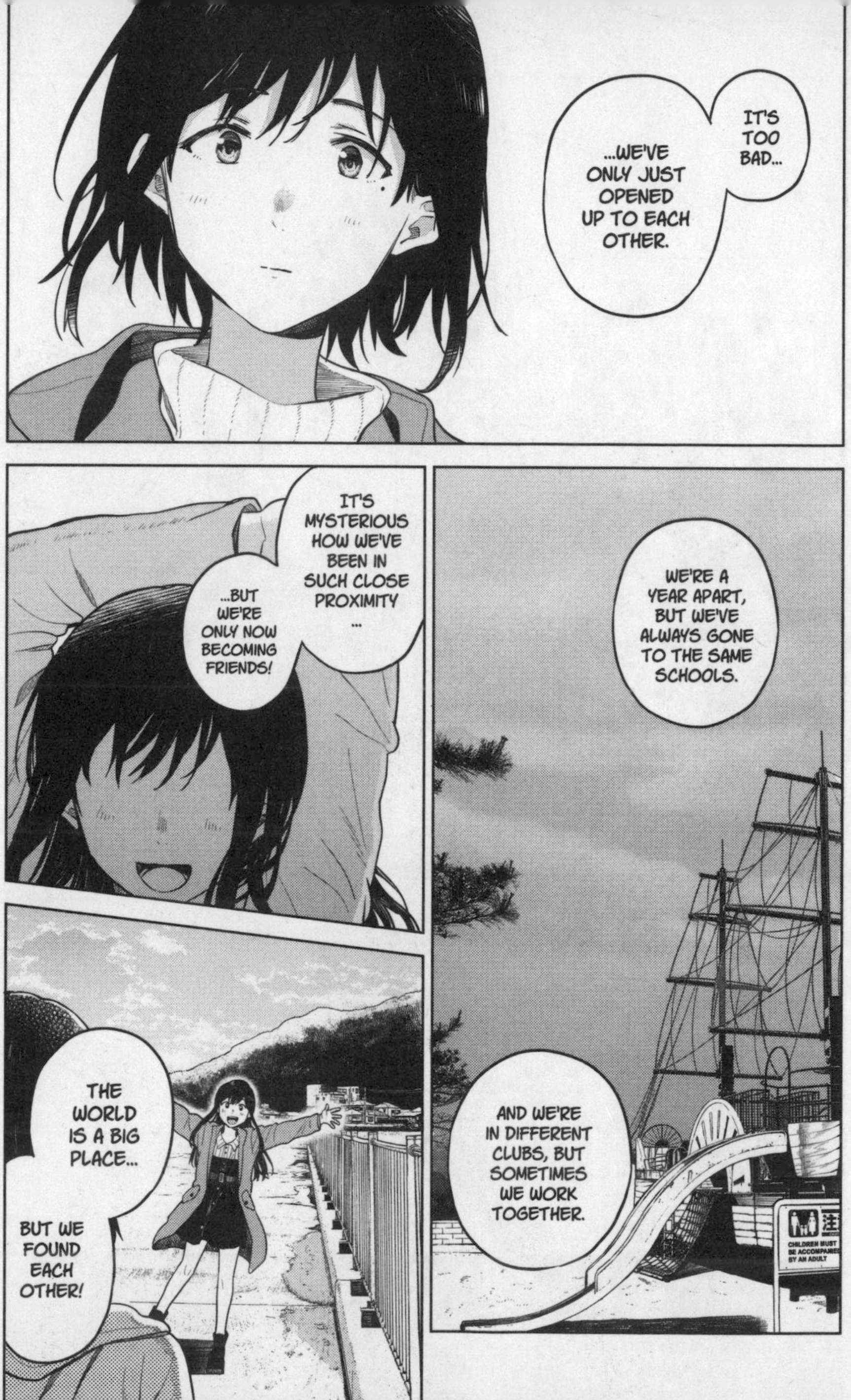
IT'S TOO BAD...
...WE'VE ONLY JUST OPENED UP TO EACH OTHER.
WE'RE A YEAR APART, BUT WE'VE ALWAYS GONE TO THE SAME SCHOOLS.
AND WE'RE IN DIFFERENT CLUBS, BUT SOMETIMES WE WORK TOGETHER.
CHILDREN MUST BE ACCOMPANIED BY AN ADULT
IT'S MYSTERIOUS HOW WE'VE BEEN IN SUCH CLOSE PROXIMITY ...
...BUT WE'RE ONLY NOW BECOMING FRIENDS!
THE WORLD IS A BIG PLACE...
BUT WE FOUND EACH OTHER!

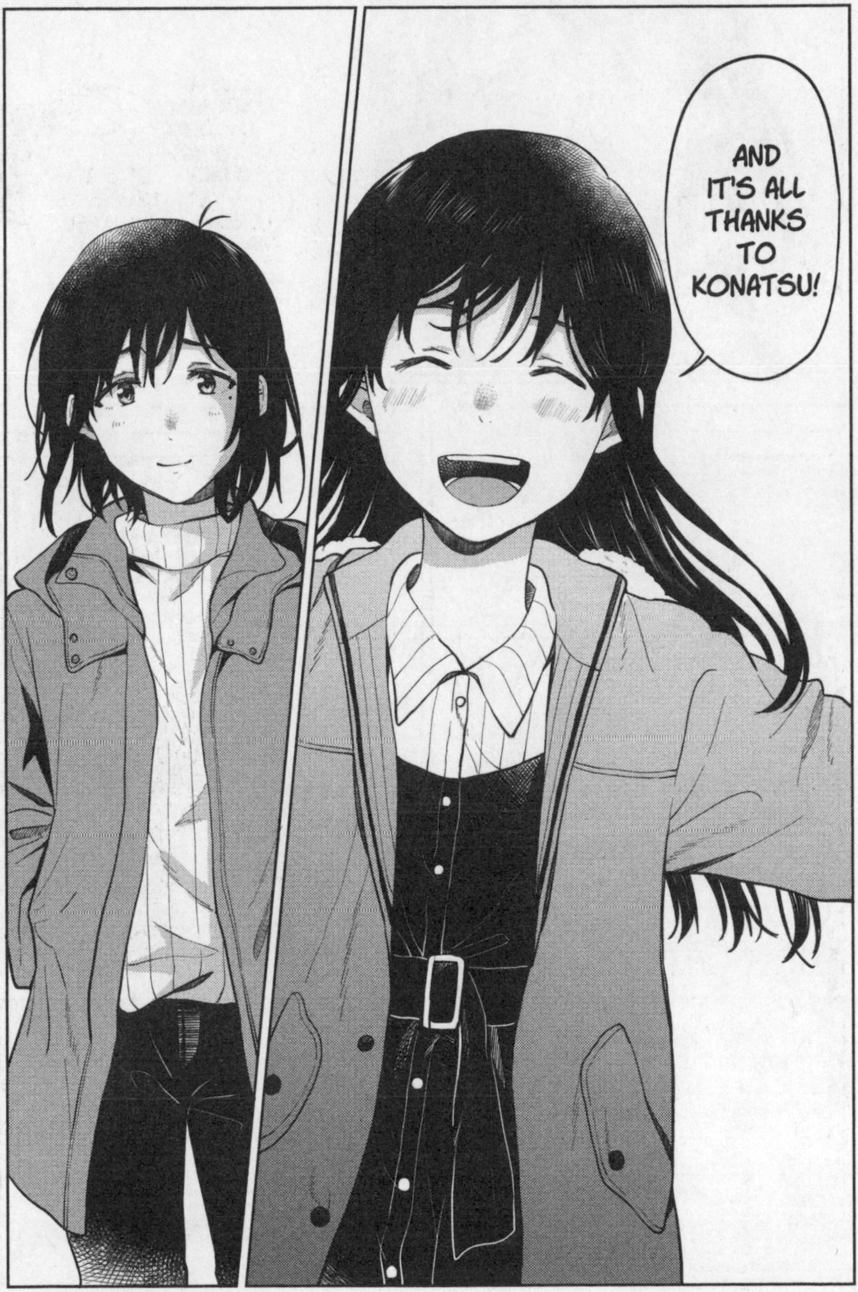
AND IT'S ALL THANKS TO KONATSU!

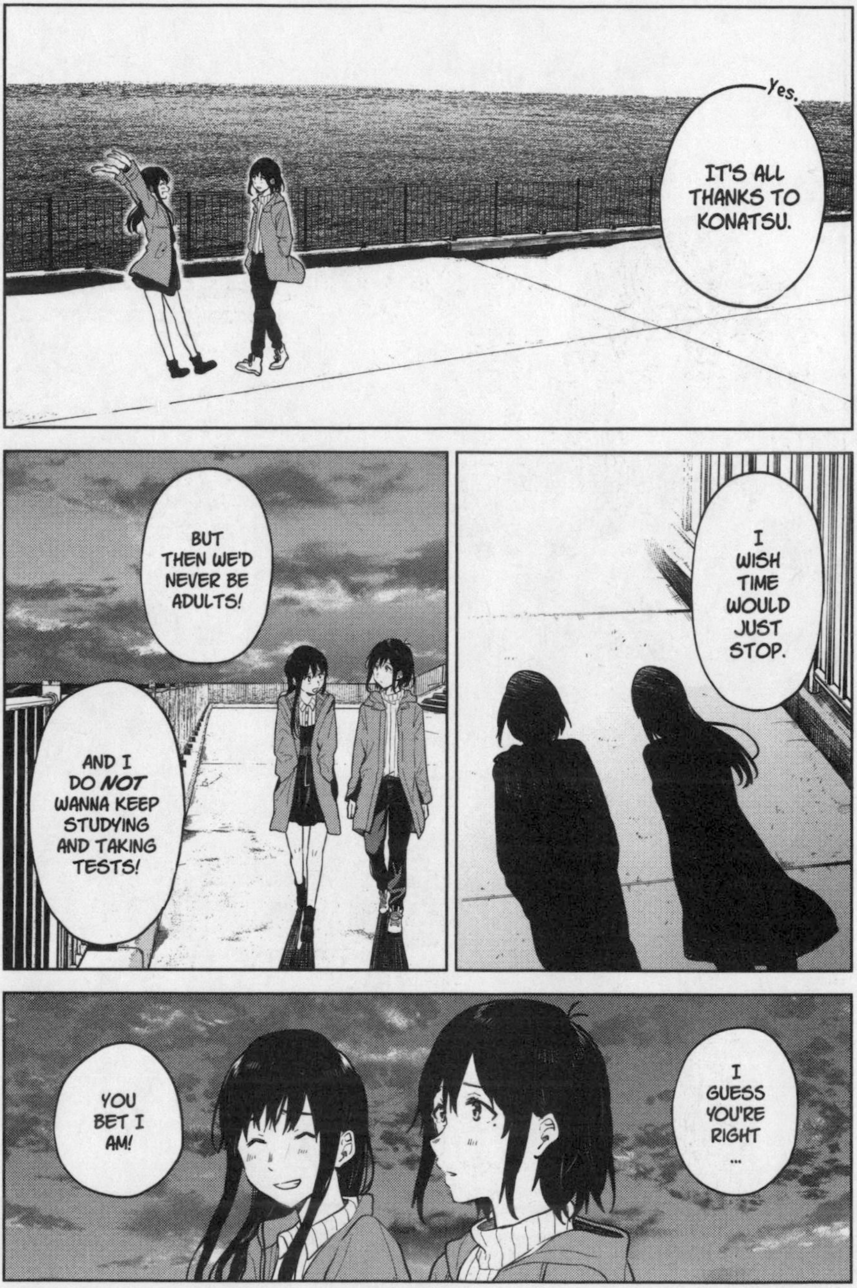
Yes.
IT'S ALL THANKS TO KONATSU.
I WISH TIME WOULD JUST STOP.
BUT THEN WE'D NEVER BE ADULTS!
AND I DO NOT WANNA KEEP STUDYING AND TAKING TESTS!
I GUESS YOU'RE RIGHT ...
YOU BET I AM!

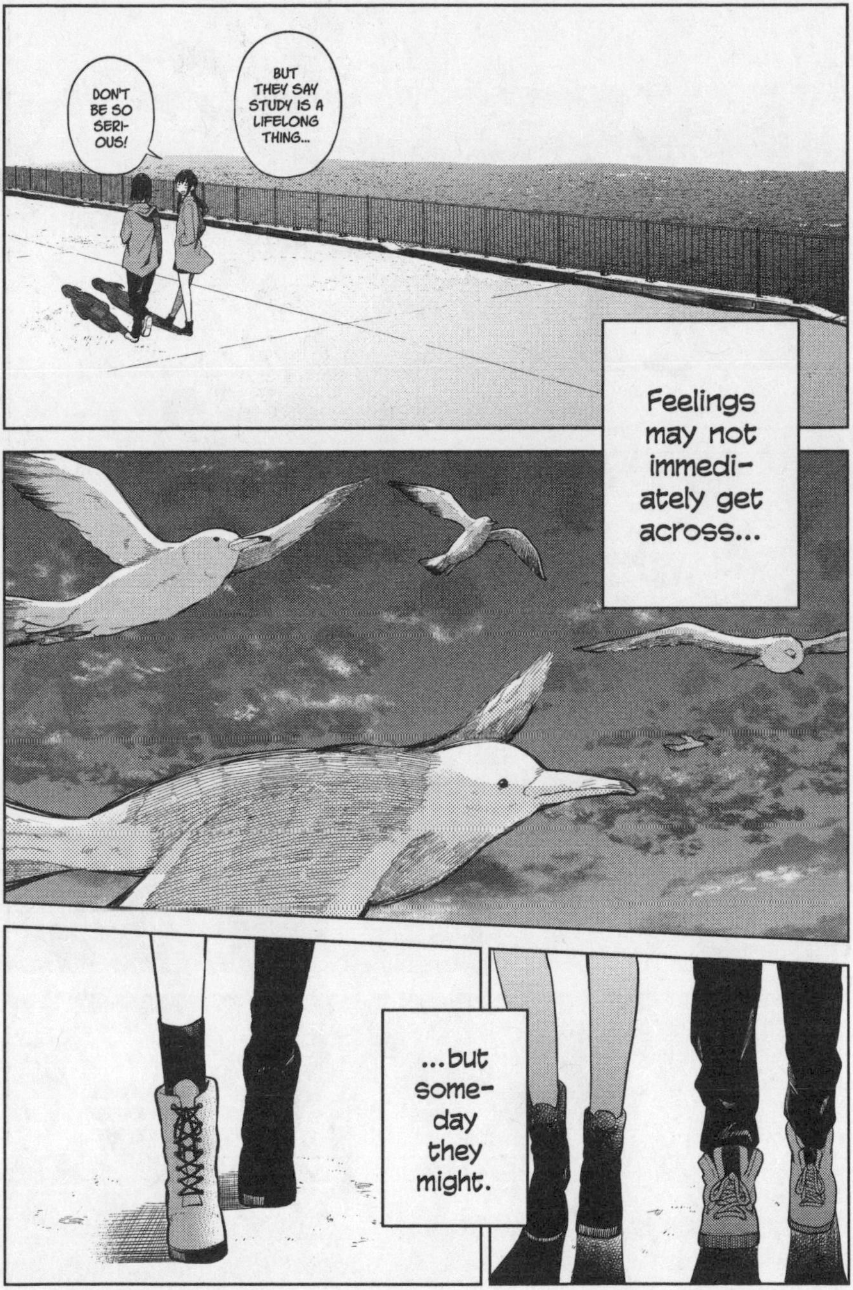
BUT THEY SAY STUDY IS A LIFELONG THING...
DON'T BE SO SERIOUS!
Feelings may not immediately get across...
...but someday they might.

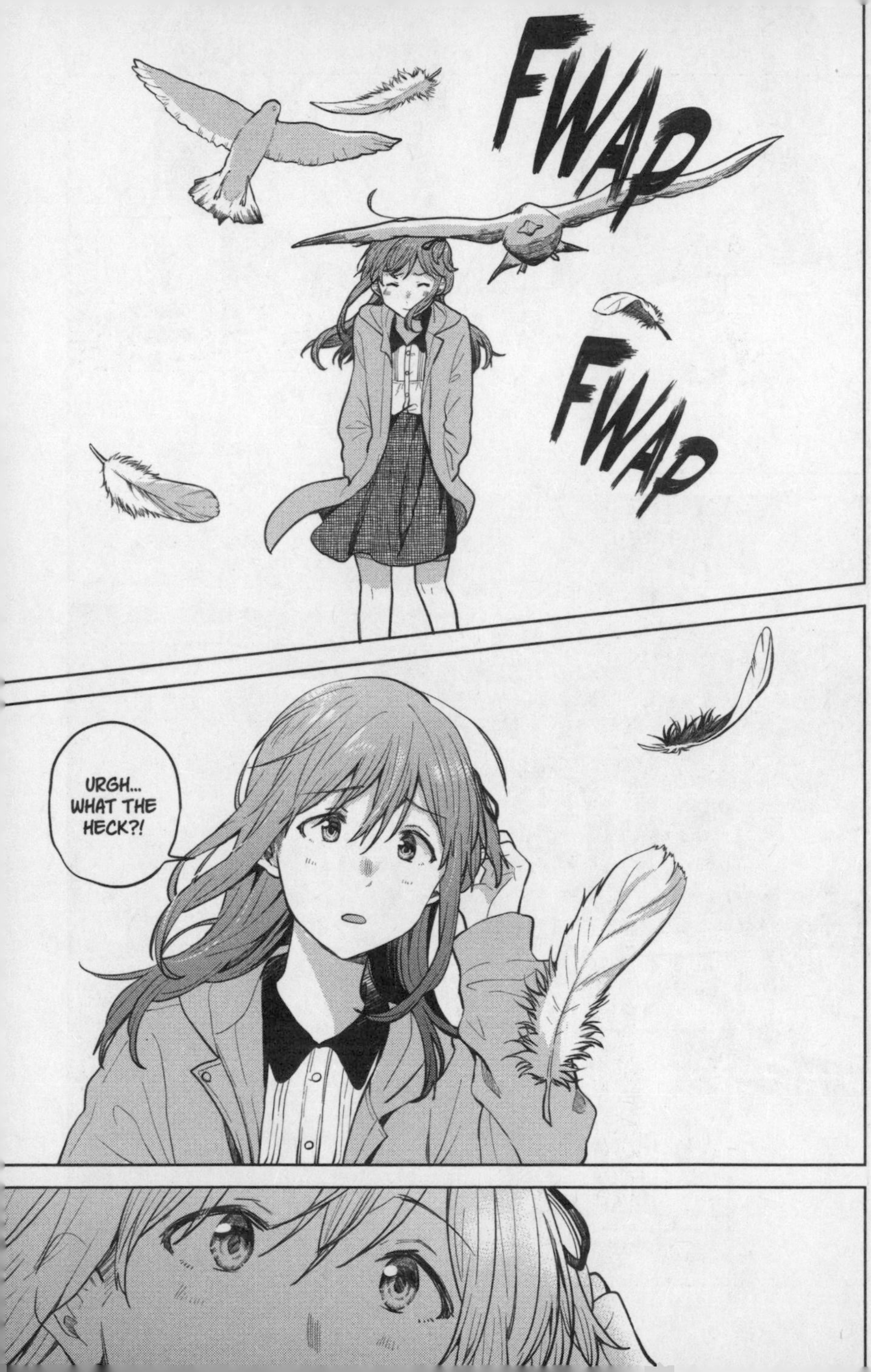
FWAP
FWAP
URGH... WHAT THE HECK?!

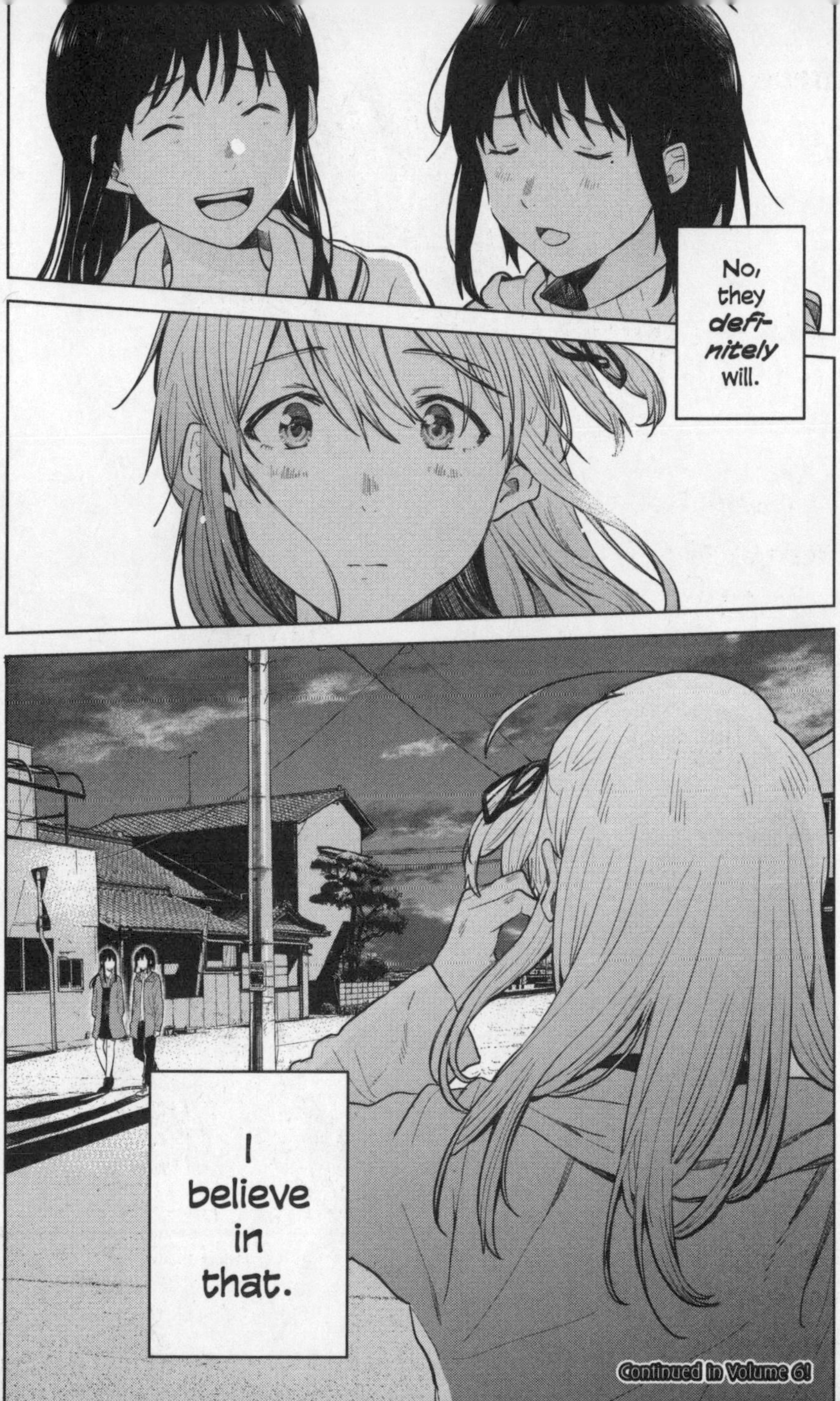
No, they *defi-nitely* will.
I believe in that.
Continued in Volume 6!

Afterword

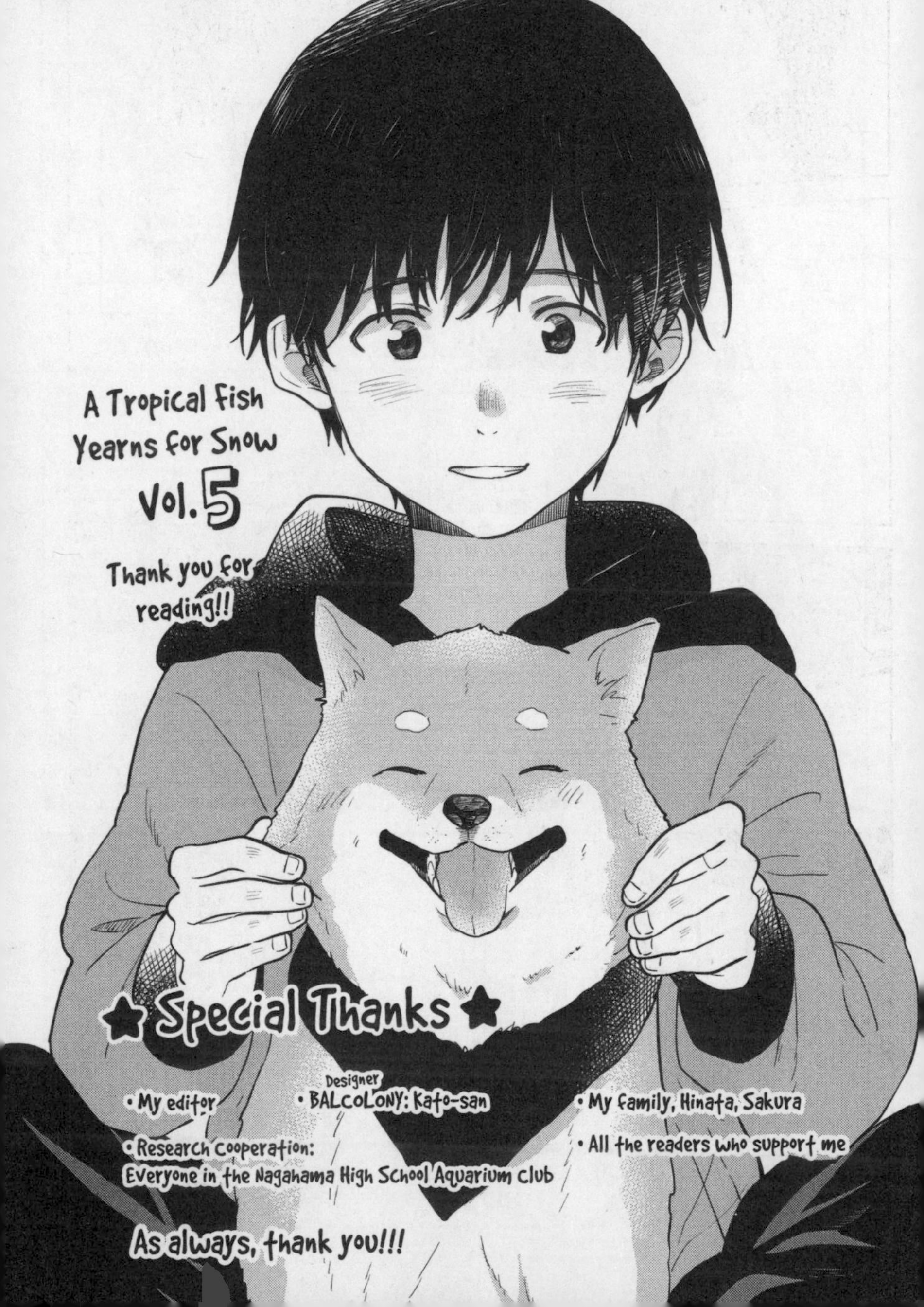
A Tropical Fish
Yearns for Snow
Vol. 5
Thank you for
reading!!
★ Special Thanks ★
• My editor
Designer
• BALCOLONY: Kato-san
• My family, Hinata, Sakura
• Research cooperation:
Everyone in the Nagahama High School Aquarium Club
• All the readers who support me
As always, thank you!!!

A Tropical Fish Yearns for Snow vol. 5 Bonus Manga Writer: Makoto Hagino

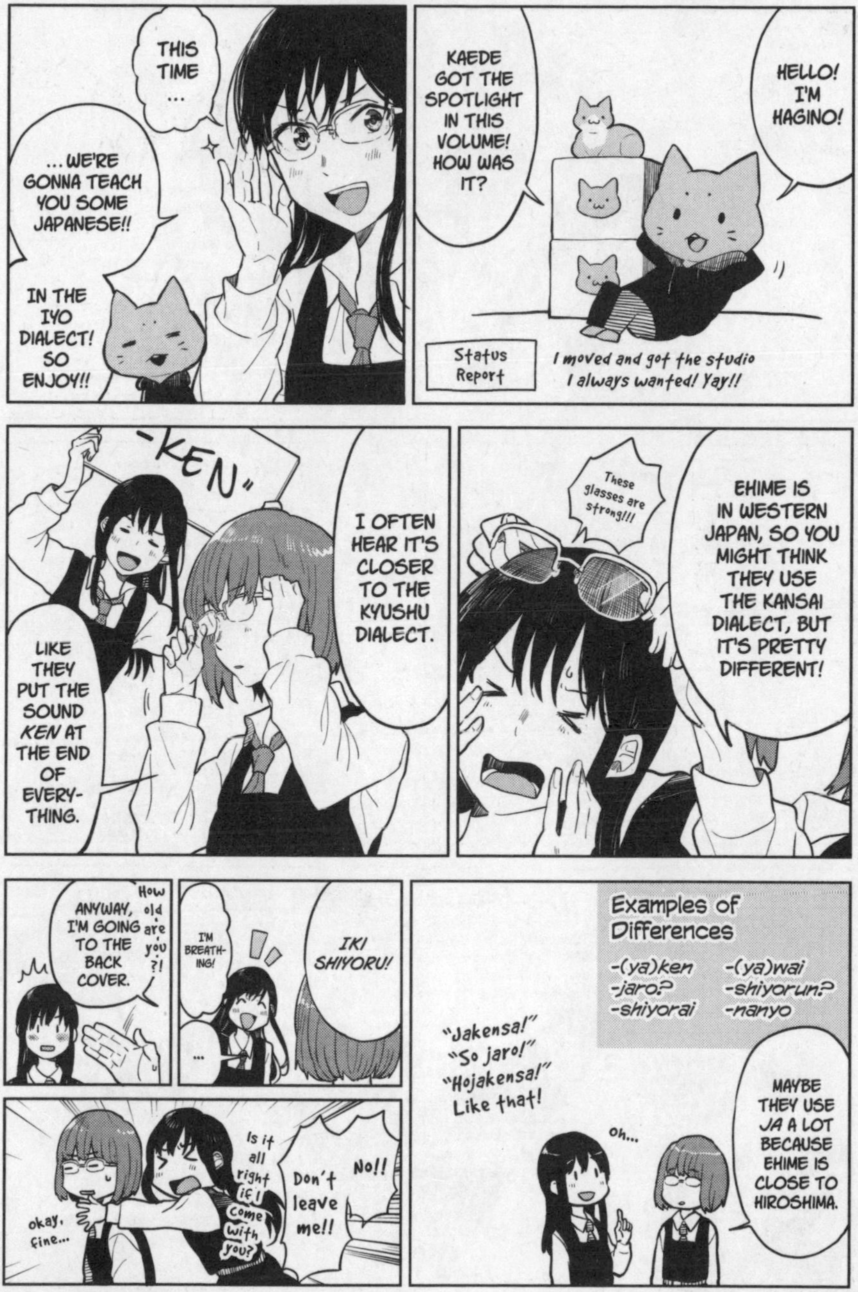
HELLO! I'M HAGINO!
KAEDE GOT THE SPOTLIGHT IN THIS VOLUME! HOW WAS IT?
Status Report
I moved and got the studio I always wanted! Yay!!
THIS TIME ...
... WE'RE GONNA TEACH YOU SOME JAPANESE!!
IN THE IYO DIALECT! SO ENJOY!!
EHIME IS IN WESTERN JAPAN, SO YOU MIGHT THINK THEY USE THE KANSAI DIALECT, BUT IT'S PRETTY DIFFERENT!
These glasses are strong!!!
I OFTEN HEAR IT'S CLOSER TO THE KYUSHU DIALECT.
-KEN"
LIKE THEY PUT THE SOUND KEN AT THE END OF EVERY-THING.
Examples of Differences
-(ya)ken -jaro? -shiyorai
-(ya)wai -shiyorun? -nanyo
MAYBE THEY USE JA A LOT BECAUSE EHIME IS CLOSE TO HIROSHIMA.
Oh...
"Jakensa!" "So jaro!" "Hojakensa!" Like that!
IKI SHIYORU!
I'M BREATHING!
...
ANYWAY, I'M GOING TO THE BACK COVER.
How old are you?!
No!!
Don't leave me!!
Is it all right if I come with you?
okay, fine...

▲ • Nani shiyorun? → Nani shiteruno? (What are you doing?)
• Ikan! → Dame! (No!)
• ottemo → itemo (if I be)
• Kaman? → Ii? (Is it all right?)

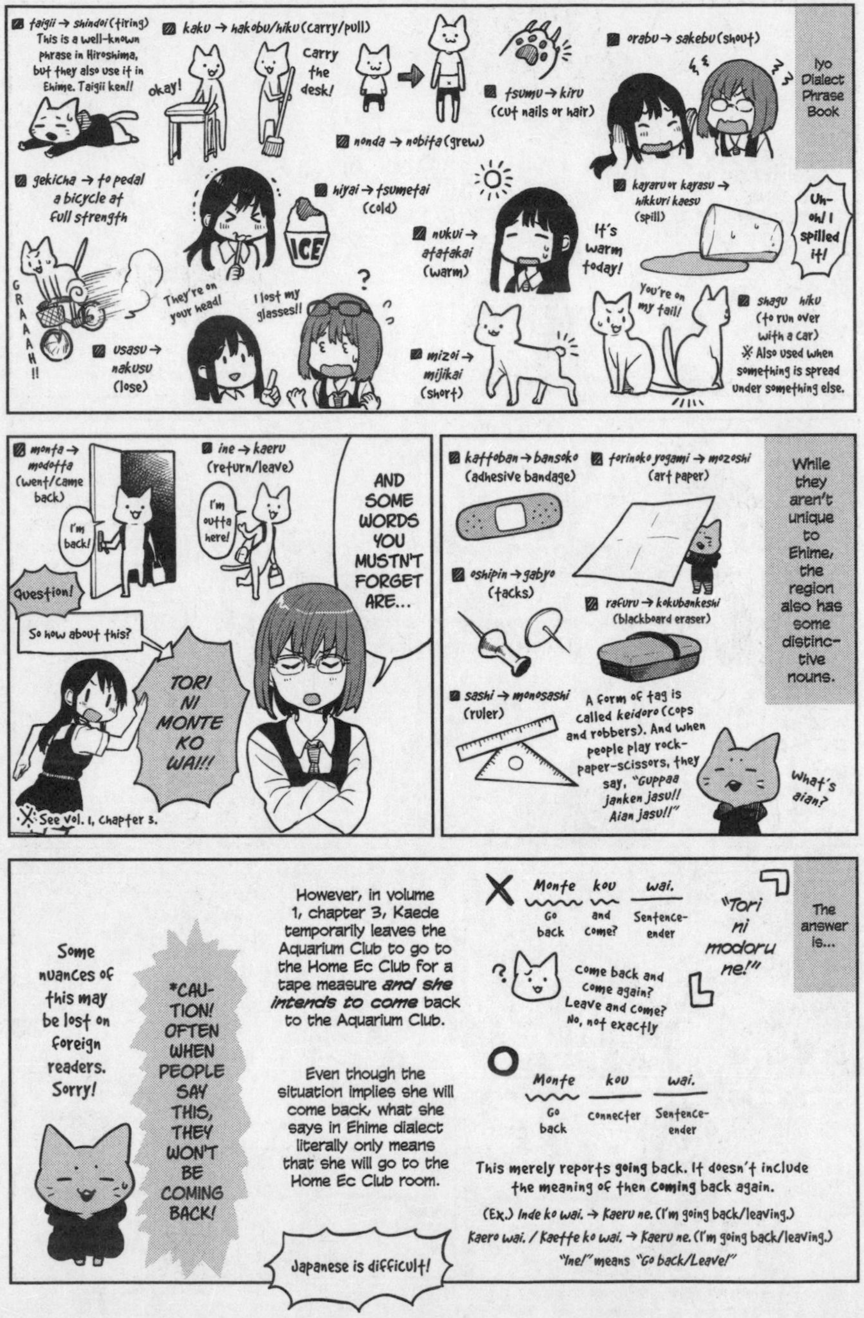
Iyo Dialect Phrase Book
orabu → sakebu (shout)
tsumu → kiru (cut nails or hair)
nonda → nobita (grew)
kaku → hakobu/hiku (carry/pull)
Carry the desk!
okay!
taigii → shindoi (tiring) This is a well-known phrase in Hiroshima, but they also use it in Ehime. Taigii ken!!
kayaru or kayasu → hikkuri kaesu (spill)
Uh-oh! I spilled it!
nukui → atatakai (warm)
It's warm today!
hiyai → tsumetai (cold)
ICE
gekicha → to pedal a bicycle at full strength
GRAAAAH!!
shagu hiku (to run over with a car) ※ Also used when something is spread under something else.
You're on my tail!
mizoi → mijikai (short)
?
I lost my glasses!!
They're on your head!
usasu → nakusu (lose)
While they aren't unique to Ehime, the region also has some distinctive nouns.
kattoban → bansoko (adhesive bandage)
torinoko yogami → mozoshi (art paper)
oshipin → gabyo (tacks)
rafuru → kokubankeshi (blackboard eraser)
sashi → monosashi (ruler)
A form of tag is called keidoro (cops and robbers). And when people play rock-paper-scissors, they say, "Guppaa janken jasu!! Aian jasu!!"
What's aian?
AND SOME WORDS YOU MUSTN'T FORGET ARE...
ine → kaeru (return/leave)
I'm outta here!
monta → modotta (went/came back)
I'm back!
Question!
So how about this?
TORI NI MONTE KO WAI!!!
※ See vol. 1, Chapter 3.
The answer is...
"Tori ni modoru ne!"
✕ Monte kou wai.
Go back
and come?
Sentence-ender
?
Come back and come again? Leave and come? No, not exactly
○ Monte kou wai.
Go back
Connecter
Sentence-ender
This merely reports going back. It doesn't include the meaning of then coming back again.
(Ex.) Inde ko wai. → Kaeru ne. (I'm going back/leaving.)
Kaero wai. / Kaette ko wai. → Kaeru ne. (I'm going back/leaving.)
"Ine!" means "Go back/Leave!"
However, in volume 1, chapter 3, Kaede temporarily leaves the Aquarium Club to go to the Home Ec Club for a tape measure and she intends to come back to the Aquarium Club.
Even though the situation implies she will come back, what she says in Ehime dialect literally only means that she will go to the Home Ec Club room.
Japanese is difficult!
*CAUTION! OFTEN WHEN PEOPLE SAY THIS, THEY WON'T BE COMING BACK!
Some nuances of this may be lost on foreign readers. Sorry!

A TROPICAL FISH YEARNS FOR SNOW
Vol. 5
VIZ Media Edition

STORY AND ART BY
MAKOTO HAGINO

English Translation & Adaptation/John Werry
Touch-Up Art & Lettering/Eve Grandt
Design/Yukiko Whitley
Editor/Pancha Diaz

NETTAIGYO WA YUKI NI KOGARERU Vol. 5
©Makoto Hagino 2019
First published in Japan in 2019 by KADOKAWA CORPORATION, Tokyo.
English translation rights arranged with KADOKAWA CORPORATION, Tokyo.

Printed in Canada

Published by VIZ Media, LLC
P.O. Box 77010
San Francisco, CA 94107

10 9 8 7 6 5 4 3 2 1
First printing, November 2020

viz.com

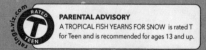

PARENTAL ADVISORY
A TROPICAL FISH YEARNS FOR SNOW is rated T
for Teen and is recommended for ages 13 and up.

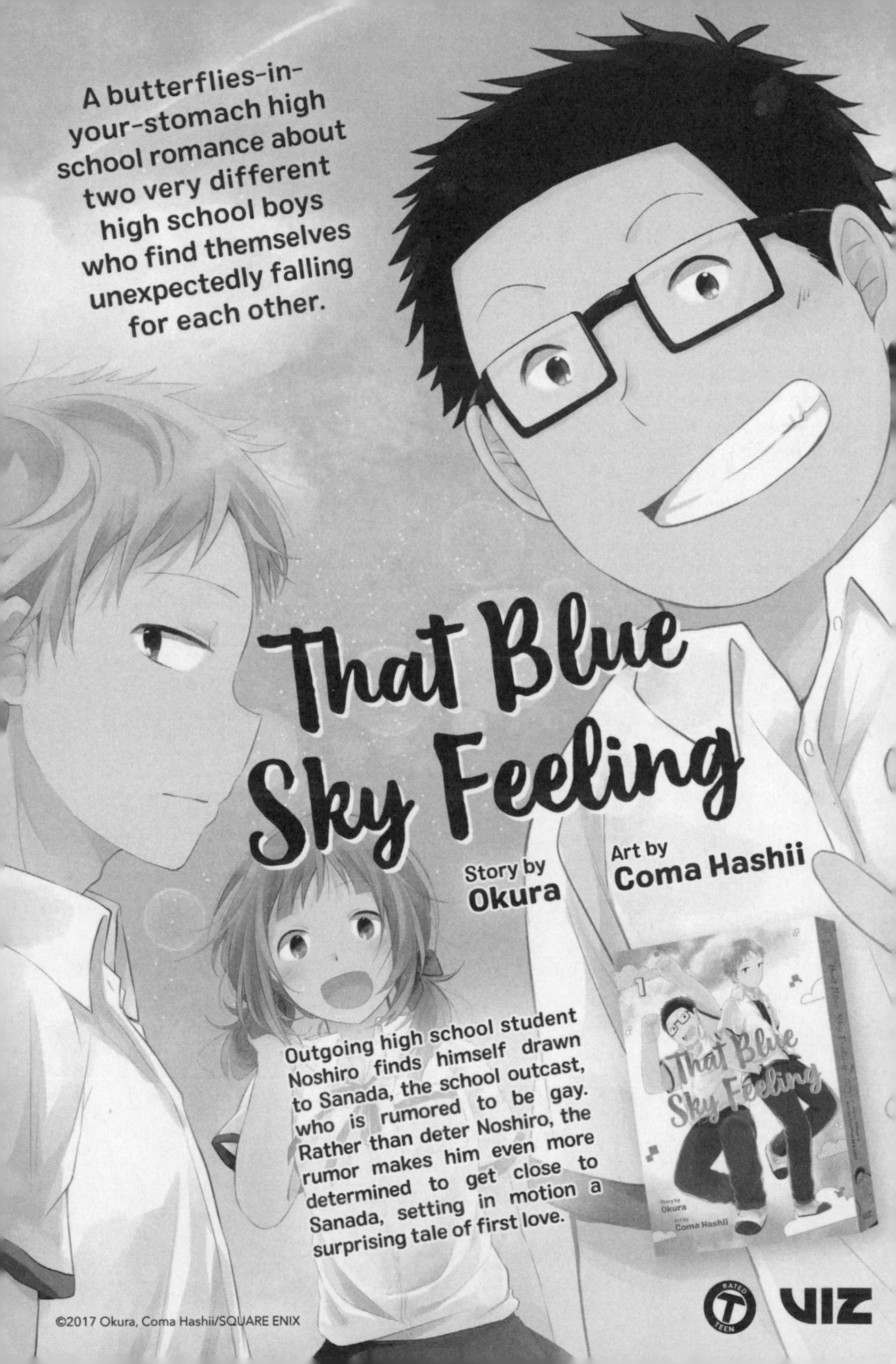
A butterflies-in-your-stomach high school romance about two very different high school boys who find themselves unexpectedly falling for each other.
That Blue Sky Feeling
Story by Okura
Art by Coma Hashii
Outgoing high school student Noshiro finds himself drawn to Sanada, the school outcast, who is rumored to be gay. Rather than deter Noshiro, the rumor makes him even more determined to get close to Sanada, setting in motion a surprising tale of first love.
©2017 Okura, Coma Hashii/SQUARE ENIX
RATED T TEEN
VIZ

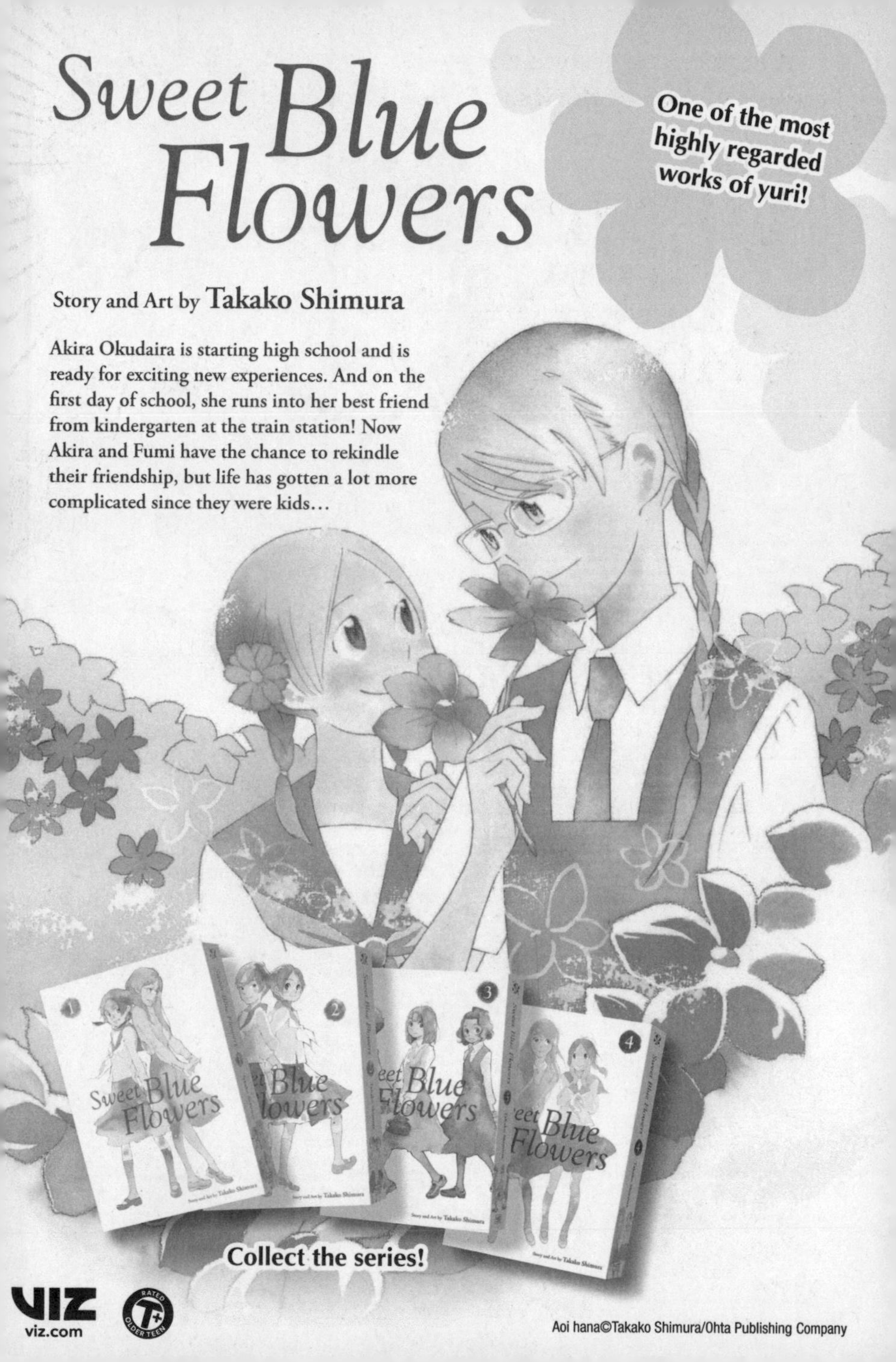
Sweet Blue Flowers
One of the most highly regarded works of yuri!
Story and Art by Takako Shimura
Akira Okudaira is starting high school and is ready for exciting new experiences. And on the first day of school, she runs into her best friend from kindergarten at the train station! Now Akira and Fumi have the chance to rekindle their friendship, but life has gotten a lot more complicated since they were kids…
1
Sweet Blue Flowers
Story and Art by Takako Shimura
2
Story and Art by Takako Shimura
3
Story and Art by Takako Shimura
4
Story and Art by Takako Shimura
Collect the series!
VIZ
viz.com
RATED T+ OLDER TEEN
Aoi hana©Takako Shimura/Ohta Publishing Company

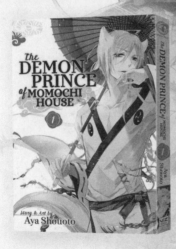
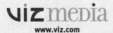

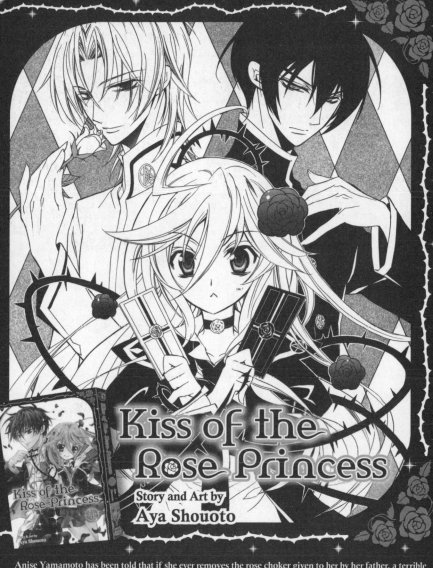

Kiss of the Rose Princess

Story and Art by Aya Shouoto

Anise Yamamoto has been told that if she ever removes the rose choker given to her by her father, a terrible punishment will befall her. Unfortunately she loses that choker when a bat-like being named Ninufa falls from the sky and hits her. Ninufa gives Anise four cards representing four knights whom she can summon with a kiss. But now that she has these gorgeous men at her beck and call, what exactly is her quest?!

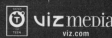

"Bloody" Mary, a vampire with a death wish, has spent the past 400 years chasing down a modern-day exorcist named Maria who is thought to have inherited "The Blood of Maria" and is the only one who can kill Mary. To Mary's dismay, Maria doesn't know how to kill vampires. Desperate to die, Mary agrees to become Maria's bodyguard until Maria can find a way to kill him.

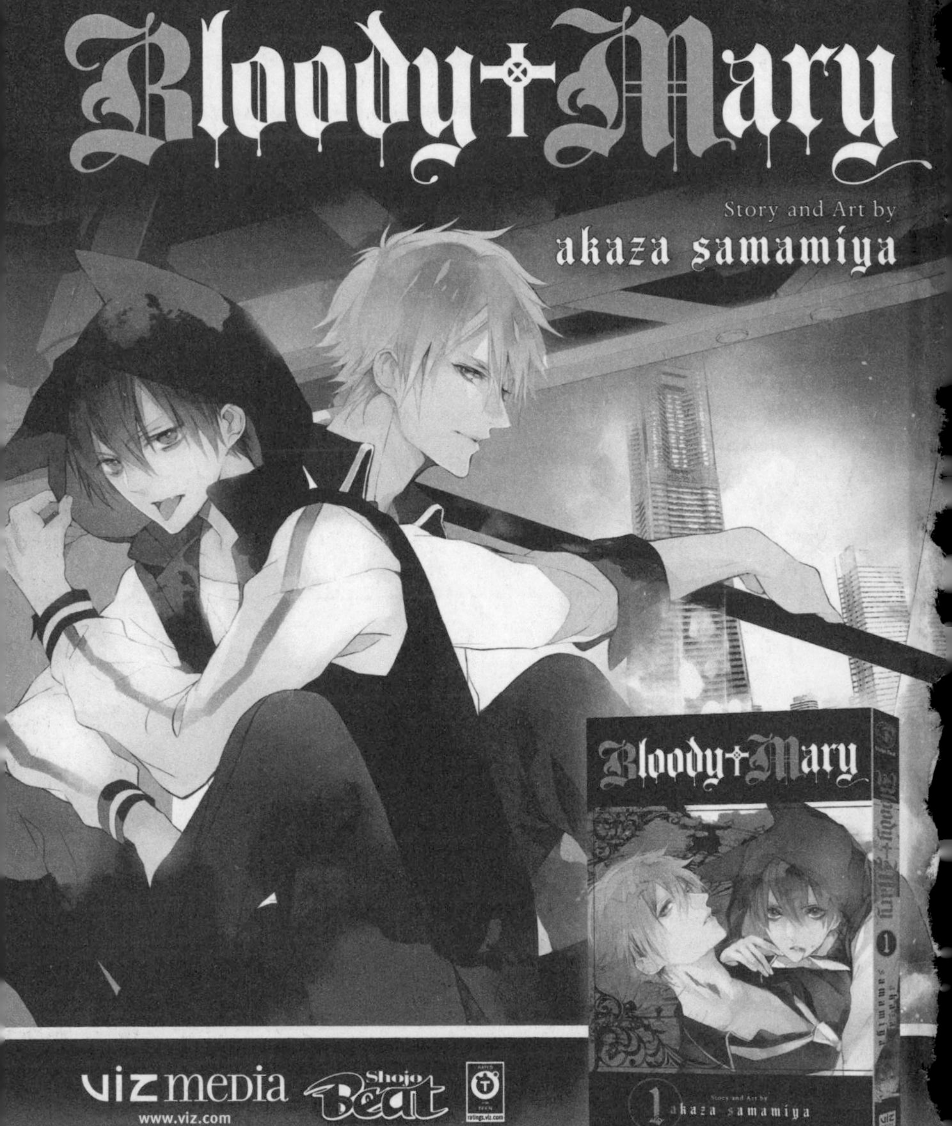

Bloody † Mary

Story and Art by
akaza samamiya

This is the last page.

A Tropical Fish Yearns for Snow **has been printed in the original Japanese format to preserve the orientation of the artwork.**

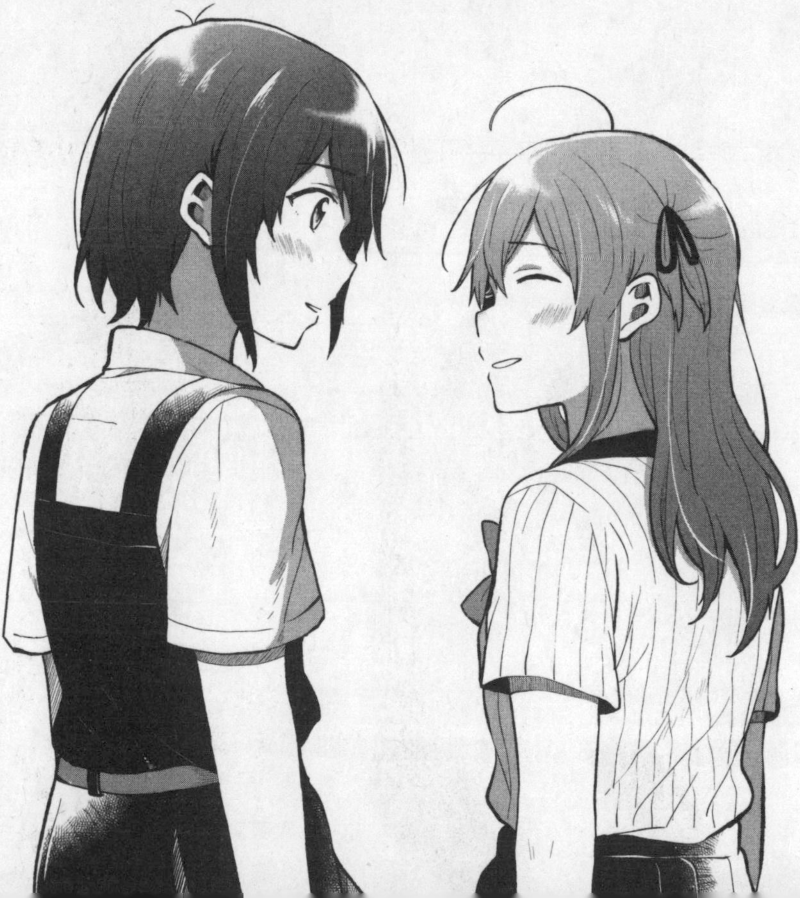